LEGAL LIMITS ON THE USE OF CHEMICAL AND BIOLOGICAL WEAPONS

An SMU Law School Study

LEGAL LIMITS ON THE USE OF CHEMICAL AND BIOLOGICAL WEAPONS

Ann Van Wynen Thomas & A. J. Thomas, Jr.

FOREWORD BY CHARLES O. GALVIN

SOUTHERN METHODIST UNIVERSITY PRESS · DALLAS

© 1970 : SOUTHERN METHODIST UNIVERSITY PRESS : DALLAS

Library of Congress Catalog Card Number 78-128123

This publication is based on research conducted
by Southern Methodist University under a contract with the United States Arms Control and
Disarmament Agency. The judgments expressed
herein are those of the authors and do not necessarily reflect the views of the United States Arms
Control and Disarmament Agency or any other
Department or Agency of the United States
Government.

CONTENTS

FOREWORD

THE SCHOOL OF LAW of Southern Methodist University is proud to have a part in the sponsorship and publication of this study by Professor Ann Van Wynen Thomas and Professor A. J. Thomas, Jr. The Thomases have an impressive list of publications to their credit in the international law field, with special concern for those legal institutional arrangements useful in the promotion of international order and peace.

This present work is another major contribution of the Thomases in a particular area of study and research not heretofore collected and analyzed. It will provide an excellent reference for agencies of government and private institutions concerned with the complex problems of public international law.

CHARLES O. GALVIN

School of Law
Southern Methodist University
May, 1970

PREFACE

THE POSSIBLE UNLEASHING of chemical and biological weapons in war has long been of international concern. In recent times this concern has increased and intensified, leading to demands for the establishment of an effective legal regime to prohibit the use and to regulate the production and possession of CB weapons lest they be employed to destroy mankind.

It is the purpose of this work to present an accurate, comprehensive, and systematic statement of the development and present status of international law as it relates to chemical and biological warfare. First, the development of conventional international legal limitations upon CB weapons is traced through analysis of the various international agreements ratified, or merely proposed, by the nations of the world. The study then delineates the development of customary international legal limitations through examination of the role of the customary law of war as it applies to CB weapons, the practices and legal policies of the major nations of the world with reference to such weapons, and the rules relating to CB weapons which can be derived from the general principles of law recognized by civilized nations.

It has not been our purpose to advance *lex ferenda,* but rather to present as accurate a statement as possible of the standing law as of 1970. Understanding of the law as it is is a vital condition precedent to any attempted extension or reformation of the law. It is our hope that this study will be of aid to those decision-makers who are presently grappling with the problem of CB warfare, as well as those who will be called upon to deal with it in the future.

Our debts for criticism and other assistance in the preparation of this book are numerous. Our particular thanks go to Dr. Edith Brown Weiss and Dr. C. Normand Poirier, whose creative suggestions were of inestimable assistance. We also wish to express our gratitude to Dr. W. Bowman Cutter for his aid on the technical aspects of chemical and biological weaponry. We happily acknowledge a most special obligation to Mrs. Margaret Hartley, our skillful and empathic editor. Mrs. Margaret Seifert deserves an accolade for having successfully undertaken the typing of the manuscript. And finally we would like to record our genuine appreciation to Dean Charles O. Galvin for his aid in making the research for and publication of this study possible.

Ann Van Wynen Thomas

A. J. Thomas, Jr.

Dallas, Texas
May, 1970

PART ONE

CB WEAPONS AND
CONVENTIONAL INTERNATIONAL LAW

CHAPTER ONE

THE NATURE AND USE OF CB WEAPONS

Background

IN APRIL, 1915, the Germans loosed a cloud of chlorine gas against the Allies in France, and therewith began the first modern massive use of chemicals in warfare. Within a short period, the Allies began to retaliate, and chemical warfare was waged with intensity throughout the remainder of World War I as each side attempted to surprise the other with new and more potent chemicals for which existing gas mask defenses were inadequate. A vast number of chemical compounds were used or considered during World War I, many of which fell within the classification of choking agents, blood agents, vomiting agents, blister agents, and tear agents. Although most of the agents used at that time are no longer of military significance, a few have been improved and refined and are still standard items in chemical arsenals.

In 1937, a German scientist made a secret and startling advance in chemical weapons (not uncovered by the Allies until after World War II) by synthesizing a group of highly toxic chemical compounds which became known as nerve agents.[2] Weight for weight these lethal nerve agents were "10-100 times as potent"[3] as the weapons used in World War I, an increase which made it logistically feasible for such agents to be disseminated on strategic targets by long-range missiles. They rendered obsolete many of the chemical agents formerly used or stockpiled. Furthermore, there is a possibility that even more powerful chemical weapons remain to be discovered. Chemists know of and can synthesize lethal chemical compounds which are far more potent than the nerve agents, although, at present, various factors limit the military significance of such compounds.[4] Nevertheless, as research continues, nerve agents may in turn become obsolete, to be replaced by more lethal chemicals.

The Nature of Chemical Weapons

In its most comprehensive sense, chemical warfare or chemical operations in war can probably best be defined as the use of, and the defense against, chemical compounds, smoke, and incendiary materials which are intentionally disseminated to reduce man's military effectiveness. Chemical compounds may affect man directly by being introduced into the body, producing death, incapacitation, confusion, or the threat thereof, or indirectly by destroying his food, his economic plants or his animals, or his materials.[5]

The chemical agents used in chemical weapons may exist as solids, liquids, or gases. Often they will change phase during dissemination; that is, some agents held in shells as liquids become gas when the shells burst. Some chemical agents are distributed as solids or liquids in the air in a very fine form so that small particles are suspended in the air for a long period of time. Such clouds, fogs, or mists, known as aerosols, are invisible and are breathed into the lungs or absorbed by the skin or eyes.[6] Most chemical agents are delivered to the target by conventional methods, such as mortar shells, bombs, rockets, missiles, cylinders, or large-caliber artillery shells.[7]

Chemical agents may be classified according to their purpose: lethal or severely injurious chemical agents; incapacitating chemical agents; riot control agents; incendiaries; screening and signaling smokes; antiplant agents; and antimateriel agents.

Although the latest United States armed forces manuals have reclassified toxins from biological agents to chemical agents, this classification would appear to be made for policy purposes, or to be premature, or to be incorrect.[8] Toxins are poisonous substances that are either (1) an integral part of the cell or tissue, or (2) extracellular products, or (3) a combination of the two situations, formed or elaborated during the metabolism and growth of certain microorganisms, as well as some of the higher plant and animal species. In general, toxins are relatively complex molecules, and, as far as is known, their chemical compositions have never been synthesized. Consequently it would appear that they are more closely related to biological agents than to chemical agents.[9] For the purpose of this study, therefore, they will be retained in the classification of biological agents.

LETHAL OR SEVERELY INJURIOUS CHEMICAL AGENTS

Lethal or severely injurious chemical agents, often called casualty agents, are chemicals or chemical compounds that are capable of producing death or serious injury when used in field concentrations. Among the lethal or severely injurious chemical agents considered to be militarily useful today are nerve agents; blood agents; the choking agent, phosgene; and the blister agents.[10]

Nerve Agents

The most lethal chemical agents so far discovered are the quick-acting casualty agents known as nerve agents. They fall into two classes, designated by the code names G-agents and V-agents.[11]

Various G-agents are known and have been investigated, but the best known consist of GA (tabun), GB (sarin), and GD (soman).[12] Although skin absorption of a G-agent great enough to cause death may occur in one to two minutes, death may be delayed for one to two hours. Respiratory lethal dosages kill in one to ten minutes, and liquid in the eye kills nearly as rapidly.

While these three G-agents differ in molecular structure, they have the same physiological action on man in that they upset his balance between the sympathetic (agrenergic) and parasympathetic (cholinergic) nervous systems, which together form the automatic nervous system. Persons who are poisoned by GA, GB, or GD display approximately the same sequence of symptoms, regardless of whether the poison entered the body by inhalation, absorption by the skin or eyes, or ingestion. These symptoms in normal order of appearance are: running nose; tightness of chest; dimness of vision and pinpointing of the eye pupils; difficulty in breathing; drooling and excessive sweating; nausea; vomiting, cramps, and involuntary defecation and urination; twitching; jerking and staggering; headache; confusion; drowsiness; coma and convulsion. These symptoms are followed by cessation of breathing and death. Symptoms appear much more slowly from skin dosage than from respiratory dosage. The number and severity of the symptoms which appear are dependent on the quantity and rate of entry of the nerve agent which is introduced into the body. Very small skin dosages sometimes cause local sweating and tremors with little other effect, and no apparent aftereffects. GB and GD are colorless in both liquid and vapor form. GA may be colorless to brownish in liquid form, but is completely colorless as a vapor. The duration of their effectiveness depends upon the munitions used to deliver them and upon the weather. Heavily splashed liquid persists from one to two days under average weather conditions.[13]

V-agents are generally colorless and odorless liquids which neither evaporate rapidly nor freeze at normal temperature. They were developed around 1950, but did not appear in unclassified literature until 1960, and their compositions have still not been disclosed. In spite of the fact that a Russian report claims that the V-agents are 100-1000 times more toxic than other nerve gases, this has been questioned by some American scientists who feel that V-agents are no more toxic than G-agents,[14] their lethal pathway being similar to that of G-agents. They are less volatile than tabun, sarin, and soman, and, because of this their vapor effect is limited but the duration of their effectiveness is increased. The time of appearance of casualties from V-agents and G-agents is roughly similar at the same dosage level. Since the process of absorption is painless, and since V-agents do not readily evaporate, drops of V-agents on the ground, foliage, buildings, and equipment remain as a hazard for a long time. Therefore V-agents are considered as quick-acting agents with a long duration of effectiveness.[15]

Blood Agents

The three World War I holdovers among the lethal agents consist of two blood agents and one choking agent. Although a good respiratory mask will provide complete protection against all three, still each has certain advantages that make it impossible to eliminate the possibility that they may be used. For example, it has been suggested that because of the readily detectable odors of these older agents, they may be released simultaneously with a nerve agent to mislead or confuse exposed personnel.[16]

The blood agents are hydrogen cyanide, designated as AC, and cyanogen chloride, designated as CK. AC is a very quick-acting casualty agent, death occurring within fifteen minutes after a lethal dose has been received. CK is slightly slower, in that death generally occurs thirty to fifty minutes after exposure.[17]

Blood agents are absorbed into the body primarily by breathing. They affect bodily functions through action on the enzyme chyto-chromeoxidase, preventing the normal transfer of oxygen from the blood to body tissues. In addition to interference with the utilization of oxygen by the body tissues, AC also brings about a marked stimulation of the breathing rate. Inasmuch as it is a highly volatile gas and lighter than air, the duration of its effectiveness is very short. CK also interferes with the utilization of oxygen by the body tissues. It differs from AC, however, in that it has a choking effect, causes a slow breathing rate, and is highly irritating to the eyes and mucous membranes. Generally the duration of its effectiveness is very short, although in jungles and forests under suitable weather conditions it may persist for some time.[18]

Choking Agents

The choking gas, phosgene, commonly referred to by the code designation CG, is also a World War I holdover, having caused more than 80 percent of all chemical agent fatalities in that war. If the concentration of phosgene is high, the victim will immediately develop characteristic symptoms and will generally die within twenty-four hours. If the concentration is low, three or more hours may elapse before any ill effects are felt.[19]

When a lethal amount of CG is received, the air sacs of the lungs become so flooded that the air is excluded therefrom. The lungs become filled with liquid so that the victim is choked to death as a result of oxygen deficiency. This is referred to as "dry-land drownings."[20] If proper care and long-term hospitalization are provided to victims of less than lethal doses, the watery fluid in the lungs may be reabsorbed, the air cell walls may heal, and the patient may recover. Hence phosgene is considered as both a delayed and an immediate acting casualty agent, depending upon the dosage received. Phosgene is generally effective only for short periods. Vapor may, however, persist for some time in low places when there is little wind.[21]

Blister Agents

A number of new blister agents have been developed since World War I, in which mustard was the major such agent.[22] The new blister agents are odorless, vary in duration of effectiveness, and are insidious in action in that there is little or no pain at the time of exposure.[23] CX (phosgene oxime) is the exception in that it causes immediate pain upon contact.

H (Levinstein mustard), HD (distilled mustard), and HT (mustard-T mixture)[24] act upon the cells first as an irritant and finally as a cell poison on all tissue surfaces contacted. Severe exposure results in systemic poisoning with malaise, nausea, vomiting, fever, cardiac irregularities, and death within twenty-four hours to two weeks. The first symptoms of H, HD, and HT usually appear within four to six hours. The higher the concentration, the shorter the interval of time between exposures to the agents and the appearance of the first symptoms. The agents act both locally and generally. Local action results in inflammation of the eyes and redness of the skin, which may be followed by blistering or ulceration and inflammation of the nose, throat, trachea, bronchi, and lung tissues. Susceptibility varies with individuals. General action of H, HD, and HT occurs because the injuries produced by these agents heal more slowly and are more liable to infection than burns of similar intensity produced by physical means or other chemicals, since these agents make the blood vessels incapable of carrying out their function of repair, and also because of the fact that dead or dying tissues act as a medium for infectious bacterial growth. Victims of these agents may take weeks or months to heal.[25]

Because of its low volatility, HT can be used only in liquid form.[26] In warm climates, depending on the munition used, the effectiveness of H, HD, and HT persists from one to two days. Under cold conditions they can be effective for a week or more.

A number of nitrogen mustard aerosols are also capable of being used as blister agents. The two most stable are the nitrogen mustards known as HN-1 and HN-3.[27] Like H and HD, they are considered to be delayed action casualty agents, since the first symptoms seldom appear until four to twelve hours after exposure. After severe vapor exposure or after exposure to the nitrogen mustards in liquid form, redness of the skin will result, followed by itching and irritation, and later blisters will develop. Effects on the respiratory tract include irritation of the nose and throat, hoarseness progressing to loss of voice, and a persistent cough. Fever, labored respiration, and bronchial pneumonia generally develop after the first twenty-four hours. Internally the nitrogen mustards cause inhibition of cell mitosis, resulting in depression of the blood-forming mechanism and injury to other tissues. Severe diarrhea, which may be hemorrhagic, occurs. The duration of the effectiveness of these agents depends upon the munitions used and the weather, but in liquid form they persist about a day under average conditions and three days under very cold conditions.[28]

CX (phosgene oxime) is a powerful irritant which produces immediate pain, varying from a mild prickling sensation to a feeling resembling a severe beesting. It causes violent irritation to the mucous membranes of the eye and nose. When it comes in contact with the skin, the area turns white in thirty seconds and is surrounded by a red ring. A wheal forms in about thirty minutes, and the white area turns brown in twenty-four hours. Normally the wheal heals in three weeks, but in some cases healing may take as long as two months.[29]

INCAPACITATING CHEMICAL AGENTS

Incapacitating chemical agents have been defined as those which temporarily produce physiological or mental effects, or both, preventing exposed military personnel from performing their primary duties.[30] While the range limit between incapacitating dosages and death-dealing dosages of lethal or severely injurious chemical agents is rather narrow (e.g., the median incapacitating dosage of sarin is 75 milligram minutes per cubic meter, while its median lethal dosage is only 25 milligram minutes per cubic meter more—100), this is not true of the incapacitating agents. It takes but a very small amount of an incapacitating agent to prostrate exposed military personnel, but it takes a large amount to cause death. In other words, the spread of the range limit between a disabling dosage and a lethal dosage of an incapacitating agent is extensive. Consequently the incapacitating agents are considered to be essentially nonlethal.[31]

Incapacitating chemical agents may be psychochemicals which produce temporary mental confusion, temporary amnesia, or temporary narcosis; physicochemicals which produce hyperthermia (heat strokes or exhaustion), orthostatic hypotension (inability to remain standing without fainting), muscular hypotonia (inability to operate many of the voluntary muscles), Parkinsonism (uncontrollable muscular tremors), inhibition of the labyrinthine reflexes (loss of sense of balance), temporary paralysis, disturbances of body temperature, or physiological blindness or deafness; or a union of psychochemicals and physicochemicals which will produce a combination of these symptoms.[32]

Little is known of the incapacitating chemical agents which are considered to be militarily feasible. The United States, for example, has published unclassified material only on the incapacitating agent BZ, stating that it provides a limited capability to produce an incapacitating effect upon man to meet military requirements by causing disorientation in addition to such physical effects as dry, flushed skin, tachicardia, urinary retention, constipation, headache, giddiness, fever, and drowsiness.

BZ functions as a slow-acting incapacitating aerosol and apparently has a nonpersistent effect.[33]

Speculation exists as to the military feasibility of a number of other incapacitating agents. Among those which may have militarily promising effects are some of the hallucinogenic drugs such as LSD-25 (Lysergic acid diethylmide), mescaline, psilocybine (psilocin), and DMT (dimethyltryptamine), which are often called psychotomimetic because some of the symptoms which they produce create resemblances to schizophrenic illnesses.[34] For example, very small doses of LSD-25—approximately 1/16,000,000 of an ounce—when inhaled or taken orally can bring about such an effect. The lethal dose is estimated to range from a hundred to a thousand times this amount.

On this basis, if the agent were disseminated through a depth of three meters of atmosphere and the personnel, breathing at a rate of 30 litres per minute, were required to inhale five times the oral dose within 15 seconds of exposure, then 1,000 kg. would provide effective coverage of an area of about half a square kilometre. In the case of personnel not protected by respirators, the time required for inhalation of the dose could be increased by two orders, reducing the agent load to 10 kg.[35]

All of these hallucinogenic drugs create an apparent indifference to relevant material in the environment by increasing the subject's awareness of trivial items, from the outside world or in his own mind, so that they become distracting factors, making the filtering and sorting mechanisms of the brain ineffective. The conscious mind is overwhelmed by an intense fusillade of irrelevant and distorted impressions.

LSD-25 was first synthetized in 1938 by a Swiss chemist who was looking for a new drug with which to treat migraine headache. After a series of tests with various derivatives of lysergic acid, on the twenty-fifth try he discovered the chemical combination that now has become famous as LSD, but which militarily is called LSD-25.[36] The effects of LSD-25 are difficult to predict, since so much depends on the subject's state of mental and physical health at the time he is exposed to the chemical. The extremes range from euphoria to manic depressive states. During a single exposure an individual may progress from the deepest feeling of impatience, restlessness, and anxiety to a highly exaggerated sense of well-being; from delusions of persecution or grandeur to a catatonic state in which he lacks the will to talk or move, but which may be punctuated by violent outbursts, hallucinations, or panic.[37] LSD-25 is odorless, tasteless, and colorless.[38] Generally it takes effect within about half an hour and the effect disappears in about twelve hours, but instances have been recorded where the effect was delayed for as long as two days. Although it has been contended that LSD-25 has few after-effects, in recent times scientists are discovering that it may produce serious long-range mental problems, and that it may cause chromosomal abnormality resulting in genetic damage for coming generations.[39]

Mescaline is a simple compound found naturally in portions of a small cactus plant. Large doses of it can bring about deep hallucinations. It seems to be of only minor military importance.[40] Dimethyltryptamine (DMT), on the other hand, is one of the newer hallucinogenic drugs, which produces the same effects as LSD-25 but is much more powerful, and hence requires even smaller dosages.[41] JB-314, popularly known as STP, is another new hallucinogenic drug. It, too, is much more virulent than LSD-25, and it can cause respiratory paralysis, convulsions, and possible death.[42]

Psilocybine (psilocin) is derived from a Latin American mushroom, which ancient pre-Colombian civilizations called *teonanacatl*, the divine mushroom, because of hallucinations experienced with its use in religious ceremonies. It produces effects similar to those of LSD-25, but not as easily.[43] The dialkyltryptamine called bufotenine is a comparatively new drug obtained from the skin of the toad, *bufo bufo bufo*.[44] Like psilocybine, it is a substituted indoleamine chemically related to seronin, but both compounds are inferior in potency to LSD-25. There are indications that prior to 1958 the United States Army had prepared a substance which had effects similar to those of all these drugs, but much more potent even than LSD-25. Whether this substance was a synthetic, or synthesizable, chemical or one of the bacterial lipopolysaccharides is not clear;[45] if the former, it may be BZ or JB 314. The latter was developed by the Dow Chemical Company. The formula was stolen from their research center in Walnut Creek, California, and thereafter JB 314 appeared among drug users in various parts of the United States.[46]

It has been said that the development of psychochemical agents as chemical weapons has recently been deemphasized in view of their unpredictable effects on rational or decision-making processes. In warfare which may involve nuclear retaliation, this is obviously an important consideration.[47]

There are in existence many physicochemicals which induce abnormal body conditions. Such chemical compounds as certain orthostatic hypotensive agents, which produce marked hypotension when the subject is standing up; or drugs which induce hyperthermia to increase body heat production or decrease heat loss; or certain benzothiazoles and benzoaxazoles which bring about muscular hypotonia causing the skeletal muscles to relax and become temporarily flaccid, have been mentioned as being potential chemical weapons. In 1959, the United States announced that it had discovered a compound which in minute dosages produced a marked ascending spinal paralysis and that with increasing dosage the subject lost the ability to stand and the function of his upper extremities and sank quietly to the haunches. At no time did the respiratory muscles cease to function, and the subject spontaneously recovered within one to twenty-four hours.[48]

These potential physicochemical weapons present a broad range of time period within which they will take effect and over which they will remain effective. Investigation is also being carried out on the possibility of using for chemical weapons new anesthetic agents which act in seconds and have an effect lasting from several hours to several days. Such agents would act in a manner similar to a powerful anesthesia and would make a victim unconscious.[49]

Speculation also exists as to how some of these incapacitants can be administered. Some of them, such as the newer variants of LSD-25, might be introduced into a water supply, for they are said to resist the effects of boiling and chlorination in the purifying process.[50] Others might be dispersed as dry agent clouds or by penetration of the skin by a hypodermic dart.

RIOT CONTROL AGENTS

A number of chemical compounds developed during World War I as harassing agents later proved to be effective for the purpose of riot control. They may still have combat uses under special conditions. The three major riot control agents are CN (Chloroacetophenone), CS (O-chlorobenzalmalononitrile) and DM (Diphenylaminochloroarsine also phenarsazine chloride).[51] All three are solids in their normal state, but when heated vaporize and then condense to form irritating aerosols. They may also be disseminated in powdered form.

CN is a tear gas which irritates the upper respiratory passage and eyes, causing an intense flow of tears within seconds of exposure. In high concentrations it is irritating to the skin and can cause a burning, itching sensation, especially on moist parts of the body. Exposure to heavy concentrations can cause death. Some persons experience nausea following exposure to CN.[52] In aerosol or powdered form its effectiveness is very short. But recently a new distillant was discovered making it possible to disperse CN as heavy liquid droplets which cling to the victim and render him helpless for 10 to 15 minutes. This new compound is known as Chemical Mace.[53]

CS is referred to as a super tear gas whose effects are felt almost immediately. It causes extreme burning of the eyes accompanied by a copious flow of tears, coughing, difficulty in breathing and chest tightness, involuntary closing of the eyes, stinging sensation of moist skin, running nose, and dizziness or swimming of the head. In addition, heavy concentrations will cause nausea and vomiting.[54]

DM is a sneeze or vomiting agent which acts more slowly but more violently than either CS or CN. Under field conditions some minutes after exposure it brings about severe headache, sneezing, coughing, eye irritation, pain in the chest, nausea and vomiting. If the concentrations are moderate, the effects last about thirty minutes after the victim leaves the contaminated atmosphere. At higher concentrations the effects may last up to several hours, and excessive exposure will lead to death. Therefore DM is seldom used alone in situations where death is not desirable.[55]

INCENDIARIES

Incendiaries are flammable materials and devices that are used to set fire to tactical and strategic targets, such as buildings, industrial installations, fuel and ammunition dumps. Flame warfare extends also to antipersonnel use in the case of flamethrowers and fire bombs. Modern incendiaries can be classified as either those which owe their effect to a self-supporting chemical reaction or those which depend on atmospheric conditions to support combustion.[56]

Petroleum incendiaries are based on gasoline as a fuel. The gasoline may be either straight or mixed with other petroleum fuels. It must, however, be thickened to be an effective incendiary. This thickening is necessary to confine the burning material to the target, and when used in flamethrowers, to increase the range of the ejected rod of fuel and to prevent its being consumed before reaching the target. Thickened fuel is sometimes called jellied gasoline.[57]

One of the first practical fuel thickeners was napalm, a mixed aluminum soap in which the organic acids are derived from coconut oil, naphthenic acids, and oleic acid. Gasoline thickened with napalm becomes a firm jelly when undisturbed but in motion, as when it is forced through a flamethrower nozzle, it acts as a viscous liquid. This thixotropy is characteristic of all thickened fuels. Napalm is also used in bomblets that are dispersed over a target area by missiles, rockets, or planes, and as fillers for cluster bombs released from an aircraft dispenser. These bombs contain built-in explosive elements designed to detonate with killing force while fires are being kindled, effectively deterring the approach of fire fighters.[58]

Flamethrowers are devices which force petroleum fuels through nozzles, igniting them as they emerge. The driving force is usually compressed air carried in a small tank which is an integral part of the device. Portable flamethrowers carried by soldiers have a range of over fifty yards under ideal conditions. Mechanized flamethrowers mounted on vehicles can throw fuel much farther. Emplaced remote control flamethrowers can be used to guard airfields and beaches—at least for a short time, for they do suffer from having a limited range and fuel capacity. Although flamethrowers have been employed to destroy vegetation, they are considered to be primarily antipersonnel weapons to be used against enclosed fortifications such as tunnels, buildings, and caves.[59] Over and above the penetration of the flaming fuel itself into such areas, there is a lethal concentration of carbon monoxide, a sudden jump in temperatures, and a dangerous lowering of the oxygen content in the air, leading quickly to unconsciousness and death.[60]

SCREENING AND SIGNALING SMOKES

Certain other chemical weapons have been found to be militarily useful. Smoke clouds have many uses in warfare, ranging from screening military operations to marking and signaling. Military screening smokes are produced by three general means: combustion, chemical reaction, or physical condensation.[61]

The most notable example of combustion smoke is that generated by white phosphorus (WP), which ignites spontaneously in the presence of atmospheric conditions and produces a dense white cloud of smoke as well as flaming particles which streak through the air.[62] Because it is easily ignited and has a fairly high burning temperature, white phosphorus is also considered an incendiary weapon, and because of the flaming particles which it casts off, it is also an antipersonnel weapon, for it can be used to wound or injure enemy soldiers.[63]

Smokes by chemical reactions are made from several chemicals. HC (hexachloroethane) smoke is made by the reaction of zinc oxide with hexachloroethane. The reaction is ignited by heat and produces a dense screen. This type of chemical smoke has been used in grenades or smoke pots. Long exposure to field concentrations of this smoke may irritate or incapacitate unprotected personnel.[64]

FM (titanium tetrachloride) and a mixture of sulphur trioxide and chlorosulphonic acid (FS) are examples of chemicals that produce smoke under conditions where the atmosphere contains much moisture. Under extremely dry conditions, these are not effective. In humid areas a dense screen is produced. These chemicals are especially adaptable to airplane spray dissemination at low altitudes. They are, however, highly corrosive as liquid and as smoke.[65] All chemical smokes, being acidic, are irritating to the respiratory tract.

Condensation smokes came out of the need for a screening smoke that was nonirritating and inexpensive. A major one was SGF—fog oil—produced by purely physical means. When high-boiling petroleum oil is vaporized by heat and the vapor is cooled rapidly it condenses into numerous fine droplets that form a stable cloud, the life of which depends solely on meteorological conditions. Generally these oil smokes are harmless by inhalation.[66]

Colored smoke can be employed in signaling troops in the field, and can also be used to communicate with planes providing close air support, thus preventing accidental bombing of friendly troops. Furthermore, they can be used for marking in pattern bombing by squadrons of planes flying in formation.[67]

ANTIPLANT AGENTS

Chemical agents effective against plants possess potential for destroying or seriously limiting food production, for defoliating vegetation, or for poisoning the soil. There are three major classifications, principally based on use, of chemical antiplant agents: herbicides, defoliants, and soil sterilants.[68]

Herbicides

Herbicides, also known as plant growth regulators, include compounds such as 2,4-dichlorophenoxyacetic acid (2,4-D), 2,4,5-trichlorophenoxyacetic acid (2,4,5-T), cacodylic acid, tordon (4-amino-3,5,6-trichloropicolinic) and isopropyl N-phenyl carbamate (ICP). These compounds are effective in killing plants when used in concentrations as low as 0.5 pounds per acre. This concentration is alleged to be nontoxic to man and animal. Because the damage to the plant has been done by the time the symptoms appear, the effects are hard to control. These compounds lose their effectiveness in the soil after a period of several weeks to several months.[69]

2,4-D produces injury to all broadleaf plants such as cotton, sweet potatoes, beans, sugar beets, potatoes, flax, nut and fruit trees, and soybeans. Plant injury may occur within an hour after spraying and usually will be evident within twenty-four hours. Some plants die within a short time, but others take several weeks. 2,4,5-T has effects on plants similar to those of 2,4-D. The two compounds differ in their ability to affect certain plant species. 2,4-D for example is more effective on beets, while 2,4,5-T is more effective on potatoes and certain woody plants. ICP affects small grains such as wheat, rye, rice, oats, barley, grasses, and a few broadleaf species. When ICP is applied to small grains as a soil contaminant in concentrations of one to two pounds per acre, the leaves of the cereal become a darker green within two weeks, then the leaf tips die, and the leaves dry out progressively until the plants die. Death usually occurs within three weeks after the first noticeable plant injury.[70]

Defoliants

Chemical herbicides may also be employed to defoliate or to desiccate. These chemicals may require a few weeks to defoliate or desiccate depending on the particular plant species, its age, environment, and vigor of growth, and the concentration or dosage sprayed on the plants. In some cases the vegetation does not die, in others it does. Where chemicals do kill plants, some are indiscriminate in killing, while others kill selectively.[71]

Defoliants are used to remove prematurely the leaves from plants. The leaves fall for an extended period of one to three weeks or more. In some species such as certain oaks, however, the leaves may die and shrivel but remain attached to the trees until separation is forced by expanding buds of new growth. Some chemical compounds require two to four weeks or more to defoliate some species, while others act within a few days. In field tests a brush control formulation comprising esters of 2,4-D and 2,4,5-T (known as "Purple") brought about complete defoliation within a week after the spraying of one and a half gallons per acre over mangrove targets. Defoliation is useful in decreasing enemy concealment through exposing him, his fortifications camouflaged with vegetation, and his lines of communication. Moreover, more accurate firing of weapons becomes possible in a cleared area.[72]

Desiccant defoliants are chemical antiplant agents used to dry up plant foliage. With this type of agent a range of susceptibility is also shown by various species of plants. Chemical drying of foliage does not invariably lead to leaf drop. On the contrary, leaf drop may be somewhat delayed. The use of desiccants would not necessarily be very effective in killing vegetation unless extended, repeated applications were employed. Most chemical desiccants cause a change in the color of foliage within an hour to a few hours, depending on the plant species and the agent. Since this color change is readily apparent from the air, desiccation is used at times to mark target release points, drop zones, and bomb release lines.[73]

Soil Sterilants

Among the antiplant materials should also be listed soil sterilants. Soil sterilants may be classified into two general groups—temporary and permanent. However, these terms are only relative, and the persistence of toxicity from any one chemical depends upon many factors. Principal among these are rainfall, textural grade of the soil, organic matter in the soil, height of water table, seasonal differences in temperature, differences among plant species, and volatility of the agent.

Normally the chemicals employed as soil sterilants consist of arsenic, borax, boron ores, and sodium chlorate; the latter two are often used in combinations. Arsenic is the most permanent of the soil sterilants. It may be applied dry as white arsenic (arsenious oxide) or in solution as sodium arsenite. The latter is poisonous and also attractive to cattle, so that it may also be used as an antianimal agent. Arsenic sterilization of soil has been known to last for as long as ten years.

Borax or boron ores, such as kramerite or colemanite, are less toxic to plants than arsenic and are less persistent. They are not poisonous to man or animal, and they are easy to handle. These materials are often used alone or in combination with sodium chlorate.

Sodium chlorate is only temporary in its effects in the soil. But it is readily soluble in water and hence moves freely with the moisture in the soil. Therefore it may be used to kill deep-rooted plants. Sodium chlorate is hazardous to use by itself because when it is combined with organic material such as straw, wood, or cloth, it forms a highly flammable mixture that ignites from friction and burns with an intense flame that cannot be smothered. Borax or sodium pentaborate reduces this flammability so that the mixture is safer to use. Also the boron compounds are toxic and are less readily leached from the soils. Borate-chlorate mixtures are used in very great quantities for soil sterilization in industrial areas all over the world.[74]

ANTIMATERIEL AGENTS

Present United States military manuals establish antimateriel agents as the final group of chemical warfare agents and define them as agents which cause deterioration of or damage to materiel. Antilubricants and catalytic agents have elsewhere been classified as chemical antimateriel agents. These apparently would cause little or no injury to enemy personnel but would be aimed mainly at causing his military equipment to break down or become useless. Antilubricants can be sprayed into the air and cause the lubricating elements in weapons to adhere together and form a tarlike substance or cause their molecular structure to break down, so that they lose their vital lubricant features. A catalytic agent accelerates a reaction produced by a chemical substance; for example, if it were possible to spray fine particles of platinum in the air near a combustion engine, it would cause instantaneous instead of controlled combustion, thereby destroying the engine.[75]

The Nature of Biological Weapons

The concept of biological warfare, popularly referred to at times as germ warfare or bacteriological warfare, consists of the deliberate dissemination of pathogenic microorganisms or their toxic products to produce noneffectiveness or death of a military or civilian population, or to bring about the destruction of an animal population, or the destruction of food crops or other vegetation, or to cause the deterioration of materiel.[76] Potential biological weapons are, therefore, divided into four classes, depending on the object of attack: (1) antipersonnel weapons; (2) antianimal weapons; (3) antiplant weapons; and (4) antimateriel weapons. Their scientific classification consists of microorganisms such as fungi, bacteria, rickettsia, viruses, and probably the toxic products of these.[77]

ANTIPERSONNEL WEAPONS

The most common agents suggested for potential antipersonnel biological weapons are the pathogenic microorganisms. Most microorganisms are not harmful, and some are even beneficial to man, animal, or plant life. The relatively few that produce disease are called pathogens.[78] The basis of fatal or nonfatal disease is infection which occurs when a pathogen invades a body and multiplies, or when it invades a body and produces toxin. Pathogens are generally parasites; that is, they are dependent on a living host for food and shelter. Nonparasitic pathogens are those microorganisms which multiply in dead matter and produce toxins. Pathogenicity, then, is the ability of an organism to enter a host and cause disease. A pathogen must penetrate its target if it is to be effective. The human body has many natural avenues of infection: microorganisms enter through the eyes, nose, throat, hair follicles, and sweat ducts. Abrasions of the skin are another common portal or entry for some. Tetanus spores, for example, may be swallowed with impunity by man, but if they are introduced into a lacerated wound, tetanus may develop.

The degree of pathogenicity—that is, the comparative ability to cause disease—is known as virulence.[79] Pathogens range in virulence from those producing mild and temporary disturbances to those causing incapacitation or death. Virulence of certain microorganisms can be increased by repeated passage from host to host. In general, virulence is dependent on two factors: invasiveness and toxicity. Invasiveness is the ability of microorganisms to enter the body and spread through the tissues, while toxicity is the quality of being poisonous. The toxicity of microorganisms depends on the potency of the toxins they produce. In some microbes invasiveness is of less importance than toxicity.[80]

In the case of antipersonnel military biological operations, a disease agent, to be an effective biological weapon, must have certain characteristics. It must have a high infectiveness; have a high degree of resistance to such destructive forces of nature as heat, sunlight, drying; be adaptable to rapid dissemination; have the ability to cause high initial mortality or lasting debilitating effects among intended victims; and be an agent foreign to that particular part of the world against which it is directed so that natural immunity has not been built up against it.[81] Although the deliberate transmission of disease organisms can take place by physical contact through contamination of food and drink, in most cases the most efficient method of transmission is through the lungs by means of dispersed aerosol particles in the atmosphere. Numerous studies have been made which show that many viral, rickettsial, bacterial, and fungal diseases can be introduced in man and experimental animals through the inhalation of artificially contaminated aerosols.[82]

Microorganisms

Fungi are a division of the plant kingdom ranging in size from microscopic single-celled forms to large and elaborate structures. They range in properties from such useful organisms as yeast and penicilin producers to pathogenic fungi which cause serious diseases or death. Fungi include molds, mildews, smuts, rusts, mushrooms, toadstools, puffballs, and yeasts. The fungi causing most of the more severe systemic mycoses are spread by inhalation of airborne spores, ingestion, and implantation of the fungus under the skin as the result of an injury. The many granulomatous diseases found throughout the world are caused by fungi and range in effect from benign to fatal infections.[83] There are three major fungal diseases considered as potential antipersonnel agents: coccidioidomycosis, histoplasmosis, and nocardiosis.[84] None of these diseases spreads from man to man or from animal to man. Rather, infection occurs by inhalation of fungus spores residing in dust from soils or dried organic matter, or infection may be transmitted by ingestion or by entry through skin scratches.[85] Consequently they are apparently suitable for aerosol dissemination.

Bacteria, microscopic unicellular organisms, are widely distributed in nature, being found in soil, air, water, the bodies of living animals, and dead or decaying organic matter.[86] They are responsible for many of the common diseases of man, animals, and plants; hence some bacteria are considered to be potential biological warfare agents, particularly the bacteria which cause the following diseases: anthrax (pulmonary); brucellosis; cholera; diphtheria; dysentery (bacillary); glanders; plague (pneumonic); tularemia (rabbit fever); and typhoid fever.[87] These diseases are normally transmitted in various ways. Many of them can be caught by inhalation of a sufficient quantity of the bacteria and are regarded as potential weapons dispersible via the aerosol method. Some are caused by eating contaminated food, some by direct contact with carriers of the disease, and some by bites from infected vectors such as flies, lice, and ticks.

Rickettsiae, intracellular parasitic microorganisms, are less prevalent throughout the world and produce fewer diseases than bacteria and viruses.[88] Nevertheless they cause such diseases as typhus fever, the spotted fevers, and Q fever. They are more difficult to produce in quantity than bacteria because they require living cells for growth. In addition, they are normally dependent upon some insect like fleas, lice, or ticks for transmission. But they can be distributed by the aerosol method, and hence are considered potential biological warfare agents.[89]

Viruses are complex organic substances which live and multiply only in susceptible living host cells. They are ultramicroscopic, and many of them are pathogenic.[90] They are responsible for such diseases as parrot fever, influenza, smallpox, yellow fever, dengue fever, encephalitis, and infectious hepatitis; hence they cannot be readily dismissed from the category of potential biological weapons.[91]

Toxins are complex organic substances, protein in nature, that are produced by living organisms and are poisonous for other living organisms.[92] It should be pointed out:

[T]he term poison is difficult to define because any material, if used in large enough amounts or administered in certain ways, will produce harmful effects on some structure or function of the body. . . . For all practical purposes, poisons are substances which cause tissue damage or malfunction of a potentially serious degree when given to an average individual in small amounts.[93]

Toxins are to be differentiated from the simple chemical poisons such as arsenic and cyanides and from the poisonous alkaloids such as strychnine.[94]

The microbin toxins are manufactured by bacterial action rather than by plant or animal action; the damage they do is caused by the action of the toxin itself rather than by the disease-infecting action of the bacteria. Microbial toxins are classified as either exotoxins or endotoxins;[95] the exotoxins are the more poisonous. The microorganism that produces them has little or no power of invasion, but once inside the body is absorbed into the tissue and causes serious or fatal illness. These microorganisms are among the most poisonous substances known.[96] On the other hand, endotoxins are rather weak poisons, but they do have greater powers of invasion than their exotoxin-producing counterparts. The two toxins considered to be potential weapons are botulinum toxin and staphylococcus food poisoning toxin.[97]

The Variable Elements of Microorganisms

Biological agents are subject to certain variables; they vary in range of rates of fatality; they have differing incubation periods, differing ability to survive and remain infectious or toxic after they are disseminated. They also vary in the number of organisms required to produce infection, in their clinical effects upon the individual, and in their ability to produce an epidemic.[98]

Potential antipersonnel biological agents are generally categorized as being incapacitating or lethal. An example of the former is the virus causing influenza, while at the lethal end of the scale are the naturally induced bacterial diseases such as glanders, pneumonic plague, and pulmonary anthrax, all of which are usually fatal if untreated and often fatal if treated. Bacillary dysentery, on the other hand, is seldom fatal, while typhoid fever and cholera have low fatality rates if treatment is prompt and adequate, and moderate fatality rates if untreated. Rickettsial diseases have moderate fatality rates ranging from 20 percent in cases of Rocky Mountain fever to 2 percent in Q fever. All progressive types of fungal diseases have very high mortality rates; on the other hand, most of the viral diseases, except for smallpox and yellow fever, have low mortality rates, particularly if a population has adequate immunization by vaccination. The fatality rate of botulism ranges between 60 and 70 percent, while the death rate from staphylococcosis is low.[99]

Incubation periods of the various diseases also show a wide range of diversity. Botulism and salmonella gastroenteritis, for example, have incubation periods of a few hours, while brucellosis may have an incubation period of several months. Some diseases such as anthrax, cholera, bacillary dysentery, glanders, influenza, melioidosis, plague, Rift Valley fever, and yellow fever have incubation periods which range from one day to eight days, while typhus, Rocky Mountain spotted fever, psittacosis, encephalomyelitis, and coccidioidomycosis have incubation periods ranging from one to three weeks. Whether the incubation period be a matter of hours, days, weeks or months, for any particular disease it is relatively constant and predictable, although it frequently depends upon the size of the dose.[100]

Since biological agents are living microorganisms, they are affected by environmental or meteorological conditions during storage, shipment, and dissemination. The rate at which each microorganism dies off is fairly predictable. Thus fungus spores are highly resistant to temperature changes, relative humidity, and drying. Some bacteria are very stable and may remain alive in contaminated air, dust, soil, or water for many years. Anthrax bacteria, for example, are so stable that no special measures are needed to insure their survival once they are dispersed. Most bacteria can be destroyed by boiling, by exposure to intensive heat, or by exposure to ordinary disinfectants. The ability of viruses to withstand environmental stress varies among the different types. All apparently can withstand freezing temperatures, but most are inactivated by heat, wet or dry, above 140 degrees Fahrenheit. Some may remain viable for days and even years under ideal conditions; e.g., hepatitis Virus B survives in a frozen state for several years and resists desiccation at room temperature for at least a year, but it can be inactivated by exposure to ultraviolet light for an hour. Rickettsiae organisms are highly susceptible to heat, light, and moisture and are thus easily destroyed under normally occurring conditions.[101]

Nevertheless, it is possible to increase the organisms' ability to withstand various stresses through laboratory techniques.[102] It has been found that various chemicals and smokes added to the biological weapon aerosol often protect the organism from the destructive effects they meet on exposure.[103] Variations may be added to the nutrients upon which the microbes grow, bringing about mutations resulting from continual exposure to gradually increased severity of the particular stress involved.[104] Mutant strains of microbes can be developed which resist or overcome the utility of protective vaccines.[105] Thus special strains of biological agents resistant to a wide variety of antibiotics can be developed so that the treatment of casualties infected by these organisms would be difficult if not impossible.[106]

Furthermore, as far as bacteria are concerned, through manipulation of their properties it is possible to breed strains which might fulfill the requirements of biological warfare agents better than their naturally occurring counterparts.[107] It has recently been proven, for example, that it is possible to make bacteria of different strains conjugate sexually, even though they normally reproduce by binary fission. During this process the genetic material of one bacterium is transferred to the other, and consequently a completely new species may be evolved without antigenetic qualities, or a new infective bacterium may be produced in one which would normally be a completely harmless strain.[108] Microbiologists have also discovered means to alter the structure of viruses,[109] which means that certain natural or induced protection against virus diseases may no longer be useful.[110] It may, therefore, be possible to reconstruct a virus of, say, smallpox which could bypass the normal immunity granted by conventional vaccines.[111]

It has been stated:

Microbial genetics, one of the most active and rapidly changing fields of contemporary biology, may rapidly develop other new ways of altering or manipulating characteristics of viruses and bacteria for BW use. The phenomena of "transformation," "transduction," and "recombination," all concern the heritable characteristics of viruses and bacteria. These are processes which can occur naturally, or can be carried out in the laboratory and can all be used to juggle factors determining virulence and immunological specificity among related and unrelated species.[112]

The quantity of an organism needed to produce a specific disease is very small.[113] Q fever can be produced in half of the persons in an exposed group if each inhales fewer than ten organisms. It has been calculated that in one gram of culture medium in which the organisms are grown there are one billion human-infective doses of this disease. Similarly, inhalation of fewer than ten organisms can infect a man with tularemia. Minimal inhalation infective doses for the dengue viruses and smallpox are probably only a little higher. Plague probably requires about 3,000 organisms and anthrax about 20,000 to infect one person. With one dozen chicken eggs as a culture medium, enough psittatosis virus can be produced to provide a theoretical infective dose for every person on earth.[114] On a weight for weight basis the bacterial doses are several thousand times more potent than toxins; yet the toxins too are fantastically potent.[115]

The effect of a BW agent on a human population differs drastically with the route by which an infecting organism enters the human body. An important factor here is the induction into the body of the infecting organism in an unnatural way. For example, the bacterium which causes anthrax in livestock is generally infectious to man only incidentally and is caused by direct contact with infected animals or animal products. The worldwide incidence of human anthrax is very low and is generally of the cutaneous form, which causes few deaths if modern anti-biotic therapy is administered. However, anthrax also occurs in an inhalation form. Although anthrax by inhalation is a rare natural infection in man, the mortality rate is high, ranging between 80 and 100 percent. Thus it is quite possible that the anthrax organism may prove a highly lethal biological agent if disseminated in aerosol form.[116] This is also true of tularemia, the rickettsial diseases, and brucellosis, which would have little or no military value in natural form but which become much more virulent when introduced into the human body via the aerosol method.[117]

Even when inhalation is the normal method of contracting the disease, the fact that the intensity of the dose concentration may be much greater via the aerosol method may increase an organism's potential as a biological weapon. A good example would be the fungal infections which result from inhalation of fungi spores but which are not of widespread importance under natural conditions. By heavy concentration of such spores, the fungal diseases may infect a great number of people and also cause increased host response. That is, although the death rate of fungal diseases varies considerably not only between the different types of fungal diseases, but also in the disease caused by one fungus, a concentrated dosage may change the clinical picture completely, drastically increasing the incidence of fatality.[118]

The bypassing of natural infective routes for most diseases has proven to bring about quite different symptoms and quite different virulence when such diseases are introduced by unnatural means such as inhalation of microbial aerosols. This, of course, would make detection of the infecting organism more difficult, and hence delay countermeasures to combat the disease. For most diseases, identification must be made quickly in order to identify the type of prophylaxis needed. While bacterial, fungal, and rickettsial diseases can all be cured by chemotherapy if treated immediately, this is not true of viral diseases or diseases caused by toxins. There is a total lack of effective treatment of these latter; as a result, only if a population has had a preventive vaccine would the effects of biological attack by such agents be minimized. If virus agents or toxins were combined with bacterial, fungal, or rickettsial diseases, and applied simultaneously, not only would the exact agents be extremely difficult to detect, but in addition little or no therapeutic treatment could be undertaken in time to prevent disability or death.

Following a large-scale dissemination of a biological agent, an initial outbreak of disease of epidemic proportions may occur. This will not be a true epidemic in that the disease is not spread from one person to another, but rather all subjected to the BW attack will become ill at approximately the same time. This may or may not be followed by a secondary or truly epidemic spread of the disease depending upon the contagiousness of the agent, the presence or absence of favorable environmental conditions, and other factors. During such a true epidemic, some microorganisms may change as they pass from person to person or from person to animal host and back to person. This change might bring about a variant of the disease which was new to the world population, for which no immunology and no immediate chemotherapy would be available. As so little is known about the long-range effects which could result from covering a large area with biological aerosols, one can only speculate that it might well be that animals which under normal environmental conditions would never encounter the microorganism used might be wiped out. On the other hand, they might serve as hosts apparently unharmed by the microorganism, but when the evolutionary cycle of the microorganism brought it back into contact with persons, it might have so changed its properties as to bring about far more lethal epidemics than have yet been experienced by the world.[119]

ANTIANIMAL WEAPONS

Animals are also considered to be potential targets for biological weapons, for animal products are important sources of food and clothing for civilian and military personnel. In addition, the production of many biological and pharmaceutical products, such as adrenalin, insulin, pituitary extracts, cortisones, vaccines and antisera, is entirely dependent upon an adequate supply of glands, organs, and secretions from healthy animals. Epidemics of animal populations, known as epizootics, occur more readily than epidemics among men. Most of the infectious animal diseases are readily transmitted from one animal to another or from herd to herd by direct contact; by contact with contaminated food, water, or excreta; or by exposure to aerosols created by coughing or sneezing.[120]

The biological agents with the greatest potential as antianimal weapons would be those which produce illness through viral infections. Prevalent viral diseases of animals are rinderpest, attacking cattle, sheep, and goats; hoof-and-mouth disease, attacking cattle, sheep, swine, goats, and other cloven-footed animals; Rift Valley fever, which attacks both sheep and man; hog cholera and African swine fever, attacking swine; fowl plague and Newcastle disease, attacking fowls; equine encephalomyelitis, attacking both horses and man; vesicular exthema, attacking swine; and vesicular stomatiatis, attacking horses, mules, and cattle.[121]

Important bacterial diseases are anthrax, attacking cattle, sheep, and man; brucellosis, attacking cattle, swine, goats, and man; contagious pleuro-pneumonia, attacking cattle; and glanders, attacking horses and man. Rickettsial diseases of domestic animals are rare; however, some are tick-borne, such as veldt disease, which has a high mortality rate in cattle, sheep, and goats in South Africa, and Q fever, a rickettsial disease which attacks man, cattle, and sheep.[122]

Although some are quite destructive, fungal diseases of animals do not seem to offer important biological and antianimal agent application. Serious protozoan diseases of animals are rare except for trypanosome diseases in horses and cattle and Babesia infections in horses, cattle, and sheep. Botulism toxins will poison certain animals and birds, but they are rarely produced under natural conditions.[123]

ANTIPLANT WEAPONS

Biological warfare might be carried on against plants to attack and destroy those crops used by an enemy population for food, economic purposes, medicine, fodder, or clothing. The potentially most effective biological agents are those which are present in one part of the world, but not in another, and which when introduced to a new environment will therefore cause extensive losses or be expensive to control. The most effective method of keeping down losses from known or native plant disease is often the development of new strains which are resistant to specific disease. Successful introduction of new organisms to which crop varieties are not resistant can therefore create a great deal of harm.[124]

Potential biological anticrop agents are those such as the parasitic fungi of the cereal grains. These agents achieve their results by producing disease in the host plants so that the grain yield is sharply reduced, even to such an extent that it is not sufficient to harvest. Some fungal diseases of plants are the various cereal stem rusts, late blight of potato, rice blast, southern blight of root crops, and smuts. The pathogenic fungi form large numbers of spores that are stable upon drying and that are readily spread by the wind and insect vectors. Fungi can initiate infections easily, because their spores and filaments can invade not only through natural openings in the leaves but also through the intact surfaces of the epidermis of leaves and roots.[125]

Bacteria attack the conducting tissues of plants and interfere with water movement, causing plants to wilt. They may also invade the soft tissues of leaves and roots, causing rotting or galls.[126] Viruses are important as plant pathogens because most crop plants are subject to attack by one or more virus diseases. Viruses are usually spread by insect vectors or by direct contact. Plant viruses can cause economic loss. Tobacco, potato, sugar beet, peach, orange, and elm are only a few of the economic plants which viruses can affect. In many cases a single virus can infect a number of different kinds of plants, and a single kind of plant may be infected by a number of viruses. Among the numerous virus diseases of plants, the tobacco mosaic virus (TMV) is well known. This virus affects many members of the nightshade family, which includes tobacco, tomato, and potato, and also some thirty other species of plants.[127]

Generally the microorganisms causing disease of plants are not agents of disease in animals or man. Some fungus structures are poisonous, however, if eaten. Ergot infected rye was used in cheap bread until the poisonous nature of the infected grain was understood. Ergot poisoning, which induced gangrene, swept France at least fifteen times in the seventeenth and eighteenth centuries.[128] Grain infected with scab fungus is also toxic.

There are also numerous parasitic seed plants which affect other plants. Among them can be listed dodder, mistletoe, and witchweed, all of which can be widely distributed as a contaminant in seed. Dodder, better known as strangleweed, is a threat to clover, alfalfa, and flax; mistletoe is a parasite dangerous to certain deciduous and coniferous trees; while witchweed lives as a parasite on the roots of a wide host range, including corn, sorghum, sugar cane, rice, rye, and oats.[129]

Insect vectors might also be employed to destroy plants. Such pests as the boll weevil, the corn borer, the Mediterranean fruit fly, the Japanese beetle, aphids, leafhoppers, apple maggots, and cucumber beetles might be used as biological weapons against a number of crops.[130]

Some microorganisms which attack plants are also potential antimateriel weapons. For example, mildew, which is defined as a morbid destructive growth consisting of minute fungi, having the appearance of a whitish coating, will attack paper, leather, and wood when these are exposed to dampness.[131]

OBJECTIVES TO BE ACHIEVED BY CHEMICAL AND BIOLOGICAL WEAPONS

Any nation which resorts to the use of chemical or biological weapons does so with the objective in mind that such weapons will persuade the enemy that further attack or resistance is useless. This is the military objective of any weapon.[132] Another broad military objective is the ability to subdue one's enemy with the least possible loss of life among one's own troops and at the least possible cost.[133] And in the economically interdependent world of today it may be desirable that a nation gain its victory with the least possible damage to the enemy in terms of life or property.[134] It has been contended that chemical and biological weapons may be able to achieve such objectives more efficiently and at a cost less than that of other available weapons systems.[135]

CHEMICAL WEAPONS

Over and above these broad objectives, there are a number of more specific objectives which might be achieved by resort to chemical weapons—objectives relating directly to the weapons used. Usually it is stated that chemical munitions may be employed separately or integrated with other munitions in military operations to cause casualties among enemy troops, to reduce enemy effectiveness through harassment, or to restrict use of terrain and materiel.[136]

Each class of chemical weapons has its own specific objectives. Nerve agent GB would be employed primarily as a nonpersistent vapor to cause casualties upon inhalation by unmasked troops, or to harass enemy troops by compelling the enemy to wear protective masks and clothing for prolonged periods, thereby impairing his effectiveness through fatigue, heat stress, discomfort, and decrease in perception.[137]

Nerve agent VX, employed as a liquid contaminant to cause casualties by penetration of liquid droplets through the skin, could be used for direct attack on targets composed of masked troops in the open or in foxholes without overhead protection. Because of its low volatility VX can be used with the objective of harassing enemy forces by means of the continuing casualty threat posed by liquid droplets on the ground or on equipment. Contamination with VX would also hamper or restrict the use of terrain by enemy forces.[138]

The objectives of blister agent HD (which comes in both liquid and vapor forms) would be to cause delayed casualties in direct attack targets containing masked or unmasked troops. Because HD droplets and vapor pose a continuing casualty threat, another objective of this agent is to harass enemy forces and to create an obstacle to traversal or occupation of the areas involved, and finally it can be used with the objective of hampering or restricting use of terrain.[139]

When incapacitating chemical agents are resorted to, they will be employed with the objective of incapacitating enemy forces when the use of lethal or destructive munitions is undesirable. Incapacitating chemical attacks can be made against hard targets, such as fortifications, to obtain delayed and relatively long-term neutralization of personnel. It has been said that incapacitating chemical attacks may seek to reduce overall fighting capabilities of intermingled enemy and friendly military units, when location of these units is not well known. This would permit the identification and delayed selective follow-up and physical separation of friendly military units from enemy units without incurring heavy casualties among friendly troops. This would also be the objective when there is intermingling of civilian population and enemy forces. When the objective is to capture vital or sensitive enemy installations for the purpose of intelligence, resort may be had to incapacitating chemical agents.[140]

Riot control munitions may be resorted to when it is necessary to disable hostile troops or rioting personnel for limited periods of time, or to control rebellious prisoners of war, or when the military objective is to "flush out" unmasked enemy troops from concealed or protected positions.[141] Preinstalled CS munitions may also be employed by locating them around the perimeter of a defended position. Furthermore, when the objective is to conduct raids and ambushes against insurgent or guerrilla forces, or to defend against insurgent or guerrilla attacks and ambushes, riot control munitions at times may prove useful.[142]

The object of incendiary agents is to start fires that will destroy the usefulness of the target.[143] The portable flamethrower has been used as a close-support weapon to advance on enemy positions when it might not be possible to use the fire of other weapons because of proximity. When the objective is to search and clear an area, it may also prove useful.[144]

When chemical antiplant agents are used, their objectives are either to destroy or to limit seriously the production of crops for food or for their economic value, to modify the normal pattern of growth of plants, or to damage or defoliate plants to prevent ambush of friendly forces along routes in jungle and forest and to deny concealment to the enemy or to mark areas of forest for reconnaissance or as guidance for aircraft.[145]

Another objective sought by resort to chemical weapons may be the anticipatory psychological reaction, in that their use may lower the morale of the enemy armed forces and the civil population and may induce a will to compromise or surrender by causing widespread fear and anxiety.[146]

BIOLOGICAL WEAPONS

Although biological weapons have probably not been used in modern wars, their employment in future conflicts is not inconceivable. Potential biological weapons include a whole spectrum which vary greatly as to incidence of fatality, length of incapacitation, and nature, degree, and period of discomfort or suffering.[147] When an objective of a military operation is to leave equipment, facilities, and structures reasonably intact, both lethal and incapacitating biological agents might be resorted to, since they primarily affect living things.[148] Another objective which might be obtained through the use of lethal and nonlethal biological weapons would be a preliminary preparation for a large-scale coordinated attack by other weapons, e.g., in advance of airborne, air-mobile, or amphibious operations scheduled to take place after the incubation period of the disease-producing agent had passed.[149] Such biological agents could also weaken strongly defended enemy positions which were impenetrable by conventional weapons. Moreover, biological weapons could be used to produce casualties among enemy troops held in reserve, gathered in assembly areas, or located on logistical bases in rear artillery and missile positions, on observation posts, or in communications facilities, with the objective of hindering support of enemy combat units.[150] A possible objective of resort to incapacitating biological weapons would be to cause numerous casualties with few deaths in attacks on enemy-occupied friendly territory. Biological weapons might well be used on a civilian population with the objective of seeking to halt all activity in an area by incapacitating but not necessarily killing from 10 to 20 percent of a population simultaneously. The effects would be quite different from those of a normal epidemic, because these agents would presumably strike the entire population at about the same moment; hence all vital services, both public and private, would be dangerously retarded.[151]

Although the agent itself might have an extremely low mortality rate, undoubtedly such a disruption of vital services would cause numerous secondary deaths through, for example, an insufficiency of doctors or nurses for other emergencies, of fire or police protection, etc.[152] The psychological effects of exposure to biological weapons might add materially to the chaotic situation, for fear and misunderstanding could grow with rumor and false self-diagnosis.[153] The effectiveness of a biological attack might be greatly enhanced by the panic and hysteria of an uninformed and untrained general population. It is possible that the psychological effects might even prove as damaging as the physical effects of such an attack.

When the military objective is sabotage or subversion, an enemy might resort to biological weapons, for they are not easily detected, inasmuch as they produce no immediate physiological reaction, nor can they be detected by normal physical means.[154] Since there is a delayed casualty effect for the incubation of biological agents, there is a lag period of several days or even months before the casualties are produced, which must be taken into account in planning military strategy in such situations.

Factors Governing the Use of Chemical and Biological Weapons

physical factors governing the use of chemical weapons

A chemical agent must have certain physical characteristics before it can be used militarily.[155] First, it must have the ability to accomplish the mission for which it is designated as well and as cheaply as other available military weapons systems.[156] This highlights a number of problems involved in the use of chemical weapons. Unlike most conventional weapons systems, chemical agents are highly dependent upon weather variables such as wind, temperature, humidity, and precipitation.[157] In turn, these variables are affected by the general weather distribution over an extensive area, topography, vegetation, and soil. Micrometeorological variables are extremely important in determining when chemical agents can be employed, in determining how many and what types of chemical agents can be used, and in determining the effectiveness of the agents and the possible downwind hazards.[158] Although the travel and diffusion of an agent cloud are not significantly affected by meteorological elements during the first thirty seconds, the dosages and rate of dosage buildup are influenced by the weather. At high wind speeds the dosages are reduced during all time intervals. At high air temperature, the rate of dosage buildup from volatile agents is faster and the total dosage may be obtained within fifteen seconds.[159]

For the most part chemical agents are dispersed as a vapor, and/or as an aerosol, or as a liquid. When disseminated as a vapor, the initial toxic chemical cloud is heavier and cooler than its surroundings and clings to the earth, and the concentration gradient decreases with height. The cloud then mixes with the surrounding air, assuming a temperature and weight similar to those of its environment. In the case of an agent normally utilized for persistent effect—liquid—evaporation produces an agent cloud only in the vapor form. These clouds are usually of low concentration, having the same temperature as the surrounding air and tending to remain near the surface because of high vapor density.[160]

High wind speeds cause the quick dispersion of vapors or aerosols, thereby decreasing the effective coverage of, and the time of exposure to, the agent in the target area.[161] More munitions are required to insure high concentrations in a limited time. When wind speeds exceed certain velocities, some chemical agents are no longer economical to employ. The limiting velocities are eight miles per hour for artillery and twelve miles per hour for aerial bombs. Above these speeds, other weapons systems must be resorted to.[162]

The terrain contour and surface cover influence the flow of toxic clouds as they do the flow of air. The toxic cloud released in a narrow valley subjected to a mountain breeze retains a high concentration of the agent as it flows down the valley; on the other hand, high concentration is difficult to obtain on the crests or sides of ridges and hills. Rough ground tends to deflect toxic clouds; ground covered with tall grass or brush retards their flow; obstacles such as buildings or trees set up eddies that tend to break up the clouds and cause them to dissipate more rapidly.[163]

When the chemical agent is to be dispersed in liquid form, weather and terrain conditions are also factors governing its use, for weather and terrain affect the rate of evaporation which, in turn, affects the persistency and concentration of vapor. Most weather conditions do not affect the amount necessary for an effective initial liquid contamination, but persistency may be affected by wind direction, speed of wind, and air turbulence, by surface temperature, and by precipitation.[164]

The rate of evaporation of agents utilized for persistent effect in liquid state is proportional to the speed of the wind. If the speed increases, evaporation increases, shortening the persistency of the contamination. Furthermore, agents utilized for persistent effects acquire the temperature of the ground and the air with which they are in contact. Their rates of evaporation are proportional to the vapor pressure at any given temperature.[165] For effective employment of bombs, shells, rockets, and land mines in releasing toxic liquid chemical agents, the temperature is of vital importance. Generally toxic liquid agents are not effective when used at temperatures below their freezing points.[166] Light rains may distribute liquid agents more evenly over a large surface, while heavy rains or rains of long duration tend to wash away toxic liquid chemical agents, which often collect in areas not meant to be contaminated, such as stream beds, so as to endanger civilians or friendly troops.[167] A thick jungle or forest canopy prevents liquid toxic agent spray from airplanes from reaching the ground in sufficient quantities to be militarily useful.[168]

Weather and terrain are also limiting factors governing the use of smoke for screening and signaling.[169] A high wind speed carries the smoke rapidly from its source and permits rapid establishment of a screen, but at the same time more munitions are required to maintain the screen.[170] When winds are too high smoke is torn apart into small clouds and loses its effectiveness. The effect of temperature upon smoke is slight, but the effect of humidity is important because all smokes absorb moisture and increase in size, thereby increasing in density and effectiveness. The same amount of smoke munitions produces a denser smoke when the humidity is high than when it is low.[171]

Incendiary munitions are not appreciably influenced by weather conditions. The combustibility of the target and its susceptibility to the spreading of fire, however, may be influenced by wind and precipitation. Incendiaries are also affected by soil, vegetation, and topography. The type of soil affects the impacting of the munitions, combustibility of the vegetation affects the efficiency of the incendiary, and topography influences wind speed and direction.[172]

It would seem therefore that many situations do not lend themselves to chemical operations, and the unique skills and judgment required in resorting to chemical weapons make many of them militarily inconvenient in comparison with more conventional weapons.

Another factor to be taken into consideration in resorting to the use of chemical agents is that their range of effects and destructive power should be reasonably calculable. It has been stated by some authorities that chemical agents can be used flexibly in a measured and restrained response to varied military situations without "spill over effects."[173] Others have questioned this. For example, it has been pointed out that certain unprecedented pharmacological problems arise in connection with the use of psychochemicals as weapons. There are several factors which modify drug actions, accounting for the diverse responses of different individuals or of the same individual at different times to the same drug.[174] Assuming that psychochemical weapons, to be effective, will require dosages appropriate for large, healthy males, how will the optimum dosages be selected if total reversibility of effects is sought? Numerous individual variables may prove significant: age, body weight, sex, state of health—including pregnancy—rate of excretion, prior and concurrent drug exposure, and method of administration. Infants and the infirm can be expected to suffer more toxicity than others receiving the same amount of a drug. Since the concentration of a dispersed gas or water-borne agent varies greatly according to time and place, dosage control becomes very complicated and may even be impossible.[175] Occasionally a person is tolerant to a drug never taken before. This could be of crucial importance to combatants in psychochemical warfare. Like the tolerance phenomenon, hypersensitivity and other idiosyncrasies are met whenever drugs are used. Atypical and allergic reactions occur with varied frequency and severity even with drugs which are nontoxic to most people.[176]

It is clear, therefore, that the effects of psychochemical agents on random troops or populations will depend on many variables, and this fact detracts considerably if not crucially from efforts to predict and control their use. Furthermore, at present scientists can only brief military commanders on the overall and long-term effects of the newer chemical weapons as demonstrated by controlled laboratory experiments, and "no military commander," so it is argued, "would base his strategy on information as scanty as this."[177]

Still another factor governing chemical weapons is that they should be economically producible on a militarily significant scale from available materials.[178] Certain chemical weapons can be manufactured at a moderate cost by a nation with advanced scientific laboratories, whether that nation be a small power or a nuclear power. Even a nation with limited scientific knowledge possessed of a supply of gasoline and a soap factory can probably produce napalm on a militarily significant scale. But many of the newer chemical agents, such as nerve gas, must be manufactured under very advanced scientific conditions and are expensive to produce: for example, in 1950, the United States paid $90 million for the designing and building of a plant for the production of highly toxic alkyl fluorophosphonates, which are the basic constituents of nerve gas. Probably only the great powers could afford expenditures of this magnitude.[179]

The capabilities and availability of chemical munitions and delivery systems also govern the use of chemical weapons systems.[180] Chemical weapons systems may be grouped under three headings: point source, multiple-point source, and line source. A point-source munition disseminates the agent from a single point, e.g., from a massive chemical bomb delivered by aircraft. Chemical land mines are also a point-source munition.[181]

A multi-point-source weapon system is characterized by a quantity of point-source munitions which are distributed at random over a target area. Each point-source munition disseminates the agent as an aerosol or a vapor that merges with other aerosols and vapors downwind. Line-source chemical munitions are delivered by aircraft which disseminate chemical agents along a line of release, either from a spray tank or from bomblets impacting on the ground in a line.[182]

Even though conventional delivery systems can be adapted for chemical agent use, the experiences of the United States and its allies during World War II proved that many chemical weapons and chemical munitions were difficult to handle logistically. Most of the chemical agents were highly corrosive, difficult to store:

Generally speaking, the problem of safely containing bulk quantities of highly reactive chemicals under wartime conditions was never solved. There was no certainty that existing containers for toxics would not burst or corrode, and the ever present possibility of leakers in lots of toxic-filled drums or munitions imposed a perpetual state of alert on depot and transportation personnel.[183]

In the South Pacific area weapons and ammunition used for incendiary purposes and for screening smoke were hard to maintain because of the heavy rain, intense heat, and high humidity. In all theaters it was discovered that potentially explosive smoke pots could not be safely stored with other ordnance items. When the M1A1 portable flamethrower was first put into combat use, it was found that in 75 percent of the weapons pinhole corrosion of the nitrogen, hydrogen, and fuel cylinder occurred, leading to their failure when most needed. It took months of readjustment or redesigning to bring them into true military usefulness.[184]

During the processing of the newer chemical agents such as nerve gas, it has been found that the compounds also produce highly corrosive conditions. To prevent destruction of process equipment, wide use has been made of such expensive metals as Monel, Hastelloy, Karbate, stainless steel, tantalum, and silver. If these agents can be produced and stored only in containers of these materials, they might prove to be too costly for many nations to contemplate.[185]

On the other hand, not all chemical weapons are difficult to ship, store, or construct. Napalm fire bombs, for example, can be made of readily available material. Napalm can be shipped in a dry state, mixed with gasoline when required, placed in spare airplane tanks made of processed paper, supplied with an igniter such as a white phosphorus grenade, and loaded on a conventional bombing plane for use.[186] Chemical defoliants and soil sterilants do not need complex weapons systems; they can be dispersed from crop-duster airplanes.[187]

PHYSICAL FACTORS GOVERNING THE USE OF BIOLOGICAL WEAPONS

A biological agent must also have certain physical characteristics before it can be employed as a military weapon. The ideal biological agent would produce a disease for which there was no known treatment and for which only the user possessed a vaccine—one which would be long lasting and would protect against even massive doses. Such a disease in its naturally occurring form is probably unknown. Any resort to biological weapons must be in the nature of a gamble, because they have never been used on a large scale and testing has been essentially confined to a laboratory.[188] It is obvious that no laboratory research can guarantee anything more than a probability that a particular agent will be dependable in the production of the effects desired. And as experiments on humans have probably been kept to a minimum, some biological agents which it is assumed will cause no permanent injury may prove in wide usage to have unexpected lasting side effects.[189]

A physical factor governing the potential employment of biological weapons is the time lapse before the agent acts. An incubation period is always required from the time the agent enters the body until it produces disease; accordingly, biological weapons are delayed-effect weapons, and any resort to them must involve long-range planning to assure delivery of the agent in sufficient time to achieve desired results. Because of this delay, biological weapons are most effective against animals and crops, or against unsuspecting civilian concentrations, and probably least effective against front line troops.[190]

In addition, the effect itself must also be serious, producing either incapacitating symptoms over a fairly lengthy period or a high proportion of fatalities. Indeed, it has been said that the United States military requirements appear to be very stringent.[191] Lethal agents might be expected to kill 25-50 percent of the population in the area attacked and incapacitating agents to affect 20-30 percent. On this score alone, many of the naturally occurring strains of infectious diseases can be ruled out, for they produce clinical results in less than 5 percent of a human population.[192]

Although some biological agents are contagious in that they spread from one human being to another, it would be almost impossible to assure that an epidemic would result in any locality from the use of biological weapons. There are so many factors which must dovetail to make an epidemic (e.g., chance, susceptibility of the populace as a whole, hygienic and public health measures, nutritional background) that basing military planning on a predicted epidemic would probably be hazardous in the extreme.[193]

It has been contended that there are substantial barriers to the perfection of effective biological weapons;[194] but if the technical problems associated with the effective dissemination of biological agents can be solved, enormous destructive capability could become available at radically low costs, since the amount of an agent potentially sufficient to attack great areas is incredibly small, and existing systems of delivery could be used without radical expenditures.[195]

Dissemination of biological agents could be accomplished in a variety of ways, but perhaps the potentially most effective is the dissemination of pathogenic microorganisms in aerosols.[196] The transmission of disease by the airborne route presents a number of problems which have a common basis whether the transmission is contrived, as by biological weapons, or by chance, as in nature. For airborne infections to occur the causative microorganisms must withstand a number of stresses. These are, in sequence: the physical stress of becoming airborne; the physico-chemical stresses of aerial flight (e.g., light, humidity, heat); the biological stresses at the site of deposition in the host body; the consequent attack by the body's defense mechanisms.[197] Throughout this sequence at least some of the organisms must remain both viable and infective. Biological agents are extremely susceptible to ultraviolet radiations, fluctuations in temperature and relative humidity, and other natural environmental factors. Consequently they die at a rate which is characteristic for specific microorganisms under prevailing environmental conditions. This rate of dying for many microorganisms of military interest ranges from a fraction of a percent per minute to 6 or 7 percent per minute.[198] It is possible to increase an organism's ability to withstand various stresses through laboratory techniques. These include variations in the nutrients upon which the microbes are grown and mutations resulting from continual exposure to gradually increased severity of the particular stress involved.[199] Some organisms have the property of forming spores as a means of surviving unfavorable conditions. This type of spore is a cell, surrounded by a tough envelope resistant to many stresses, which remains in this state until conditions are favorable. It then reverts to the active state and again starts reproducing. If not subjected to direct sunlight, spores may live for several days. Direct sunlight will kill them in a matter of hours. Organisms which do not form spores have much shorter lives.[200]

Since biological aerosol particles tend to diffuse in much the same manner as a chemical cloud, the biological cloud will move with the wind, and the terrain will affect cloud travel of biological aerosols in the same general manner as it does a toxic chemical cloud. The ground contour of rough terrain, for example, will create wind turbulence, which in turn influences the vertical diffusion of the aerosol cloud.[201]

When a pathogenic microorganism is disseminated by the aerosol method, the size of the agent becomes exceedingly important. The natural defensive features of the upper respiratory tract are capable of filtering out the larger infectious particles to which people or animals are ordinarily exposed in their daily existence. Particles larger than five microns in diameter are useless as far as human beings are concerned. Furthermore, particles smaller than one micron are usually exhaled from the lungs before they have time to settle. Thus biological agents, to produce the desired disease, must be dispersed in particles ranging from one to five microns to pass through the defensive barriers of the upper respiratory tract and be retained in that area of the lungs which is highly susceptible to infection. The number of microorganisms required to produce infection via the respiratory route has been estimated for man on the basis of the number of these microorganisms required to produce infection in various laboratory animals: this ranges between ten and ten thousand, depending on the microbial characteristics of the specific microorganism involved.[202] Since they are extremely small, the weight of the microorganisms required for one dose is something on the order of a millionth of a millionth of a gram or less.[203] Personnel may be exposed to a massive overdose of the agent through the use of an aerosol; thus the acquired immunities of the target personnel may possibly be overcome by the use of a selected agent.[204]

Another physical factor influencing the potential employment of biological weapons is the fact that such weapons should be economically producible on a militarily significant scale from available materials. Up to the present time this has apparently not as yet come about, although recent scientific discoveries[205] indicate that in the future such obstacles may eventually be overcome.[206] Even so some authorities would contend that many biological agents cannot be stockpiled because they have a "relatively short shelf life."[207] This, of course, is not true of those species of bacteria which form spores. They are very stable under storage conditions.[208]

Another physical factor governing biological weapons is the fact that the effects of spreading disease agents are not exactly calculable.[209] Marked differences in susceptibility to biological agents occur not only in different geographical locations, but also in different age groups or in groups protected or unprotected by artificially induced or naturally acquired immunity. A biological agent that might be effective in one section of the world or against one particular group might not be effective against another group or in another geographical area.[210] It may be impossible to immunize friendly troops or allied civilian populations against a backlash. For example, despite worldwide efforts, there are many virus diseases for which no effective vaccines are available. In addition, unexpected problems may arise from the effects biological agents would have on the ecology of the strike area; for example, very little is known of the range of susceptibilities of many species of wildlife to specific microorganisms which have been dispersed via infectious aerosols and have lodged in their respiratory systems.[211]

The bite of an arthropod vector (mosquitoes, flies, fleas, lice, ticks, and mites) can also spread disease. Although they have been referred to as potential biological weapons, it would seem that many physical factors restrict their use. Many of them can survive only in tropical or subtropical areas; they would be useless against nations with colder climates.

Where public hygiene is reasonably well developed, common insect vectors would stand little chance of surviving and multiplying. Furthermore, the control of these vectors after release is difficult; they may move out of the target area and thus cause loss of the agent.[212]

POLITICAL FACTORS GOVERNING THE USE OF CHEMICAL AND BIOLOGICAL WEAPONS

Before the decision-makers of a nation agree to permit military resort to chemical and biological weapons, they are likely to take into consideration the possible political effects of the decision both abroad and at home. If, for example, the object of the attack was not the destruction of an enemy population, but rather its subjugation, the decision-makers would have to reckon the cost of maintaining the enemy after the use of CB weapons had forced surrender.[213] In a free society there is considerable concern that such weapons as psychochemical compounds might be used in brainwashing procedures. Unquestionably any attempt to use drugs to persuade men and women against their convictions or to further a particular ideology would be repugnant and contrary to every concept of individual liberty in a civilized society.[214]

Internationally the use of nonlethal chemical and biological agents might be counterproductive in certain military situations. A carefully directed publicity campaign at home and abroad might well bring about such an indignant outcry that the political decision-makers would be forced to withdraw the CB weapons,[215] or the use of nonlethal CB weapons might lend support to false enemy charges claiming the use of lethal gases.[216]

On the other hand, when there is a deep division among the major powers of the international society and their attention is deeply engaged in certain potentially explosive international situations, it is not inconceivable that a political decision-maker of a smaller nation might well feel that a propitious moment had arrived for advantageous resort to CB weapons in some minor peripheral conflict, for such use would probably be largely disregarded in view of the power struggle going on elsewhere.[217]

The fact that CB weapons are almost universally referred to, with undisguised horror, as terror weapons would in many instances give rise to serious psychological problems for decision-makers contemplating their use, even though campaigns have been carried on in an attempt to prove that such weapons are more humane than high explosives, shrapnel, or bullets.[218] The psychology of the acceptability of a weapon is an obscure area of learning, although it has been suggested that the more closely a weapon "approaches the basic effects of fang and claw, the more readily it is accepted."[219] Oldendorf has stated, for example:

It is especially interesting that when these devices are individually spotlighted, scrutinized and dissected, and their merits are weighed, the explosive weapon seems so *right* and the quietly lethal so wrong. The basis of this view escapes me, but perhaps it is only that we are accustomed to the use of the violent variety.[220]

Another political factor in the use of CB weapons might relate to the technique used in delivering the agent. If the attack were on the homeland of one of the nuclear powers and if it were made by an intercontinental ballistic missile, immediate nuclear retaliation could result because the enemy would be unable to distinguish between chemical and biological warheads and other types of warheads. Consequently one writer has suggested that large power political decision-makers would probably sanction the use of CB weapons only in minor wars in which the other side could not retaliate.[221]

Another writer has contended that a nation which decides to permit its military commanders to employ nonlethal CB agents under certain limited conditions must face the fact that it has opened a dangerous door, for military commanders would seek permission to use a militarily more promising range of weapons, and political decision-makers would be hard pressed to hold them in line.[222]

The final political factor which must be taken into consideration is the effect of CB weapons on the morale of the enemy. The morale of an army and of a nation depends in decisive measure on their faith in victory. There is a widespread opinion that by the use of CB weapons morale will be broken quicker than by resort to any other arms or means of combat. Soldiers can be trained in certain defensive measures against CB weapons, but training for the broad masses of the population presents great difficulties, and hence the population will admit defeat in face of occurrences of strange phenomena of death or disease not amenable to the customary means of detection or control. On the other hand, it has been said:

It seems to be possible that if the use of biological weapons were to inspire aversion or hatred rather than terror, its effect might be to strengthen morale, rather than destroy it. Assuming that an attack, of which BW was strongly suspected to be a part, did not bring total devastation in its train, then the effect of a weapon considered particularly loathsome might be to arouse the attacked population so that they would gather up all their remaining strength and mobilize every latent resource to resist the attackers.[223]

The highly potent factor of morale, therefore, would seem to remain an unknown quantity.

LEGAL FACTORS GOVERNING THE USE OF CHEMICAL AND BIOLOGICAL WEAPONS

A final factor in any decision to employ chemical or biological agents will be the decision-makers' views on the legality of resort to such weapons.[224] The conduct of modern warfare, including the nature and type of weapons employed, is governed by certain international rules and regulations, called the law of war, which are principles acknowledged as binding by states of the international society. The law of war is found in certain international treaties, in the customs and practices of states which have gradually obtained universal recognition, and in the general principles of law recognized by civilized nations. This law is not static, but by continual adaptation follows the needs of a changing world.

It has never been the function of a principle of law to point the way to a specific result with catechistic certainty, and this is true of the law of war:

The realistic function of those rules, considered as a whole, is accordingly, not mechanically to dictate specific decision but to guide the attention of the decision-makers to significant variable factors in typical recurring contexts of decision, to serve as summary indices to relevant crystallized community expectations, and, hence, to permit creative and adaptive, instead of arbitrary and irrational, decisions.[225]

Therefore, the decision-makers must review the law of war broadly, as well as in the light of the nature of the specific weapon contemplated, for each chemical agent and each biological agent varies from others in nature of effects as well as in the gradation of effects.[226] As any weapon, even the most conventional rifle, can be used in an illegal manner, the makers of any decision as to whether or not resort can legally be had to CB agents must, in addition, review the elements of time, place, and circumstance.

CHAPTER TWO

SOURCES OF THE LAW OF WAR

LAW AND WAR

THE EXTENT TO WHICH chemical-biological weapons are proscribed, permitted, regulated, or not regulated by international norms is governed by the law of war, which confers rights and imposes duties upon the participants. The two major categories of norms[1] which form the law of war are rules and principles. A rule, used here in its narrow sense, is definite and precise, and for this reason its application admits of little discrimination; e.g., if a weapon is absolutely and unconditionally prohibited by a rule of war then it is unquestionably illegal to resort to it under any condition. Rules constitute only a small part of the normative content of the law of war. Principles are more complex. They are authoritative starting points for legal reasoning, employed continually and legitimately where cases are not covered or are not fully or obviously covered by rules in the narrow sense. Principles, therefore, are often involved with consideration of the ends and purposes of the law of war, i.e., the humanization of international armed conflicts. Consequently it may be deduced that a weapon, even though not specifically banned by a narrow rule of the law of war, may still be prohibited if it violates certain fundamental principles of the law of war.

The rules and principles encompassed by the international law of war set forth the procedures which the belligerents are to observe in carrying on the war, and thus place legal limitations within which the force necessary to injure and overcome the enemy may be employed. Broadly speaking the procedural norms as formulated bear upon the commencement of war, its immediate legal effects, and the determination of the belligerent participants; the conduct of hostilities, which would be inclusive of treatment of the victims of war, military occupation, weapons and methods of destruction, and intercourse between the belligerents; neutrality and neutrals; and finally the conclusion of hostilities. By these norms the international society has attempted to curtail with legal fetters the unrestricted exercise of belligerent power.[2]

To speak of war in terms of law may be considered paradoxical. Law suggests an orderly society wherein the conduct of its members is governed by certain rules of behavior. War on the other hand connotes disorder, violence, and a casting off of restraint, legal or otherwise. Despite the anomaly, however, civilized man has since an early time sought to ameliorate the harshness of war by the moderating influence of law. Although warfare in ancient periods was waged with cruelty and little scruple, still the law of certain ancient peoples did attempt to prescribe legal rules of war. For example, and speaking with respect to weapons of a chemical-biological nature, the Indian Code of Manu prohibited poisoned arrows or flaming throw-torches, and Islam forbade the poisoning of water.[3] However, the modern international law of warfare has as its source the practices and customs which arose in Western Europe. Writers generally point to the Middle Ages[4] as a starting point when the influence and doctrine of Christianity and the standards of chivalry began to impose some restraints upon procedures of warfare, although the historians are quick to point out that the period was one of harshness and cruelty in the conduct of war, and any softening influence of the laws of chivalry was probably much overrated.[5]

In the relatively peaceful and stable period which existed from the end of the Napoleonic Wars until World War I, an important effort was made to moderate the conduct of hostilities by various international bodies and international conferences which took up the problems involved in the humanization of warfare.[6] At this time the three basic principles which are said to underlie the law of war became evident. The first principle would justify a belligerent to apply that amount and kind of force necessary for the purpose of war, i.e., the defeat of the enemy within the shortest time and with the least possible expenditure of life and money. The second principle is that of humanity which prohibits violence as to both kind and degree not necessary for the purpose of war. Third is the principle that a certain amount of chivalry, of the spirit of fairness, should prevail in the conduct of hostilities and that resort to certain fraudulent and deceitful practices should be avoided.[7] The latter principle, a relic of medievalism and knighthood, has probably gone by the board today. In an age of mechanized warfare, it is difficult to think of chivalry as a principle distinct from humanity.[8]

Of the two main complementing principles, the first stresses necessity, i.e., military necessity, which admits of all direct destruction of life or limb of the armed enemy and of those whose destruction is incidentally unavoidable in the armed contest. The second stresses the fact that because of humanitarian considerations any violence not necessary for that destruction is prohibited. The kind or degree of force, which of course is directly related to any weapons system including CB weapons, which is proscribed is that not absolutely necessary in the circumstances involved in the operation.

The principle of military necessity does not signify the *Kriegsraison* doctrine which the German Army adopted as early as 1902.[9] Under the German theory, the ordinary laws of war cease to be binding upon a belligerent whenever their observance would defeat the attainment of the object of war; hence a belligerent may use any weapon and any means which will enable him to win the war.[10] This varies radically from the generally accepted doctrine of international law, that belligerents are considered to be bound by the law of war and cannot resort to a plea of military necessity to justify a violation of the rule that belligerents are not unlimited in their choice of weapons or means to overcome an opponent.[11] The concept that military necessity may not overcome the prohibitions of the law of war is accepted by the United States Army Field Manual, *The Law of Land Warfare*, which defines military necessity "as that principle which justifies those measures not forbidden by international law which are indispensable for securing the complete submission of the enemy as soon as possible."[12] It follows from this statement that military necessity loses all importance and a plea thereof is not legally permissible where a clear-cut, firmly established rule of warfare prohibits the employment of certain weapons or methods of war. However, certain customary and conventional rules of international law give sanction in advance to the principle of military necessity as an excuse. Some weapons and conduct are absolutely prohibited by these rules, while others are prohibited conditionally, i.e., they may be resorted to if "imperatively demanded by the necessities of war."[13] In such an instance, where the rule contains a more or less definite built-in recognition of the principle of military necessity, the principle remains cogent.[14]

It also remains valid as a standard to determine the legality of weapons or methods of warfare not already expressly regulated by rules of customary or conventional international law.[15] Hence, the principle may well become of import to a study delving into the legality of chemical-biological weapons under international law. A Calvinistic approach to law might be taken, that law prohibits what it does not command.[16] Such an approach would outlaw any new weapon until expressly sanctioned by a specific rule of law. This theory of law has in general been rejected, at least in a free society, and it is thought that if the law does not legally prohibit, it legally permits.[17] If this be correct, can one conclude that all new weapons not expressly covered by existing prohibitions are to be automatically considered legal? Such a conclusion is unwarranted, for existing prohibitions not only emanate from detailed and express *rules* of warfare established by international custom or set forth in treaties, but in addition they may also be derived from a third law-creating source,[18] namely the general principles of law recognized by civilized nations.[19] Furthermore, there are other international elements which must be taken into consideration in probing the legality of resort to chemical and biological weapons. For example, judicial decisions and the teaching of publicists of various nations, although not in themselves international law–creating sources, have been legally acknowledged to be "subsidiary means for the determination of the rules of law."[20] Other subsidiary means for determination of the laws of warfare are the military manuals or codes issued by states to guide their own armed forces. These manuals have had far-reaching effects on the law of war, in that many of the rules which they authoritatively set forth were usages of war which had already hardened into norms of international customary law and their publication exerted influence on the law-creating process in that it led gradually to codification into international conventions.

MILITARY MANUALS

Until the middle of the nineteenth century no serious attempt had been made to codify that body of tradition and custom governing warfare, but during the early months of the American Civil War, questions involving a knowledge of these customs and usages were constantly arising. Hence President Lincoln issued the first army manual, "Instructions for the Government of the Armies of the United States in the Field."[21] This manual, having been drawn up during a civil war in which both sides had approximately the same type of weapons, tended to emphasize the regulation of the conduct of hostilities rather than to prohibit or limit the use of certain weapons. (Poison was an exception.) It was actually the first codified attempt to distinguish between combatants and noncombatants, with an accompanying limitation on the permissible type of hostilities directed solely against noncombatants. It stated:

Military necessity admits of all direct destruction of life or limb of *armed* enemies, and of other persons whose destruction is incidentally *unavoidable* in the armed contests of the war . . . it allows all destruction of property . . . and of all withholding of sustenance or means of life from the enemy. . . . Military necessity does not admit of . . . the use of poison in any way. . . .

War is not carried on by arms alone. It is lawful to starve the hostile belligerent, armed or unarmed, so that it leads to the speedier subjection of the enemy. . . .

Unnecessary or revengeful destruction of life is not lawful. . . .

The use of poison in any manner, be it to poison wells, or food, or arms, is wholly excluded from modern warfare. He that uses it puts himself out of the pale of the law and usages of war.[22]

Although it was very useful during the American Civil War, if one were to apply these portions of the code to the employment of CB weapons today, one would immediately be faced with the fact that the code contained latent ambiguities. If it is lawful to starve the hostile belligerent, would it be lawful to do so by destroying his food crop through the use of CB weapons? If they fall within the category of poison,[23] it might be argued that it would not be lawful, but would defoliants or soil sterilants, or plant fungi, fall within the concept of poison? Furthermore, it could be argued that food crops do not fall within the definition of food, as crops are only potential food. If it is legal to withhold all means of life from an enemy, would this include polluting the air with chemicals that destroy oxygen, thus asphyxiating him?

Internationalists hoped other nations would immediately follow the lead of the United States and adopt military codes governing the conduct of their armed forces. Only a few did so.[24] It was not until the last decade of the nineteenth century that most of the military powers began to issue manuals which attempted to define, systematize, and reduce to writing many of the rules governing the conduct of war.[25] Even then, the rules laid down in one manual often varied drastically from those in another. These manuals and regulations were, of course, unilateral acts binding only the commanders and the troops of the nation which issued them,[26] and were without international effect. Except insofar as the obligatory character of the principles or rules was established by international law, there was no international legal duty on the part of the government which promulgated them to observe their provisions. In many instances the regulations laid down in manuals were similar, and two nations in conflict might then agree to refrain from a particular action or from the use of a particular weapon (even though not banned by the international laws of war) on the basis of reciprocity, for presumably such reciprocal action would be of benefit to both sides. In spite of the fact that many of the rules which nations enacted as standards of conduct for their own guidance were direct copies of the rules of other nations, this did not in and of itself imply the creation of international law. Nevertheless these expositions of government views of rules of warfare did have important repercussions on the continuing development of conventional and customary international law of war, including the norms governing the employment of weapons of warfare, the method of warfare, and the degree of permissible force. For the similarities and the discrepancies among the various manuals led to attempts on the international level to establish an authoritative international code of the law of war, which it was hoped would be sanctioned by all nations and consequently would be binding on all of them.

CHAPTER THREE

EFFORTS AT TREATY CONTROL OF CB WEAPONS

CONVENTIONAL INTERNATIONAL LAW

A PRIME SOURCE of the norms making up the international law of war is the international treaty or convention.[1] Through the lawmaking treaty entered into by groups of states and later adhered to by other states, international legislation or codification has been achieved.[2] Until the beginning of the twentieth century the law of war was almost wholly customary. At that time, however, a spirit of humanitarianism made itself felt, and in an era of relative peace a series of international conferences assembled and set down a substantial portion of this law in treaties or conventions.[3] The instruments codified to a degree already existing customs of war. They also created new rules for the future conduct of participating states. Unlike customary rules, which are binding upon all states, new conventional rules bind only the contracting parties, and then only to the extent that they consent to be bound in their ratifications. However, such new treaty norms may themselves be transformed into customary rules recognized by nations and thus become applicable to noncontracting parties. As such they may provide seeds from which international customary law springs.

This movement for the codification of war law has from its beginning sought to limit or regulate the use of certain weapons in war, including those which could fall into a category of chemical or biological. An early conference concerned with the methods of warfare and their humanization was that which met in St. Petersburg in 1868 and resulted in the Declaration of St. Petersburg.[4]

THE DECLARATION OF ST. PETERSBURG

With the invention of a bullet which exploded when coming into contact with the human body, the Russian minister of war, believing that such a weapon would add unnecessarily to the sufferings of war, proposed to Czar Alexander II that its use be renounced. The czar convoked an international military commission with the stated purpose contained in the ensuing Declaration of St. Petersburg, "to consider the desirability of forbidding the use of certain projectiles in time of war among civilized nations. . . ."[5] The parties specifically were able to agree to renounce the employment by military or naval forces of any projectile of a weight less than four hundred grams, which is "either explosive or charged with fulminating or inflammable substances."[6]

44

The parties also set forth in the declaration certain broad principles which have relevance to weapons in the CB area. The preamble among other things would prohibit "the employment of arms which uselessly aggravate the sufferings of disabled men, or render their death inevitable . . . as contrary to the laws of humanity."[7] Following this language the viewpoint has been advanced by legal writers that chemical and biological methods of warfare would cause cruel and unnecessary suffering and could also have the effect of rendering death inevitable.[8] These words would seem to be in the main simply a restatement of the principle of humanity—military necessity, as applicable to the legality of new weapons and their use, i.e., that the suffering caused by a new weapon must not be disproportionate to its military effect.[9] It was this theory that formed the basis of choice of the only weapons specifically prohibited by the declaration—small bullets of an explosive or inflammable nature. These projectiles were needlessly cruel in proportion to their military importance or tactical effect. Larger shells of this nature were not forbidden, for they had military advantages sufficiently great in proportion to the suffering which they might cause.[10]

One writer has even advanced the proposition that the provision of the declaration banning small bullets of an explosive or inflammable nature would by implication outlaw the use of chemical incendiaries as direct antipersonnel weapons.[11] A belief that a stipulation constraining the use of explosive and inflammable bullets weighing less than fourteen ounces can be interpreted to prohibit flamethrowers and fire bombs seems farfetched.

The St. Petersburg Declaration is obligatory only upon the contracting parties in instances of war between or among themselves. Its adherents were seventeen European states as well as Persia, Turkey, and Brazil.[12] The preambulatory principles are, however, enumerations of general principles of the international law of war, military necessity, and humanity, and are applicable as principles binding international society.[13]

THE HAGUE PEACE CONFERENCES OF 1899 AND 1907

BACKGROUND

In 1874, at the invitation of the czar of Russia, the Conference of Brussels, composed of representatives of all of the European powers of importance, met and drew up a code entitled "Project of International Declaration Concerning the Laws and Customs of War."[14] Although this declaration did not directly mention weapons of chemical or biological nature, it did expressly forbid the "[e]mployment of poison or poisoned weapons."[15] The feasibility of a stipulation which would ban the diffusion of contagious diseases or the employment of substances of a nature to develop such diseases in enemy territory was considered during the conference, but no express prohibition was believed warranted, inasmuch as it was thought that military commanders would use all means to prevent their own troops from being infected with diseases, and thus would not be instrumental in starting an epidemic which might backfire and spread to men under their own command. It was also thought that a provision forbidding the use of poison and poisoned weapons would cover substances of a nature to spread contagious disease.[16] In any event, the only prohibition stated in the declaration related to poison and poisoned weapons. The Brussels Declaration failed to be adopted by the governments represented,[17] but it exercised a strong influence on the law of war, forming the basis of the conventions respecting the laws and customs of war adopted by the Hague Conferences in 1899 and 1907, both of which were convened under Russian initiative.[18]

Certain agreements reached at these conferences have significant bearing on the international legality of resort to CB weapons in time of war. These include the Hague Gas Declaration of 1899, which endeavored to ban a specific weapon of chemical warfare, and the provisions related to poison and poisoned weapons of Convention II of the 1899 conference which was readopted as Convention IV at the 1907 conference.[19]

THE HAGUE GAS DECLARATION

The Hague Gas Declaration provided in part that the signatories,

[i]nspired by the sentiments which found expression in the Declaration of St. Petersburg . . . [d]eclare as follows:
The Contracting Powers agree to abstain from the use of projectiles the sole object of which is the diffusion of asphyxiating or deleterious gases.[20]

When that part of the Russian program for the 1899 conference which would prohibit "new explosives, or any powders more powerful than those now in use" was defeated by a vote in the subcommittee to which it had been referred, the Russian delegate changed his tactics and presented a plan to forbid the employment of projectiles charged with explosives which diffuse asphyxiating or deleterious gases. Objection was raised that any high explosive shell would generate certain amounts of asphyxiating or deleterious gas. It was therefore agreed that the ban should apply only to those weapons the object of which was to diffuse such gases and not to those which might incidentally upon explosion spread them. This interpretation would prohibit the projectile only if after comparison of the gaseous and splinter effects it was found that the gaseous exceeded the splinter effects.[21] The final declaration then applied the ban to projectiles with the *sole* object of diffusing asphyxiating or deleterious gases.

This declaration was accepted by all of the states represented at the

1899 conference except the United States and Great Britain. Great Britain agreed to it in 1907. Twenty-seven states finally adhered or ratified.[22] Agreements in support of the ban on such gas weapons were based on the thought that gas projectiles were of a barbarous character, treacherous and cruel, similar to the poisoning of drinking water; that if they were directed against cities they would cause a greater number of deaths than would ordinary shells; that death from asphyxiating gas was more cruel than death from bullets; and finally that means should be sought to put enemies *hors de combat*, but not to certain death.[23] The opposition of the delegates of the United States to this declaration was based on their official instructions, which took a dim view of the Russian proposals to prohibit the use of certain weapons such as new firearms, new and more powerful explosives, submarines, torpedo boats, and vessels with rams.[24] The defense of the United States stand on the gas projectiles was forcibly stated by Captain Mahan. His reasons are set forth in the following words:

1. That no shell emitting such gases is as yet in practical use, or has undergone adequate experiment; consequently a vote taken now would be taken in ignorance of the facts as to whether the results would be of a decisive character, or whether injury in excess of that necessary to attain the end of warfare, the immediate disabling of the enemy, would be inflicted.

2. That the reproach of cruelty and perfidy, addressed against these supposed shells, was equally uttered formerly against firearms and torpedoes, both of which are now employed without scruple. Until we know the effects of such asphyxiating shells, there was no saying whether they would be more or less merciful than missiles now permitted.

3. That it was illogical, and not demonstrably humane, to be tender about asphyxiating men with gas, when all were prepared to admit that it was allowable to blow the bottom out of an ironclad at midnight, throwing four or five hundred into the sea, to be choked by water, with scarcely the remotest chance of escape. If, and when, a shell emitting asphyxiating gases alone has been successfully produced, then, and not before, men will be able to vote intelligently on the subject.[25]

Unanimity was not present within the United States delegation, for Ambassador White wished to support the declaration on grounds of humanity, and he was particularly impressed with an argument against a thesis of Mahan to the effect that asphyxiating bombs would be used against cities and could destroy large numbers of noncombatants, while torpedoes were used only against enemy military and naval forces. However, he deferred to the opinions of military and naval experts on the delegation.[26]

As an instrument creating clear-cut obligation to bar the use of chemicals in war, the declaration is limited and deficient. First, the very restricted language of the declaration makes it of little use even among parties obligated. The declaration forbids projectiles the *sole* object of which is to spread the asphyxiating or deleterious gas. The use of the words *sole object* permits a literal interpretation to the effect that any projectile diffusing even gravely injurious gases which had objects other than the diffusion of such injurious gases would be permitted, although as noted above this was not the interpretation intended by the drafters. To have effectuated their true intention, the drafters should have written "primary" or "main" rather than "sole" object. Too, the declaration bars projectiles which diffuse gas; it does not prohibit generating tanks or cylinders. A projectile would apparently be a missile or a shell from firearm or cannon. The Germans neatly avoided the declaration's literal wording in their first use of gas in World War I by employing canisters or containers fired from the ground, from which gases were released into the wind and reached the enemy troops by being blown against them. Actually the delegates at the First Hague Conference were not thinking in terms of instruments other than shells or projectiles for the spreading of gas and thus failed to cover other means. The conference, if it meant to interdict noxious gas in war, should have prohibited the use thereof no matter how it might be diffused. Therefore, the narrow language of the declaration makes it of scant value as an international prohibition of the use of gas in war.[27]

A second problem of interpretation arises from the declaration's terminology as to the type of gas to which it applies. It forbids projectiles having as object the spreading of asphyxiating or deleterious gas. An asphyxiating gas would be a lethal or severely injurious gas with a suffocating effect. The addition of the word "deleterious" would extend the meaning to any gas which would be hurtful or injurious to life or health. This would broaden the definition to include not only the killing or gravely injurious gases, but also those such as some incapacitating and riot control gases which may have injurious or harmful effects on health. A division of opinion, however, has resulted as to the exact meaning of the language. Kunz speaks of nontoxic irritant gases as being excluded from the definition,[28] while others would include them on the ground that their use in heavy quantities can well be capable of injuring health.[29]

A third deficiency is that the obligation of this declaration extended only to the contracting states and then only "in the case of a war between two or more of them." Moreover, should a contracting belligerent be joined by a noncontracting belligerent in armed conflict between contracting powers, the obligation established by the declaration would cease to be binding.[30] Since a limited number of states have adhered and accepted the obligation, this has been said to restrict the significance of the declaration.[31] Another view to the contrary, however, has indicated that the obligation of the declaration is so universally recognized as to be an accepted prohibitory rule of international law independent of treaty obligation, as an expression of the principles of the law of war which prohibit poison and materials causing unnecessary suffering.[32] This may be, but these two principles do not depend upon the declaration.

Finally, the import of this declaration is further diminished by the fact that it did little to prevent the use of gas during World War I; and further, it would appear that it has been largely superseded by the more absolute ban of the Geneva Gas Protocol of 1925.[33]

POISON AND POISONED WEAPONS

Convention IV respecting the laws and customs of war on land of the 1907 conference, like its counterpart Convention II[34] of the 1899 conference, has relevance in the development of legal limitations on CB weapons. Article 23 of the Annex to Convention IV established Regulations Respecting the Laws and Customs of War on Land in language almost identical to that of the same article of the 1899[35] instrument. It provides in part:

In addition to the prohibitions provided by special Conventions it is especially forbidden

(a) To employ poison or poisoned weapons;
(b) To kill or wound treacherously individuals belonging to the hostile nation or army;

. . . .

(e) To employ arms, projectiles, or material calculated to cause unnecessary suffering. . . .[36]

Sections (b) and (e) of Article 23 pertaining to treachery and unnecessary suffering can be equated to the principles of chivalry and humanity, general principles of the law of warfare to be discussed as pertaining to CB warfare under those headings.[37] The prohibition of the use of poison has been said to be a declaration of customary international law,[38] but nevertheless in the two Hague Annexes the prohibition of a specific instrumentality of warfare, poison, is codified through international convention, and the language of the ban is often cited as a legal limitation against the use of CB weapons.

The interdiction against the use of poison and poisoned weapons of the Hague Regulations was accepted expressly by some forty-eight states including the United States,[39] but since it is simply a codification of a customary rule of international law, it in effect confirms a rule already obligatory upon all states.

The rationale behind the outlawing of the use of poison or poisoned weapons is said to rest upon various legal principles, such as those relating to unnecessary suffering or those established by the rules of chivalry which would condemn their use as treacherous or dishonorable.[40] As these are principles of the law of war, whether CB weapons fall within them should properly be discussed under that heading. But separate consideration must be given to the question of whether any or all CB weapons fall within the absolute rule expressly forbidding the use of poison or poisoned weapons which emerged in customary law and was codified by the Hague Regulations. Therefore attention must be given to CB weapons as poison, to determine whether the word poison encompasses CB instrumentalities. And, if so, a further determination must be made as to whether the Hague Regulations were drawn up with the intent to include CB weapons.

Few writers of international law, in discussing the rule against the use of poison in warfare, define the meaning of poison for the purpose of interpreting the rule. Resort must be had to the popular and technical meanings attributed to the term, which, to a degree, coincide, although an exact and legalistic definition as to what constitutes poison is not possible.[41]

Definitions do stress, however, that poison is a substance or agent which when introduced into or absorbed by a living organism causes death or injury thereto. It is also common to speak of poison as an agent which acts on the organism chemically or by physicochemical mechanisms.[42] The action must not take place by mechanical means, but by the inherent qualities of the substance. This terminology would exclude from the meaning of poison agents causing physical damage only, i.e., those killing or injuring by means of force such as that caused by the cutting of the body with a sword or knife, the penetration of the body with a bullet, or the injury caused by explosions or explosive shells.[43] Also worthy of note is the fact that the dosage is stressed; it is stated that the agent must kill or injure with a small dosage. This is said to be requisite because almost any substance can be harmful if administered in sufficiently large amounts. Dosage would appear, however, to be a somewhat relative factor, for harmful effects and the quantity necessary to bring them about may depend upon that which is the subject of the poison. In an individual dosage may vary depending upon his health, his age, sex, or previous exposure (which may increase tolerance or through cumulative effect may render him more susceptible).[44] Therefore, possibly a definition is more nearly accurate that defines poison as a substance producing chemically an injurious or deadly effect when introduced into an organism in relatively small quantities.

Toxic chemical agents which make up a large part of chemical warfare would automatically be poisonous under the various definitions. A toxic substance is a poisonous substance, one which kills or injures through chemical or physicochemical action on the body;[45] and the use of such a substance to reduce the military effectiveness of the enemy by killing or injuring the members of the armed force would constitute a use of poison in warfare. The nerve agents, the mustard agents, the blood agents, and the choking agent phosgene all fall within a category of toxic or poisonous chemical agents.[46]

As to incapacitating chemical agents and riot control chemical agents, it has been contended in some quarters that these should not be classified as toxic agents, nor should they be included within the concept of chemical warfare, since they are not designed to be death-dealing or to inflict permanent injury.[47] General Rothschild indicates that there is disagreement as to the poisonous effects of hallucinogenic mental incapacitants. "At present," he writes, "there is some controversy among doctors and scientists as to whether LSD-25, and other hallucinogenic drugs such as mescaline and peyote, induce a true toxic psychosis."[48] Some writers have even gone so far as to contend that not only do such agents escape the odium of the toxic classification, but also their use in warfare should be considered beneficial.[49]

Although accepting a definition of poison including not only substances which cause death, but also those which cause injury to health, a French writer concludes that the psychochemical drugs are neither death-dealing nor injurious to health and therefore are not poisons. He states that the psychochemicals "do not bring about any malady and that the state of disorientation which they provoke is only of short duration. . . ." As a result they do not qualify as poisons for purposes of the Hague Regulation interdiction.[50]

Another author has rather straddled the fence, calling these chemical mental incapacitants less toxic than other agents; and with respect to LSD-25 he has noted that serious harmful effects on the brain chemistry or of a biophysical nature were not present.[51]

Disagreements with these positions exist. In the literature the psychochemicals have been called toxic, poisonous, and hazardous.[52] The notion that they are not injurious to health has been questioned, for recent reports on LSD-25 indicate that this particular drug may well create long-range mental problems in a user, and genetic problems as well. Moreover, mescaline is listed as an organic poison; bufotenine is called a toxic;[53] and psilocybine is derived from a toxic mushroom.[54]

The physical chemical incapacitating agents and the riot control agents resemble each other to the extent that it is intended that they produce a temporary physical disability without permanent harm or injury. They prevent enemy exposed personnel from performing primary military duties, but there is said to be complete recovery from these effects.[55] If one accepts the argument that a substance which has effects for a limited time only and from which no permanent injury ensues is not a poison, then these agents may not fall within the meaning of the term. However, these incapacitating and riot control agents are toxic, with chemical reactions on the system which may, in cases of overexposure, cause serious illness or death. They would fall under the label of poison.

Furthermore, it is doubtful if one can accept the short duration of the agent's effect as removing it from the poison category. Under a broad definition of poison there is included the "impairment" of the organism, and such agents are used to and do impair by causing vomiting and lachrymation. The fact that one may recover from a poison would not seem to be conclusive as to whether he was poisoned. Although little is known about other incapacitating agents, they too would appear to have a toxic chemical reaction on the system causing temporary paralysis, blindness, or deafness.

For the purposes of Article 23(a) of the Hague Regulations, inquiry must also be made to determine whether or not all biological agents or certain biological agents can be categorized as poison. It will be remembered that the Brussels Conference did concern itself not only with a prohibition of poison, but also with forbidding the spread of contagious disease. The latter prohibition was, however, abandoned, and only poisons were expressly banned, although at least some belief seemed to be present that this could also cover substances which spread contagious disease.[56] The Brussels text outlawing poisons and poisoned weapons only was accepted by the Hague Regulations. No mention is made in the minutes of these conferences of contagious diseases or germ warfare. If biological agents are restrained, they must fall under the language inhibiting poison. Biological warfare can be described as "the military use of living organisms or their toxic products to cause death, disability or damage to man, his domestic animals or crops. . . ."[57]

Apart from antimateriel agents (either biological or chemical), which would not appear to be poisonous because they are not applied to living organisms,[58] the issue of biological agents as poisons narrows to a consideration of the use of microorganisms to infect with disease or of the use of toxic biological products, especially those produced by microorganisms. The latter are called toxins, and they are poisons. A United States Department of the Army and Air Force Manual has declared this expressly, stipulating that toxins are "poisonous substances chemically allied to proteins."[59] A legal commentator has stated that toxins are "inanimate substances which meet the definition of poison" and are for that reason prohibited by Article 23(a) of the Hague Regulations.[60]

A distinction might be made between toxins and disease-causing microorganisms. One legal authority, for example, has stated that while toxins are poisonous, disease-causing microorganisms are not because they only create infection through direct contact with a victim.[61] The author making this distinction may be drawing the line too narrowly, for although he speaks broadly of toxins (apparently all toxins) as poisons, which they are, he still seems to be thinking primarily of botulinum toxin, which is noninfectious and which is not grown or reproduced in the body. The poisoning in this case is due to the toxin which has formed in the ingested material. He may also be thinking of staphylococcus toxin, which produces a food poison, not an infection, the poisoning following ingestion of food in which staphylococci are growing. These are, of course, poisons; but other toxins, also poisons, are formed by bacteria coming into direct contact with the human body and are characterized by infection. For example, diphtheria is a disease described as one where "bacteria lodge in the mucous membranes of the throat producing virulent toxins that destroy tissue."[62] It is also infectious.[63] It would seem best simply to say that any such infectious agent which also produces a toxin would come within the meaning of poison. But this would fail to cover those biological agents which do not produce toxins. Can these latter microorganisms qualify as poison? Another commentator has flatly concluded that all such biological agents, whether toxin-creating or not, are to be characterized as poison in accordance with the definition thereof. They are substances causing death or injury in living organisms, and these effects are the results of chemical changes in the host produced directly or indirectly by the bacteria.[64] Moreover, an infectious disease is said to invade the tissues, and the damage is done by pathogenic organisms.[65] Thus the disease acts not mechanically but by its own inherent qualities.[66] Nevertheless, in common usage non-toxin-producing diseases are not generally equated with poison.

Even though biological agents may be considered as poison, a further issue arises as to whether or not the Hague Regulations proscriptions against poison in general were intended to affect or apply to biological agents so as to outlaw them all in war. In this connection inquiry can first be directed to the use of disease-producing biological agents (as well as chemical agents) to produce casualties or death in animals or to damage or destroy plants. The antipoison rule is commonly said to encompass and forbid the poisoning of food, water, and supplies and, of course, the use of poisoned weapons.[67] To the extent that certain animals and plants are utilized as food, it might be thought that their poisoning would be prohibited. However, such a generalized conclusion can hardly be reached. Antianimal agents are those used to incapacitate or destroy domestic animals so as to limit the enemy's food supply and his use of the animals in transportation and crop cultivation, and to decrease the amount of useful animal products. Antiplant agents, in causing disease or damage to crops, also reduce food supply, and destroy economically valuable plants. In addition they are used as defoliants.[68] Article 23(a) relates to the use of poison to injure or destroy the *person* of the enemy, rather than the destruction of his property. To the extent that antianimal, antiplant agents are used to deprive the enemy armed forces of property valuable to them and upon which they are dependent, there would seem to be no serious objection.[69] Thus, rule 37 of the U.S. Army Field Manual declares that the antipoison proviso does not apply to the use of "chemical or bacterial agents harmless to man, to destroy crops intended solely for consumption by the armed forces (if that fact can be determined)."[70] This does not mention the destruction of animals, but there would appear to be little legal distinction that can be made between the destruction of animals and that of plants. If destruction of one type of property is permitted to deprive the enemy of its use, destruction of the other should also be permitted.

If chemical or biological agents which are poisonous also to man are used to destroy crops or animals, would the result be the same? To contaminate such food and also water deliberately so as to poison enemy forces would of course offend against Article 23(a). Possibly the use of such poison harmful to man would not offend if taken to deprive the enemy forces of use of stocks of food and water, if warning is given or other steps taken to apprise the enemy that such supplies have been poisoned.[71] But some legal authority would view such poison as illegal even if notice of the poisoning were given; and this position seems to be the correct one, for warning notices may be removed or destroyed.[72] Moreover, those supporting legality if notice is given change their position if civilians are completely deprived of water supplies or food supplies.[73] Here, even if steps are taken to warn of the poisoning, the pollution has been regarded as unlawful. Garner, taking this latter position, states: "As a belligerent may not lawfully requisition for his use the entire food supply, leaving the inhabitants to starve, so it may be doubted whether he has a right to destroy their water supply, which is as essential to their existence as food."[74]

There would seem to be nothing in the rules of warfare which prohibits one belligerent from depriving the other belligerent nation, including its civilian population, of essential supplies if military necessity demands. A blockade is meant to accomplish such a result, although the Geneva Conventions of 1949 do attempt to require free passage of certain supplies embracing essential foodstuffs for children, expectant mothers, and maternity cases.[75] Even a general devastation of a country —usually absolutely forbidden—may be permitted in exceptional cases when demanded by the necessities of war. The rule to which Garner refers is applicable to enemy occupation of territory after active military operations therein have come to an end, for here all food and water may not be requisitioned from enemy noncombatants. To the contrary, there is a duty upon the occupying belligerents to insure adequate supplies.[76] The rule which prohibits poisoning of food and water supplies stands on its own feet and is not derived from a rule concerned with depriving enemy civilian personnel in some instances of such supplies. This is well exemplified by the fact that a cut-off of the water supply of a besieged place is permitted, even though civilians may be found there, but the poisoning of the water to deprive them of its use would be violative of the rule against poisons.[77] Thus, any deliberate contamination of food and water supplies which would make them poisonous to man appears to be prohibited; but the question as to whether such contamination is prohibited if notice is given and there is no deception is open.[78]

A second subject for examination is whether there can be derived from the broad general terms "poison or poisoned weapons" of Article 23(a) of the Hague Regulations particular prohibitions of chemical or biological agents in war when those agents fall into the category of poison and when they are used as antipersonnel agents. Schwarzenberger and Greenspan take a clear-cut stand, educing from the Hague Regulations Article 23(a) a proscription against chemical or gas and bacteriological warfare which has now become an international customary law binding on all states.[79] Kelsen is similarly inclined, adhering to the position that insofar as asphyxiating gases as well as biological weapons have toxic effect, they fall within the rule forbidding poison or poisoned weapons.[80]

Stone and McDougal and Feliciano are skeptical of this position.[81] The last two writers are of the opinion that where ambiguities, gaps, or contradictions in a treaty exist, the instrument must be restrictively interpreted; i.e., it must not be carried beyond that which is absolutely necessary to implement its major purposes, for to do so would impose new purposes and unnecessary detailed obligations upon the contracting parties. They further contend that the words of a treaty must be interpreted in light of the facts and policies surrounding the period of the treaty-making and state that such words should not be given "absolutistic meanings which can be projected into the future without regard to original and contemporaneous contexts."[82] They conclude that the Hague language forbidding poison or poisoned arms was "historically directed against poisoned arrows and javelins" and thus can hardly form a basis for a prohibition of modern chemical or biological methods.[83]

O'Brien[84] adopts a somewhat similar attitude, contending that it was not the intention of the framers of Article 23(a) "to establish broad, conventional prohibitions to weapons and weapons systems non-existent at the time the conventions were drafted."[85] He goes on to say, in this vein, that the article could be interpreted to include biological warfare, but only in forms which had come into existence and which had been used in war previous to 1907.[86] Spelling this language out, the proviso against poison in warfare would apply to chemical-biological agents categorized as poison if they were pre-1907 substances and if they had been used in war prior to that time. Post-1907 substances would not be disallowed. Such a restricted view appears to be somewhat broadened by this same author, for he agrees that the customary law as declared by Article 23(a) would prohibit the use of poisons to assassinate enemy leaders as well as poisoned weapons such as spears, arrows, swords, bayonets,[87] etc. As another publicist has pointed out, a prohibition of poisons and poisoned weapons constitutes a very extensive ban which could cover most means of biological and chemical warfare, pre- or post-1907.

Thus, Neinast has asked:

What is the difference between secreting a lethal dose of pre-1907 poison in the drinking glass of an enemy general and infesting the water supply for his entire headquarters with an infilterable germicidal-resistant virus that produces an incurable, fatal illness? If it is illegal to make bayonets infectious with germs which produce very slow healing wounds, why is it not also illegal to immunize friendly troops against tetanus and then spray all battlefields with tetanus spores which can enter the wounds of the enemy and delay healing?[88]

This statement shows that although there may be little relation of the new CB weapons to the old the results may be the same. It is something of an absurdity to include some and exclude others depending upon an arbitrary date. The position that a conference through a convention cannot regulate methods of warfare unknown at the time is open to some question.[89] There would appear to be no rule of international law which would exclude regulation of future technological scientific developments. This would be a prerogative of sovereign states. This is borne out by the fact that the parties in 1899 regulated shells which had never been used before for the diffusion of gases. Indeed, the 1899 Hague Conference had as one of its purposes the interdiction of new firearms and explosives.[90] In fact, it has been reasoned that agreement was reached to prohibit such shells only because they had not reached military utility, inasmuch as the conference refused proposals to eliminate weapons which had become militarily useful.[91] A more cogent argument is that which would seek to determine whether it *was intended to regulate* means of warfare unknown at the time. Strong argument can be made that the conferences at the Hague did not actually intend to encompass the use of chemical-biological agents in warfare within the prohibitions of Article 23(a).[92] As to chemical and gas warfare, the contracting parties at the 1899 conference sought to provide for its regulation by the Hague Gas Declaration. It would be strange to think that the parties intended gas to fall under the more general prohibition of poison if they felt obliged to provide for it specifically in another regulation.[93] Evidence as to biological agents is somewhat more equivocal, for there seemed to be some belief that the Brussels Declaration against poison impliedly included the spreading of contagious disease,[94] although at the same time there seemed to be some notion that this was primarily a sanitation measure to be followed by commanding officers in occupied territory.[95] Nevertheless, the United States Army manuals of 1914 and 1940 accepted the view that Article 23(a) of the Hague Regulations in its prohibition of poison prohibited "the use of means calculated to spread contagious diseases."[96] The current United States Department of the Army field manual has now, however, reversed itself and proclaims as the military point of view that "[t]he United States is not a party to any treaty, now in force, that prohibits or restricts the use in warfare of toxic or nontoxic gases, of smoke or incendiary materials, or of bacteriological warfare."[97]

Strong evidence that biological warfare was not regulated previously by convention or by custom is provided by the fact that some forty nations felt it necessary to ratify the later Geneva Gas Protocol extending the prohibition against gas "to the use of bacteriological methods of warfare."[98]

CONCLUSION

This, then, is the unsatisfactory state of the law relating to CB weaponry as set down in conventions prior to World War I. The Hague Gas Declaration would appear at first reading to establish a fairly clear-cut prohibition of projectiles having as sole object the diffusing of asphyxiating or deleterious gas. But its wording is so restrictive, as is its application among states, that it has been of little usefulness as a ban on gas weapons. The Hague interdiction of poison has been subject to so many differences of opinion among legal authorities in relation to chemical-biological agents that it becomes impossible to point with any certainty to its relevance as to any prohibitory effect in the chemical-biological field. It can be said with assurance that it is not applicable to agents which clearly fall without a poison classification or to anti-materiel agents. In other areas disputes exist as to whether certain agents are poison so as to fall within this rule; whether agents would be encompassed if not in existence prior to 1907; and whether the rule was intended to apply to chemical-biological weapons in any event.

This divergent thought makes these pre-World War I conventional principles of extremely limited utility as legal fetters on the use of chemical-biological agents in war.

CHAPTER FOUR

ATTEMPTS BETWEEN THE WARS TO OUTLAW CB WEAPONS

WORLD WAR I PEACE TREATIES

IN JANUARY, 1919, after the end of World War I, the successful Allied nations gathered in Paris to draw up a treaty of peace with Germany and its associated states.[1] Finally, on June 28, 1919, the treaty with Germany was signed at Versailles.[2] Thereafter a series of treaties, known as the "treaties of the Paris suburbs" were signed with the other defeated nations. On September 10, 1919, the peace treaty between the Allies and Austria was concluded in Saint-Germain-en-Laye.[3] There followed on November 27, 1919, the Treaty of Neuilly-Sur-Seine between the Allies and Bulgaria;[4] on June 4, 1920, the Treaty of the Trianon[5] between the Allies and Hungary; and on August 11, 1920, the Treaty of Sèvres between the Allies and Turkey.[6] This treaty was never ratified by Turkey and hence was never effective.

The working system of the peace conference had a direct effect on the development of international legal limitations on chemical weapons. The full conference, which consisted of plenipotentiaries of all the Allied powers, proved too bunglesome a working body to draft a treaty. Consequently, the large powers, to maintain control of the principal problems, established a Council of Ten, who devoted themselves to the task of drawing up the military and armaments section of the treaty. This Council of Ten consisted of the heads of governments and foreign ministers of the United States, Great Britain, France, and Italy, and two representatives from Japan.[7] Once they approved the wording of the various portions of the treaty, these were presented to the Plenary Conference for final approval.

A preliminary question faced by the Council of Ten was that of which language version of the treaties should be authoritative.[8] No agreement was reached at the beginning of this conference, but in the final treaty with Germany it was stated that the "French and English texts are both authentic." It should be noted that Italian texts were prepared only for the Austrian and Bulgarian treaties, but in these treaties the French text was stated to be superior to all others.[9]

Once the Council of Ten came to a unanimous decision on a certain point, this decision, often loosely worded, was turned over to a drafting commission, which would then convert the substance of the decisions into legal phraseology for insertion into the treaty.[10] In some instances the drafting commission went farther in interpretation than apparently was intended,[11] and this is possibly the case with the articles in the various treaties dealing with chemical weapons.

The first draft of the article in the Treaty of Versailles on chemical weapons was drawn up by a commission of military experts of the major powers and was placed in the chapter which dealt with disarming Germany and with placing limitations on future armaments for Germany.[12] This chapter was viewed as an ingenious method to limit Germany's power for aggression and offense. The English version of the first draft stated: "Production or use of asphyxiating, poisonous or similar gases, any liquid, any material and any similar device capable of use in war are forbidden."[13] In view of its location in the draft treaty, it would seem to have been understood "are forbidden to Germany."

The Council of Ten considered this draft in conjunction with the importation of arms into Germany, which it agreed to ban in the following words: "Importation into Germany of arms, munitions and war material of every kind shall be strictly prohibited. The same applies to the manufacture for and export of arms, munitions, and war material of every kind to foreign countries."[14] The British foreign minister inquired how it would be possible to forbid the importation of materials required for the manufacturing of asphyxiating gases, since many of these were innocent chemicals which later could be perverted to nefarious uses. After pondering this problem, the French foreign minister came up with the suggestion that the following sentence be added to the ban on the production or use of gas: "The same applies to materials *specially intended* for the manufacture, storage and use of said products or devices."[15] This was agreed upon and the article was turned over to the drafting commission. The drafting commission apparently had ideas of its own, for in the second draft of the treaty, it was stated:

The use of asphyxiating, poisonous or other gases and all analogous liquids, materials or devices being prohibited, their manufacture and importation are strictly forbidden in Germany.

The same applies to materials for the manufacture, storage and use of said products or devices.[16]

In reviewing this language, the Council of Ten realized that the drafting commission had not grasped what the council desired: therefore, on its own initiative the council rephrased the second paragraph to include "materials *specially intended*." This became the final English version. But the complete English text of Article 171 was not an accurate translation of the French text. The English prohibition on "asphyxiating, poisonous or other gases" is not identical to the French prohibition of "gaz asphyxiants, toxiques ou similaires," for the English implies a general prohibition on the use of all gas, while the French has been said to prohibit only gases of a specific type.[17] Since both languages are authentic, it would be impossible to say which is the correct interpretation.

Furthermore, some legal writers imply that this article of the treaty establishes that the nations gathered in Paris were in effect acknowledging the fact that all employment of gas in time of war had been prohibited by international law.[18] For example, Van Eysinga states that this particular wording indicates that the drafters were setting forth a declaration of existing law, and were not putting out a new regulation or law.[19] This would seem to be difficult to support in view of the history of the article, which was mainly, as we have seen, an attempt to place armament limits on Germany. The drafting commission had changed the wording of the original version from "are forbidden" to a broader statement, "being prohibited," but it is doubtful in view of the lack of discussions on this matter that the signatories of the treaty intended this to be a statement of what they considered the established rule of international law. Certainly if they did so intend, then the proviso goes much farther than that of the Hague Conventions, and the legitimate question then arises as to when this prohibition came into effect.

After completion of the military terms of the German treaty,[20] the military clauses of the Austrian and Hungarian treaties were drawn up.[21] Article 135 of the Austrian treaty and Article 119 of the Hungarian treaty were modeled in part after Article 171 of the Treaty of Versailles, but a new weapon was added and there were some word changes:

The use of flame throwers, asphyxiating, poisonous or other gases, and all similar liquids, materials or devices being prohibited, their manufacture and importation are strictly forbidden in Austria [Hungary].

Material specifically intended for the manufacture, storage or use of the said products or devices is equally forbidden.[22]

Because of the slow progress on the German treaty made by the Council of Ten, some speedier system had to be devised for the other treaties. It was decided that the foreign ministers should be dropped, and the four heads of state—British, United States, French, and Italian—should be the only participants.[23] When the military experts presented the Committee of Four with the disarmament section of the Austrian and Hungarian treaties, one of the four suggested that flamethrowers be added, and this was done.[24] This would seem to be additional evidence of the fact that the framers of the treaties did not intend to imply that they were setting forth established principles of international law relating to prohibited weapons, for flamethrowers were new weapons, invented by Germany during the war.[25] No conventions were in existence that regulated flamethrowers, nor could they be said to be specifically outlawed by customary international law. Only if they fell within the unnecessary suffering principle or the principle of humanity of the laws of war could they be said to be banned,[26] and no claims to this effect were made. It is not unreasonable to conclude that the Committee of Four was intent only upon placing an additional arms limitation on Austria and Hungary.

As in the Treaty of Versailles, the French text refers to "gaz asphyxiants, toxiques ou similaires," while the British text would seem to be more extensive in its inclusion of all other gases or analogous liquids. Of course, here, the French text is the authoritative one. The Bulgarian treaty followed the wording adopted by the Austrian and Hungarian treaties, in that it, too, prohibited flamethrowers.

Although the United States was a signatory of all these treaties, and in spite of the fact that President Woodrow Wilson had been very active in their drafting, when they were presented to the Senate for ratification the requisite two-thirds of the senators did not favor them, for the reason that they incorporated the Covenant of the League of Nations—an organization opposed by many conservative Democrats and a majority of the Republicans.[27] The United States never ratified these treaties, and, absurd as it might appear, had to negotiate new peace treaties. In the Treaty Restoring Friendly Relations Between the United States and Germany of August 25, 1921, certain portions of the Versailles Treaty were incorporated, including the English version of the article on asphyxiating gas.[28] This was also true of the Austrian and Hungarian treaties.

Another error in translation occurred in the Versailles Treaty, when "tous liquides, matières ou procédés analogues" was translated into all "analogous liquids, materials or devices." A *procédé* is not a device; it is a process, while a device is a mechanism. It has been intimated by some writers that both the English and French versions would prohibit bacteriological weapons.[29] The only foundation for such a statement would seem to be that bacteriological weapons would fall under the classification of "analogous liquids, materials or devices—or processes." This would be rather a difficult proposition to uphold, for bacterial agents and chemical agents are dissimilar,[30] although the weapons system which delivers them may be the same.[31] Biological agents in and of themselves are not "liquids" or "devices." It is possible that they might fall under the interpretation of "materials" or "process," if these terms are given a very elastic meaning—but it is doubtful whether the treaty drafters had any intent to cover biological agents in the treaty. According to the records of the conference, this phrase was employed in an attempt to extract from the Germans[32] a disclosure of their secret processes for the manufacture of chemical agents.[33]

The Paris Peace Treaties were signed by twenty-six of the Allied Nations,[34] China being the only one refusing to sign.[35] And, of course, each treaty, except that of Turkey, was signed by the defeated power to which it applied. Among the signatories, only the United States failed to ratify the treaties.[36] But the treaties were denounced, criticized, and broken so many times prior to World War II that it was generally conceded that they were no longer a relevant portion of conventional international law. Following the rise of Hitler, Germany breached all of the military clauses of the treaty by the amassing of forbidden weapons; this was known to all the signatory nations, yet they did nothing to stop Germany. By implication they condoned the assumption that the treaty was a dead letter. McNair points out

that most governments would recognize that failure by one party to invoke a treaty, or acquiescence by it in acts or conduct prima facie constituting violations of a treaty, would in time justify the other in regarding the treaty as having lapsed, provided that such failure or acquiescence
(1) had been frequently repeated,
(2) could be imputed to a government and not merely to individuals,
(3) was incapable of reasonable explanation, and
(4) had not been negatived by protests reserving the rights of the party affected; and it is probable that in time even a protest which was not accompanied or followed up by some other action would not suffice to keep the treaty alive.[37]

THE 1922 WASHINGTON DISARMAMENT CONFERENCE

As we have seen, one of the major objectives of the Allies at Versailles was to disarm Germany. In addition, the two English-speaking nations, Great Britain and the United States, wanted to reduce the burden of national armaments through international agreements for general disarmament.[38]

Nevertheless, following the war, instead of reducing armaments, the United States, Great Britain, and Japan entered into a naval competition. Japan, as an ally of Great Britain during the war, had extended her sphere of influence in the Far East, and with her increased sea power even threatened the Philippines (which were then American possessions) with encirclement. This was viewed with apprehension by American citizens who had financial and commercial interests in the Far East.[39] France, while not entering into a naval armaments race, continued to build up her land forces because the Senate of the United States had refused to ratify a treaty signed at Paris whereby the United States and Great Britain would guarantee French security against future German aggression.[40] Furthermore, all of the arming nations were engaged in adding to their armaments the new weapons which had been used in World War I, such as airplanes, submarines, flamethrowers, and poisonous gases.

Recognizing the danger of the situation, the Senate of the United States suggested to President Harding that he invite interested nations to a conference which was to be charged with the duty of reducing armaments.[41] Secretary of State Hughes felt that the conference should be somewhat broader; hence, the invitation covered questions concerning the Pacific and Far East (principally Japanese imperialism) as well as arms limitations. The latter included questions of naval armament, and, in the words of the invitation, ". . . it may also be found advisable to formulate proposals by which in the interest of humanity the use of new agencies of warfare may be suitably controlled."[42] Holland, Belgium, and Portugal, having interests in the Far East, were invited along with Britain, France, Italy, Japan, and China. The first session of the conference took place in Washington on November 12, 1921.[43]

The British wanted to discuss disarmament of land forces, but France absolutely refused. As an emollient, Secretary of State Hughes suggested that the conference turn to the issue of the use of new agencies of war, and a subcommittee composed of the technical experts of the United States, Great Britain, France, Italy, and Japan took up the issue.[44] The Japanese expert proposed that the use and manufacture of poisonous gases should be prohibited. The Italian expert agreed, while the experts of Great Britain, the United States, and France strongly opposed any prohibition of poisonous gases, arguing that due to the increasingly wide peacetime use of several warfare gases, it would be impossible to restrict the manufacture of any particular gas or gases. This entailed, as a logical consequence, the impossibility of preventing any country from arming itself in advance against the unfair use of those gases which an unscrupulous enemy might secretly prepare for sudden use upon an unprotected enemy. The Japanese and Italian representatives suggested that proper laws might limit the quantities of certain gases to be manufactured. Opinion was divided between the representatives of the United States, Great Britain, and France on the one hand, and those of Japan and Italy on the other, as to the status of gas warfare. The former contended that gas warfare was a method of warfare similar to other methods such as shrapnel, machine guns, rifle bayonets, bombs, hand grenades, and other older methods, while the latter refused to admit this contention.[45]

The subcommittee came to the conclusion that the kinds of gases and their effects upon human beings could not be taken as a basis for limitation, and that "the only limitation practicable is to wholly prohibit the use of gases against cities and other bodies of non-combatants in the same manner as high explosives may be limited, but that there could be no limitation on their use against the armed forces of the enemy, ashore or afloat."[46] In other words, the subcommittee decided that it could not agree on the limitation of the use of poisonous gases on the ground that such use caused unnecessary suffering of men, and, therefore, it was impossible to prohibit the use of poisonous gases as weapons of war. Consequently, they admitted that poisonous gases were legitimate weapons similar to other weapons of war.

The conclusion of the subcommittee at the Washington Conference was entirely unsatisfactory to the Advisory Committee of the American Delegation.[47] The Advisory Committee established its own subcommittee, which produced a report, adopted by the Advisory Committee, stating:

Whatever may be the arguments of technical experts, the committee feels that the American representatives would not be doing their duty in expressing the conscience of the American people were they to fail in insisting upon the total abolition of chemical warfare, whether in the Army or the Navy, whether against combatant or noncombatant.[48]

The same committee proposed a resolution to be submitted to the Committee on the Limitation of Armament, to the effect that

[c]hemical warfare, including the use of gases, whether toxic or nontoxic, should be prohibited by international agreement, and should be classed with such unfair methods of warfare as poisoning wells, introducing germs of disease and other methods that are abhorrent in modern warfare.[49]

The American delegation, therefore, overriding the opinion of the subcommittee on poisonous gases, proposed the following resolution, which was accepted by the conference on January 11, 1922:[50]

The use in war of asphyxiating, poisonous, or analogous liquids or other gases and all materials or devices having been justly condemned by the general opinion of the civilized world, and a prohibition of such use having been declared in treaties to which a majority of the civilized powers are parties;

Now, to the end that this prohibition shall be universally accepted as a part of international law, binding alike on the conscience and practice of nations, the *signatory powers declare their assent to such prohibition, agree to be bound thereby between themselves,* and invite all other civilized nations to adhere thereto. [Italics added][51]

From the imperative phrasing of this resolution, it might be contended that all of the signatory nations were henceforth to be bound by its terms. But from a juridical standpoint the binding nature of resolutions adopted at an international conference has been open to controversy and doubt. A number of authorities take the position that a mere conference resolution or declaration, no matter how strong the language used therein, does not have the force of law as would be the case if the same language were used in a ratified treaty. It is claimed that resolutions and declarations at best create only moral obligations, not legal obligations.[52] If this be true, then resolutions and declarations cannot be equated with international legislation. On the other hand, there is a strong body of authoritative opinion which declares that resolutions and declarations are juridical in nature and have an obligatory force upon signatory nations.[53] Support for this view may be found in a passage which occurs in an Advisory Opinion given by the Permanent Court of International Justice: "From the standpoint of the obligatory character of international engagements, it is well known that such engagements may be taken in the form of treaties, conventions, declarations, agreements, protocols or exchange of notes."[54] It might, therefore, be contended that the language of the resolution establishes its obligatory character immediately binding upon all of the signatory nations. Nevertheless, most authorities would issue a word of caution against jumping to such a conclusion with regard to any resolution adopted at an international conference, pointing out that it must always be determined whether or not the parties actually intended to create legal rights and obligations. In order to make such a determination it is necessary to seek evidence of the intention of the parties as expressed at the conference, and the decision of the parties to embody the results of their deliberations in one or another form may constitute particularly valuable evidence of their intentions.[55]

The best expression of the intention of the conferees at the Washington Conference was a statement by Secretary of State Hughes:

> . . . certain of the resolutions . . . adopted by the Conference, are put in treaty form, and other resolutions are not put in that form. The distinction is that those engagements which it is deemed require the sanction of a treaty are put in the form of a treaty and proposed for execution by the powers. In other cases, the resolutions are of a character not requiring such sanction in the form of a treaty, and are deemed to be binding upon the Powers according to their tenor when adopted by the Conference.[56]

Inasmuch as no objection was raised to this statement at the conference, it can be assumed that the signatory powers did not feel that their resolution on gases was binding upon them. At the conclusion of the conference they incorporated the ideas of the resolution in a treaty. Article V of this treaty reads as follows:

> The use in war of asphyxiating, poisonous or other gases, and all analogous liquids, materials or devices, having been justly condemned by the general opinion of the civilized world and a prohibition of such use having been declared in treaties to which a majority of the civilized Powers are parties,

> The Signatory Powers, to the end that this prohibition shall be universally accepted as a part of international law binding alike the conscience and practice of nations, declare their assent to such prohibition, and agree to be bound thereby as between themselves and invite all other civilized nations to adhere thereto.[57]

In analyzing this article one is again impressed with the fact that it is exceedingly nebulous. In the first place, the assertion that the use of all gases "had been justly condemned by the general opinion of the civilized world" would probably not even serve as evidence of an assumption that the nations at the conference intended to set forth an accepted principle of law derived from practice or custom of states, for a *just* condemnation is not the equivalent of a *legal* condemnation. This, then, would appear to be merely an expression of the opinion of the signatories. Furthermore, "a prohibition of such use having been declared in treaties" is also a disputable statement. The Declaration of St. Petersburg refers to arms which "uselessly aggravate the suffering of disabled men or render their death inevitable." This would not be true of all gases used in wartime; thus the Washington Convention cannot be referring to that declaration.[58] In the Hague Declaration the powers agreed to abstain from the employment of *projectiles* having for their sole purpose the diffusion of asphyxiating or deleterious gases. It can be argued, as we have seen, that the use of gases through instruments other than projectiles was not explicitly forbidden. On the other hand, it may also be argued that the Hague rules forbid, not a particular instrument for introducing gases, but the use in any manner of deleterious gases which are calculated to cause unnecessary suffering, in view of the fact that Article 23 of the convention prohibits the employment of poisoned projectiles as well as of materials calculated to cause unnecessary suffering.[59] But even this would not outlaw the use of all gases in wartime, for it would not prohibit those which did not cause unnecessary suffering, or, if there be any which fall within the classification of nontoxic, would possibly not prohibit their use. Furthermore, the prohibition of poisonous gases in the peace treaties of World War I apparently was intended to apply only to Germany, Austria, Bulgaria, and Hungary.[60]

The second paragraph of Article V would seem to acknowledge the fact that previous treaties on gas warfare were not generally considered to be codifications of customary international law, for had they been so, they would automatically have been "universally accepted as a part of international law."[61] This was demonstrated to some extent by discussions in the Washington Conference. Both British and Italian representatives pointed out[62] that if one of the five signatory powers should find itself in war with another of the five signatory powers, and the latter should be allied with a nonsignatory or nonadherent power, it was clear that the first-mentioned power could not afford to find itself bound by the duties imposed by the treaty, for in effect the nonsignatory or nonadherent power would be free to make unlimited use of poisonous gases, and would do so not only in its own interest but also in the interest of the powers to which it was allied. In other words, these gentlemen were definitely of the opinion that there was no universal international rule of law prohibiting resort to poisonous gases. To whatever limited extent existing treaties might bind nations, they bound only ratifying nations.[63]

Finally, Article VI of the Washington Treaty stated that the treaty was to go into effect when all the signatory nations deposited their ratifications in Washington. This treaty was ratified by Great Britain, Italy,

Japan, and the United States, but France refused to ratify; hence, the treaty never went into effect.[64]

THE 1923 HAGUE AIR WARFARE RULES

The Washington Conference also resolved that the participating nations should appoint a Commission of Jurists to undertake a study at the Hague[65] of the laws of war in the light of the new weapons which had been used during World War I.[66] It was agreed that the commission should not reconsider the rules of international law pertaining to the use of noxious gases or chemicals, for these had already been set forth in the Washington Treaty.[67] In effect, the commission's work boiled down to a study of the rules of air warfare.[68] Of interest to a review of the legality of CB weapons was the question of whether military aircraft should be permitted to use tracer bullets for the purpose of determining the correctness of their aim, and of incendiary bullets as a means of attack against lighter-than-air craft for the purpose of setting fire to the gas which they carried.[69]

Both of these bullets had been used in World War I, weighed less than fourteen ounces, and were fired from the same gun. The rule as originally proposed by the experts to the commission simply declared that the use of tracer bullets against aircraft generally was not prohibited, but it said nothing about incendiary bullets, implying that standard bullets only would be acceptable. Against this proposal objections were raised, mainly on the ground of the impracticability of aviators changing, during the course of a flight, the ammunition used by them in aerial machine guns. The commission finally came to the conclusion that the most satisfactory solution of the problem would be a rule declaring specifically that the use of tracer, incendiary, or explosive projectiles by or against aircraft is not prohibited. And this is the form in which the statement appears in the draft code. It also added that the rule applied equally to states which were parties to the Declaration of St. Petersburg of 1868 and those which were not.[70] In other words, whatever legal implications can be deduced from the renunciation of projectiles of a weight of less than fourteen ounces which is "either explosive or charged with fulminating or inflammable substances" as it appears in the Declaration of St. Petersburg would be virtually abolished by the draft code with regard to the use of such weapons against or by aircraft.

The reason for this loosening of the St. Petersburg Declaration is to be found in the experience of World War I. The Germans used observation balloons to check on enemy troop movements, and zeppelins to bomb Britain. The ordinary machine gun bullet was almost innocuous against such lighter-than-air craft, for it simply pierced the gas bag, went through it, and failed to do any harm.[71] As an alternative method of destroying these balloons and zeppelins, a new bullet was developed from the tracer bullet. A tracer bullet is a bullet that contains incandescent material but does not explode. From this the British developed an incendiary bullet containing at the base an inflammable charge which was definitely intended to set alight the object struck. As its nose was soft, when it struck an object it flattened out and made a much larger perforation than that of a standard bullet. Thus not only was it doubly prohibited by the Declaration of St. Petersburg, which condemned both explosive and incendiary bullets of less than fourteen ounces, but it probably also fell within the prohibition of the Hague Declaration of 1899 on dumdum bullets. It was with these facts in mind, therefore, that the Commission of Jurists drafted the proposed section.[72]

The Washington Conference had agreed that once the report of the commission was received, the signatory powers would confer as to its acceptance, and upon the course to be followed to secure consideration of its recommendations by the other civilized powers. But after the Draft Code had been received by the participating governments, and after it was widely circulated to other nations, no move was made to embody it in an international treaty. It remained a draft and never became conventional international law.

THE CONFERENCE OF CENTRAL AMERICAN STATES, FEBRUARY, 1923

In an effort to prevent an outbreak of war among Central American states in 1922, the United States secretary of state invited the five Central American republics to meet in conference early in 1923 in Washington to discuss their differences.[73] By February 7, 1923, the delegates had drawn up agreements on "everything that the tropical imagination of the delegates could invent,"[74] including a treaty on the limitation of armaments which contained the following provision:

The Contracting Parties consider that the use in warfare of asphyxiating gases, poisons, or similar substances as well as analogous liquids, materials or devices, is contrary to humanitarian principles and to international law, and obligate themselves by the present Convention not to use said substances in time of war.[75]

The treaty was signed and ratified by all the Central American nations, but it was never registered with the Secretariat of the League of Nations.[76] Under the Covenant of that organization it was clearly stipulated that every treaty entered into by any member of the League was to be registered with the Secretariat, and no such treaty would be binding until so registered.[77] All the Central American nations were members of the League at the time of ratification of the treaty; consequently it can be argued that in spite of such ratifications, the treaty had no binding effect.[78] In any event, by 1930 two of the nations had denounced the treaty, and, as Article 8 stipulated that it would remain in force only so long as four of the five nations agreed to it, the treaty lapsed.[79] It is not today considered to be a limitation on its signatories.

THE FIFTH INTERNATIONAL CONFERENCE OF AMERICAN STATES

From 1899 on,[80] the nations of this hemisphere occasionally met in conference to discuss common problems.[81] The date of the fifth such conference had originally been set for 1914, but with the coming of World War I it was delayed until 1923. When it was finally convened in Santiago, Chile, Latin American dislike of United States interventionary actions in the Caribbean was at its height,[82] and many of the projects upon which the United States had hoped to obtain binding agreements, including a treaty on the limitation of arms, were rejected.[83] The best that could be obtained was a weak resolution on gas warfare:

The Fifth International Conference of American States,

Resolves: . . .

c) To recommend that the Governments reiterate the prohibition of the use of asphyxiating or poisonous gases, and all analogous liquids, materials or devices, such as are indicated in the Treaty of Washington, dated February 6, 1922.[84]

Although in some instances inter-American resolutions have clearly been lawmaking resolutions,[85] it would be difficult to sustain that position with regard to the above statement. A resolve "to recommend" that a government "reiterate" cannot be viewed as authoritative legal language setting forth a definite rule of international law. Accordingly, this resolution in no way changed the existing conventional law status of chemical or biological weapons.

In spite of the weakness of the resolution, Colombia refused to sign it. In 1922 an international arbitral award had given Colombia title to disputed territory lying at a point where Colombia, Peru, and Brazil met. Peru agreed to the award, but Brazil did not. Colombia was unwilling to commit itself in even the slightest manner to any indication that there might be a limitation on its choice of weapons in the event war broke out between Brazil and Colombia.[86]

LEAGUE OF NATIONS EFFORTS TO LIMIT RESORT TO CB WEAPONS

FIRST CONSIDERATIONS

In its first year of operation the League of Nations directed its attention to the problem of the use of chemical weapons in time of war, and in the following years it concerned itself with both chemical and biological agents. The Permanent Advisory Commission for Military, Naval and Air Questions was asked, in 1920, by the Council of the League to advise it concerning, among other things, the "use of poisonous gas in warfare."[87] In its report the commission expressed the opinion that gas was a cruel method, but its use could not be prevented in war simply by prohibiting or limiting its manufacture in peacetime or by prohibiting experiments in laboratories.[88] The council thereafter saw fit to condemn the use of poison gas in war, and called upon governments to consider the penalties to be imposed upon any state making the first use of gas in war in contravention to the laws of humanity. It also decided to seek, with the help of competent scientists, ways to prevent the manufacture of poisonous gas.[89] In this connection consideration was given to the usefulness of securing full publicity for chemical inventions. The thought was present that if the world's scientists published their discoveries relating to chemical warfare, the danger that such discoveries might be used for aggressive purposes would be minimized, inasmuch as through publicity and knowledge all nations would be on the same footing. The conclusion was reached, however, that such an invitation to scientists was impracticable.[90]

The Temporary Mixed Commission,[91] which had been entrusted with the problem of reduction of armaments, in giving its attention to the problem of gas warfare concluded that treaties prohibiting the use of gas would not actually prevent secret preparation of gas or its employment in time of war. It was admitted that such treaties might have some moral value. The commission did consider it to be vital for the people of the world to understand the magnitude of the problem of chemical warfare. A special committee of experts was appointed "to study the development of chemical warfare and to prepare a report upon its probable effects in any future war."[92]

The report of this committee included a discussion not only of chemical warfare, but also of bacteriological warfare.[93] It was based on a questionnaire which had been sent to leading chemists and scientific experts of the world. The questionnaire sought to discover what the possible results would be to combatants, to civilians, to animal life, to vegetable life, and to the wealth and resources of a nation which was attacked, whether or not such attacks were permitted by the laws of war,

(1) By chemical warfare by means of the most powerful explosives, chemical products and gases, as already practiced and as further developed since the last war;

(2) By bacteriological warfare by means of microbes or any other agent, if, in defiance of all human laws its effectiveness should induce nations to adopt it.[94]

The report examined the effects of the various known chemical agents on man, declared that their effects would be about the same on animals, and concluded that there was no gas known at the time which would injure vegetation and no chemical agent which would produce direct chemical destruction of sources of wealth.[95] Nevertheless, it did not overlook the possibility that new substances with greater military value would be discovered, and prophetically predicted that such substances might strike at vegetation, at sources of wealth, and also at functions of the body other than those affected by the then known gases.[96]

As to bacteriological agents, the report concluded that the existing knowledge of hygiene and microbiology would limit the spread of epidemics so that they could not be considered as having potential decisive influence on future hostilities. Furthermore, bacteriological agents were viewed as double-edged weapons and therefore not particularly formidable.[97] A word of caution was uttered to the effect that future developments in bacteriological science would warrant keeping in touch with its progress, for if such agents could be used in warfare, they would know no frontiers and "would be aimed directly against all mankind."[98]

Earlier, in 1922, the Assembly had sought to bring the governments into agreement not to resort to chemical warfare by calling upon members as well as nonmembers of the League to accede to the Treaty of Washington, which would pledge against the use of asphyxiating, poisonous, or other gases or any analogous liquid or device.[99]

THE GENEVA PROTOCOL OF 1925

In 1925 the League of Nations called together at Geneva a Conference for the Supervision of the International Trade in Arms and Ammunition and in Implements of War.[100] The agenda as set and a draft convention on supervision of trade in arms which had been prepared gave no consideration to an interdiction of chemical or biological weapons.[101] The delegates of the United States had been given strong instructions by their government to seek a ban on the international trade in chemical warfare materials and implements.[102] As a result, at the Second Plenary Meeting, a United States delegate informed the conference that the United States sought amendments of the draft convention so as "to deal with the traffic in poisonous gases with the hope of reducing the barbarity of modern warfare."[103] When the proposal was presented, the United States delegation availed itself of the opportunity to state the desire of the United States to seek a universal ban on the use of asphyxiating gases in warfare;[104] but, since the conference was called to deal with international traffic in arms, the proposal was presented in more limited terminology, designed to prevent international trade in asphyxiating gases, for otherwise the instructions of the delegates might be exceeded. The proposal as presented read:

The High Contracting Parties agree to prohibit the export from their territory of all asphyxiating, toxic or deleterious gases, and all analogous liquids, exclusively designed or intended for use in connection with operations of war.[105]

The Polish delegate then submitted an addition which read:

Any decision taken by the Conference concerning the materials used for chemical warfare should apply equally to the materials employed for bacteriological warfare.[106]

Objections were raised to the proposed amendments. In some quarters, as De Madariaga tells us, it was believed that the League should not "meddle with the laws of war." He states that for the League of Nations to say: "'Thou shall not wage war with chemicals' is tantamount to a government enacting that 'no one shall murder with arsenic.'"[107] The opinion was also held that the League should not make laws which would not be respected. The Norwegian delegate stated:

. . . you cannot regulate war; you can only abolish it. . . . [Y]ou cannot humanize a tiger; you can only kill it. Once war is let loose, it is impossible to prevent the use of the most horrible methods. Our problem therefore is not the regulation of war; it is the abolition of war. . . . [T]he formula which will be adopted [i.e., to prohibit chemical and bacteriological warfare] will merely be another stone on that road paved with good intentions which leads to a place of which we have all heard.[108]

These objections proved fruitless. A final objection did win the day. The argument was made that the proposal to prohibit the export of certain chemical weapons would not prevent states which had large chemical industries capable of producing such weapons from resorting to them. Indeed, unless the manufacture of such materials of war were prohibited and prevented, the proposals would simply result in the granting to the producing nations of an exclusive monopoly in the ability to use such methods. Moreover, it was pointed out that such a prohibition on export would be difficult to enforce, inasmuch as chemical war substances were very similar to or the same as those in constant use for industrial or pharmaceutical purposes. It was contended that the simplest method to restrain CB weapons would be to obtain a pledge from all nations to abstain from their use.[109]

It was decided to proceed along these lines, and it was agreed that rather than making the pledge an amendment to a convention for the supervision of international trade in arms, it should be placed in a special protocol of its own. It was also decided that a special conference to consider the adoption of the prohibition was not necessary. Thereafter a protocol was drafted. The first so prepared condemned the use of gases only,[110] no mention being made of bacteriological agents, although during conference discussions references had been made to their prohibition. The Polish delegate drew attention to the omission and called for the application of the conference decisions to bacteriological warfare.[111] The United States delegation accepted the Polish amendment, stating: "Bacteriological warfare is so revolting and so foul that it must meet with the condemnation of all civilized nations."[112]

The French delegate was of the opinion that the broad words of the draft, "asphyxiating, poisonous or other gases, and of all analogous liquids, materials or devices," would also cover bacteriological warfare, but agreed that an express reference to the latter might be advantageous.[113] It was agreed to include the restriction on bacteriological warfare. The final instrument entitled "Protocol for the Prohibition of the Use in War of Asphyxiating, Poisonous or other Gases, and of Bacteriological Methods of Warfare" reads in part as follows:

Whereas the use in war of asphyxiating, poisonous or other gases, and of all analogous liquids, materials or devices has been justly condemned by the general opinion of the civilized world; and

Whereas the prohibition of such use has been declared in treaties to which the majority of Powers of the world are Parties; and

To the end that this prohibition shall be universally accepted as part of International Law, binding alike the conscience and the practice of nations;

Declare:

That the High Contracting Parties, so far as they are not already Parties to Treaties prohibiting such use, accept this prohibition, agree to extend this prohibition to the use of bacteriological methods of warfare and agree to be bound as between themselves according to the terms of this declaration.[114]

Most of the then existing powers of the world saw fit to accept the protocol. Japan and, ironically, the United States, which had pressed the prohibition on the conference, failed to ratify it. The United States Senate refused to ratify the protocol, despite the fact that the United States delegation had been officially instructed to submit and sponsor it in every way, and that this position had at the time been approved by the War and Navy Departments. However, when the protocol came before the Senate for ratification opposition was so strong, apparently on the ground that gas warfare was no more cruel than any other weapon and might be more humane and effective, that the proposal was withdrawn without definite action.[115] This was done despite support for the protocol from General Pershing, who wrote:

I cannot think it possible that our country should fail to ratify the protocol which includes this or a similar provision. Scientific research may discover a gas so deadly that it will produce instant death. To sanction the use of gas in any form would be to open the way for the use of the most deadly gases and the possible poisoning of whole populations of non-combatant men, women and children. The contemplation of such a result is shocking to the senses. It is unthinkable that civilization should deliberately decide upon such a course.[116]

The Geneva Protocol is the most significant international agreement banning the use of CB weapons, for it has been adhered to by a large number of states.[117] Its broad proscription on chemical agents far exceeds the very restrictive prohibition of the Hague Gas Declaration. It is the only general treaty in effect expressly prohibiting bacteriological warfare. Nevertheless, an analysis of its language reveals that its actual meaning, significance, and extent of inhibition are confusing and not easily understood. The English language version of the Protocol prohibits "the use in war of asphyxiating, poisonous or other gases, and of all analogous liquids, materials or devices." This ban has been said to apply to the employment in war of all methods of chemical warfare[118] including the means by which the forbidden chemical substances can be emitted and applied to the enemy, i.e.,

projectiles or apparatus of any sort, aerial bombardment, land or aerial dissemination, emission of clouds of fogs, mines, etc., as well as all other techniques imaginable by which these substances could be placed in contact with enemy personnel.[119] [Authors' translation]

This extensive character of the interdiction may be seen to be warranted when one notes the general prohibition of the use in war of chemical agents and combines this with the broad language later used of prohibiting "bacteriological methods of warfare."[120]

The comprehensive scope of the protocol's terminology would embrace a bar against the use in war of all chemical agents or substances. No distinction is made as to the consistency of the substance. Thus it makes no difference whether it is gaseous, liquid, or solid. The words "gases" and "liquids" are expressly used; and solid substances would fall under either "analogous materials" or "procédés," the latter word being used in the French version instead of the somewhat unintelligible English term "devices." "Procédés" would apply to the nature of the substances employed and not to a mechanism or a technique employed.

The definition would not only outlaw the use of chemical agents classified as toxic, lethal, or severely injurious, but would also cover and disallow nonlethal chemical agents such as riot control agents and the incapacitating agents which are said to produce only temporary physical disability without permanent injury. Spaight, for example, is of this opinion. He says:

The argument that, because the effect of a gas is not to kill but merely to stupefy temporarily those within its radius of action, its use is permissible, cannot be sustained in face of the definite terms of the treaty. If, therefore, any nation which is a party to that treaty resorts in a future war to the use of gas in any kind or form, whether it be chlorine, phosgene, mustard or any less harmful variety, that nation is breaking its solemn undertaking and sullying its national honour. It is necessary to emphasize this unquestionable truth in view of the prediction (in 1922) of an able military writer that non-toxic gas, sprayed by aircraft, would be the munition of the future.[121]

Reasoning behind contentions that the ban on chemical agents extends to lethal and nonlethal but injurious agents as well as to those which do not injure severely rests upon practical conclusions to the effect that the frontiers between irritating gases and those injurious to health or death-dealing are nebulous and variable, and that it is most difficult to determine with any certainty an enemy's use of lethal or nonlethal substances. It therefore becomes necessary to prohibit the use of all.[122]

A British view expressed in the post-World War I era, though it was in accord with the contention that all forms of gases are included and prohibited, took a somewhat different tack. Although it was recognized that certain gases, e.g., the tear gases, were less deadly or cruel than others, still it was believed that gas warfare should be blotted out completely, since the recognition of any gases as legitimate would in turn legalize the manufacture of the equipment for using them, which would then be available for the lethal gases also.[123]

A literal reading of the English language version of the protocol could be taken to preclude other chemical agents such as certain smokes, like white phosphorus, and incendiaries, such as flamethrowers, which may give off gas, even asphyxiating gas.[124] It can also be argued, as in the case of the Gas Declaration of 1899, that the language could extend to high explosives which give off fumes of gas incidentally. One commentator would find that the protocol banned fire weapons because they might be gaseous, and, also under the broader language of the protocol, because they are "analogous liquids, materials or devices."[125] Also as analogous liquids or materials might be considered the antiplant agents such as the defoliants and sterilants (soil poisoners) which are aimed at wiping out vegetation.

Since these various extensive prohibitions may be read into the far-reaching language of the English text, confusion and doubt are created as to the scope of the obligation actually assumed by the contracting parties. The attempts to bar the use of poisonous and asphyxiating gases have been based principally on the unnecessary suffering principle. It becomes somewhat difficult to stretch this principle so as to conclude that all of the above-mentioned agents were intended by the parties to be prohibited.[126] This is particularly true as to the gas agents such as incapacitants and riot control agents,[127] although, as we have seen, the view has been taken that all such agents are barred, and the literal language of the protocol does incorporate this position.[128]

A reading of the French text creates some additional perplexity. The French version, which is equally authentic with the English, forbids the use in warfare of "gaz asphyxiants, toxiques ou similaires, ainsi que de tous liquides, matières ou procédés analogues. . . ."[129] This terminology appears upon first examination to be more restricted than the English text, the latter forbidding all forms of gas while the French prohibits specific types of gases: toxics and asphyxiants and analogous materials. It can be argued that the reference here is only to lethal gases which are asphyxiating or toxic. Nontoxic gases would not be included, and it has been implied that the French version would not pertain to the so-called innocuous nonlethal gases such as tear gas.[130] One cannot be sure, for, as we have seen earlier, certain of the riot control and incapacitating chemical agents may be considered as toxic, although perhaps in lesser degree.[131] Moreover, the chemical antiplant agents may be toxic to plant life. Are they prohibited here? And finally, chemical agents not thought of as gas agents, such as smokes, flamethrowers, and high explosives, may give off asphyxiating and toxic gases. To the extent that they do, are they also forbidden? The fact that the French and English versions are not identical in terminology has raised questions, but actually they seem after study and from literal reading expressive of a prohibition of all chemical substances in war. Meyrowitz, a French author, comments to this effect concerning the French version:

Finally, the extensive character of the text is evident in the definition of the *properties* which are interdicted: asphyxiants, toxics or similars. What is meant by *similars*? Medically speaking an asphyxiant gas is a gas which is toxic in its suffocating effect. . . . The term *toxic gas* . . . (the word toxic is understood to signify something which injures health or brings on death) is a general term, which encompasses gases (or other substances) which have a toxic effect generally, a suffocating effect, a vesicant effect or an irritant effect. The expression, "asphyxiant, toxic or similars" must therefore be read as *toxic gases or similars*. If the expression "or similars" is to signify here other gases injurious to health or lethal, it would not seem necessary to place these words here because they would be understood within the word "toxic." This expression cannot be given any meaning other than that it aims to extend the enumeration to products that are not *asphyxiating* or *toxic*.[132] [Authors' translation]

At a later date a French representative before a League of Nations organ accepted a broad meaning to be ascribed to the French version which would include all gases having some toxic action on the human organism whether such effects were temporary, serious, or fatal.[133]

At first glance the protocol's inhibition of bacteriological agents in warfare seems clearer. Both the French and English texts declare that the prohibition extends to the use of "bacteriological methods of warfare." But difficulty as to meaning prevails here also. As defined, biological warfare is the deliberate dissemination of pathogenic microorganisms or their toxic products.[134] It might be thought that microorganisms and their toxic products would all fall within the terminology of the protocol "bacteriological methods of warfare." Strictly speaking this is not so. Bacteriological agents are microorganisms, and these agents would obviously be barred by the protocol's language. But modern science classifies other agents such as fungi, rickettsiae, and viruses as microorganisms.[135] These are agents of biological warfare, but they are not bacterial agents; and an exact scientific interpretation of bacteriological methods would have to count fungi, rickettsiae, and viruses out. To ascribe such a limited meaning to the protocol would be an absurdity. The parties at Geneva in 1925 surely meant to abolish germ warfare, or warfare, in the words of the Polish delegate, with the cultures of microbes.[136] Such words as well as those of the report from the Temporary Mixed Commission which used the term "microbes" in connection with bacteriological agents would encompass microorganisms.[137] If biological agents as presently delineated which infect with disease signify more than the then known bacterial agents, they also should be considered within the proscription; but a word of caution is warranted to the effect that the narrower interpretation might be advanced.

Further, with regard to the scope of the protocol as related to bacteriological warfare, the question has been raised whether it should be applicable to biological agents which merely disable or incapacitate and do not impose permanent injury, or to those directed against enemy food sources, the latter comparable to a food blockade in time of war.[138] Speaking more broadly, was the protocol intended to prohibit antiplant and antianimal or even antimateriel biological weapons? These biological agents, i.e., the disabling ones, or the antiplant, antianimal, and antimateriel, might not offend the principle of humanity and unnecessary human suffering; therefore some doubt exists whether the protocol is applicable to them. This might be borne out to some extent by the Polish delegate's draft text, wherein it was stated that bacteriological warfare was an "arm that is discreditable to modern civilization. . . ."[139] This would seem to say that bacteriological methods should be prohibited only where they violate the principle of humanity. However, when discussing his reasons for seeking the inclusion of bacteriological weapons in the ban, the Polish delegate spoke not only of the dangers of its use against humans, "but also of its use against animals which he said could be infected in large numbers . . . by cultures of the germs of glanders, cattle plague, etc." He spoke also of plants: "Bacteriological warfare can also be waged against the vegetable world, and not only may corn, fruit and vegetables suffer but also the cultivation of useful plants, that is to say, vineyards, yards, orchards and fields."[140] Thus all agents for the deliberate spread of disease in warfare would appear to be subsumed within the meaning of bacteriological methods—at least all bacterial agents, whether they be antipersonnel, antiplant or antianimal.

Over and above the difficulty involved in arriving at an exact conclusion as to the meaning of the protocol as it related to CB agents is a further problem involving the obligatory effect of the protocol. The fact that the protocol itself makes it binding only upon contracting parties creates something of a Chinese puzzle when read in conjunction with other language of the protocol. The instrument states that the use of gases in war has been condemned by the general opinion of the civilized world and in treaties to which the majority of states have become parties. If gas is condemned by the general opinion of the civilized world, an expression of the signatories' belief might appear to be present that a rule of customary international law prohibiting the use of gas had come into existence. Grave doubt can be expressed as to the correctness of such a view, but in any event if customary international law had already outlawed gas warfare it is paradoxical that the present protocol should be so concerned with a provision stating that it came into force for each signatory power only from date of deposit of ratification. This is like saying that a customary rule of international law must be accepted by states in a treaty before it is binding at international law.

The Geneva Protocol, in stating that the use of gas warfare had previously been declared outlawed in treaties to which the majority of the powers had adhered, as in a similar declaration in the Washington Treaty noted above, also seems overoptimistic. The only treaty expressly speaking of gas which was binding upon a number of powers was the Hague Gas Declaration of 1899 which, as we have seen, was limited in scope and the nonobservance of which during World War I makes it of little value as a precise legal prohibition of the use of gas or of chemical agents in warfare.[141] The interdiction of gas warfare in the peace treaties was meant to apply only to the disarmed vanquished states,[142] and the Central American instrument was temporarily binding, if at all, only upon that small group of states.[143] That leaves only the Washington Treaty of 1923, which did condemn the use of gases in war, but which never entered into effect.[144]

There is a further problem involving the obligatory effect of the protocol. It would seem that those states which have ratified or adhered to it would be bound as between and among themselves; but many of the powers adhered with reservations,[145] all of which emphasized the contractual nature of the protocol. Some of the reservations followed the form of the French one, which is a double reservation first stating that the protocol will bind France only as to states which have signed or ratified it or which may accede thereto, and second, that it shall cease to be binding in regard to any enemy state whose armed forces or whose allies fail to respect the prohibitions laid down in the protocol. The first reservation may be merely an understanding in that it repeats an idea appearing in the protocol itself; namely, that the protocol will be binding only with reference to states which have signed, ratified, or acceded to it. This reservation would, therefore, probably not change the effect or purport of the protocol. It may have been added because, in view of the ambiguities in the text, the French wished to emphasize the contractual and relative nature of the agreement.[146] Nevertheless the idea it contained limiting the binding force of the agreement to ratifying nations is inconsistent with another clause in the protocol which seeks to establish the prohibition as universally accepted customary international law. If there is in existence a customary and universal rule, a statement implying that the prohibition ceases to be binding vis-à-vis nonratifying states, even though such states have not resorted to CB weapons, would seem to be an attempt to limit or condition the binding effect of the customary rule. This would be a backward step and something nations cannot legally do. Customary law regulates the conduct of *all* states, and if a treaty is actually only a codification of customary law, then any attempt to limit its application and obligatory effect would appear to violate the principle of equality of states.[147] The second reservation, at first glance, might seem to incorporate the idea of a reciprocal reprisal—that is, when a state is injured by a violation of a rule of the law of war, it may under certain conditions respond to that illicit act by taking exactly the same measures against the violating state. In such a condition, the rule remains valid, and both sides are required to abide by it after the act of reprisal has taken place. But actually, there is in the second reservation no mention of meeting an illegitimate act with what otherwise would be an illegitimate act. The second reservation is much more extensive than reciprocal reprisal, for apparently it suspends the treaty under conditions in which the resort to CB weapons might not be an illegal act. For example, if State A, a noncontracting party and an ally of State C, a contracting party, uses CB weapons against State B, a contracting party, State A would not be violating the treaty because it is not bound by it. Thus, only if there were a customary international law banning CB weapons would State A's action be illegal; if there is no such customary international law, then the use of CB weapons by State B would not be meeting an illegal act by reciprocal reprisal. Furthermore, the reservation suspends the treaty whenever an enemy resorts to CB weapons, whether the weapon was used against a signatory or a nonsignatory. If signatory State B used CB weapons against nonsignatory State A, which was an ally of signatory State C, then under the reservation, State C would no longer be bound by the treaty. This too would be different from a reprisal.[148] Question might also be raised as to what happens after the war is over, for no reinstatement provisions are included in the reservation. Once the treaty ceases to be binding between two signatories, unless provision is made for its reinstatement in peace settlements, presumably it remains a dead letter as between those parties.

The Russian reservation appears broader than that of France. After stipulating that the protocol binds the U.S.S.R. only as to other ratifying or acceding states, it goes on to declare that the protocol will cease to be binding with regard to all enemy states whose armed forces or whose allies "*de jure* or in fact do not respect the restrictions which are the object of this Protocol."[149] Under normal methods of treaty interpretation, any nation which has not ratified the protocol could readily be equated with a nation which *de jure* does not "respect" its restrictions, for note, nothing is said about violating its restrictions. Russia probably would feel free to resort to the prohibited weapons against any enemy signatory of the protocol which was allied to a nonsignatory, such as the United States, even though neither of the latter nations had resorted to chemical or bacteriological weapons.

The increase in the practice of making reservations to multilateral instruments has brought about many international studies on the effect of such reservations. Most traditional authorities seem to agree with the statement made by Hackworth:

. . . ratifications with reservations in order to be binding must be brought to the knowledge of the other contracting powers and receive their approval, unless otherwise specified in the treaty, since they constitute a modification of the agreement. As to signatories whose ratifications had been deposited prior to the receipt by them of notice of the deposit of a ratification with reservations, acceptance by such states of the reservation by some positive act would seem to be necessary in order to give the treaty binding force as between the parties who had already deposited their ratifications and the party subsequently ratifying with reservations. There is authority for the proposition that failure to object to a reservation should be regarded as acceptance thereof. The better view, however, would appear to be that the mere failure to object to a reservation, in the absence of some act by the party which has already deposited its ratification indicating that it regards the treaty as operative between it and the party making the reservation, does not constitute acceptance of the reservation. As to signatories whose ratifications are deposited subsequent to the receipt by them of notice of the deposit of a ratification with reservations, acceptance of the reservations would seem to be implied from failure to object.[150]

There has never been any clarification of the status of the various reservations to the protocol. The protocol is probably binding among those nations which have no reservation to it, and it and the reservations are probably binding among those nations which have similar reservations; but beyond this, clarity ends.

A glance at some of the early ratifications and adhesions[151] will demonstrate the confusion in the international status of the protocol created by reservations:

May 9, 1926	France ratified with reservations, consequently all subsequently ratifying states were on notice of these reservations and acceptance thereof is implied.
April 2, 1927	Liberia acceded without reservations, hence is bound with all other nations which ratified or acceded without reservations, as well as with France.

February 8, 1928	Venezuela ratified without reservations. Same status as Liberia.
April 3, 1928	Italy ratified without reservations. Same status as Liberia.
April 5, 1928	The Soviet Union acceded with reservations which varied in language and purport from those of France; consequently it can be argued that no contractual relationship exists between Russia and any of the previously ratifying nations, although all subsequent ratifying states would be on notice of the Russian reservations.
May 9, 1928	Austria ratified without reservations. Bound with Russia, France, and all other nations which ratified without reservations.
December 4, 1928	Belgium ratified with reservations similar to those of France; consequently there is a binding treaty between these two nations, and all subsequently ratifying states would be on notice of the Belgian reservations. But good legal argument can be made that as far as Venezuela, Italy, Russia, and Austria are concerned, Belgium is not bound.
December 6, 1928	Egypt ratified without reservations—bound by above ratifications and subsequent ratifications without reservations.
February 4, 1929	Poland ratified without reservations. Same as Egypt.
April 12, 1929	The Kingdom of the Serbs, Croats, and Slovenes ratified without reservations. Same as Egypt.
April 25, 1929	Germany ratified without reservations. Same as Egypt.
June 26, 1929	Finland ratified without reservations. Same as Egypt.
July 4, 1929	Persia acceded without reservations. Same as Egypt.
August 7, 1929	China acceded without reservations. Same as Egypt.
August 22, 1929	Spain ratified with a reservation which differed from that of France, Belgium, or the Soviet Union, hence it can be said that none of the previous

	ratifying states are bound as far as Spain is concerned although subsequently ratifying states are so bound.
August 23, 1929	Rumania ratified with reservations similar to those of the Soviet Union; consequently it can be contended that as to previously ratifying or acceding states, she is bound only to Russia.
October 5, 1929	Turkey ratified without reservations. Bound by above ratifications and subsequent ratifications without reservations.
January 22, 1930	The Union of South Africa, Australia, and New Zealand all acceded with the same reservations, but these varied from any previous reservations; hence they are probably bound only to subsequently ratifying states.
April 9, 1930	Great Britain and India both ratified with reservations which varied slightly in wording but not in meaning from those of South Africa, Australia, and New Zealand; thus she would probably be bound as to these nations, but not as to the other previously ratifying nations.
April 25, 1930	Sweden ratified without reservations. Bound by above ratifications and subsequent ratifications without reservations.
May 5, 1930	Denmark ratified without reservations. Same as Sweden.
May 6, 1930	Canada ratified with reservations which, strangely enough, did not follow the wording of the British or Indian reservations, or of those of South Africa, Australia, and New Zealand. Rather, it copied the Russian reservations, and therefore among the previously ratifying or acceding nations Canada may be bound only to Russia and Rumania.

A further problem with regard to reservations has arisen with the successor states, particularly those which became independent after World War II in Asia and Africa. It is generally said that multilateral conventions of a humanitarian character are binding on successor states without a specific declaration of adhesion.[152] The 1925 Protocol could probably be classified as a multilateral convention of a humanitarian character, to be considered binding on the new nations. But it should be noted that while Pakistan, in April, 1960, declared that it considered itself bound by the protocol since its date of independence, Ceylon and Tanganyika, in notifying their adherence to the protocol, did so stating that the date of adherence was the date of notification—indicating that they did not think the protocol binding until they had formally adhered to it.[153] These states were British colonies prior to the war, and not one mentioned whether their adhesions included the reservations of the mother country. This gives rise to the presently unresolved question whether failure to mention the original reservation in the express declaration of a successor state implies acceptance or rejection of that reservation.

Another series of problems relating to the extension of treaties to successor states was posed by the United Arab Republic (U.A.R.).[154] In February, 1958, Syria, a nonsignatory nation, merged with Egypt, a signatory nation, to form a new international entity called the United Arab Republic. Normally this would result in the extinction in fact and in law of the right of international personality of each of the merging states and the birth of a new international personality—the new nation arising out of the union.[155] Thereupon, only such treaties as were not incompatible with the political constitution and public law of the new state, or were considered to be of a universal humanitarian nature, would remain in force.[156]

A note dated March 1, 1958, from the Permanent Mission of the U.A.R. in New York to the secretary general of the United Nations stated:

It is to be noted that the Government of the United Arab Republic declares that the Union henceforth is a single member of the United Nations, bound by the provisions of the Charter, and that all international treaties and agreements concluded by Egypt or Syria with other countries will remain valid *within the regional limits prescribed on their conclusion* and in accordance with the principles of international law. [Italics added][157]

This notion of limited territorial application of existing treaties was repeated in Article 59 of the Provisional Constitution of the U.A.R. adopted four days later.[158]

There are some treaties which may no doubt have limited territorial extension. Others, however, must apply to a nation as a whole.[159] Certainly the 1925 Geneva Protocol would seem to fall within this classification, for it would be meaningless if a government could limit its application to only one sector of the national patrimony. If the phrase, "remain valid within the regional limits prescribed on their conclusion" implied that the Egyptian portion of the new nation continued to be bound by the 1925 Protocol, while the Syrian portion was not so bound, then good argument could be made that the U.A.R. was not acting "in accordance with principles of international law." Obviously either the whole nation had to be bound under the earlier Egyptian ratification or it was not bound at all, because the protocol in and of itself logically required complete territorial coverage and therefore was incompatible with the constitution of the new international entity, which only maintained treaties in force which applied to each sector of the new nation. The issue was never clarified.

The United Nations practice with regard to the status of multilateral conventions of which its secretary general acted as depository was to list under the U.A.R. the two subdivisions, Syria or Egypt, according to whether one or the other or both were parties to the treaties.[160] But as the depository for the Geneva Protocol was not the United Nations but France, this convention was not listed in the U.N. publications relating to the status of multilateral conventions. A representative of the government of the U.A.R. assured the 1958 International Labor Conference in Geneva, with respect to the variations in multilateral labor conventions signed by Syria and Egypt, that when "the transitional period was over all conventions would be equally applicable in the two regions."[161] It might be alleged that this was indicative of the fact that a similar attitude existed concerning the application of other humanitarian multilateral conventions: Egyptian ratification was meant to extend to the Syrian portion of the new nation. But it would be difficult to come to any completely certain conclusion.

The birth of the U.A.R. gave rise to another question with regard to the Geneva Protocol. Without doubt it was possible for Egypt and Syria to agree as between themselves that their treaty rights and obligations with foreign powers were to remain binding on each territorial sector of the new international entity; but would this be binding on such foreign powers? In other words, are foreign powers who were parties to such treaties bound to fulfill their obligations thereunder, or can they repudiate the treaties on the ground that the U.A.R. declaration was *res inter alios acta*—a matter which, in law, exclusively concerns others?[162] The merger of the two nations did change the nature of the contractual relationship, and therefore it can be legally pleaded that the consent of all other signatories to the Geneva Protocol was necessary either to limiting its territorial extent to the Egyptian sector or to extending it to the whole of the new nation, and that without such consent other signatories were no longer bound as to the Egyptian sector or as to the total entity of the U.A.R.

It was apparently the view of the United States in regard to such treaties to which it was signatory, either on a multilateral or bilateral basis, that the U.A.R. was under a duty to extend them throughout the whole nation or probably they would lapse. Because of its extension of recognition it diplomatically took issue with the U.A.R. statement relating to the territorial scope of existing treaties:

The United States Government, having taken note of the assurance of the United Arab Republic to respect and observe its international obligations *including all international obligations of Egypt and Syria, respectively*, existing at the time of the formation of the United Arab Republic, extended recognition. . . . [Italics added][163]

Even further doubt was cast on the validity of such territorial limitations by a memorandum of the Secretariat of the United Nations in 1962 which posed the very cogent question—which it did not answer—of whether or not a state such as the U.A.R. or Tanzania (which had made similar statements *re* treaties relating to Tanganyika and Zanzibar) could thereafter be, in reality, considered a *party* to any multilateral treaty which of necessity had to apply throughout a nation's territory.[164]

Even if it is accepted, in spite of the territorial limitation stipulations in both the Provisional Constitution and the U.A.R. note to the United Nations, that the U.A.R. inherited the Egyptian ratification, binding the whole of the new nation, problems still remain. In 1961 a coup d'etat separated the Syrian portion from the Egyptian portion and Syria returned to independent nation status. At that time, did Syria return to nonsignatory status? As far as the United Nations was concerned, the new Syrian Arab Republic was readmitted as an independent nation and was deemed to be the same as the pre-1958 Republic of Syria whose international commitments, like the state itself, were viewed as having been in a situation of suspended animation.[165] From this it may be rationalized that its noncommitments were also reinstated.

The same rationale might be applied to the Egyptian sector of the U.A.R., but note should be taken of the fact that the U.A.R. did not attempt to reinstate itself as Egypt, rather continuing to maintain its membership in the United Nations under the aegis of the United Arab Republic. As a result the status of former Egyptian treaty commitments is less clear. If Egypt lost its international personality when it entered the U.A.R. and if, in spite of its assertions, its multilateral treaties were terminated by that fact, then it might be argued that the mere loss of territory by the U.A.R. (i.e., the loss of the Syrian portion of the nation) would not in and of itself subsequently reinstate the Egyptian ratification of the Geneva Protocol, and the U.A.R. would no longer be a party thereto.

The best that can be said, therefore, of the Geneva Protocol is that it does not constitute a completely legal obligation even between and among its signatories. It establishes a whole host of legal regimes which seem to be impossible to untangle.[166]

LEAGUE DISARMAMENT PROPOSALS AND THE LIMITATION OF
CB AGENTS IN WARFARE

The Preparatory Commission and Its Subcommissions

In 1925 the League of Nations again commenced to plan for a general disarmament conference, and a new organ was created to take over from the Temporary Mixed Commission. This organ was designated the Preparatory Commission for the Disarmament Conference and usually called the Preparatory Commission.[167]

At its first session in May, 1926, the Preparatory Commission submitted to two subcommissions a series of questions on the problems of disarmament, including some related to chemical and biological weapons.[168] In the reports issued by the two subcommissions[169] covering these issues, it was again concluded that it would not be feasible to draw up an international convention compelling the publication of all inventions which could be utilized in chemical or bacteriological warfare. It was agreed that existing chemical facilities could be quickly converted into agencies for the production of war gases, although the rapidity of this transfer would vary in accordance with surrounding circumstances, including the availability of sufficient raw material, machinery, and skilled personnel, and the industrial, scientific, technical, and material resources of the country. The subcommissions further agreed that it would be impossible in time of peace to prevent the manufacture of chemicals which could be quickly converted to weapons of war. In consequence Sub-Commission A suggested that there should be drawn up a universally effective and absolute international prohibition against the employment of chemical weapons of war. Sub-Commission B, on the other hand, suggested that the problem of chemical weapons could be controlled by an international industrial agreement among manufacturers, backed by each nation, rationing the production of chemicals adaptable for war purposes. It was recognized that such an agreement might be faced with two distinct types of violations: (1) that brought about by competition between industries, the settlement of which would not require state intervention but only accord between the parties on a basis of regulations set forth among the industrial groups of the various countries; and (2) that resulting from secret manufacture for export for military purposes or from the exercise of pressure by a state on its own industry which could demand international objections, investigations, and sanctions.

The reports suggested that each state should undertake to establish as a crime, to be punished with suitable penalties, any exercises or training by military persons or civilians in the use of poisons and bacteria, particularly such training or exercise by air squadrons.

There was a split of opinion concerning a reply to the question, "What effective sanctions can be proposed for the enforcement of the international undertaking not to employ poisonous gas or bacteria in warfare?" The representatives of some eight states believed that the only effective sanction to prevent a state from violating its agreement not to use such agents in war would be the possibility of immediate and forceful reprisals by the same means against a violator. They stated:

All states in possession of a chemical industry should therefore undertake:
(a) to put at the disposal of any State which is attacked by gas the raw materials, chemical products and means of operation necessary for reprisals;
(b) to engage in joint reprisals themselves, so far as distance permits, by the use of other chemical means against the State which has committed an act of aggression by the use of gas.[170]

Other than reprisals, this grouping of nations expressed the view that there were no technical means to prevent chemical warfare. Ten other nations, including the United States, refused to associate themselves with this proposal, the Netherlands and Germany stating specifically that gas as a means of warfare should not be legalized in any manner, whether it be in the form of reprisals or sanctions or otherwise.[171]

In the years following these reports, the Preparatory Commission worked on the agenda for the General Disarmament Conference, and by 1930 had come up with a draft disarmament convention.[172] Article 39 of this proposal dealt with CB weapons in the following words:

The High Contracting Parties undertake, subject to reciprocity, to abstain from the use in war of asphyxiating, poisonous or similar gases, and of all analogous liquids, substances or processes.
They undertake unreservedly to abstain from the use of all bacteriological methods of warfare.[173]

This language, although adopted by the commission by a majority vote, was a subject of much discussion and contention. Reservations were made by several representatives expressive of their discontent with the draft and of their right to submit to the conference their proposals concerning CB arms and to amplify the scope of the Geneva Protocol.[174]

Discussion by the commission was directed to the question of whether the prohibition of chemical arms or of any type of weapons had any place in a Disarmament Convention which had as its aim the regulation of armaments in peacetime, not the codification of rules applicable in wartime.[175] However, the view prevailed that it was wise to renew the obligations concerning chemical and biological warfare and, in the words of a delegate, to forbid "the use in warfare of all weapons which are generally considered those of savages."[176] The German representative objected to the designation "chemical warfare," preferring the term "chemical arm" because there was no exclusive chemical warfare, but only a chemical arm used in conjunction with other arms.[177] The final draft was entitled "chemical arms."

Attention was called to the existence of the Geneva Protocol, which prohibited chemical and bacteriological arms in almost identical language. Therefore, it was suggested that a draft resolution should be made urging its adoption, and that any expansion of the protocol should be done by a special treaty coming into force before the Disarmament Convention. Otherwise the ratification of the protocol would be retarded, since states failing to ratify would wait until the draft agreement in the convention was adopted—which might be never.[178] A contrary view prevailed, on the ground that it would be good to secure uniform obligation on the part of all states acceding to the Disarmament Convention.[179]

The draft recognized that the duty to abstain from the use of asphyxiating, poisonous, or similar gases was to be observed *subject to reciprocity* only. This phrase "subject to reciprocity" was not included in the original draft. Its omission was remarked upon. Although it was believed that if a contracting party were attacked with gas weapons by a non-contracting party the contracting party could resort to gas in defense, still it was felt desirable that the implication should be expressly recognized by the insertion of the reciprocity language.[180] Some delegates were, however, uncertain as to the inclusion of a statement making the prohibition applicable only to contracting parties, on the ground that this would change or diminish the force of the character of the prohibition as a rule of the international law of war.[181] Their objection was disregarded because it was believed that in any event international law would permit latitude to disregard the prohibition against an opponent disregarding it and resorting to first use of gas weapons.[182]

No mention was made of the phrase "subject to reciprocity" as to bacteriological methods. The undertaking to refrain from these methods was made absolute. The Belgian delegate explained the reason for the differentiation:

In the case of gases . . . the Convention would be contemplating a method of warfare which essentially could not be employed except in war. If an army projected asphyxiating, poisonous or similar gases into the ranks of the enemy, it would thus kill a certain number of men; but the shells it sent over would do quite as much damage. That, therefore, was a method which was not in itself intended to be used against the innocent, *i.e.*, civilian population, and which would therefore be admissible—at any rate, subject to reciprocity.

On the other hand, it was beyond question that bacteriological methods would inevitably affect everybody, and that was why it was essential to prohibit such methods absolutely. If a country resorted to such horrible methods against another country, that was no reason why this country should be entitled to use them in turn against the attacker. . . . It was really inconceivable that countries should ever be entitled to send to others poisons which would attack the entire population. Any really civilized Government would refuse to employ such methods.[183]

The British raised objection to the language of the draft which incorporated the French language version of the Geneva Protocol of 1925 forbidding the use of asphyxiating, poisonous, or *similar* gases rather than forbidding the use of asphyxiating, poisonous, or *other* gases. The British held to their view that all gases, including tear gases, were prohibited by the Geneva Protocol and that the Geneva instrument and the present draft should conform. They desired a definite opinion as to whether the use of tear gas was regarded as contrary to the Geneva Protocol.[184] The commission felt unable to express an opinion and decided to leave this matter to the coming conference.

The French delegation set forth its opinion that tear gases were covered by the words of the protocol (French version) as well as the words of the draft, for the language would be applicable to "all gases employed with a view to toxic action on the human organism, whether the effects of such action are a more or less temporary irritation of certain mucous membranes or whether they cause serious or even fatal lesions." Listed as such gases were suffocating gases, blistering gases, irritant and poisonous gases in general, the irritant gases being defined as those causing tears and sneezing. It was stressed, however, that the use of tear gas by police in the maintenance of internal order would not be included within either instrument, for the prohibition was of the use of gases *in war* only. Certain other delegates agreed with the broad British proposal, that of Czechoslovakia setting forth his accord because it would be difficult to distinguish clearly between lethal and nonlethal gases.[185]

The American delegation was in disagreement with this broad connotation. It declared:

The problem before us is essentially one of doing away with agencies which cause unnecessary suffering, and it is important, if our prohibition of these inhumane agencies is to be all-inclusive and applicable, that we have definite knowledge of these various agencies and their effects, and of the ramification of any decisions we may take. On the other hand we seek a maximum prohibition of unhumane agencies, but, at the same time, we should not be led to bring into disrepute the employment of agencies which not only are free from the reproach of causing unnecessary suffering, but which achieve definite military or civil purposes by means in themselves more humane than those in use before their adoption. I think there wonld be considerable hesitation on the part of many Governments to bind themselves to refrain from the use in war, against an enemy, of agencies which they have adopted for peacetime use against their own population, agencies adopted on the ground that, while causing temporary inconvenience, they cause no real suffering or permanent disability, and are thereby more clearly humane than the use of weapons to which they were formerly obliged to resort to in times of emergency.[186]

In addition, proposals were made that the draft should also prohibit the preparation in peacetime for the utilization of gas and bacteriological methods of warfare, and further, should restrict the importation, exportation, and manufacture of substances therefor.[187] Accord as to the first proposal could not be reached because prevention of preparation in peacetime would preclude preparation for defense against gases and preparation for their use against an enemy who first employed them. That part of the French proposal to prevent preparation in peacetime which would call upon the parties to take "effectual steps to prevent private persons from making preparation in their territory for the use of such methods in war," as well as the importation-exportation ban,[188] brought a United States objection. This was based upon the lack of power of the federal government to act and to supervise or intervene, since such measures could be taken only by the individual states.[189] This objection would be a doubtful one, for the war power, the foreign commerce power, or the treaty power of the Constitution would probably cover the exercise of federal power in this area.

As to the second proposal, the difficulty of determining in advance whether such substances were imported, exported, or manufactured for use in war or for entirely innocent purpose was highlighted.[190]

A Soviet proposal suggested the destruction within three months after the convention entered into force of "methods and appliances for chemical aggression (all asphyxiating gases used for warlike purposes, as well as all appliances for their discharge, such as gas projectors, pulverisers, balloons, flamethrowers and other devices) and bacteriological warfare, either available for the use of troops or in reserve or in process of manufacture. . . ."[191] This was not adopted by the commission, nor was a Polish endeavor to provide practical and preventive measures so that violations could not be committed without involving unpleasant consequences for a guilty state.[192] The delegations making these proposals reserved their rights to present them to the Conference.

Conference for the Reduction and Limitation of Armaments

The Disarmament Conference finally opened on February 2, 1932.[193] The General Commission of the Conference appointed a Special Committee to consider the problem of CB methods and warfare and report back to the General Commission. Three criteria were formulated for determination as to whether certain weapons should be included in a system of qualitative disarmament: whether they were among those specifically offensive in character, most efficacious against national defense, or most threatening to noncombatants.[194]

1. Report of the Special Committee, May 31, 1932

The Special Committee agreed that chemical weapons and methods of warfare met all three criteria,[195] especially number three, because once gas is released it can no longer be controlled by its users and may reach civilians a considerable distance away. Thus, chemical substances used to injure an adversary should be included in a system of qualitative disarmament, specifically

all natural or synthetic noxious substances, whatever their state, whether solid, liquid or gaseous, whether toxic, asphyxiating, lachrymatory, irritant, vesicant, or capable in any way of producing harmful effects on the human or animal organism, whatever the method of their use.[196]

Also included would be appliances, devices, or projectiles especially constructed to utilize these noxious agents for use against an adversary. Explosives as such, or noxious substances arising from their detonation, unless the explosives were designed or used to produce the noxious substances, did not come within the definition, nor did smokes or fog used to screen objectives or for other military purposes if they did not produce harmful effects under normal conditions of use.[197]

Attention should be directed to certain aspects of this report. The committee speaks of chemical weapons and methods of warfare, not merely gas or gas warfare, and extends its definition to all harmful chemical substances, natural or synthetic, whether solid, liquid, or gaseous. The degree of harmfulness was not considered. It was said that to create a distinction on the ground of degree of harmfulness so as to include substances with little harmful effect would weaken the system of disarmament. Such a distinction would permit good faith allegations by one who had used the substances that the user had not actually violated the ban. Moreover, it was pointed out that it would be difficult to distinguish chemicals on the basis of their relative harmful effects. Tear gases used internally by police forces were, however, excepted by the committee, but not if used for war.[198]

It should also be noted that the interdiction applies not only to human beings but also to animals. Plants were not mentioned. It was believed at that time that any substance employed against plants would also be harmful to human beings or animals or would make the plants harmful to them.

Finally, the prohibition of the use of such chemical substances is applicable only if its use is designed to injure the enemy.

Bacteriological weapons and means of warfare should, according to this committee, also be included in qualitative disarmament.[199] The spread of infectious disease affects all human beings, since there is no sure method of stopping the effects once disseminated; therefore, bacterial methods met criterion three quite clearly as a method of war most threatening to civilians. The committee believed, however, that this method should be included in a system of qualitative disarmament even had it not fallen within any of the criteria for it was "so particularly odious that it revolted the conscience of humanity more than any other form of warfare."[200] To be included within the ban were all methods of injuring an adversary by the projection, discharge, or dissemination in inhabited as well as uninhabited places of pathogenic microbes (virulent or capable of becoming so), of filter-passing viruses, or of infected substances whether the purpose be to bring them into immediate contact with human beings, animals, or plants, or to infect them indirectly by polluting the atmosphere, water, food, or any other objects.[201]

Stress should be laid upon the fact that the committee used the broader and more modern term "pathogenic microbes," which would include not only bacteria but the other microorganisms. Moreover, the committee also declared that methods of bacteriological warfare should be prohibited whether used directly against human beings, animals, or plants or indirectly as by pollution of water, the atmosphere, foodstuffs, or other objects.

Also included in the committee's restrictions in a system of qualitative disarmament were incendiary projectiles if specifically intended to cause fires, with the exception of those used for exclusive defense against aircraft. Also restrained were appliances like flamethrowers designed to attack human beings by fire.[202] Incendiaries were likened to *chemical* rather than ordinary weapons, for it was said that they did "not act by shock or trauma."[203] It was felt that these weapons particularly threatened civilians, since they were effective in destroying urban areas, the fires caused by them being liable to considerable spreading. Flamethrowers used against persons were called weapons of unnecessary suffering.[204]

The General Commission accepted the report of the Special Committee and concluded in a resolution of July 23, 1932, that chemical, bacteriological, and incendiary warfare should be prohibited and that rules of international law should be formulated in connection with these prohibitions, supplemented by measures to deal with violations of them.[205] Therefore, as directed, the chairman of the Special Committee submitted a report in October, 1932, on problems of the use of chemical, bacteriological, and incendiary warfare, to the bureau which had been set up to assist the president of the conference in his work.

2. Report Submitted to the Bureau on the Prohibition of Chemical Warfare and Violations of the Prohibition to Use Chemical, Bacteriological, and Incendiary Weapons

This report[206] embodied provisions which if agreed upon by states would extend their obligations in relation to chemical and biological methods in war far beyond any previous international undertaking. According to its conclusions the parties would renounce as against any state, whether party to the convention or not, and in any war, even though it be unlawful on the part of their adversaries, the use of chemical and bacterial methods to injure an enemy, and the use of projectiles specifically intended to cause fires or the use of appliances designed to attack persons by fire. Excepted were those projectiles made and used specifically for defense against aircraft, as well as projectiles constructed to give light, pyrotechnics which were not intended to cause fires, and projectiles which produce fires accidentally.[207] The report accepted the previous definition of the Special Committee in its report of May 31, 1932, of chemical and bacteriological methods and agents to be included within the prohibition.[208]

In failing to include a phrase making the undertaking of the contracting parties subject to reciprocity, which would bind such parties only as to states accepting the obligations of the convention, the report differed from the Geneva Protocol, which did not expressly exclude reciprocity (although many of the signatories, of course, adhered with express reservations),[209] and the Preparatory Commission's previous draft, which absolutely forbade bacteriological methods, but which created a less restrictive prohibition as to chemical methods, for the ban on these was expressly conditioned upon reciprocity.[210] Moreover, this report to the bureau did not distinguish between the legality and illegality of wars. A state, victim of an illegal war, would be forbidden the use of CB methods. Reprisals against an adversary making first use of such weapons were permitted. Reprisals could take the form of chemical or incendiary weapons, but not bacteriological ones.

Such a new absolute prohibition was believed necessary because if a convention permitted use of CB agents in certain instances, states would be reluctant to consent to a restraint on the preparation for chemical warfare in peacetime. If these weapons were permitted under certain conditions and against certain adversaries, states would contemplate recourse to CB warfare, which in turn would demand preparation. Consequently, it would not be possible to preclude preparation. It was further recognized that such a denial of CB weapons would necessitate the establishment of satisfactory forms of control in each state, and that the penalties to be made applicable against violators must be effective.[211]

This draft sought to prohibit also all preparations for chemical, incendiary, and bacteriological warfare in peacetime and in wartime. The prohibition would be absolute in peacetime, but in wartime an exception was recognized. Chemical and incendiary weapons were permitted as reprisals under certain conditions. As a consequence, some preparation for such use might, perhaps, be permitted. The prohibition of preparation was expressly extended to the institution and training of armed forces in the use of chemical, bacteriological, and incendiary weapons. It would also apply to the manufacture, import, export, or possession of "chemical appliances and substances exclusively suited to the conduct of chemical, incendiary and bacteriological warfare."[212] As discussed in the report, the chemical appliances falling within the prohibition would be special apparatus used to project gases or propel gas shells.[213] Also barred would be the manufacture, import, export, or possession of chemical appliances and substances capable of being used for both peaceful and military purposes with the intention of using them in war should occasion arise. Here it would be not the nature of the substances but the intention to use them in war which was reprehensible.[214] The prohibition in the proposed instrument did not extend to material to be used for protective purposes against CB warfare, such as gas masks, or to the training of persons to protect themselves against CB attacks, for such material and training would lessen the injury caused by use of these weapons, would lessen the military advantage to be gained by their use, and would make resort to them less tempting.[215]

The report also sought to provide supervision to assure that the nations observed the prohibition against preparation for chemical, bacteriological, and incendiary warfare. A special section of the Permanent Disarmament Committee was to be created for this purpose and empowered to collect all useful information from official or private statistics on manufacture, import, export, and possession of the means of such warfare. Moreover, it could request governments to supply it with additional information and explanations, and receive applications from states for explanation regarding the importation or manufacturing of chemical substances in another state. After examination of such applications, the section could decide to drop the matter, or, if warranted, to lay it before the Permanent Commission, which could take certain steps in accord with the powers to be conferred upon it by the convention.[216]

Supervision was intended to prevent breaches of the prohibition. But cognizance was taken of the difficulties involved in creating an effective system, particularly with respect to substances used in chemical warfare which could be manufactured by any country with a well-developed chemical industry, in some cases without conversion of the peacetime producing process, and in others with simple and rapid adaptation. Supervision of chemical substances exclusively for war would necessitate inspection of producing factories and study of the processes taking place there. It was acknowledged that such supervision could not be efficacious because of ease of concealment and because products of exclusive use for war would not become so until a final and simple transformation. Such inspection could lead to malpractice and frictions particularly involving a risk of industrial espionage. Supervision of appliances and substances utilized for both peace and war would be equally difficult and complicated, for it would be necessary to establish capabilities of output and plant production over and above what was actually in use, to discover any excesses of production over consumption, and to determine whether the excess was produced because of accident such as an erroneous economic forecast, a depression, or new inventions in the manufacturing process, or because of intent to produce new stocks for use in war. In view of these complications, it was believed that the limited system of supervision advanced above, although admittedly incomplete and defective, would be all that could be created. It was acknowledged that reliance should not be placed essentially on observance and supervision, but rather upon severe penalties to be applied in the event of employment of chemical, bacteriological, and incendiary methods of warfare.[217]

The establishment of the fact of the use of these methods was to be entrusted to the Permanent Disarmament Commission, a neutral authority, not to the state which had been the subject of the infringement. Since establishment of the fact of infringement would have to precede measures of retaliation, it was realized that the fact must be established rapidly, for if it were not the state resorting to such infringement would gain great military advantage. However, a few days' delay was acknowledged to be needed to permit investigation. Until the facts were established with certainty, third states could not be expected to act against the delinquent state. It was also pointed out that even though the victim might retaliate in kind, preparation for such retaliation would take a few days.[218] Thus the procedure to establish the facts of use and violation of the prohibition was set forth as follows:

The State which alleges that chemical, incendiary or bacteriological weapons have been used by its adversary will immediately inform the Permanent Commission, which will notify the State against which the charge is brought. The complainant State will at the same time appeal to the doyen of the Diplomatic Corps accredited to it. The doyen of the Diplomatic Corps will appeal for assistance in establishing the actual facts to agents such as the consuls or military attachés, for whom he will, if necessary, secure the assistance of doctors and chemists. He will then report to the Permanent Commission. The Permanent Commission will have the right to carry out any preliminary enquiries both in the territory subject to the authority of the complainant State and in the territory subject to the authority of the State against which the charge is brought.[219]

Upon the establishment of the fact of infringement of the ban on employment of chemical, bacteriological, or incendiary weapons, the problem of the imposition of penalties or sanctions upon the violator would become vital. The belief was expressed in the report that, in view of the inadequate supervisory and preventive action in time of peace, severe penalties should be provided as offset. It was reasoned that immediately after the establishment of infringement third states should be permitted and obligated to take measures such as diplomatic representations, rupture of diplomatic, economic, and financial relations, or blockade, to force discontinuance of the use by the delinquent of chemical, bacteriological, and incendiary methods. Rapid consultation would be requisite to secure agreement on appropriate methods to stop the infringement and to assist the victim state.[220] Whether states should be bound to take measures ordered after consultation was deemed a political question, and one which should be deferred so as to permit the conference itself to make its attitude known.[221] As a result, rather weak wording which could be subject to varying interpretations was inserted. This language would require consultation to decide on the punitive action and "to address injunctions or recommendations to the States at war."[222]

The state victim of the illegal use of the banned weapons was given the right to retaliate with chemical or incendiary, but not bacteriological, weapons. It could also make use of other methods of reprisal. It was required that reprisals take place within the fighting area. The Permanent Disarmament Commission and the consulting states were empowered to request the victim state to refrain from specified measures of retaliation.[223] The report—not the draft convention of the report—thought it not desirable to permit the victim state to retaliate in kind but stressed the fact that it should be compensated by third states for the disadvantages accruing from the use of the forbidden weapons. Nevertheless, since states might not assist, and in any event since the time for consultation might permit the victim to be crushed before collective actions were taken, a prohibition of reprisals in kind on the part of the victim was not believed warranted. Thus the victim was permitted to defend itself so as not to be placed in a position of inferiority.[224] Retaliation in kind by the victim was, it should be stressed, confined to chemical and incendiary weapons. Bacteriological weapons would not be permitted to the victim even if their use by another belligerent were established, for such weapons would strike at all indiscriminately and were not regarded as "an appreciable element of military superiority."[225]

In discussion of the bureau's report as related to sanctions, differences of opinion came to the fore. Consensus was reached that sanctions for infringement of the prohibition were called for, but those to be applied and the methods of application brought on disagreement and had to be reserved. Much of this discord centered around the granting of any right of retaliation or reprisal in kind.[226]

Thereafter the Bureau of the Conference requested the Special Committee to reconsider the problem of prohibiting preparations for the use of these three methods of warfare as well as the measures to be taken in the event of a breach of the ban on use. This was to be done on the basis of a submitted questionnaire.[227] The Special Committee was of the opinion that outlawing the manufacture, import, or possession of implements and substances *exclusively* suitable for chemical warfare would be of limited value. The reasons given were those stated in previous studies, such as the rapidity with which a chemical industry could turn to the manufacture of these substances and the fact that there were no means of projection used exclusively for chemical warfare. Moreover, the prohibition of the manufacture, import, or possession of apparatus and substances used in both peace and war would not be possible. It was reported that the training of troops in chemical warfare could be prohibited, but the practical effects would be small, since they would be so trained in the normal course of their general training.

The committee examined tear gases separately, and concluded, as before, that they could not be treated apart from a prohibition of the use of poisonous substances in wartime. It was admitted that tear gas could be used by police in internal operations, and that police could be so armed. Since this was just a step from actual preparation for chemical warfare, and to avoid abuse, the Permanent Disarmament Commission was to be informed of a state's intention to use such substances, the substances used, the implements employed, and their number. The commission could then determine whether there was disproportion between the facts given in this notification and the police requirements. The state itself would be expected to supervise and regulate strictly the manufacture or sale of implements with tear gas substances for private use.

The committee was most discouraging as to the effectiveness of attempts to prohibit preparations for chemical warfare. A consultation of the commercial statistics of each country relating to that country's chemical industries was said not to suffice. Even if it might be possible to entrust supervision of all of the chemical factories of the world to an international body, the prevention of all preparation for chemical warfare could hardly ensue, for the measures of supervision could be evaded by "the preparation of products similar to those that were really aimed at, or by the formation of states of semi-finished products, or by the masking of the real capacity of the factories by the accumulation of spare parts for the plant."[228] To limit the chemical output capacity of states or some of them would be a difficult undertaking and in some instances not desirable economically, for some states possessed natural favorable conditions for such production, and others, even though at a disadvantage from the standpoint of raw materials, had built up chemical complexes to insure economic independence. These states would hardly want to give up such industries. It would be possible to limit stocks of chemical substances suitable *only* for chemical warfare, but as regards others it would be difficult. It was further pointed out that an attempt to prohibit preparations of certain chemical products useful in peace and in war on a basis of intention to use them in war could never be really successful because of the difficulty of determining the intention of the state.

Turning to incendiary warfare, the committee concluded that the manufacture, possession, import, or export of incendiary *methods* could be prohibited and that such a prohibition would be an effective obstacle to the preparation for incendiary warfare. But it would not preclude states from resorting to this type of warfare once hostilities had begun, for they could easily and rapidly construct the implements necessary, and the substances could quickly be manufactured. It would not, however, be possible to prohibit the manufacture, import, export, or possession of incendiary *substances*, inasmuch as these substances are used for numerous purposes. Manufacture of flamethrowers might be prohibited, if it were possible to define such apparatus.

A prohibition of training in incendiary warfare could be provided, but it would be of little effect, for training in bomb throwing is the same whether it is an incendiary bomb or not; hence, no special training for the incendiary weapon would be needed. Training to use flamethrowers would hardly be needed anyway, for they were said to be simple implements.

The committee stated bluntly that it would not be "possible to prevent preparations for bacteriological warfare."[229] It was admitted that bacteriological warfare was an unknown factor, that there had been no experience of it, that it was a hypothesis. There could be no effective supervision of bacteriological research, for hindering the progress of medical bacteriology by supervising and restricting experiments would not be in the interests of humanity. The Permanent Disarmament Commission was warned, however, that it should not lose sight of the dangers of this type of warfare.

The recommended procedure for establishing the fact of violation through the use of the outlawed weapons was somewhat similar to that of the former report to the bureau. A Commission for Urgent Initial Investigation was to be constituted to make immediate inquiries and report to the Permanent Disarmament Commission. The latter body would then inform the accused state, and if necessary order an inquiry into its territory.

In attempting to fix penalties for breaches, the committee did not consider penalties for violation of the prohibition against preparation, but only those for violating the prohibition against use of the weapons. The committee believed that it would be effective for signatory states to give the state subjected to a breach scientific, medical, and technical assistance to repair, attenuate, or prevent the effects of the use of the prohibited weapons, and that supplies to the violating state of raw materials, implements, and products of such warfare should be stopped. In the event of the use of such weapons, reprisals in the form of incendiary or chemical weapons would be permitted, but rigid conditions for such reprisals should be established to guard against nullification of the prohibition of preparation for chemical and incendiary weapons. Retaliation by bacteriological weapons was precluded.

There was disappointment among certain delegations as to the negative conclusion of the Special Committee to the effect that it was impossible in peace to provide guarantees against the use of chemical, bacteriological, or incendiary weapons in war. Some delegations, including that of the United States, believed that the imposition of penalties for breach of the prohibition against use of the weapons under consideration raised political questions and involved decisions upon other questions and prohibitions under consideration by the Disarmament Conference. The French delegate thought otherwise, believing that the question of penalties for use of these weapons was a special problem demanding special action, and the bureau agreed.[230] The bureau then instructed a drafting committee to frame articles for inclusion in the draft Disarmament Convention.[231] The articles so drafted formed a basis for the chemical, bacterial, and incendiary warfare provisions of the draft Disarmament Convention submitted by the British delegate on March 16, 1933.[232]

British Draft Convention

This draft convention went farther than the report to the bureau with respect to an interdiction of the use of chemical, bacterial, or incendiary warfare, and that report had gone farther than previous prohibitory provisions. In the previous report to the bureau, any contracting state renounced the use of such weapons against any other states. The British draft provided:

The following provision is an established rule of international law. The use of chemical, incendiary or bacterial weapons as against any State, whether or not a Party to the present Convention, and in any war, whatever its character, is prohibited. This provision does not, however, deprive any Party which has been the victim of the illegal use of *chemical* or *incendiary* weapons of the right to retaliate, subject to such conditions as may hereafter be agreed.[233]

As to this right of reprisal, it was recalled that the Special Committee had originally proposed that such right should not be accorded until the use of such weapons by the adversary had been established. The delegation of the British defended the provision it had advanced because there might be delay involved before the fact of use and violation could be established. The German delegate opposed any use of chemical and gas weapons even as a measure of retaliation.[234] The prohibitions set forth as to the application of chemical, bacterial, or incendiary weapons for the purpose of injuring an adversary were similar to those set forth in the previous reports of the Special Committee,[235] including not only toxic and asphyxiating substances, but also tear, irritant, or vesicant substances.

The draft prohibited all preparations for chemical, incendiary, or bacterial warfare in time of peace as in time of war. This prohibition would apply in general to the manufacture, import, export, or possession of the prohibited substances and training in their use. Possession of quantities of chemical substances necessary for protective purposes and therapeutic research was excepted, although the Permanent Disarmament Commission was required to be informed of the quantities necessary for protective experiments. Also excepted from the prohibition were material and installations intended for defensive protective purposes, and tear gas intended for police operations. Some debate was forthcoming as to whether these provisions prohibiting manufacture, import, export, or possession of these forbidden substances were really necessary, in view of the fact that previous committee reports concerning the impossibility of effective supervision demonstrated that the only reliance for their observance would be on the good faith and goodwill of the contracting parties. This was particularly true of the provision which extended the prohibition as to manufacture, import, or export to substances or appliances suitable both for peace and for war where there was intent to use them for war. It was pointed out that it would be difficult to adopt legislation grounded upon intention.[236]

In order to avail itself of the exception made of tear gas for police purposes, a party would be required to furnish information as to such use and the number of appliances required. The United States delegate objected to the provision. He stated that in the United States the use of tear gas for police purposes was very widespread. If the furnishing of information were made a contractual obligation, he believed the United States could not carry out the obligation for it would not be able to obtain such information short of taking a complete census of the country.[237] The language of this draft provision was later changed and softened to provide that the parties would undertake to supply the commission with information if such substances were used by governmental agencies or instrumentalities for police operations.[238]

The contentions as to the impossibility of establishing a truly effective system of supervision of the observance of the prohibition of preparation for chemical, incendiary, or bacterial warfare apparently bore fruit, for the provision in this regard was extremely simple: The Permanent Disarmament Commission would be empowered to examine complaints of any party alleging that the prohibition against preparation had been violated.

A party claiming that chemical, incendiary, or bacterial weapons had been used against it was called upon to notify the Permanent Disarmament Commission, and at the same time notify the authority named for the purpose of the commission. Where such authority had not been named, the dean of the diplomatic corps accredited to it should be notified with a view to immediate creation of a commission of investigation.

This latter commission was to act speedily with inquiries to determine whether chemical, incendiary, or bacterial weapons had been used, and then report to the Permanent Disarmament Commission. This latter body could invite explanations from the party against whom the complaint had been made. It could also carry on an inquiry as to use of the forbidden weapons, and could send commissioners into the territory of the accused to undertake an investigation there. As a result of all these operations the Permanent Commission was to establish whether such weapons had been used.

No sanctions for resort to chemical, bacteriological, and incendiary weapons were included, although the delegations of France and Yugoslavia emphasized the necessity for sanctions to enforce the prohibitions against *both* preparation and use.

This British Draft Convention on disarmament was never accepted. The Disarmament Conference itself held its last meeting in 1934 without agreeing upon a general disarmament convention. The withdrawal of Germany from the League of Nations in October, 1933, its rearmament, and the uncertainty of its intentions as to peace and war had ruptured any unity which might have existed and which might have been conducive to any disarmament.[239]

Conclusion

From the foregoing discussion, the conclusion can be reached that there was a determined and concerted effort to outlaw chemical, bacteriological, and even incendiary warfare by international treaties or conventions in the period between the two great wars. During the course of deliberations, the official views of many nations were stated and restated to the effect that these methods of warfare were odious, uncivilized, contrary to the laws of humanity, or conducive to unnecessary suffering and therefore were prohibited or should be prohibited, by the rules and principles of the law of war. The last activities of the League of Nations in this field sought not only to establish a simple prohibition against the use of these methods, but also to limit preparation for them in peacetime, supervision to assure that there would be no such preparation, and sanctions not only against the resort to the use of CB weapons but also against preparations for their use.

In spite of the many attempts to bring into force an international convention, only the Geneva Protocol was signed and ratified by a great enough number of states to make it at all expressive of a multilateral rule of international law on the use of chemical and biological agents in war. And even so, its status is uncertain because of the dispute as to the meaning of the language of the protocol, accentuated by the somewhat differing French and English versions regarding chemical methods— although a comparative analysis of the two versions can lead to the conclusion that all harmful chemical methods in war, whether lethal, severely injurious, or merely temporarily disabling, are forbidden. This conclusion would seem to be borne out by later discussions and the various versions of later draft conventions which took place or were considered at various international conferences and in the League of Nations. Even the United States official representatives appeared to accept the fact that all harmful chemical methods in war, including the use of tear gas, were prohibited, after it was generally accepted that tear gas could be lawfully used for internal police purposes. It must be stressed, however, that because of the difference in the English and French versions, and because of the fact that the treaty is based on the unnecessary suffering principle of the law of war, a strong legal argument has been made that the protocol applies only to the use in war of those chemical agents which are lethal or severely injurious.

Over and above this dispute, the international regime set up by the Geneva Protocol is clouded by the fact that many nations ratified or acceded to the Protocol with reservations, and no agreement has ever been reached on the status of these nations vis-à-vis nations which ratified without reservations. In addition the protocol itself and many of the reservations to it appear to create a gap as to nonratifying nations. Finally, it should be added that approximately one-third of the nations of the world have not ratified the protocol and are not bound by it. As of this writing, among the nonratifiers are two major powers—Japan and the United States.

CHAPTER FIVE

CB WEAPON REGULATION EFFORTS SINCE WORLD WAR II

UNITED NATIONS ATTEMPTS TO REGULATE CB WEAPONS

PRIOR TO THE END of World War II, the leaders of the Allied Nations had little interest in any postwar general disarmament movement. At the Potsdam Conference stress was laid[1] on imposing rigid control over German industries to eliminate Germany's war potential, and, along with other factories, all plants and equipment engaged in the production or manufacture of biological or chemical weapons were to be destroyed or removed. The Charter of the United Nations drafted at San Francisco in 1945 gave very low priority to the question of general international disarmament.[2] But thereafter the United States perfected the atomic bomb and employed it against Japan, thereby ending the war. Upon the advent of this weapon, disarmament again became important, international attention being diverted at the time from chemical and biological weapons to nuclear arms. When President Harry Truman met with British Prime Minister Clement Attlee and Canadian Prime Minister Mackenzie King in November, 1945, a principal item on the agenda was the possibility of international control of nuclear weapons.[3] The resulting "Three Nation Agreed Declaration on Atomic Energy" recommended the setting up of a commission under the United Nations to prepare recommendations relating to the control of atomic energy for peaceful purposes, and added, as an afterthought, that "all other major weapons adaptable to mass destruction" should be eliminated from national armaments.[4] Presumably certain lethal chemical and biological agents would fall within the classification of "weapons adaptable to mass destruction," but not all chemical and biological weapons would appear to fall within this grouping.

Following this declaration, the United Nations General Assembly created the Atomic Energy Commission, charging it specifically with the duty to make treaty proposals looking to "the elimination from national armaments of atomic and all other major weapons adaptable to mass destruction."[5] From its inception, the commission was rocked with dissent because of the wide divergence between Soviet and Western views on the international control of atomic weapons.[6]

At the second half of the first session of the United Nations, in October, 1946, the U.S.S.R. introduced into the General Assembly a resolution calling for the general reduction of armaments, including the production and use of atomic energy for military purposes.[7] This resolution in fact disregarded the previous authorization given by the General Assembly to the Atomic Energy Commission concerning the control of atomic weapons. After much negotiation, the General Assembly reaffirmed the authority of the Atomic Energy Commission over nuclear weapons and weapons of mass destruction, but suggested that the Security Council give prompt consideration to the formulation of the practical measures essential for the general regulation and reduction of armaments.[8]

To comply with this resolution, the Security Council on February 13, 1947, created the Commission for Conventional Armaments.[9] Upon convening, this commission sought to prepare a plan of work outlining its jurisdiction. Despite the decision of the General Assembly reaffirming its original grant of authority to the Atomic Energy Commission in regard to weapons of mass destruction, the Soviet Union sought to include in the work plan of the new commission the elimination of weapons of mass destruction and atomic weapons.[10] Months of heated debate were devoted to the problem of the commission's jurisdiction; but finally, over Russian objections, the majority of the commission adopted, on August 12, 1948, a resolution which defined the competence of the commission and excluded from its jurisdiction consideration of weapons of mass destruction, which were defined "to include atomic explosive weapons, radioactive material weapons, *lethal* chemical and biological weapons."[11] (Italics supplied) By logical implication, therefore, nonlethal chemical and biological weapons seemed to be equated with conventional armaments. Under normal procedure, the work of the commission would be placed in a report, including the resolution adopted, and sent to the Security Council for approval and transmission to the General Assembly. But because of Russian opposition, the commission delayed for more than a year the sending of the resolution and its accompanying progress report to the Security Council for deliberation.[12] When transmission finally occurred, the Security Council sought to obtain approval. A vote of nine in favor, two against (the U.S.S.R. and the Ukranian Soviet Socialist Republic) was the result. Since one of the votes in opposition was that of a permanent member of the Council, it acted as a veto. Consequently the resolution was not adopted.[13] Thereafter, it was agreed that the Security Council was to transmit the report and resolution to the General Assembly without expressing approval thereof. There was, then, no Security Council endorsement of the definition of weapons of mass destruction.[14]

Although such an endorsement by the Security Council would not have the effect of establishing once and for all the legal definition of weapons of mass destruction, nevertheless it would have exerted certain influence on the law-creating process. In any legal review dealing with the scope and content of the phrase, such an endorsement would have become an obligatory item of consideration in the process of decision-making, as an authoritative statement relating to the meaning and intent of the phrase. Failure to endorse the definition, on the other hand, implies that legal decision need give it no weight.[15]

Even though the problem of international treaty control of chemical and biological weapons has taken something of a back seat as compared to nuclear arms, still, since World War II, there have been rounds of debates relating to the necessity for legal control of such weapons. Speaking at the United Nations in December, 1946, the United States delegate, Senator Tom Connally, urged that any treaty for the international control of armaments should cover chemical and biological weapons: "We see no reason why these other deadly measures should not be included in any plan of disarmament."[16] At that time the Soviet representative declared that gas and bacteriological warfare had already been prohibited by international agreements, but stated that the Soviet Union would reaffirm these if necessary.[17]

In August, 1948, in the Introduction to his Annual Report to the United Nations, Secretary General Trygvie Lie urged action by the United Nations looking toward the adoption of a treaty for preventing or controlling the manufacture of chemical and biological weapons,[18] and two years later he complained that the Atomic Energy Commission, which the General Assembly had entrusted with the responsibility of working out treaty proposals for the elimination from national armaments not only of atomic weapons, but of all other major weapons, had never discussed biological and chemical weapons, which he believed might be more destructive of human life than atomic weapons.[19] Still nothing was done. Discussions in various United Nations bodies remained oriented toward atomic weapons. At the Assembly's sixth session in 1951, agreement was, however, reached among the major powers that a single disarmament commission should be established to deal with the whole question of the regulation of all armed forces and all armaments, including atomic and "all major weapons adaptable to mass destruction."[20]

In June, 1952, the Russians presented a resolution to the Security Council which noted "the fact that differences of opinion exist among statesmen and public figures in various countries concerning the admissibility of using bacterial weapons," and requested that the Security Council appeal to all states which had not ratified or acceded to the Geneva Protocol to do so.[21] During the debate in the Council, the representatives of Chile, China, Greece, Turkey, the United Kingdom, and the United States maintained that however praiseworthy and humane the provisions of the Geneva Protocol might have been, they were now obsolete, for they contained no safeguards or guarantees and were not accompanied by any system of international control.[22] Mere declarations, they argued, could not secure any real or effective inhibition. They suggested that the question be referred to the Disarmament Commission.[23]

The representative of France, however, declared that his government considered the Geneva Protocol as retaining all of its legal value and moral authority. He admitted that it should be merged in a wider system for the control and abolition of weapons of mass destruction, but pending the achievement of such a desirable result, the Geneva Protocol remained the chief international instrument which could, if respected, strip war of its more barbarous aspects. Its provisions were as binding as ever on the states parties to it. Nevertheless, he agreed that the only body competent to discuss the U.S.S.R. proposal was the Disarmament Commission.[24]

The Brazilian representative also supported the motion to refer the draft resolution to the Disarmament Commission and stated that the standards of international morality had become such that the protection supposedly afforded by the protocol had become illusory.[25] The representative of the Netherlands was of the opinion that the U.S.S.R. was raising the wrong question in the wrong United Nations organ. The problem of bacterial warfare was a disarmament problem and did not belong to the Security Council. It belonged in the Disarmament Commission, which had clear instructions to prepare a draft treaty, *inter alia*, "for the *elimination* of all major weapons adaptable to mass destruction including bacterial weapons." He stressed the word *eliminate* in that it went further than prohibition. The aim, therefore, was to eliminate the weapons themselves so that they could not be used. Thus, the Disarmament Commission had a broader mandate than the Geneva Protocol, which was limited to the prohibition of the use of such weapons.[26]

When the Security Council voted upon the Russian resolution, it was rejected by one vote in favor and ten abstentions. In view of this decision, the United States representative withdrew his motion to refer the U.S.S.R. draft resolution to the Disarmament Commission, noting that the matter was in any case under discussion in that commission.[27] Thereafter the commission adopted a plan of work, stipulating that it should cover the "elimination of weapons of mass destruction and control with a view to ensuring their elimination."[28]

The subject of bacteriological warfare did come to occupy a large portion of the time of the Disarmament Commission, because of its association with a vast propaganda campaign being carried out at the time by the Soviet Union against the United States, accusing the latter country of employing germ warfare.[29] The Soviet representative in the Disarmament Commission constantly sought to associate the failure of the United States to ratify the Geneva Protocol with the Soviet charge that the United States had engaged in bacteriological warfare in Korea.[30] The United States representatives categorically denied the charges and pointed out that because of the confused status of the Geneva Protocol and because it did not provide inspection and control safeguards, it was of little value.[31] In any event, in view of the constant discussion of bacterial weapons, in August, 1952, the commission amended its work plan to read "weapons of mass destruction, including bacterial weapons."[32]

At its seventh session the General Assembly, having considered the reports of the Disarmament Commission, adopted, on April 8, 1953, a resolution which encouraged the continuation of disarmament negotiations and referred to chemical and biological weapons as a part of a general phrase on "the elimination and prohibition of all major weapons, including bacteriological, adaptable to mass destruction."[33]

Again on November 28, 1953, the General Assembly instructed the Disarmament Commission to prepare a disarmament treaty which included the elimination and prohibition of bacteriological, chemical, and all other weapons of mass destruction.[34] In 1954, the General Assembly reaffirmed that the Disarmament Commission should prepare a draft international disarmament convention which would include the total prohibition of the use and manufacture of weapons of mass destruction of every type.[35] For the next few years, disarmament negotiations in the United Nations included provisions for the control and elimination of chemical and biological weapons, but actually no in-depth discussions of this subject took place.

Disarmament negotiations were completely suspended during 1958 and 1959, despite a speech to the United Nations General Assembly in September, 1959, by Premier Khrushchev of the Soviet Union proposing a general and complete treaty which, among other things, would provide for the removal and destruction, under international control, of all stockpiles of chemical and bacteriological weapons in the possession of states. This was to take place in the third stage of a three-stage plan.[36] Early in 1960, a Ten-Nation Committee on Disarmament,[37] meeting in Geneva, began to discuss two alternative general and complete disarmament treaty proposals, that of the Western powers[38] and that of the Soviet Union,[39] both of which included, *inter alia*, the cessation of manufacture of chemical, biological, and other types of weapons of mass destruction, and the reduction of the existing stockpiles of these weapons, but which differed greatly on the stages in which this should be brought about and on the inspection and control measures to be taken to assure compliance with the proposed treaty terms.[40] The Russians declared that the Western proposals were merely a treaty screen under which espionage activity could take place, and in June, 1960, withdrew from the conference.[41]

Disarmament negotiations lagged for over a year, but on September 20, 1961, a joint letter from the representative of the U.S.S.R. and the representative of the U.S.A., addressed to the president of the General Assembly, set forth a statement of the basis upon which multilateral disarmament negotiations could again begin.[42] Included among these principles was that of seeking early agreement on a treaty which would cover "the elimination of all stockpiles of nuclear, chemical, bacteriological and other weapons of mass destruction, the cessation of the production of such weapons, and the elimination of all means of delivery of weapons of mass destruction." This agreement led to the establishment of the Eighteen Nation Disarmament Committee (ENDC).[43]

This committee began meeting in Geneva in March, 1962, and has met intermittently since. Various draft general and complete disarmament treaties have been discussed, all containing reference to the need to eliminate stockpiles of chemical, biological, and other weapons of mass destruction, the cessation of the production of such weapons, and the elimination of all means of delivery of such weapons. But in the area of chemical and biological weapons no tangible progress has been made toward these professed goals.

The issue of resort to chemical and biological weapons was raised again in the First Committee (Political and Security) of the General Assembly in 1966. The ambassador of Hungary presented to the committee a draft resolution,[44] the preamble of which would have the General Assembly (1) note that it was guided by the principles of the United Nations Charter and of contemporary international law; (2) consider that weapons of mass destruction constituted a danger for all mankind; and (3) recall that the Geneva Protocol for the Prohibition of the Use of Asphyxiating, Poisonous or other Gases and of Bacteriological Methods of Warfare of June, 1925, had been signed, adopted, and recognized by many states. Under the operative paragraphs of the resolution, the General Assembly would: (1) demand strict and absolute compliance by all states with the principles and norms established by the Geneva Protocol; (2) condemn any action aimed at the use of chemical and bacteriological weapons; and (3) declare that the use of chemical and bacteriological weapons for the purpose of destroying human beings and the means of their existence constituted an international crime.

In presenting this resolution, the Hungarian ambassador accused the United States of employing chemical and bacteriological weapons in Vietnam, citing numerous examples of the use of tear or riot-control gas, napalm, and herbicides.[45] The United States representative, exercising his right of reply, described the draft resolution as propaganda and denied the charges that the United States was engaged in chemical and bacteriological warfare. For the next two weeks major speeches came from both Hungary and the United States, each offering rejoinders to the other. The argument revolved around two questions: (1) Are riot-control gases and herbicides generally thought of as asphyxiating or poisonous gases? (2) Do they fall within the term "other gases, and of all analogous liquids, materials or devices," banned by the General Protocol?[46]

The representative of the United States answered both questions in the negative. It was pointed out that more than fifty countries have used tear gas for domestic riot-control purposes, and that the Geneva Protocol "does not apply to all gases, and it certainly does not prohibit the use of simple tear gas where necessary to avoid injury to innocent persons."[47] Furthermore, the herbicides used in Vietnam, he said, involve the same chemicals and have the same effect as those commonly used in the United States and a great many other countries to clear weeds and control vegetation. This being true, their use was not contrary to international law.[48]

The ensuing debate was acrimonious, the Communists asserting that there was no international legal distinction between incapacitating and lethal weapons,[49] and claiming that the United States refused to ratify the Geneva Protocol because it wanted a free hand to use all types of chemical and biological weapons.[50] The United States representative pointed out[51] that it was up to each state to decide whether or not to adhere to the Geneva Protocol in the light of constitutional and other considerations which might determine the adherence of states to any international instrument, particularly one which dated back to 1925. However, he went on to say that if the members of the committee were genuinely concerned over the dangers of chemical and bacteriological warfare, and if they were anxious to maintain international law and standards of civilized conduct, it would be possible to obtain from all the countries represented in the committee a formal public expression of intent to observe the objectives and principles of the Geneva Protocol.[52]

The Russian representative stated that the Geneva Protocol had in fact established a rule of international law even for those states which had not ratified it.[53] This was challenged by the French delegate, who pointed out that only if the Geneva Protocol were a codification of existing customary law would this be true.[54] He had grave doubts that this was the case; consequently it was difficult for him to see how states which had not signed or ratified a treaty could be required to undertake its provisions. Furthermore, the Hungarian draft resolution extended the scope of the Geneva Protocol to the point of including a condemnation of chemical weapons in general, and such an interpretation could not be derived from the text of the protocol.[55]

The delegate from the Netherlands said that after more than forty years, the moment had come to give serious consideration to a possible review of the Geneva Protocol by an appropriate body, since, "in the light of the scientific and technological developments of the postwar era, such a review is not only warranted but in fact overdue."[56] Thereupon the representative from Malta suggested that the ENDC be given the task and be asked by the General Assembly to study the procedures necessary to "give effective publicity through the UN to the national production and to the stocks of chemical and bacteriological weapons in national arsenals."[57] He went on to say that within the not too distant future the United Nations would be asked to study the effects of such weapons of mass destruction, and that sooner or later the ENDC would have to tackle the task of regulating research, production, and stockpiling of such weapons.

Eventually an amendment to the original Hungarian draft resolution was proposed by a group of "nonaligned" nations:

Whereby the General Assembly, guided by the principles of the United Nations Charter and contemporary international law, considering that weapons of mass destruction constitute a danger for all mankind and are incompatible with the accepted norms of civilization, affirming that the strict observance of the rules of international law on the conduct of warfare is in the interest of maintaining these standards of civilization:

Demand strict and absolute compliance by all states with the principles and norms established by the Geneva Protocol of June 17, 1925, which prohibits the use of chemical and bacteriological weapons; deplores the use of chemical and bacteriological weapons for the purpose of destroying human beings and the means of their existence; and invites all states to accede to the Geneva Protocol of 17 June 1925 on Prohibition of the use of asphyxiating, poisonous and other gases and bacteriological methods of warfare.[58]

This revised resolution was attacked by representatives from the Western powers on the grounds that (1) the phrase "contemporary international law" was meaningless;[59] (2) the phrase "deplores the use of chemical and bacteriological weapons" implied that such were in fact being used by the United States, and hence was condemnatory propaganda;[60] (3) the phrase "the Geneva Protocol . . . prohibits the use of chemical and bacteriological weapons," was inaccurate; (4) the phrase "destroying human beings and the means of their existence" was nonsensical, as all wars sought such destruction; and (5) the term "chemical and bacteriological weapons" should be clearly defined, for in the light of modern science and technology without definition there could be no international agreement on what was covered by the term.[61]

Thereafter the Western powers submitted their own draft resolution[62] which substituted for the preambular paragraph a statement noting that ENDC had the task of seeking, in the context of general and complete disarmament, a ban on chemical and bacteriological weapons, and which substituted for the two operative paragraphs a terse clause calling for "strict observance by all states of the principles and objectives" of the Geneva Protocol. This draft resolution was adopted by the committee by a vote of 101 to 0 with three abstentions (Cuba, France, and Gabon).[63]

When the First Committee's resolution was presented to the General Assembly for action, the delegate from Cuba declared that in view of the fact that

[a]t the time when this Assembly is in session, the chemical and bacteriological weapons used by the United States Air Force are destroying harvests and fields, and Yankee troops continue to disembark in South Viet-Nam, bringing war and death . . . Cuba considers that these discussions are mere dreams and, under present conditions, will not lead to any practical results. . . . Because of all that . . . my delegation will abstain in the vote. . . .[64]

The Hungarian delegate declared that the basic intention of the drafters of the resolution, and in fact of the drafters of the Geneva Protocol, was to prohibit the use of whatever gases can be used in warfare, for "they are all poisonous in one degree or another. Some of them kill everybody and some of them kill only some people. So there is a difference only of degree in their danger."[65]

The United States delegate disagreed, pointing out that the Geneva Protocol was framed to prohibit the use of poisonous gases such as mustard gas and phosgene. It was not intended to apply to all gases. Furthermore, he stated:

It would be unreasonable to contend that any rule of international law prohibits the use in combat against an enemy, for humanitarian purposes, of agents that Governments around the world commonly use to control riots of their own people. Similarly, the Protocol does not apply to herbicides, which involve the same chemicals and have the same effects as those used domestically in the United States, the Soviet Union and many other countries to control weeds and other unwanted vegetation.[66]

On December 5, 1966, the General Assembly adopted a resolution following the tenor of that recommended by the First Committee:

THE GENERAL ASSEMBLY

Guided by the principles of the Charter of the United Nations and of international law,

Considering that weapons of mass destruction constitute a danger to all mankind and are incompatible with the accepted norms of civilization,

Affirming that the strict observance of the rules of international law on the conduct of warfare is in the interest of maintaining these standards of civilization,

Recalling that the Geneva Protocol for the Prohibition of the Use in War of Asphyxiating, Poisonous or Other Gases and of Bacteriological Methods of Warfare of June 17, 1925 has been signed and adopted and is recognized by many States,

Noting that the Conference of the Eighteen-Nation Committee on Disarmament has the task of seeking an agreement on the cessation of the development and production of chemical and bacteriological weapons and other weapons of mass destruction, and on the elimination of all such weapons from national arsenals, as called for in the draft proposals on general and complete disarmament now before the Conference,

1. *Calls* for strict observance by all States of the principles and objectives of the Protocol for the Prohibition of the Use in War of Asphyxiating, Poisonous or Other

Gases, and of Bacteriological Methods of Warfare, signed at Geneva on June 17, 1925, and condemns all actions contrary to those objectives;

2. *Invites* all States to accede to the Geneva Protocol of June 17, 1925.[67]

The preamble of this resolution is not imperative in nature. Such verbs as *guided by, considering, affirming, recalling,* and *noting* merely indicate the motivation for the body of the resolution. And the wording in the operative paragraphs ("calls for strict observance," "condemns all actions contrary," and "invites all States to accede") is also not legally mandatory in nature, being rather a solicitation, request, or solemn entreaty. Even if one accepts the view that certain of the United Nations resolutions are binding, this could not be the intent of the parties in this instance, because the language of the resolution does not establish a firm enough ought.[68]

The United Nations concerned itself again with the problem of chemical and biological weapons in 1968, following a report of the Eighteen Nation Committee on Disarmament which recommended the appointment of a committee of experts to study the effects of a possible use of these weapons. After the secretary general stated a belief that there was not sufficient consciousness by the international community of the dangers inherent in chemical and biological weapons because due attention had not been focused on them, and after a discussion in the First Committee of the General Assembly, the latter body adopted, on December 20, 1968, a First Committee resolution asking the secretary general to prepare, with the assistance of qualified expert consultants, a report on these weapons and on the effects of their use.[69]

In pursuance of this resolution, the secretary general appointed a group of fourteen consultants to survey the entire subject from the technical and scientific points of view so that these weapons could be placed in proper perspective. With the appointments the secretary general expressed his personal hope that "an authoritative report could become the basis for political and legal action by the Members of the United Nations."[70] Specifically, the experts were asked to provide a scientific appraisal of the characteristics of chemical and biological weapons, of the effects they could have on military personnel and civilians, and of their long-term effects on health and physical environment. They were also asked to speak concerning the economic and security implications of the development, acquisition, and possible use of such weapons and associated weapon systems.

The committee of experts completed its work on June 30, 1969. On July 1, 1969, the secretary general transmitted the report to the General Assembly, to the Security Council, to the Conference of the Eighteen Nation Committee on Disarmament, and to the governments of the member states. In his foreword the secretary general declared:

I also feel it incumbent upon me, in the hope that further action will be taken to deal with the threat posed by the existence of these weapons, to urge that the Members of the United Nations undertake the following measures in the interests of enhancing the security of the peoples of the world:

1. To renew the appeal to all States to accede to the Geneva Protocol of 1925;

2. To make clear affirmation that the prohibition contained in the Geneva Protocol applies to the use in war of all chemical, bacteriological and biological agents (including tear gas and other harassing agents), which now exist or which may be developed in the future;

3. To call upon all countries to reach agreement to halt the development, production and stockpiling of all chemical and bacteriological (biological) agents for purposes of war and to achieve their effective elimination from the arsenal of weapons.[71]

The second recommendation, interpreting the ban of the Geneva Protocol as extending to tear gas and harassing agents, is disputable and could well meet opposition.

Within a matter of days the British submitted to the Eighteen Nation Disarmament Conference a draft convention concerned with biological weapons only.[72] The British delegate implied that the secretary general's interpretation of the Geneva Protocol as covering lethal as well as the nonlethal incapacitating and riot control agents would doom to long delay, if not failure, any attempt to ban both chemical and biological weapons in a single treaty. He also had reservation to the second recommendation, because only about half of the members of the United Nations were parties to the Protocol. It would therefore be odd for nations which were not parties to the protocol but were members of the United Nations to interpret its meaning. The British delegate was of the opinion that only the parties to the protocol were empowered "to say what the protocol means." He went on to add that it would be difficult in any event to secure unanimous agreement of all the parties to the secretary general's interpretation, and it would be even more difficult to secure the unanimous agreement of all of the members of the United Nations.[73]

Article I of the British proposal provided:

Each of the Parties to the Convention undertakes never in any circumstances, by making use for hostile purposes of microbial or other biological agents causing death or disease by infection or infestation in man, other animals or crops, to engage in biological methods of warfare.

The dual purpose of this article was to set forth the central prohibition on the use of biological methods of warfare and to define what was meant by that term. It would cover not only microorganisms which could be used for biological warfare but also biological agents which are not microbes, such as crop-destroying insects or hookworm. Its awkward wording was explained on the ground that "if it read . . . never in any circumstances to engage in biological methods of warfare, by making use . . . ,' that might give the impression that there were other ways of engaging in biological methods of warfare that were permitted."[74]

The British aim was to outlaw biological warfare completely. Consequently it was stated that Article I was framed so as to prohibit the use of biological methods even in self-defense.[75] But this may be questioned. The phrase "by making use for hostile purposes" modifies "to engage in biological methods of warfare." If self-defense is not considered a hostile purpose, as would seem to be the case, then biological methods would still be permissible if used in self-defense.

The second article of the British draft would bar the production of biological agents and of acquisition or research aimed at the production of biological agents having no peaceful justification of an independent nature, as well as ancillary equipment or vectors to facilitate the use of such agents. Destruction of agents and equipment within three months after the convention becomes operative for a party would also be demanded.

Supervision and verification of parties' compliance with the production-possession ban was considered not possible in relation to biological agents because "agents which might be used for hostile purposes are generally indistinguishable from those which are needed for peaceful medical purposes, and militarily significant quantities of a biological warfare agent could be produced clandestinely in a small house or large garage."[76]

It was provided by Article III, however, that complaints of breach of Article II, i.e., production, acquisition, or possession of biological agents as well as facilitating equipment for their use, could be taken to the Security Council for investigation. Complaint to the secretary general would also be possible by any party believing itself to be a victim of the use of biological weapons. Evidence of the use was to be submitted along with a request for investigation and request for a report of the investigation's result to be submitted to the Security Council. Not only a party victim, but any other party as well would be empowered to lodge a complaint before and a request for investigation by the Security Council.

Full support of the secretary general and his representatives in the investigating proceedings was demanded by Article IV, as was appropriate assistance to a party found by the Security Council to have been a victim of the use of biological warfare. The latter was explained as an obligation of assistance to the victim rather than one of action against an aggressor. It was of course recognized that the Security Council could decide on such collective action.[77]

Finally, a draft Security Council Resolution was proposed which would obligate the Security Council to authorize the secretary general to investigate and report in accordance with the terms of the draft convention, which would also declare the Security Council's readiness to consider complaints and recommend action if the complaint were well-founded.

As might be expected, criticism of the British proposal was forthcoming. Objection was raised to the exclusion of chemical methods of warfare from the proposal and the disassociation or separation of chemical and biological weapons in a regulatory scheme which resulted from such exclusion. As to the former, accession by all states to the Geneva Protocol was urged, with clear understanding and affirmation that its prohibitions were applicable to *all* biological agents and to *all* chemical agents including tear gas and other harassing agents and to existing or future chemical and biological agents.[78] To back up this all-inclusive conclusion, the secretary general's report was used which propounded the impossibility of drawing definite limits between lethal or nonlethal agents, inasmuch as some lethal agents could leave survivors and some merely incapacitating agents could cause severe casualties or death. Reference was also made to the fact that chemical or biological agents would be used along with conventional weapons, so that even safe incapacitating agents, if used for military purposes, would enlarge the kill effects of the conventional weapons. The danger of escalation was stressed, in that any use of these weapons would invite retaliation with the risk of the employment of a more deleterious agent in the retaliation. A difference in use within a nation in contrast to external use of riot-control or incapacitating agents was noted, for control of rioting citizens in case of internal commotion in a country would not necessitate killing. External enemies, it was believed, would not be likely to meet the same treatment, for in war "the chain of action-reaction-responses does not stop in the same way."[79]

In making a draft convention applicable to biological weapons only, a separation of chemical and biological weapons for purposes of international regulation would be effected. The British, to justify this separation, made use of the secretary general's report which brought out differences between the two.[80] It was pointed out that differences exist as to toxicity, speed of action, duration of effect, specificity, controllability, and residual effects. Thus biological agents were shown to have potentially a greater contaminating power and to be more difficult to control than chemical weapons. The ability of biological weapons to self-propagate—to multiply themselves, and as a living weapon to seek out victims for destruction—was said to make of them the most horrifying and inhumane of all weapons.[81] The British representative stated:

The area affected by a nuclear weapon would be up to 300 square kilometres; for a chemical weapon the area would be up to 60 square kilometres; but for a bacteriological (biological) weapon the figure is of a different order—up to 100,000 square kilometres. It is clear from this that chemical weapons can be used with a certain amount of precision, but that in the nature of things biological weapons are totally indiscriminate. This in itself seems to me to be a good reason why we should try to tackle biological weapons first.[82]

This attempt to separate or draw limits between chemical and biological warfare was censured. Indeed, the idea was expressed that if separation was to be made and one method sought out for prohibition the chemical method should be given priority, for it was more highly developed and there was more possibility of its use.[83] The linkage which often caused chemical and biological weapons to be placed under a single heading, "biochemical weapons," was emphasized as militating against separation[84] and reference was made, to support the continued association of the two for regulatory purposes, to a quotation from the French jurist Meyrowitz:

In international law, as well as in the law of war and in the field of disarmament, biological weapons are closely linked to chemical weapons. The same applies in military theory and practice. This is also true of public opinion, in which chemical and biological weapons are united in one and the same image. This link is not based only on general usage or on an automatic association of ideas. It is founded on strong factual reasons deriving from both the technical and military characteristics and the effects of these weapons. It is usual in military literature and practice to include in the definition of biological weapons hormones or other chemical substances employed against vegetation. Toxins secreted by bacteria can be manufactured industrially; their composition can be modified and their pathogenic power increased by genetic and chemical processes. Military circles foresee the combined use of aggressive chemical and biological agents.[85]

Fear was also expressed that separation would adversely affect the Geneva Protocol. By failure to condemn both methods in one international convention, positions of states and their attitudes would be changed. Some states, for example, could be bound to the biological convention only, some to neither the Geneva Protocol nor the biological convention, and some to the Geneva Protocol only.[86]

The Swedish delegate was firm in the belief that chemical and biological weapons could not be separated as to their use and that both should be condemned—indeed, the Geneva Protocol was said already to condemn both. Nevertheless, it was thought that a separate treaty prohibiting production, possession, and acquisition was feasible and that such a prohibition could be applied to biological weapons first, one reason for the priority being that there was no need to produce biological weapons for domestic use.[87]

On August 26, 1969, the British representative offered certain amendments to the United Kingdom draft convention. The prohibition only of biological methods of warfare remained as before.[88] A clause was added to Article I to make clear that there was no derogation from the Geneva Protocol and that its existing commitments as to state parties remained unaffected. Thus Article I, in setting forth the undertaking to refrain from engaging in biological warfare, would have the addition, ". . . insofar [as a party] may not already be committed in that respect under Treaties or other instruments in force prohibiting the use of chemical and biological methods of warfare. . . ." This would permit parties to the biological convention to have a uniform obligation as to nonuse of biological weapons—a new commitment for some and a preexisting one for others. This was the most important amendment; others merely set forth minor clarifications.

The consensus of the representatives at the disarmament committee conference seemed opposed to the British draft in its exclusion of chemical weapons. Other proposals were also placed before the committee,[89] an important one being a working paper introduced by twelve nations.[90] This was a proposal to be adopted by the General Assembly whereby that body would, among other things, recognize that a customary rule of international law had come into existence prohibiting the use of *all* biological and chemical methods of warfare and would condemn as contrary to international law the use in international conflicts of

any chemical agents of warfare: chemical substances, whether gaseous, liquid, or solid, which might be employed because of their direct toxic effects on man, animals or plants, and
any biological agents of warfare: living organisms, whatever their nature, or infective material derived from them, which are intended to cause disease or death in man, animals or plants, and which depend for their effects on their ability to multiply in the person, animal or plant attacked.

This latter definition of chemical and biological agents of warfare was that contained in the secretary general's report.[91]

Outer Space Treaty

Although negotiations leading to a universal multilateral treaty aiming at the control of chemical and biological weapons on earth has made little headway since World War II, the prospects of the control of such weapons in outer space may be slightly better. Late in 1963, the Soviet Union and the United States reached a gentlemen's agreement not to orbit nuclear weapons or weapons of mass destruction in space.[92] This agreement was made mainly with an eye to restraining nuclear weapons, but it would also cover chemical and biological weapons which fall within the definition of "weapons of mass destruction." Eventually negotiations between the two nuclear powers brought about a draft treaty which stipulated that the parties to the treaty agreed "not to place in orbit around the earth any objects carrying nuclear weapons or any other kinds of weapons of mass destruction, install such weapons or any other kinds of weapons of mass destruction, on celestial bodies, or station such weapons in outer space in any other manner."[93] This draft treaty was placed before the First Committee of the United Nations General Assembly for approval, with little opportunity granted to other nations for debate. It was endorsed by acclamation on December 19, 1966, and eventually was ratified by the Soviet Union, the United States, and eleven other nations, going into effect on October 10, 1967.[94]

Even though the main purpose of the treaty was to keep outer space free from nuclear weapons, apparently the negotiators were farsighted enough to see that the day might come when it would be possible or feasible to place other critical weapons, such as certain chemical and biological weapons, in outer space. Hence they attempted to make the wording of the treaty broad enough to cover such future contingencies by including "weapons of mass destruction." This gives rise to the question of which chemical or biological weapons would fall within the international legal classification of weapons of mass destruction.

In treaty interpretation, it is permissible to look to antecedent acts to determine the meaning of an obscure phrase.[95] In international intercourse, the first use of the words "mass destruction" appeared in the Truman-Attlee-King statement of November, 1945, which recommended that the United Nations prepare regulations for the control of atomic energy as well as for other "major weapons adaptable to mass destruction."[96] In subsequent disarmament negotiations, the term was eventually shortened to "weapons of mass destruction." But no universal agreement was ever reached on what was included in the phrase.

It can be argued that if the treaty had intended to speak of widespread, extensive damage to people, crops, animals, and property, the adjective *massive* would have been employed, making the phrase "weapons of massive destruction." Hence *mass*, being a noun, can relate only to its dictionary sense, namely a large body of persons, for only in that manner would the sentence be grammatically correct. *Destruction*, when used with reference to a mass of people, is defined as the slaying of them.[97] If this is what is meant by "weapons of mass destruction," there would be *excluded* from the prohibition of the outer space treaty those chemical and biological weapons which mainly destroy vegetation, materiel, or property, i.e., certain incendiary weapons, smoke weapons, chemical herbicides and soil sterilants, antianimal biological weapons, antiplant biological weapons, and antimateriel chemical and biological weapons. Also excluded would be those weapons which are not intended to be lethal to large groups of people, such as incapacitating chemical agents, riot control agents, and biological agents with low mortality rates.

It might be argued that the phrase "weapons of mass destruction" applies only to chemical and biological weapons which destroy property.

Since indiscriminate slaying of the civilian population is, supposedly, contrary to the customary laws of war, and since the purpose of all war is to destroy the enemy's troops, a weapon which slays a large number of men in the field would not be considered a weapon of mass destruction; hence it refers only to the destruction of property and should be interpreted as "massive" destruction.[98] Under this line of reasoning, few chemical or biological weapons would be banned by the outer space treaty, because on the whole they do not destroy property. Consequently one would reach almost the opposite conclusion from the above; i.e., only certain incendiary weapons, antimateriel weapons, and some antiplant and antianimal agents would probably fall within the ban.

Finally it can be argued that as the phrase is ambiguous, it can be translated into a commonly accepted meaning—namely, that there are various categories of weapons of mass destruction; some indiscriminately destroy people, others indiscriminately destroy property, and others indiscriminately destroy both. This apparently was the position taken by the Commission for Conventional Armaments when it defined weapons of mass destruction as atomic explosive weapons (which would be both antimateriel and antipersonnel), radioactive materiel weapons (which would also be both antimateriel and antipersonnel), and *lethal* chemical and biological weapons (which would be antipersonnel only). But until an authoritative definition has been agreed upon, no one can definitely stipulate which weapons do fall within the classification of weapons of mass destruction.

Less than a month after the treaty became operative, the United States secretary of defense acknowledged that the Soviet Union was developing a fractional orbital bombardment system (FOBS) which would be operational in 1968. This system could place a vehicle in orbit around the earth, in either direction, about one hundred miles high. Upon signal there could be launched from it a missile with a nuclear warhead or a warhead "of mass destruction."[99] It was alleged that this would not be a breach of the treaty, for the wording of the treaty prohibits only the *stationing* of such weapons on celestial bodies or in outer space, or the *orbiting around the earth* of such weapons. As the FOBS system is not stationary, it would not fall within the first prohibition, and according to the secretary of defense, as it is merely a fractional and not a full orbit, it would not fall within the second prohibition.[100]

The secretary of defense was apparently implying that when, in treaty interpretation, it appears that words are employed in a technical sense, their ordinary meaning will give way to their technical meaning.[101] Still there could be a question of whether or not the phrase "in orbit around the earth" was being used in a completely scientific and technical manner. It could plausibly be alleged that it should be construed according to its general and naturally accepted signification, and as the treaty does not speak of a complete orbit, but rather of *placing* into orbit any object carrying nuclear warheads or weapons of mass destruction, it would be violative of the meaning of the treaty to place such weapons into fractional orbit. This position would be strengthened by the fact that in treaty interpretation one must bear in mind what may be called the overall aim and purpose of the treaty, which in this instance was the peaceful use of outer space.[102]

It might be argued alternatively that the treaty reflects the intention of the parties. Although apparently no mention of FOBS was made during negotiations between the Soviet Union and the United States, both nations were probably aware of this potentiality and failed to guard against it.[103] Consequently the old maxim *expressio unius est exclusio alterius* comes into play.[104] By express reference to orbit around the earth, partial orbits were excluded. This argument is pertinent as between the two major parties—Russia and the United States—but other nations enter into the picture, for they have signed and ratified the treaty. If these nations were unaware of FOBS, then they were not deliberately excluding the partial orbit from the treaty. As it is accepted that an *ambiguous phrase* must be construed against the party or parties which drafted or proposed the provision and in favor of the other parties, here the joint United States-Russian draft would be construed in favor of the other ratifying states, i.e., to the effect that there was no intent to exclude the fraction when mentioning the whole.[105]

And finally, argument might be advanced that all ratifying nations understood that this article was placed in the treaty only to guard against weapons in outer space which would be used at some indefinite time in the future, i.e., those having the capability of posing a *continuing threat* of bombardment from space against nations on earth. The FOBS system, once launched, has a defined time of arrival at a target, and consequently would not pose such an indefinite threat from outer space.

All this adds up to the fact that even the most recent treaty which might be interpreted as placing some conventional international legal limitations on possible future resort to chemical and biological weapons is far from perfect. It not only fails to define the phrase "weapons of mass destruction," but also fails to indicate whether it does or does not cover fractional orbit of such weapons. The only certainty, apparently, as far as chemical and biological weapons are concerned is that the treaty does prohibit objects carrying weapons of mass destruction (if ever agreement is reached on the meaning of this phrase) from being placed in complete orbit around the earth or from being stationed in outer space or on celestial bodies.

POSTWAR EUROPEAN TREATIES

Prior to the end of World War II, Russia, France, England, and the

United States agreed to impose rigid controls on Germany's industries to eliminate her war potential. Consequently, immediately at the end of the war plants engaged in production of chemical or biological materials for war purposes were destroyed or dismantled.[106] Shortly thereafter, political differences developed between Russia and the other Allied Nations, and the status of Germany remained in limbo for some time. In April, 1949, France, the United States, and the United Kingdom promulgated a tripartite agreement relating to prohibited and limited industries in the western zones of Germany. The prohibitions were to remain in force until a peace settlement or until January 1, 1953, whichever was the earlier.[107]

Among the war materials whose production was prohibited by this agreement were weapons capable of projecting lethal or destructive liquids, gases, or toxic substances, as well as the substances themselves such as poison war gases (including liquids and solids customarily included in this term). Nevertheless, the ban was far from absolute, for it was recognized that some war chemicals were required by Germany's peacetime economy. Therefore, manufacture of essential peacetime requirements was permitted of chlorine, phosgene, hydrocyanic acid, chlorinated ketones, cyanogen halides, lachrymatory halogen derivatives of hydrocarbons, halagenated carboxylic acids and their esters, white phosphorus, incendiary compositions such as thermites, and smoke-producing substances, such as titanium tetrachloride and silicone tetrachloride.[108] The treaty also prohibited "highly toxic products" from bacteriological or plant sources, but again an exception was made of those bacteriological and plant products which are used for therapeutic purposes.[109]

Although there was no formal peace treaty between the Allied Powers on the one side and Germany on the other, such treaties were signed by the Allied Nations on February 10, 1947, with Italy, Bulgaria, Finland, Hungary, and Rumania.[110] All contained similar stipulations relating to chemical and biological weapons: the defeated nation agreed not to manufacture or possess, either publicly or privately, certain types of war materials including asphyxiating, lethal, toxic, or incapacitating substances intended for war purposes or manufactured in excess of civilian requirements; propellants, explosives, pyrotechnics, or liquefied gases destined for the propulsion, exploding, charging, or filling of, or for use in connection with war materials in the above categories, not capable of civilian use or manufactured in excess of civilian requirements; and factories and tool equipment especially designed for the production and maintenance of the material enumerated and not technically convertible to civilian use.[111]

These treaties were worded with much more care than those following World War I, and no claim has thus far been lodged that any nation has breached these particular provisions, although Bulgaria, Hungary, and Rumania have breached other provisions of the treaties—a fact which might give rise to a question of whether such breaches, although strongly protested, have not been sanctioned and as a result may in effect abrogate the treaties.[112]

When Austria regained its independence in 1955, a peace treaty, signed and ratified by the Soviet Union, France, the United Kingdom, and the United States, stipulated that Austria was not to "possess, construct or experiment" with "asphyxiating, vesicant or poisonous materials or biological substances in quantities greater than or of types other than, are required for legitimate civil purposes, or any apparatus designed to produce, project, or spread such materials or substances for war purposes."[113] Thus, the Austrian treaty specifically mentioned "biological substances," which were not so spelled out in the other peace treaties.

By September, 1950, the foreign ministers of the United Kingdom, the United States, and France issued a statement declaring their wish to include a democratic Germany on a basis of equality in a continental European community as a major step toward European unity.[114] Included in this concept was a treaty arrangement which would establish a European Defense Community with a commissariat in charge of the production, importation, and exportation of all war materials including atomic, biological, and chemical weapons. The draft treaty specifically provided that the commissariat could not grant licenses for such weapons without unanimous approval of the European Defense Community Council. The treaty was ratified by Belgium, the Federal Republic of Germany, Luxembourg, and the Netherlands. Although France and Italy signed the treaty, they did not ratify it; consequently it never entered into force, and therefore it was necessary to seek a new way of achieving an organization for European defense.[115]

In 1948, when many Europeans still feared the possibility of German aggression, a collective defense treaty had been signed in Brussels and had been ratified by France, the United Kingdom, Belgium, Luxembourg, and the Netherlands. With the downfall of the European defense community, it was suggested that the Brussels treaty be revised to include Italy and Germany among the members of the organization.[116] In order to make German rearmament acceptable to France, various commitments were to be made, including a German agreement not to manufacture on German territory atomic, chemical, or biological weapons. In return for this promise the other signatories would not give up the right to produce such weapons, but rather agreed:

When the development of atomic, biological and chemical weapons in the territory on the mainland of Europe of the High Contracting Parties who have not given up the right to produce them has passed the experimental stage and effective production of them has started there, the level of stocks that the High Contracting Parties concerned will be allowed to hold on the mainland of Europe shall be decided by a majority vote of the Council of Western European Union.[117]

Furthermore it was accepted that the supervision of the nonproduction of such weapons by Germany and the supervision of the "effective production" by the other parties were to be controlled by an Agency for the Control of Armaments. Thus came about the Paris Protocols of October, 1954, which amended the earlier Brussels Treaty and established an administrative organ, the Council of Western European Union, made up of ministers appointed by each government, and a parliamentary organ, the Assembly of Western European Union, made up of parliamentarians elected by the parliaments of member countries.[118] These agreements were ratified on May 6, 1955, and the Western European Union came into existence. Protocol IV established the Agency of Western European Union for the Control of Armaments, giving it a twofold task:

1) to check that the level of armaments subject to control in each of the member countries did not exceed the appropriate levels laid down in accordance with the provisions of the treaty (quantitative control);

2) to satisfy itself that the undertakings given by Germany not to manufacture certain types of weapons including CB weapons were being observed (non-productive control).[119]

The protocol further stipulated that the inspection and control functions of the agency were to be conducted in a spirit of harmony and cooperation under the regulations providing for the due process of law in respect to private interests.[120] The agency was directly responsible to the Council of the Western European Union, which in turn was required to present to the Western European Union Assembly an annual report on the agency's activities in the matter of supervision of armaments.

The agreements modifying the Brussels Treaty defined both chemical and biological weapons, but these definitions were not all-exclusive for it was agreed that they were to be "more closely defined and the definitions brought up to date by the Council of Western European Union."[121] But for initial purposes, as to chemical weapons it was stated:

a) A chemical weapon is defined as any equipment or apparatus expressly designed to use, for military purposes, the asphyxiating, toxic, irritant, paralysant, growth regulating, and anti-lubricating or catalysing properties of any chemical substance.

b) Subject to the provisions of paragraph c), chemical substances having such properties and capable of being used in the equipment or apparatus referred to in paragraph a), shall be deemed to be included in this definition.

c) Such apparatus and such quantities of the chemical substances as are referred to in paragraphs a) and b) which do not exceed peaceful civilian requirements shall be deemed to be excluded from this definition.[122]

As to the definition of biological weapons, the agreements declared:

a) A biological weapon is defined as any equipment or apparatus expressly designed to use, for military purposes, harmful insects or other living or dead organisms or their toxic products.

b) Subject to the provisions of paragraph c), insects, organisms and their toxic products of such nature and in such amounts as to make them capable of being used in the equipment or apparatus referred to in a) shall be deemed to be included in this definition.

c) Such equipment or apparatus and such quantities of the insects, organisms and their toxic products as are referred to in paragraphs a) and b) which do not exceed peaceful civilian requirements shall be deemed to be excluded from the definition of biological weapons.[123]

Although the definition of chemical weapons was far more extensive than any previously set out in proposed or existing international conventions, it was not broad enough to cover agents such as incendiaries or smokes. In addition to lethal or severely injurious agents, it also included irritant or paralyzing agents, which could cover such nonlethal agents as tear or incapacitating weapons. Furthermore, it should be noted that certain antimateriel weapons were included, i.e., antilubricants and catalytic agents designed for military purposes.

Biological weapons were also very broadly defined to include not only weapons delivery systems but all insects, living or dead organisms, or their toxic products designed for military purposes. No limitation on degree or nature of injury was stipulated. Even mildly incapacitating biological agents would fall within the definition.

The Control Agency was initiated on June 21, 1955, with a staff recruited in equitable proportions from nationals of the seven member countries.[124] It ran into immediate difficulties in that without permission from each government, as well as each private industry, surprise on-the-spot inspections could not be made. After two years of negotiating, a treaty, called "the due process treaty," was signed, setting forth the necessary legislative measures each country was to pass to grant permission for unannounced agency investigations of private as well as public enterprises engaged or suspected of engaging in manufacture of biological or chemical weapons. Private interests were to be safeguarded by the establishment of an impartial tribunal with power to determine claims for compensation against the Western European Union submitted by physical or juridical persons whose private interests might have been damaged by excess or abuse of authority on the part of the agency or its officials. Since France never ratified this treaty, it never went into effect; consequently, the agency was always required to obtain prior consent of authorities concerned before making its visits of inspection in the armaments factories, and this has been a factor severely limiting the agency's effectiveness. The agency has therefore limited its control to the scrutiny of statistical and budgetary information (control from documentary sources) supplied by member states in answer to a questionnaire annually circulated by the agency, and by certain inspections carried out when and where agreement can be reached with the governmental authorities and the factory managements concerned.[125]

Furthermore, it was not until April, 1959, that any agreement was reached on which chemical or biological products were to be controlled, either under "nonproduction" by Germany or in a "controllable stage," in the other countries which had not given up the right to produce chemical weapons but had only agreed to certain controls when "effective production" of those weapons had begun.[126] A working party of legal and chemical experts appointed by the governments of the member countries drew up the following list of chemical products which were to be subject to Agency control:

GROUP I—Chemical Products which CANNOT be used for civilian purposes

1. Alkyl alkylphosphonofluoridates   (certain of the chemi-
2. Alkyl N-dialkyl phosphoramidocyanidates cal components of nerve
                                            agents)
3. Mustard Gas
4. Nitrogen mustard
5. Lewisites[127]

In 1965, three more classifications were added to this group:

6. Tabun
7. Sarin
8. Formulas of the Amiton Families.[128]

GROUP II—Chemical Products which CAN be used for civilian purposes:

1. Hydrocyanic acid (blood agent AC)
2. Cyanogen chloride (blood agent CK)
3. Parachlorophenyldimethylurea (herbicide—Monuron)
4. Malleic hydrazide (plant growth regulator)[129]

In spite of the broad definition given in the treaty, the experts refused to include such agents as tear agents and incapacitating agents. Furthermore, they could come to no agreement on a definition of "controllable stage" or "effective production" under the agency's quantitative control function; or on the possibility of the Agency taking samples in either quantitative or nonproductive control; or on the adoption of a directive to enable the agency to carry out nonproductive control exercises for chemical weapons pending the entry into force of the treaty provisions for due process of law.[130]

The list of biological agents to be controlled by the agency was drawn up by a group of military and biological experts. They agreed that there were no biological products which could be used exclusively as weapons and not for civilian purposes, and hence decided that *approximate quantities* of production should be established, after which the products should then become subject to agency control as biological weapons, for the notion of quantity was an essential factor in defining biological weapons.[131] The experts assigned quantity quotas for each state, which were to be the basis of control by the agency "unless greater civilian requirements were duly reported by member states."[132] The biological products to be controlled consisted of the following:

1. Botulic toxins
2. Malleomyces mallei (glanders)
3. Malleomyces whitmori (melioidosis)
4. Bacillus anthracis (anthrax)
5. Brucella
6. Pasteurella tularensis (tularemia)
7. Rickettsia burneti (Q fever)
8. Pasteurella pestis
9. Pestis bovina (cattle plague or rinderpest)[133]

Certain others were discussed but were not included for technical reasons, such as their uncontrollability against the user's own forces.

Inasmuch as the aforementioned due process of law treaty never entered into force, the agency was limited in its effectiveness, and the annual reports of the Council to the Assembly were subject to a great deal of criticism. The Assembly pointed out that without the right of surprise inspections, some of the fundamental provisions of the treaty remained unapplied, thereby endangering the validity of the whole treaty.[134]

There were criticisms of the treaty. It was said, for example, in a debate in the British parliament, that although Germany had renounced the right to manufacture chemical and biological *weapons*, it had not renounced the right to manufacture such chemicals and biologicals as might be needed for civilian purposes. German factories or establishments manufacturing biological and chemical products for civilian use would therefore be exempt from surprise inspection if the due process treaty ever came into force.[135] It was also pointed out that although Germany had agreed not to manufacture *in its territory* chemical or biological weapons, there was nothing in the terms of the protocols to prevent Germany from engaging in the joint production on Spanish territory, for example, of such weapons, nor was there any inclusion of a ban against

Germany's importing them, or even purchasing them directly from abroad.[136]

The French pointed out that the protocols applied only to continental Europe, excluding the United Kingdom. France refused to ratify the due process of law treaty by stating that unless Britain submitted to control, France would not do so. France's reluctance, of course, can be traced to that nation's determination to become a nuclear power. In mid-1963 France's manufacture of nuclear bombs passed the experimental stage and entered into "effective production," which automatically should have brought about application of Article III of Protocol III, for this covered not only chemical and biological agents but also nuclear weapons. This article stipulated that the level of stocks of such weapons was then to be decided by a majority (not a unanimous) vote of the Council of the Western European Union.[137] This was never done in the case of France's atomic weapons, because of French opposition and refusal to cooperate.

The best that can be said about the Western European Union's attempt to control chemical and biological weapons is that even among friendly allied nations, because of the policy of certain member states, it was found to be impossible to apply the provisions of the treaty in full. One authority has written:

The experience of the Armaments Control Agency has been largely disappointing and the lessons to be drawn from it are largely negative. It has dedicated, efficient servants, and they have acquired a great deal of valuable experience in cross-checking budgetary and other data. But political considerations have prevented them from widening their experiences. Little has been learned, for example, about techniques of physical inspection and control that would be useful in training those who will one day have to police a general and comprehensive disarmament agreement.[138]

THE WORK OF THE INTERNATIONAL RED CROSS

The International Red Cross possesses a large measure of international personality and the capacity to operate on an international plane.[139] It has been the primary mover toward the making of new international treaty law dealing with what are called the "Geneva" laws of war—the humanitarian laws of war—as distinguished from the "Hague" laws of war, which deal with norms concerning the actual conduct of the war. In 1949, after the International Red Cross had prepared four new draft treaties, the Swiss government convoked the Geneva Diplomatic Conference to discuss them.[140] This conference adopted the Red Cross drafts as new multilateral treaties dealing with the protection of "war victims," that is, with the protection of persons outside of the fighting formations (civilians), or with persons of the armed forces who are at the time or permanently not able to fight. These treaties have been ratified by over 109 nations.[141] Nonetheless, it was felt by some that the four Geneva

Conventions of 1949 were not complete because they failed to revise rules of warfare completely in an age of total war, and because they did not forbid the use of certain weapons.[142] The International Red Cross was therefore requested in 1954

to make a thorough examination and propose at the next International Conference of the Red Cross the necessary additions to the Conventions in force in order to protect civilian populations from the dangers of atomic, chemical and bacteriological warfare.[143]

Under the auspices of the Red Cross, a fifteen-man commission of experts met in Geneva in 1954. In a declaration of principles it was pointed out that all of the Geneva Conventions on the humanitarian laws of war might remain inoperative if the belligerents were not limited in any way in their choice of methods and weapons of war. Consequently, the work done by the commission of experts went beyond the Geneva Conventions into the Hague laws of war.[144]

The experts confirmed that certain basic principles of the laws of war were still in force, such as that relating to military necessity, which must in certain cases give way to laws of humanity. They also agreed that the draft rules which they drew up would be more effective if all states would agree in advance to renounce the use of weapons of mass destruction against enemy troops.[145] The draft rules stated that acts of violence were to be justified only if their object was the destruction or placing out of action of enemy forces; acts directed against a civilian population were prohibited. Furthermore, certain weapons, even though employed only against enemy armed forces, were prohibited under all circumstances, namely weapons of unpredictable or uncontrollable effects such as asphyxiating, poisonous, or other gases, and the use of bacteriological agents.[146]

This draft of rules was submitted to all governments for approval prior to a planned Swiss convocation of another international conference to convert them into treaty law. But instead of accepting them as they had the draft Geneva Conventions of 1949, many governments protested that the new draft rules went beyond the proper sphere of action of the International Red Cross, which was conceived of as relating only to civilians and noncombatants.[147] Thereupon the Red Cross invited another group of experts to meet in Geneva in 1956. This group drew up another draft, trying to restrict it to the "Geneva" laws of war; consequently this draft differed in some aspects from the draft rules of 1955. Article 14 of the new draft stated:

Without prejudice to the present or future prohibition of certain specific weapons, the use is prohibited of weapons whose harmful effects—resulting in particular from the dissemination of incendiary, chemical, bacteriological, radioactive or other agents—

could spread to an unforeseen degree or escape, either in space or in time, from the control of those who employ them, thus endangering the civilian population. This prohibition also applies to delayed-action weapons, the dangerous effects of which are liable to be felt by the civilian population.[148]

This draft was placed on the agenda of the Nineteenth International Conference of the Red Cross, which took place at New Delhi in 1957.

There were strong differences of opinion on the whole draft, but particularly with respect to Article 14, some claiming it was a disguised attempt to erase the dividing line between "Geneva" and "Hague" laws of war, others demanding a return to the 1955 draft rule absolutely prohibiting the use of certain weapons under all circumstances, while still others demanded the right to use such weapons under certain circumstances, such as in case of self-defense.[149] At the plenary session of the conference, a resolution was adopted stating that the underlying principles of the draft were in conformity with Red Cross ideals and their requirements of humanity, but rather than approving them, it was requested that the Red Cross transmit them to the governments for consideration.[150] The Red Cross sent the texts to all governments, requesting comments; "their replies took the form of a crushing silence, with the exception of a few well-disposed countries. The great powers, in particular, remained silent. . . ."[151]

In 1965, at the Twentieth International Conference of the Red Cross, there was no mention made of the draft code of 1956, but a resolution was adopted which declared

that all Governments and other authorities responsible for action in armed conflicts should conform at least to the following principles:

1) that the right of the parties to a conflict to adopt means of injuring the enemy is not unlimited;

2) that it is prohibited to launch attacks against the civilian populations as such;

3) that distinction must be made at all times between persons taking part in the hostilities and members of the civilian population to the effect that the latter be spared as much as possible;

4) that the general principles of the Law of War apply to nuclear and similar weapons; expressly invites all Governments who have not yet done so to accede to the Geneva Protocol of 1925. . . .[152]

The director of the International Committee of the Red Cross has declared that these four principles constitute "the only pronouncement of the kind made by an assembly in which governments are represented since World War II." They are, according to him, the general principles of customary international law which indicate that indiscriminate use of new weapons is not lawful:

The new weapons may be employed only under the conditions established by the general principles of law. The principles in question are . . . no attacks on civilian populations as such; a distinction to be made between combatants and non-combatants; and avoidance of disproportionate suffering.[153]

The fact that the 1965 Red Cross Conference felt it necessary to extend yet another invitation to nations to accede to the Geneva Protocol might add further weight to the presumption that the Geneva Protocol is not a codification of customary international law, nor has it become customary law because of long acceptance by the majority of the nations of the world. It could be reasonably argued in the alternative that the Red Cross merely sought to distill a customary rule into a conventional rule for the sake of greater exactitude and unquestionable clarity.

In spite of the prolonged and creative post-World War II attempt by the International Red Cross to establish a new regimen of conventional international law prohibiting resort to certain weapons, including many of the chemical and biological weapons, and in spite of the somewhat optimistic words of the director of the International Red Cross, in effect, the efforts of the Red Cross seem to have resulted merely in a reaffirmation of the Hague Rules of 1907, which are still the only *universal conventional* international law norms which specifically prohibit certain classes of weapons.

Conclusion

In spite of the torrents of words which have poured forth since World War II on the necessity of prohibiting the use of certain weapons of warfare, only a few faltering steps have been taken to establish new conventional international legal controls. Much of the postwar debates circled not around the need to add weapons prohibitions to the laws of war, but rather around limitation of weapons to achieve disarmament. These are two distinct areas of international law. The first relates to the need to prevent the *use* of chemical or biological weapons, while the second deals with the need to limit the *freedom to produce or possess* such weapons. Even in the disarmament negotiations, stress was laid on nuclear weapons, and the latent danger of chemicals and biological warfare was generally relegated to a subsumption under the phrase "weapons of mass destruction," which phrase was never *officially* clarified. One of the few conventional limitations agreed upon since World War II dealt with the peaceful exploration of outer space and prohibited the orbiting around the earth or the stationing in space or on celestial bodies of "weapons of mass destruction," which can be interpreted to include certain chemical and biological weapons.

The postwar peace settlements did give birth to certain multilateral treaties forbidding the national possession or manufacture of specific chemical and biological weapons by the defeated nations. Although no supervision or verification arrangements were made to assure that the nations were fulfilling their agreements, no charges have been leveled that they were not. So there is a presumption that, at least to this extent, there has been some control over chemical and biological weapons. And the Western European Union attempted through a series of protocols and treaties to establish a control system to ascertain that Germany did not engage in the manufacture of chemical and biological agents for purposes of war, together with a system of regulation of other member states, whenever they engaged in the "effective production" of chemical and biological agents for warfare. But because of the uncooperative attitude of France, the system was never fully implemented as originally envisioned.

Consequently the most optimistic conclusion that can be reached is that in the past twenty-five years only minimal and irresolute actions have been taken toward bringing into being effective international multilateral conventional limitations on resort to or production and possession of chemical and biological weapons. The results of the present efforts of the Committee on Disarmament and of the United Nations remain to be seen.

PART TWO

CB WEAPONS AND
OTHER SOURCES OF INTERNATIONAL LAW

CHAPTER SIX

CUSTOMARY LAW OF WAR

CUSTOMARY INTERNATIONAL LAW

ALONG WITH TREATIES, custom, i.e., those established usages or practices of states which have come to be regarded as obligatory, is a source of international law.[1] Indeed, until recent times custom was the principal law-creating instrument of the primitive international society, and a great portion of the detailed rules of international law in general, which would include the international rules of war, were developed from it.[2] In any study of possible international legal limitations on the use of certain weapons in time of war, such as chemical or biological agents, the customary law becomes of much import, for general customary rules, if they are inhibitory, traditionally have been thought of as binding all of the states of the international society.[3] In this respect they differ from treaty or conventional rules, which normally bind only the contracting parties.

International custom as a procedure for creating new international norms must meet two conditions: (1) usage or practice among states coupled with (2) the conviction that the practice is applied because it is legally binding.[4]

The usage that is required is a recurrence or repetition of conduct—actions or abstentions—within the realm of international relations, in time of peace or in time of war, which can give rise to a customary rule. Such conduct must be regular and repeated. Subsequential departures from the practice may well demonstrate the fact that the alleged customary rule is not in existence. In the words of the International Court of Justice, the usage or practice by the states in question must be "constant and uniform."[5] No specific duration is required; the practice does not necessarily have to be an ancient one, although passage of time may be evidence of its uninterrupted continuity.[6]

According to existing theory, the consent of states is the ultimate source of international law, such consent being express or tacit or implied.[7] Since customary law is, according to theory, tacit consent, it might be thought that it would be necessary to establish a customary rule to show that all states have consented to all norms of general customary law by their actual conduct. This is not the case. As Brierly points out, "[i]t would hardly ever be practicable, and all but the strictest of positivists admit that it is not necessary, to show that every state has recognized a certain practice. . . ."[8] The usage requisite for the formation of custom need not be universal, but it should be general. In the words of Article 38 of the

Statute of the International Court of Justice, it must be "general practice accepted as law." Thus a general rule which has been created by general practice is applicable to states which may never have had opportunity to share in the practice which established the custom. New states and pre-existing states which, previous to the coming into being of the norm, had no opportunity to apply it are still considered bound. Moreover, with respect to the actual creation of the norm in the first place, all states do not necessarily have to participate in the practice. A new norm can hardly come into being if resisted by a great power. Conversely, the great powers cannot create a rule if resisted by other powers. Still, the practice of a great number of states, including those which for various reasons are considered influential, may create the new rule. Kunz declares: "The practice must be 'general,' not universal; but a mere majority of states is not enough. The practice must have been applied by the overwhelming majority of states which hitherto had an opportunity of applying it."[9]

The second element of customary law is psychological in nature, the *opinio juris sive necessitatis*. The usage or practice constituting the first element must have been carried on in accord with a conviction that the practice is legally binding, not merely morally binding or followed because of expediency. As Brierly describes the requisite conviction or feeling, "There must be present a feeling that, if the usage is departed from some form of sanction will probably, or at any rate ought to fall on the transgressors."[10]

The *opinio juris* would seem to be most important to the creation of customary norms restricting certain means of warfare like chemical biological methods, for a practice of states which would be evidence of a prohibition of such a means would arise from the abstention of states from its use—a negative approach. The International Court of Justice has preferred positive actions or practices to demonstrate custom. In the *Lotus* case the court stated:

Even if the rarity of the judicial decisions to be found among the reported cases were sufficient to prove in point of fact the circumstances alleged . . . it would merely show that states had often, in practice, abstained from instituting criminal proceedings, and not that they recognized themselves as being obliged to do so; for *only if such abstention were based on their being conscious of having a duty to abstain would it be possible to speak of an international custom.* [Italics supplied][11]

Finally, the *opinio juris* becomes of import in the face of repeated violations of a norm. Such violations may occur without effectuating a change, if the conviction remains that the norm is the compulsory and accepted rule. On the other hand, the violations may have occurred with the conviction that a new norm is being created. It can happen that a prohibitory norm as to certain forms or methods of warfare may have come into existence. Persistent violations may occur without changing the rule, but if the *opinio juris* is present for the creation of a new norm, it may be difficult to maintain the continued unimpaired status of the old.[12]

To ascertain whether the two conditions for the law-creating customary process are met is not easy. Disagreement can well prevail as to the constancy and uniformity of the usage. The duration requisite is unsettled. The test of general practice or recognition is a vague one. How general must the practice be? How much and what kind of participation is necessary? The *opinio juris* is also a troublesome matter for determination. Is the conduct pursued because of mere political or moral expediency, or because it is believed to be legally obligatory?

Despite the uncertainty of the customary process, if a norm of customary law is to be relied upon and its validity is in issue, it must be proved. This becomes a matter of evidence. Of prime importance are the acts or practices of states. Thus, in order to determine the existence of a customary rule or rules applicable to chemical or biological agents as instruments of war, an examination into the actual practice of states must be made. A constant and uniform use of such weapons by a large majority of states in war would indicate a customary rule recognizing the legality of the use of such instruments. Large-scale state abstention might well indicate that such weapons had been banned, particularly if it can be demonstrated that the abstention springs from a sense of legal duty.

THE PRACTICE OF STATES

CHEMICAL AGENTS

Early Uses

History has long recorded resort to chemical agents in war, but their early use produced few important results and made little lasting impression in the field of weaponry.[13] With the development of the chemical industry and chemical substances in modern times, chemicals as agents of warfare have become a reality and instances of their use in conflict— in varying types and degrees and at various times—are now to be noted as among the practices of states.

World War I

The first widespread use of chemical weapons occurred during World War I.[14] The initiation appears to be attributable to the Germans, who, in October, 1914, used a chemical-type projectile which was a shrapnel modified by substituting for the matrix which bound the shrapnel balls sulfuric dianisidin which, upon explosion of the base charge, was diffused as a fine dust. Since the potency of this instrument as a tear agent was of low value, it was not used again. A tear gas shell or projectile for field howitzers was then developed. This projectile contained a chemical filler composed of a mixture of xylyl bromide and xylylene bromide. This weapon was first used against Russians in January, 1915, and later in March, 1915, on the Western Front. At about the same time, March, 1915, the French used against the Germans tear grenades filled with ethyl bromacetate and later chloracetone.[15]

Despite these uses of gas in the early days of World War I, the beginning of chemical warfare is usually thought to have occurred on April 22, 1915, at the second battle of Ypres, when the Germans used approximately 6,000 cylinders to release chlorine which was wafted over Allied lines by the wind. The attack, coming as a surprise to the unprepared Allied forces, was most successful, taking a high casualty toll and creating a great gap in the Allied line. The Germans failed to follow up the advantage thus created, for they had not foreseen the effective results to be gained from the use of gas in this instance.[16] The Germans thereafter made follow-up attacks, and by September, 1915, the British retaliated with a gas attack around Loos. Thereafter gas became a method of attack employed by both belligerents during the remainder of the war, close to 100 principal attacks occurring in total, causing over 1,000,000 injuries and 91,198 deaths. Gases other than chlorine were soon developed, the most important being phosgene and mustard gases.[17]

The first uses of gas in World War I did not technically violate the literal language of the Hague Gas Declaration of 1899 by which the parties agreed "to abstain from the use of projectiles the sole object of which is the diffusion of asphyxiating or deleterious gases."[18] The German gas projectile first employed in October, 1914, was not a projectile having as its *sole* object the diffusion of such gases, for it also projected shrapnel against the enemy. Moreover, it did not diffuse a gas but a solid in the form of a fine dust. The tear gas projectiles later resorted to by the Germans and by the French have been called projectiles having as sole object the diffusion of gas and hence in violation of the Declaration,[19] although the French at this time sought to except from the meaning of "asphyxiating and deleterious gases" the relatively harmless tear gases.[20] As has been noted previously, controversy has existed on this point, for later, in 1931, before the Preparatory Commission of the Disarmament Conference the French delegation expressed the view that it considered tear agents banned by the Geneva Protocol, which prohibits all gases.[21] But following World War II, in 1966, before the First Committee of the General Assembly, a French representative adopted a narrower position and concluded that the text of the Geneva Protocol could not include a condemnation of chemical weapons in general.[22]

In any event, no protests as to the use of these projectiles in World War I were forthcoming from either side. This failure to protest has been explained on the ground that no tactical advantage was gained by the use of these instruments. One writer surmises that their use may have gone unnoticed at the time.[23] The Allies also failed to protest the cloud-gas attack at Ypres in 1915,[24] although again a literal interpretation of the Hague Gas Declaration would not forbid this attack inasmuch as the cylinders used to launch it were not projectiles.

The British did charge violation of the laws of civilized warfare when the Germans resorted to the use of projectiles which emitted asphyxiating gases.[25] The Germans defended their action on the ground of reprisals and also claimed that such projectiles did not have a *sole* object of spreading such gases but had other purposes as well.[26] The gas shell did evolve from the earlier model, first used in 1914, which did not have the sole object of diffusing gas; still, as noted, the later projectiles developed did have such a sole purpose and would appear to fall within the ban of the Hague Declaration.

The restrictive language of the Hague Declaration made its circumvention in World War I easy, or at least permitted pious denials of its violation because the weapon was said to fall without the prohibition, whether or not such denial was truthful. However, some writers take the view that the Hague Declaration emerged from fundamental principles of the international law of war such as the prohibition of the use of poison and of weapons causing unnecessary suffering, and from these principles there emanated a more expansive customary rule of law prohibiting the use of gas, or at least particular kinds of gas of a lethal or severely injurious nature, and not just its diffusion by a particular projectile.[27] If a broader customary forbiddance did exist at the time, the use of gas during the war would be considered illegal as violation of the law, unless it was excused by the law under certain fact situations. In either instance the existence or continued existence of the rule would not necessarily be affected. On the other hand, a prolonged and repeated use of gas by the belligerents in violation of the norm would indicate a conviction that the old prohibition which might have existed at the beginning of the war had given way to a new permissive rule. Or, finally, such a general and repeated use of gas could be evidence of a conviction that no legal restraint, other than the Hague Gas Declaration, which as noted was easily evaded, was ever obligatory upon the parties. Arguments can be made to support all of these positions from the conflicting practices and statements of the belligerents regarding the use of gas during World War I.

Germany, insisting on a literal interpretation of the Hague Declaration to which she was bound, could except therefrom gases spread by cylinders with the aid of the wind, as well as her later use of projectiles which she claimed had uses other than the spreading of gas.[28] Thus, Germany legalized her position under the Hague Declaration and then sought to deny any general customary ban on gas. It might be pointed out here that the extreme German theory of military necessity, *Kriegsraison*,[29] would justify the violation of any rule of international law by the use of any weapon if necessary to overcome the enemy and to gain the victory. This theory was referred to in order to justify German conduct in this instance.[30]

The Germans were also careful to justify their use of gas as falling within the meaning of reprisals. Here it was contended that the German use of gas was in legal retaliation to a previous use of gas against German forces by the Allies.[31] In calling their action reprisals, as to the use of gas falling both within and without the literal language of the Hague Gas Declaration, the Germans intimated that a customary rule of international law banning use of gas in war did exist and had been violated by the Allies—an illegality which would legalize the German use of gas as a true reprisal.

The German accusations seem to be fabrications, for the consensus is that Germany used gas methods in warfare first.[32] This could indicate a cynical violation of a customary rule believed by Germany to exist to which a legal defense, even though false, must be made. Or it could show a conviction that no customary obligation was ever in being and that the defense of reprisals was simply an additional factor thrown into the battle of criminations and recriminations to remove the blame from German shoulders.

The Allies, in their failure to protest the first German use of gas, particularly the Ypres attack, demonstrated their belief that no customary rule had been created. For this attack technically fell without the Hague Declaration; ergo, if gas were disallowed it would be by customary international law. Failure to protest the illegality of this gas attack would indicate that it was not considered illegal either under the Gas Declaration or under a customary norm.[33]

One writer has set forth the view that the unpreparedness of the English and French for the use of gas was evidence of their belief that such use would contravene international law and would not be employed. There are conflicting reports here, for another author points out[34] that the Allied preparations for gas warfare served to turn German attention to the use of this method, although it is further noted that the Allied preparation probably consisted of no more than French possession of tear grenades.[35]

Stronger evidence of the actuality of a rule is that the English, in charging that the use by Germans of shells or projectiles emitting asphyxiating gas was violative of law, were not content to rest their case upon the Hague Declaration, but spoke of a German violation of the laws of civilized warfare.[36] Moreover, the Allies categorized their use of gas as legitimate reprisals, i.e., retaliation in kind against the illegality committed by the Germans in using gas in violation of a rule forbidding it.[37] Thus there would be demonstrated an international prohibitory norm of the laws of war with which the Allies were trying to induce compliance by the sanction of reprisals against the breach of the norm. If, then, their actions were true reprisals regarded so by those resorting to them, it would go far to indicate their belief that an antigas rule existed. However, the conduct of the Allies tends to remove their retaliatory use of gas from a reprisals characterization. In the first place, reprisals should be taken only as a last resort after all other means have been taken by the victim state to prevail upon the wrongdoing state to desist from the unlawful behavior.[38] This the Allies did not do. No complaint or protest was directed toward Germany, for example, when she employed gas at Ypres. Instead, the Allies began their preparation for the use of gas on a large scale and thereafter used it freely as a part of their weapons system. This conduct denotes an approach to the laws of war whereby the violation of those laws by the Germans through an illegal use of gas in effect terminated any continuing legal obligation and permitted *carte blanche* employment of chemical methods by those who had been subjected to the gas attack in the first instance. Since the obligation of the laws of war continues despite violations of them, such an Allied approach would be wrong and Allied reprisals could hardly, it is said, be considered legitimate, inasmuch as they would not be necessarily proportionate and appropriate measures against a specific unlawful conduct, to be discontinued when the conduct has ceased.[39] If the Allies' unlimited resort to gas was not proportionate and appropriate so as to constitute reprisals, then their actions were illegal as reprisals and would indicate a belief that no international customary norm was ever in being which would ban their use of gas, for a German violation alone could hardly abrogate the rule.[40]

The United States, after it entered World War I, also engaged in chemical warfare against the enemy. This conduct, coupled with the fact that the United States had rejected the Hague Gas Declaration, would seem to be demonstrative of the fact that no law—treaty or customary—existed prohibiting the employment of gas in warfare.

In view of these conflicting practices of states involved in the use of gas in World War I, a dogmatic answer can hardly be given as to the reality of an international norm interdicting the use of gas in warfare. On the face and in balance it would seem that the evidence shifts the scales toward a conclusion either that no such rule was ever in being, or that if it was it did not survive the war. If there was such a rule, it did nothing to restrain the use of gas.

The Interwar Period

During the Italian-Ethiopian War, the Italian military forces used chemical agents against the Ethiopians. In a series of communications to the League of Nations in 1936, the Ethiopians charged that the Italians had used "asphyxiating and similar gases" along the front and against open towns.[41] The gas most frequently used was mustard gas (yperite).[42] The emperor of Ethiopia, in a speech to the League Assembly, described the chemical attacks as follows:

At the outset, toward the end of 1935, Italian aircraft hurled tear-gas bombs upon my armies. They had but slight effect. The soldiers learned to scatter, waiting until the wind had rapidly dispersed the poisonous gases.

The Italians then resorted to mustard gas. Barrels of liquid were hurled upon armed groups. But this means too was ineffective; the liquid affected only a few soldiers, and the barrels upon the ground themselves gave warning of the danger to the troops and to the population.

It was at this time when . . . the Italian command, fearing a rout, applied the procedure which it is now my duty to denounce to the world.

Sprayers were installed on board aircraft so that they would vaporize, over vast areas of territory, a fine, death-dealing rain. Groups of nine, fifteen, eighteen aircraft followed one another so that the fog issuing from them formed a continuous sheet. It was thus that, from the end of January 1936, soldiers, women, children, cattle, rivers, lakes and fields were constantly drenched with this deadly rain. In order to kill off systematically all living creatures in order the more surely to poison waters and pastures, the Italian command made its aircraft pass over and over again. That was its chief method of warfare.[43]

Italy did not deny the existence of a rule of international law forbidding gas warfare but on the contrary stated her intention to abide by the Geneva Gas Protocol of 1925. She argued, however, that the protocol did not forbid the use of gas on legal grounds as reprisals not in kind, but against barbarians and illegal means of warfare of another nature. In a letter to the secretary general of the League it was pointed out that

His Majesty's Government has never ignored the provisions of the Protocol of 1925, although it regards that Protocol as not precluding the exercise of the right of reprisal in punishment of such abominable atrocities as those committed by the Ethiopian forces, which would be inconceivable in civilized countries (torture and decapitation of prisoners; emasculation of the wounded and killed; savagery toward, and the killing of noncombatants; systematic use of dum-dum bullets, etc.)[44]

In an earlier letter the Italian government, in speaking of the Protocol and the right of reprisal, stated even more explicitly:

The Protocol contains no provision excluding the exercise of the right of reprisal by way of exception to the general principles which admit that right. By the clause in the Protocol referring to the use of chemical weapons, the signatory Powers merely declared that they recognized the prohibition of the use of gases therein mentioned as embodied in international law, but added no clause modifying the existing legal situation in regard to the right of reprisal.[45]

It should be stressed that the rule of international law to which the Italians alluded is not a customary rule, but a conventional one, the Gas

Protocol of 1925 to which both Italy and Ethiopia were parties. The nations condemning the Italian use of gas also predicated their condemnation from a legal point of view on the Geneva Protocol. The Ethiopians in their allegations of illegality spoke rather generally of Italian violations of the laws and usages of war, international undertakings, and international conventions.[46] The British representative before the Council of the League referred specifically to the Geneva Protocol and the obligations which had been undertaken under it against the use of gas warfare.[47] The Portuguese representative stated bluntly that the protocol prohibited "asphyxiating, poisonous or other gases in war, whatever the reasons alleged for their employment."[48] Moreover, a resolution adopted by the Council of the League recalled to the two belligerents to the conflict that they were parties to the protocol, which forbade the use of asphyxiating, poisonous, or other gases in war.[49] When this emphasis was placed on the protocol, a conventional or treaty rule, as the legal basis of the gas prohibition, little credence would appear to have been given to the existence of a customary rule. One writer has said that the Italian use of gas in its relation to law was simply an aberration having no relevance in other situations.[50] From the practices and pronouncements of states at the time, it would appear to be more correct to say that the use was either regarded as a violation of a treaty rule or legally justified as reprisals excepted from the treaty rule, if indeed a valid case for reprisals could be made. In any event, a customary rule can hardly be founded on these condemnations.

Reports are conflicting, but it seems certain that the Japanese resorted to the use of gas against the Chinese during the Sino-Japanese War.[51] A House of Representatives report on Research in CBR declares categorically that the Japanese were guilty of a large number of small gas attacks upon Chinese forces from 1937 to 1943.[52] Kelly, in his article on gas warfare, states that "tremendous quantities of mustard and lewisite" were used by the Japanese against the Chinese at Ichang.[53] Chemical agents used have been said to be tear gas, vomiting gas, and smoke, but use of blistering agents, mustard, and lewisite are also reported. A few instances of Japanese use of choking and vomiting gases against United States forces on Guadalcanal and New Guinea have also been cited.[54] In 1938, in its dying days, the League of Nations did have occasion to consider the matter. The Chinese government brought before the Council an accusation against Japan with respect to the use of chemical and bacteriological methods of war. Council action was requested. In the course of the appeal it was reported that the Japanese were "on the point of using poison gas on a large scale in disregard of international law and convention,"[55] and that several Japanese chemical warfare units were en route to China. Request was made that steps be taken to forestall "the perpetration of a heinous crime."

On May 14 the Council by resolution recalled

that the use of toxic gases is a method of war condemned by international law, which cannot fail, should resort be had to it, to meet the reprobation of the civilized world; and requests the Governments of states who may be in a position to do so to communicate to the League any information that they may obtain on the subject.[56]

Various delegates, speaking to the resolution, recognized that the use of poisonous gases was a method of warfare disapproved by the conscience of the world and viewed by mankind with horror. The Polish delegate stated that the resolution embodied a rule of general application which absolutely prohibited chemical warfare.[57] It might be noted that previous to the making of this resolution the Chinese government informed the League that the Japanese forces had resorted to poison gas on a number of occasions.[58] If this be true, the fact that the ban on such use might be considered as a rule of general application did not prevent the employment of such forbidden weapons.

In 1938 the Assembly had occasion to consider the problem of the use of chemical warfare in relation to a resolution for the "Protection of Civilian Populations against Bombing from the Air in Case of War." The representative of China again alluded to the Japanese use of poison gas on various fronts in China, stating that gas attacks formed an important part of aerial warfare, and that the bomber was an instrument for that purpose.[59] Thus, after condemning the intentional bombing of civilian populations, the resolution went on to take the opportunity

to reaffirm that the use of chemical or bacterial methods in the conduct of war is contrary to international law as recalled more particularly in the resolution of the General Commission of the Conference for the Reduction and limitation of Armaments of July 23, 1932 and the resolution of the Council of May 14, 1938.[60]

None of these statements stress the Geneva Protocol, for that protocol was not binding upon Japan, inasmuch as she had not ratified it. Except for the first Chinese statement mentioned, which spoke of disregard of international law and convention, they speak of the gas prohibition as a rule of general application or of international law generally. Thus the impression can be gained that the delegates and the resolutions did believe that a customary rule of international law had come into being which Japan, through a use of gas, would violate. However, in the indictment brought before the Tokyo War Crimes Tribunal, Japan was charged with using poison gas against China in violation of conventional law only,[61] i.e., the Hague Gas Declaration of 1899,[62] Article 23(a) of the Annex to the Hague Convention on Land Warfare,[63] and Article 171 of the Treaty of Versailles.[64] The application of this particular law to Japan's use of gas would appear to be tenuous at best. Although Japan was a party to the Hague Gas Declaration, the effect of that treaty to restrain the use of gas is, as has been seen, most questionable. Doubt exists as to whether poison gas was meant to be included in the Hague antipoison rule, and Article 171 of the Versailles Treaty was in reality applicable only to Germany. Reliance solely on this treaty law as the basis of the illegality of Japan's use of gas, when its application to the case is dubious, indicates a contrary notion to that before mentioned, i.e., that no customary rule was present upon which the illegality could have been predicated.

World War II and Korea

Except for Japan, none of the major powers used chemical gases during World War II.[65] At the beginning of the war a joint Anglo-French declaration reaffirmed that these two nations would abide by the terms of the Geneva Protocol of 1925, but reserved the right to take any appropriate action if the enemy failed to observe the ban on gas warfare.[66] An inquiry was directed to the Germans for assurance of observance of the gas prohibition, and the assurances were forthcoming, although full liberty of action was reserved by the Germans if the protocol was infringed by the enemy.[67] The British sought similar assurance from the Japanese in 1941, but here they were unsuccessful.[68] At the First Meeting of Foreign Ministers in 1939, the American republics also called upon the European countries in conflict to refrain from certain methods of warfare such as

The use of poisonous gases and other chemical methods of warfare which produce irreparable and permanent injuries;
Employing of inflammable liquids;
Poisoning water and disseminating bacteria. . . .[69]

There were some unauthenticated reports of the use of gas in Europe, and fear was always present that it would be used. Spaight, for example, has stated that there was discussion by the Germans about the use of gas as an answer to Allied use of incendiaries.[70] Moreover, Germany had developed a new deadly nerve gas and had stockpiled it. General Creasy pointed out before a congressional committee that the Germans did have orders to use the nerve gas (GA) as defense against the channel crossings and landings in Normandy; but such orders were never carried out, probably because of German fear of overwhelming retaliation by the Allies.[71]

At various times the Germans were warned not to adopt gas weapons and assured that retaliation would follow if they did. In 1943 Churchill informed the Germans of Britain's formidable gas preparations. It was stated that although Britain had resolved against the use of gas, still if the Germans were guilty of employing it against Russia such an attack would be treated

exactly as if it were used against ourselves and if we are satisfied that this new outrage has been committed by Hitler we will use our great and growing air superiority in the West to carry gas warfare on the largest possible scale far and wide against military objectives in Germany.[72]

A warning by President Roosevelt that if the enemy used gas the Allies would retaliate brought an answer by the Germans in 1943 denying any intention to use gas and charging that President Roosevelt's statement probably signified that the Allies were planning to do so.[73]

The fact that gas was not resorted to in Europe is surprising, especially when one considers that this weapon had been used effectively in World War I. The German failure to employ this form of warfare has been the subject of some speculation. Germany's refraining from such use at the beginning of the war has been generally attributed to the fear of retaliation and to a belief that employment of gas would not be necessary. When she might have resorted to the use of the new nerve gas, which could have gained her military advantage so as possibly to turn the tide in her favor toward the end of the war, her decision against such use is said to have been made for fear of retaliation in kind from the air. It must be remembered that at this time the Allies had gained air superiority and all Germany lay open to air attacks with gas.[74]

A German army officer, in writing of the reasons behind the German restraint, points out that Hitler was opposed to the employment of chemical agents because he had been poisoned and temporarily blinded by Yellow Cross (vesicant) gas in 1918.[75] Moreover, he states that in the first year of the war Germany was not prepared to wage gas warfare and lacked the means to do so.[76] Later, in Russia, Africa, and Italy, tactical and climatic considerations ruled against it.[77] Ground contamination chemical agents or skin poisons called Yellow Cross might have been advantageously employed against Russian partisans and guerillas so as to flush them from hiding places in bunkers and caves and render such places inaccessible for periods of time. However, to have used such agents would, it was said, have placed a stigma upon Germany as contravening the Geneva Protocol, would in a broad sense have forced no really favorable military decision, and would have given the enemy on all fronts excuses to use gas against German forces and the German homeland.

This officer's remarks as to the reasons behind the Allied abstention are interesting. The Russians were pictured as realizing that the length of their front and the wide area involved would permit the Germans to bypass the gassed areas so that no real tactical advantage would be gained, and, further, that the Russians were inferior in gas both technically and in training.[78]

The British reasons were different. At the beginning of the war British cities were vulnerable to gas attacks from the air by German planes; undoubtedly Germany at that time possessed tremendous air superiority. Later in their campaigns on the continent and in North Africa the British and Americans engaged in blitz operations which were not conducive to the use of gas, for it would have helped the Germans more than the Allies. Moreover, the British, like the Germans, considered that climatic conditions militated against the use of gas in Africa.[79]

This writer states that since America "was not bound by the Geneva Convention and [since] the Japanese were intensely hated by the American public . . . the government would have found no opposition in public sentiment" to an American use of gas in the Far East. He speculates that climatic conditions and the great sea distances involved in transporting gas were factors operating against the use of gas, as was the development of the atom bomb, an even more effective weapon which America had, at a later stage of the war, in reserve.[80]

These reasons are primarily tactical, and thus would not indicate abstention because of respect for law. Could the decision on both sides against the use of gas have been based on legal reasons? It has been said that the legal force of the Geneva Protocol was one of the bases of the self-restraint.[81] If this were true, it would denote again that the prohibition against gas weapons was one of treaty law, not customary international law.

However, the United States refrained from the use of gas along with other belligerents who were adherents to the protocol. This failure to use gas in the greatest war in history by both ratifiers and nonratifiers of the Geneva Protocol alike is an astonishing fact and could be a manifestation of the emergence of a customary rule of international law prohibiting the use of gas in warfare. Stone has said that the abstention would be based on fear of reprisals and that the extent to which it could be "attributable to the *opinio necessitatis* supporting an established rule of international law, is still debatable."[82] Some issue can be taken with this point of view, which appears to negate a legal principle; for as O'Brien has stated, "Moreover, custom which is the consequence of fear of reprisal, i.e., of legal sanctions, need not be any less important than custom based on a deep respect for the law."[83]

In the Korean conflict, gas agents were not used in the fighting.[84] Front-line commanders did request permission to use chemicals, even if they had to be only riot control tear and vomiting agents, to flush North Korean and Chinese troops from certain entrenched fortifications.[85] This permission was not given. Tactically the use of gas agents could have aided the United Nations position, for the front, like that in World War I, lent itself to gas warfare since it was narrow and well defended. Moreover, the United States had a developed chemical industry and service, while North Korea and China did not and apparently did not even have adequate protective equipment.[86] Abstention from the use of gas when a tactical advantage was possible from its use could be evidence of respect for a legal rule prohibiting, which, in the case of the United States, would be a customary rule. On the other hand, political motivations could be behind the abstention, for the Korean conflict was a limited war with limited political objectives against the enemies, including Red China.

Cognizance should be taken of the use of riot control incapacitating tear and vomiting agents by United States military forces to control North Korean prisoners of war in prison camps. Since they were not used in war itself, they could be excluded from a rule prohibiting the use of gas in war.[87]

Vietnam

The United States and its allies have employed temporarily disabling chemical agents in the Vietnamese conflict. The Viet Cong have also been accused of using such agents against United States forces.[88] The antipersonnel agents are classified by United States military authority as riot control agents.[89] The specific ones which have been used, according to the secretary of defense of the United States, are CN, CS, and DM.[90]

South Vietnamese troops have been said to have used tear agents in late 1964 or early 1965.[91] The first use by United States forces appears to have been an unauthorized one by a United States marine battalion commander in 1965. The gas was resorted to in order to clear out Viet Cong guerrillas located in underground bunkers and caves, who, it was thought, were holding with them innocent civilians as a shield against attack. Since the group could be flushed out without the employment of flamethrowers or other death-dealing weapons, the lives of innocent persons could be saved. In October, 1965, United States and Australian troops resorted to chemical weapons against the Viet Cong, but with permission from General Westmoreland. Thus, tear gas may now be used in an operation if the local unit commander believes that resort to it will result in fewer casualties to friend and foe. Military justification of this use was found when the use of conventional arms would kill innocent women and children and other noncombatants mixed in with the Viet Cong guerrilla forces.[92] Persistent gases have been employed to make Viet Cong tunnels unusable. Crystals are placed in the tunnel which later evaporate, releasing the gas.[93]

There have also been reports of another type of use of tear gas in this conflict.[94] Here the tear gas is dropped from the air over a large area.

Then antipersonnel fragmentation bombs are dropped from the air in a saturation pattern. The gas drives persons from hiding so that they are exposed to the fragmentation bursts of the bombs. The accusation has been made that this is a use of "gas in order to kill."[95] This position is arguable. Despite the fact that the tear gas is used in the military operation, the tear gas remains a nonlethal agent. The actual killer is the fragmentation bomb. Since aerial bombardment of legitimate military targets is permitted by international law, the military action would be legal if a legitimate military objective was involved.[96] Would these Viet Cong combatants be considered legitimate military targets? Enemy fighting men—combatant troops—are obviously, under almost every circumstance, to be regarded as legitimate military targets. However, according to the Hague Regulations the killing or wounding of an enemy who has laid down his arms or, having no longer any means of defense, has surrendered is prohibited.[97] Moreover, the Geneva Conventions of 1949 provide that persons who take "no active part in the hostilities, including members of armed forces who have laid down their arms and those placed *hors de combat* by sickness, wounds, detention, or any other cause, shall in all circumstances be treated humanely. . . ."[98] Thus the issue in this Vietnamese situation reduces itself to a consideration as to whether these men are legitimate military objectives. If they are *hors de combat*, out of action, they are not. From the facts it appears that the tear gas flushes them out from hiding and temporarily disables them. They are then *hors de combat* for a short time only. If a military force could move in immediately and capture them at this time or accept their surrender so as to remove them from the fray, then obviously killing them by bombing or otherwise would be illegal. They would not be a legitimate military target. Since they are disabled by the tear gas for a short time only and can quickly return to battle, the killing by bombing would appear to be justified by military necessity as a proportionate measure necessary to bring about the submission of the enemy as soon as possible.[99]

Some comparison may be made between this situation and legitimate ruses of war such as surprises or ambush.[100] In a surprise or ambush the enemy troops might be temporarily out of action; they might, for example, be sleeping or resting without arms at hand. Attack to kill the enemy, even though the enemy might be described as disabled at the time, would be permitted.

This explanation, which would permit the military operation to be regarded as legitimate at international law and which would exonerate the use of nonlethal tear gas as the killer, might seem too pat to some, for it can be maintained, if reference is made to the law of causation, that the use of the nonlethal gas is a proximate or legal cause of the deaths by bombing. Here a sufficiently close causal connection exists between the conduct, the use of the gas, and the resulting injury or harm so that the use of the gas constitutes a proximate cause of the harm. Such a conclusion need not be defeated by the fact that an intervening factor exists, i.e., the bombing, an active operation which actually produces the result after the conduct consisting of the use of tear gas, inasmuch as the intervening cause here is one which in ordinary human experience would be reasonably anticipated, or one which the users of gas would have reason to anticipate under the particular circumstance. In other words, the users of the gas in the military operation would know of and thus would foresee the subsequent bombing.

Although a case of legal or proximate cause can be made out, still something appears to be lacking in a consideration of the illegality of the tear gas. To impose liability where proximate cause exists, there must be a duty to protect against the event which in fact did occur.[101] If the event, i.e., the bombing, was legal as a necessity of war, then legal blame can hardly be placed upon the use of tear gas in the military operation, unless tear gas is to be regarded as specifically outlawed by international law, or unless some legal fiction can be invoked to say that because the nonlethal tear gas is a proximate cause of death by other means, the nonlethal gas itself is transformed into a gas with properties of a lethal gas which may be barred by international law.

Herbicides have also been used in Vietnam. Hundreds of thousands of acres have been subjected to chemical antiplant agents to strip away jungle cover and to destroy crops. These agents have been said to be no more than weed killers. Announcement has been made that defoliants and electronic devices will be used to clear and monitor an area on the borders of South Vietnam to prevent infiltration from North Vietnam.[102]

The use of these chemical agents in the conflict has caused a great outcry of condemnation and criticism in certain quarters and denunciations of the United States as a violator of international law.[103] Official United States utterances have maintained that the policy of this nation is one of no first use of weapons of gas warfare, but the United States has defended its actions on the ground that the employment of riot control agents, such as tear gas, and the use of herbicides to control vegetation does not amount to gas warfare as prohibited by the Geneva Protocol or otherwise.[104]

Once again the issue is raised as to the meaning of the words of the Geneva Protocol which might well be considered expressive of a customary rule and which prohibit the use in war of asphyxiating, poisonous, or other gases and all analogous liquids, materials, or devices. As we have seen, those who hold one view have strongly maintained that at least first use of all gases in war is considered forbidden for various reasons, primarily because of the fear that the use of any chemical weapons would escalate to include all.[105] Though the United States has been ambivalent on this question, still during the League of Nations disarmament proceedings it took exception to this viewpoint, maintaining for example that tear gas was not banned.[106] In view of this disagreement the existence of a customary rule prohibiting the use of *all* gas in war cannot be unequivocally proclaimed, but from its practices in conflict the United States would seem to have taken the position that the first use of antipersonnel lethal or severely injurious chemical agents is now prohibited.

Yemen

As early as 1963, charges were made against the United Arab Republic of the use of poison gases against royalist villages in Yemen, where civil strife prevailed between the royalists and the republicans, the latter being aided by the United Arab Republic. The United Arab Republic denied the charge. United Nations fact finders failed to find evidence of such employment.[107]

In January, 1967, gas raids in Yemen were once again reported. Several hundred persons were said to have been killed or wounded. The press in Saudi Arabia and the Yemini royalist leaders blamed these attacks upon the United Arab Republic. United Nations intervention was requested. Various reasons were propounded to explain the gas raid. It was said that only by the use of gas could the royalists, who were sheltered in deep caves, be reached. Further, it was said that officials of the United Arab Republic hoped that this resort to terror weapons would intimidate both the royalists and their backers, the Saudi Arabians, to such a degree as to bring the fighting to a close and thus end a long-drawn-out conflict which was frustrating to the United Arab Republic and its president.[108]

In June, 1967, the International Red Cross confirmed that gas bombs had been used in northern villages of Yemen. This confirmation was based upon the report of a Red Cross team investigating the facts in Yemen. The Red Cross refrained from naming the United Arab Republic as the gas attacker, but it stated its concern at gas methods of warfare and appealed to all of the parties to the conflict—the two factions in Yemen, the United Arab Republic, and Saudi Arabia—not to use gas or similar poisonous substances.[109]

News reports have pointed the finger of blame to the forces of the United Arab Republic, despite continued denial by the authorities of that nation. These reports have stated that not only mustard but also the very lethal nerve gas was employed. Charges and suppositions have been advanced that the nerve gas was supplied by the Soviet Union. Others have said that the United Arab Republic is capable of making the substances.[110]

The Red Cross communication failed to halt the gas attacks. Later

United Arab Republic gas attacks on the royalists have been brought to the attention of the world. In July, after news of certain poison gas attacks in Yemen, the members of the British House of Commons deplored the United Arab Republic use of gas and requested the government of Britain to bring the matter before the United Nations.[111] They were informed that the government would confer with other governments on the matter.[112] After the royalists, in a letter addressed to the United States representative before the United Nations, Ambassador Goldberg, denounced the United Arab Republic use of gas, a United States Department of State spokesman stated: "We continue to be deeply disturbed by the many reports concerning the use of poison gas against civilians in the Yemen. This Government condemns such action as inhuman and entirely contrary to the laws of nations."[113] He added that "the United States would support international action to deal with this problem."

On this same date, the State Department released a letter written by Ambassador Goldberg in reply to a letter from a New York representative, Lester L. Wolff, which had requested information as to the reasons why the United States had not taken action on this reported use of gas in Yemen. In his reply, Ambassador Goldberg expressed the concern of the United States government over the growing number of indications pointing to the use of gas again by the United Arab Republic Air Force against the local population in Yemen, and then stated:

The United States position on this matter is quite clear and corresponds to the stated policy of almost all other governments throughout the world as reflected in the voting (91 in favor and 4 abstentions) on UNGA Resolution 2162 B of 1966 which condemned the use of poison gas in warfare. *The use of poison gas is clearly contrary to international law.* [Italics supplied][114]

The letter indicated that the United States government was hopeful that Saudi Arabia would bring the case to the United Nations. It was reported that American officials believed that a United States initiative in the matter would subject this country to accusations of being pro-Israeli.[115] Even Saudi Arabia, which had previously sought to focus attention on the issue, refused to press for action because of the Middle East situation.[116]

It is possible, as we have seen, that Egypt or the United Arab Republic is no longer bound by the Geneva Protocol of 1925, and it can be contended that even if she were bound, she would not be bound as to Yemen if Yemen were a nonadhering state and therefore not obligated under the protocol. This would be the case unless Yemen was obligated as a successor state under the British ratification.[117] Still, Egypt would be bound by an international customary rule inhibiting the use of lethal or severely injurious gas, if, as would seem to be the case, such a rule had come into being sometime during the period following the Geneva Protocol.

A derogation from such a rule by Egypt would ordinarily be an indication not of the nonexistence of the norm, but rather of a violation of it. Insofar as international law is concerned, what is disheartening is the indifference of the international society and its failure to take action through international organizations against the law-breaking state. This dereliction in enforcement weakens not only the force of the rule as one in being but also its continued existence, for if a majority of the members of the international society fail to register protest or to demand and take sanctions against a delinquent it could show an *opinio juris* of the international society that prohibition no longer exists. Even if the rule *qua* rule may be thought to continue unimpaired, failure to compel its observance, albeit for political reasons, sacrifices law to politics and again impairs the efficacy of the norm and of international law itself. Attention should be called to the fact, however, that the United States did through the Department of State recognize that the use of such poison gas as was made in Yemen, i.e., lethal and severely injurious agents, was "inhuman and entirely contrary to the law of nations."[118]

It is ironic to compare this situation with that of Vietnam. In the latter case, the United States and its allies, upon resort to mere temporarily disabling chemical agents, brought down upon themselves howls of criticism, not only from communist states, but also from governments of other states and groups in those states. The small outcry at the use of lethal and severely injurious gases in Yemen should well cause some conjecture.

Incendiaries and Smokes

Throughout the annals of history fire has been used as a weapon of warfare,[119] but the technical advances occurring in the twentieth century first permitted the adoption of flame, incendiaries, and smoke as weapons of war on a large scale. Thus, in World War I incendiaries were used by both sides in the form of artillery shells, incendiary grenades, trench mortar shells, and projector bombs. Stress was placed on incendiaries that could be dropped by aircraft. In 1915, London and Paris were frequently subjected to German air raids with incendiary bombs.

The first fire attacks against ground troops were made by the German army against the French at Malancourt by means of flame projectors or flamethrowers. These devices had been invented by the Germans before the war. After the German use of such a weapon, the British and French developed their own flamethrowers. However, this weapon was used only intermittently during World War I and met with little success because of its limited range and also because of lack of proper fuels. United States troops did not then resort to its use.

World War I was also to see the methodical use of smoke as a weapon of war. Smoke was first used with success at sea by navies in order to screen naval operations and movements. Planned tactical use of smoke on land began in the summer of 1915. By 1916 smoke generators were employed by all of the principal belligerent armies. Smoke fillings were loaded into every type of projectile including grenades, trench mortar bombs, artillery shells, and aviation bombs. The Allies were said to have excelled the Germans in the use of this weapon, primarily because the Germans lacked phosphorus, which was possessed and employed in large quantities by the Allies.[120]

As we have seen, there was some attempt between World Wars I and II to outlaw incendiary projectiles specifically intended to cause fires or to outlaw the use of appliances designed to attack humans with fire.[121] Smokes would apparently have been excepted from the attempted ban, and no qualms existed as to their employment in World War II. The Germans proved the effectiveness of smoke in screening operations in a war of fast movement, or blitzkrieg. Later developments permitted the use of smoke to screen rear area targets from long-range air attack, and to screen beach landings and paratroop attacks. The first American smoke screening of a paratroop assault occurred in New Guinea in 1943. Smoke as a screening agent was also used in the Korean War.[122]

Efforts to prohibit incendiaries and flamethrowers proved to be of no avail. Increasing use has been made of these weapons in conflicts occurring since World War I. Aerial incendiaries, consisting of incendiary bombs and fire bombs, were used extensively and successfully during World War II by both the Axis ond Allied Powers. Enormous quantities of incendiaries were dropped on German industrial cities, and after March, 1945, the Japanese cities were subjected to all-out incendiary aerial attacks. The Japanese premier stated in a broadcast that Tokyo had been so nearly destroyed that the city would have to be completely rebuilt. Some sixty-nine Japanese cities were targets of this type of assault.[123]

Fire bombs which consisted of large containers filled with napalm gel were successfully used in tactical air missions. In Germany they were effectively employed against point targets such as headquarters areas, vehicles, warehouses, and marshaling yards, as well as certain open fortifications and exposed enemy troops. They were also employed in the war against Japan to produce materiel destruction and casualties.[124]

At the beginning of World War II the Axis powers possessed tank-mounted flamethrowers. The Italians had employed such weapons earlier, in the Ethiopian War, and a few German flame tanks had been used in the Spanish Civil War. Intelligence reports indicated that the Germans had employed flamethrowers in Poland and in their drive across the Low Countries. The Allies, except for the Russians, were not well equipped with flamethrowers at the beginning of the war, although by 1943 the Canadians demonstrated a flame gun mounted on a vehicle.

Portable flamethrowers were slowly perfected, and were used for the first time by the Americans in New Guinea in December, 1942. After this date portable flamethrowers were used by all nations in the conflict, both in the European theater of operations and in the Pacific theater. They were most successful against pillboxes or other fixed fortifications and in house-to-house fighting.[125] Flamethrowers were resorted to in the Korean War.[126] This weapon is also employed in Vietnam. In the latter conflict, napalm has been used on a large scale both in bombs and in flamethrowers. Antiwar groups in the United States have demonstrated against the use of napalm fire weapons as inhumane.[127]

Despite this recent protest by certain members of the clergy, students, and others opposed to the war in Vietnam against the use of fire in war, it seems apparent that the actual practices of states in resorting to incendiaries and smokes demonstrate that no customary international law rule exists which would interdict the use of these weapons. On the contrary, the extensive practices of nations in employing these weapons in the wars of the twentieth century would indicate an acceptance of their legality.

BIOLOGICAL AGENTS

Crude methods of biological warfare were utilized early in the history of conflict. In ancient times bodies of cholera and plague victims were dropped over the walls of beleaguered cities, or left on the ground the enemy was expected to occupy.[128] Later in time the British supposedly spread smallpox among the Indians by giving them blankets which had covered smallpox victims.[129] In 1797 Napoleon deliberately flooded an area near the besieged city of Mantua in the hope that swamp miasmas would weaken the Italians' will to resist.[130]

Rivers and wells were often polluted so as to produce disease by throwing the carcasses of animals or corpses of men into them. Even during the American War between the States, General Johnson, retreating from Vicksburg in July, 1863, ordered the Confederate Army to throw into rivers and ponds the carcasses of dead horses, cattle, hogs, and sheep.[131]

There is no proof that biological agents were used during World War I, although it was rumored that Germany dropped garlic and sweets infected with cholera germs in Rumania and Italy.[132] It has also been alleged that the widespread glanders epidemic which affected more than 58,000 horses in the French army was caused by the first modern attempts at biological warfare by the Germans. German agents in the United States also were accused of having inoculated animals scheduled for shipment to Europe with various bacteria in the hope that they would spread disease upon their arrival.[133]

During the 1930s Germany, Japan, and the Soviet Union were engaged in active research in biological warfare. In 1941 growing concern in the United States brought forth a directive to the Chemical Warfare Service to engage in biological warfare research. By 1942, the initiation of research projects was authorized to investigate ways and means to maintain security and to retaliate should the enemy use biological methods in war. Moreover, liaison was established with British and Canadian scientists who had previously begun work in the biological area.[134] Japan, during World War II, may have made a few limited attempts to employ biological weapons. In any event, in 1949 several Japanese nationals were accused of doing so. They were tried and were convicted, mainly on the basis of circumstantial evidence, by a Soviet military tribunal of having employed plague and typhus biological agents against the Mongolian People's Republic in 1939 and against China in 1940-42. In 1950, the Soviet government proposed that a special international military tribunal should be created to try the Japanese emperor and certain Japanese generals on such a charge.[135]

During the Korean conflict the charge was made that the United Nations forces and the United States had used "cruel and inhuman" bacteriological warfare against the inhabitants of North Korea and northeast China. Through the medium of a scientific commission, claimed to be impartial, the Peking regime investigated the charges and conveniently declared them to be true, basing their case on testimony reputedly supplied by four captured American Air Force lieutenants, who, under duress, admitted dropping disease-carrying insects in certain bombs from the air. Refuting these charges as communist slander, the United States proposed a truly impartial investigation by the International Red Cross and the World Health Organization—a proposal to which the communists would not agree.[136]

Ancient and very unsophisticated forms of biological warfare have been reported in Vietnam. The Viet Cong have sought to protect their positions with camouflaged pits in the bottom of which needle-sharp bamboo slivers are placed. The tips of these slivers are covered with urine or feces, in an attempt to induce tetanus or other infection in the victims.[137]

These limited attempts by nations to spread disease in war, some authenticated and some not, have been considered by certain writers as hardly indicative of a rule of customary international law derived from the practice of states either permitting or prohibiting resort to biological weapons in warfare. It has been pointed out that, as modern weapons of war, biological agents are still too experimental to have permitted a pattern of practice to come into being. Abstention from usage does not necessarily indicate that such abstention came about because of a prohibitory legal rule; nor would such abstention at this stage of biological weapons development bring into being a customary prohibitory rule, for failure to resort to such weapons may well be based on purely military considerations such as their doubtful effectiveness when compared to the utility of existing conventional weapons and instruments of war.[138]

Such an opinion may not be taking into account the whole story. The Korean and Vietnamese conflicts have been two major ones in which resort has not been had to biological agents, despite the fact that ability to engage in biological warfare had by the time of these wars become a reality and that biological weapons were considered effective in some military operations.[139] This fact could indicate abstention based on a conscious legal duty to abstain.

Conviction That the Usage Is Binding—*Opinio Juris*

As can readily be seen from the above discussion, the actual practices of states when considered alone can often be contradictory and confusing as to the establishment of a binding rule of customary international law. For example, the use of a certain weapon in warfare by states could possibly indicate a violation of an existing prohibitory rule against such use, a legal exception to the rule, or a conviction on the part of the state user that a norm is not in being. Moreover, an abstention from use of a weapon may be evidence of a customary inhibitory rule, or may simply indicate that states have refrained from use because of political considerations, military considerations, convenience, or expediency, rather than because of a belief that a compulsory rule of international law requires abstention.[140] It is not enough to show that states follow a pattern of conduct to prove the existence of a customary rule of international law. It is also necessary to demonstrate that this practice or conduct is combined with the *opinio juris*, i.e., that the usage or practice is followed because it is felt to be legally obligatory or accepted as law.[141] One writer has contended that the true and only constitutive element of customary international law is the *opinio juris* of states. Usage and custom, according to this view, is only one of various types of evidence which may be used to establish the *opinio juris* as to the existence or nonexistence of a particular rule relating to the resort to certain weapons;[142] this approach is reinforced by the contention that a rule of international law can come into existence even without usage or practice if there is an *opinio juris* present, even though an objection might be raised that a rule without usage could not, from a strictly semantic point of view, be called customary law.[143]

Customary legal limitations on chemical and biological weapons cannot be established, therefore, without resort to *opinio juris*. State abstention from the use of certain chemical or biological agents will not in and of itself indicate the existence of a customary international norm, for, as was highlighted in the *Lotus Case*, abstention must be based on a consciousness of "having a duty to abstain." As there has been little or no resort to today's sophisticated biological weapons, it would be difficult to establish a customary norm either for or against their use based only on the practice of states. On the other hand, if the majority of nations, including those representing the major legal systems of the world, strongly feel that they are legally bound to refrain from the use of biological agents, then it would seem that the *opinio juris* in and of itself would be sufficient to indicate that there has been a development of a norm of international law banning resort to such weapons.

To discover, therefore, whether the nonuse of biological weapons in recent wars has been based upon the *opinio juris* of their being illegal under customary international law, one must seek evidence from scattered sources, such as diplomatic correspondence, policy statements, opinions of officials, writings of legal advisers to nations, official manuals, orders to military forces, and official statements presented to international conferences or international organizations.[144]

Therefore, in an attempt to ascertain customary rules pertaining to the use or nonuse of chemical and biological agents in war, attention must be directed to such evidence emanating from states, particularly the powers which have used or are capable of using such weapons in war, in order to determine whether or not an *opinio juris communis* has developed.

THE UNITED STATES

The attempt to discover an *opinio juris* of the United States as to customary international legal limitations on chemical and biological warfare is fraught with complication arising primarily from uncertainty caused by the contradictions of policy and statements of United States officialdom as they have been made over the years. Offhand, it would seem, conclusion could be safely reached that prior to World War I no conviction existed to the effect that chemical or gas agents were forbidden in war. Evidence which can be marshaled consists of the United States action and statements in relation to the Hague Gas Declaration of 1899, whereby this country strongly opposed a conventional rule in any way limiting resort to gas on the ground that it would be unwise to restrict or outlaw the use of a new weapon which might prove effective in the defense of the nation, particularly in view of the fact that since the consequences of gas were not yet known, there was no method of judging the weapon in relation to unnecessary suffering.[145] If the United States opposed the creation of a new conventional rule, it could hardly be thought that any belief was present that a customary rule had already arisen. It is somewhat surprising to discover that the 1914 Army manual, *Rules of Land Warfare*, after stating that chemical or gas weapons were excluded from Article 23 of the 1907 Hague Annexes to the Convention respecting the Laws and Customs of War on Land prohibiting use of poisoned weapons and arms and projectiles calculated to cause unnecessary suffering, went on to say that in practice the United States refrained from the use of poisonous gas.[146] Although the statement excepts poison gas from any customary or conventional prohibitory rule, still it shows some belief that this method of war should not be resorted to, not because of legal compulsion but possibly because of moral or political compulsion or possibly because the United States simply was not prepared for this type of warfare anyway, which would signify abstention because of military considerations. The statement does, however, appear to soften the policy enunciated at the 1899 Conference when the United States denied any limitation on its right to use gas weapons.

This language to the effect that in practice the United States abstained from the use of poison gas did not prevent such use by this country a few years later when it entered World War I, although in March, 1918, United States military leaders, along with those of other Allied Powers, stated, in reply to a Red Cross inquiry, that poisonous gases came under the prohibition forbidding the use of poison,[147] and in May they joined in a French note to the Red Cross comparing such gas to "cruel means of warfare according to international agreement" and stating that the Allies had resorted to its use for protection only after German first use.[148] Germany appears to have used gas first against the United States after the latter entered the war, so that United States use could conceivably be contended to constitute reprisals; nevertheless, as Kelly points out, World War I use of gas by the United States does not fairly reflect the United States attitude, for that was "a gas war long before the United States entered it."[149]

World War I proved gas to be a most effective weapon.[150] As a weapon of war, plans and preparedness for its use were thought to be necessary; therefore the Chemical Warfare Service was established in 1920 as a part of the permanent military establishment,[151] in spite of the antigas sentiment which developed after World War I and which created much hostility to chemical warfare. Moreover, the United States military was somewhat divided; certain commanding generals had developed a distaste for gas warfare during the war and, as a result, the Chemical Warfare Service had its activities severely limited for some years and came close to being abolished.[152]

This division can be noted at the 1922 Washington Conference on the Limitation of Armaments, where the United States did accept the idea of a ban on gas warfare. But such acceptance was of a rather conditional nature, for there were two distinctly opposing views represented at the conference. The United States representative on a subcommittee of military experts to study the question joined the representatives of other nations in their opposition to the outlawry of gas in war and in their statement that gas should be regarded as a legitimate weapon of war.[153]

This conclusion was contrary to the views of the Advisory Committee of the United States Delegation, which did not accept the subcommittee's report but rather followed the line of an earlier subcommittee on land warfare, chaired by General Pershing, which had concluded that "chemical warfare should be abolished among nations as abhorrent to civilization,"[154] and also of a report submitted by the General Board of the Navy which found that the use of gas in war was almost universally condemned as violative of fundamental principles of international law such as the unnecessary suffering principle and the noncombatant principle.[155] Total prohibition of gas warfare, which would pertain to nonlethal, temporarily disabling gas as well as to severely injurious or lethal gases, was recommended on the ground that a demarcation between or among gases would be difficult to make, and on the further ground that the diffusion of all gases would be beyond control and that this fact could result in the bringing of war to innocent noncombatants. The Advisory Committee, agreeing with these reports, therefore resolved that toxic and nontoxic gases should be prohibited by international agreement and "should be classed with unfair methods of warfare as the poisoning of wells, [and] introducing germs of disease."[156] The conference adopted a provision along these lines in its antigas treaty, which the United States ratified. The treaty failed to become operative because the French refused to ratify.[157]

The Pershing subcommittee report, the naval report, and the resolution of the Advisory Committee all show a conviction that gas warfare should be abolished. But it is not clear whether a conviction was also present that the use of gas in war had already been abolished by customary international law. The statements confuse. The naval statement, claiming gas warfare to be violative of fundamental principles of international law and almost universally condemned, could be interpreted to indicate a belief in a legal prohibition other than treaty prohibition. But then the recommendation goes on to say that it would be sound policy to prohibit gas warfare, which gives rise to the question of whether the use of gas was already prohibited, or whether it was to be prohibited in the future.

The same type of conflict is to be noted in the Advisory Committee's resolution wherein gas is classed with the use of poison in war. Since poison is barred by customary international law, and since the committee classified gas as poison, it would seem contradictory for the resolution to go on to demand that gas should be prohibited by international agreement. Nonetheless, the resolution does seem to regard germ warfare as prohibited means, for it is classified with poisons as an abhorrent method of waging war.

A policy contrary to that exemplified by the Washington Treaty and its ban on gas warfare came to the fore when the Senate failed to ratify the prohibition on gas as well as bacteriological methods of the 1925 Geneva Protocol.[158] This would denote a United States belief that it was not bound by any rule of international law, treaty or customary, which would limit the use of chemical or biological methods. Here the Senate is said to have returned to the realist position expressed by Captain Mahan at the Hague in 1899, which would refuse to accept any provision rejecting the use of weapons not fully developed. Emphasis was also placed in the Senate hearings upon the absence of provisions to enforce such a flat prohibition as a reason for rejection. Probably, however, the isolationist mood of the time did much to contribute to the Senate's action.[159]

A short time later, a delineation of United States policy on the civilian executive level began to be manifest. In 1926, in speaking of military preparations for chemical warfare, the secretary of state set forth his opinion that all governments recognized the necessity to be prepared for chemical warfare, particularly for defense against it, irrespective of the existence of international agreements which sought to prohibit the actual use of gas in war. He stated:

I have never seen any proposal seriously advanced by any government to provide that national preparation for the use and for defense against chemical warfare, if such warfare should be used by an enemy contrary to treaty agreements, should be abolished or curtailed in the slightest.[160]

This statement recognizes no rule of international law binding upon the United States in relation to chemical weapons, but the implication is present that United States preparedness is necessary so as to permit the United States to engage in reprisals in kind in case gas is first used by an enemy against this country. Such reprisals could be considered legal even if a rule of international law did forbid the use of chemical agents.

The language of a declaration expressing a joint Army-Navy policy in 1934, however, was not so limited. It stated:

The United States will make all necessary preparations for the use of chemical warfare from the outbreak of war. The use of chemical warfare including the use of toxic agents, from the inception of hostilities, is authorized, subject to such restrictions or prohibitions as may be contained in any duly ratified international convention or conventions which at that time may be binding upon the United States and the enemy state or states.[161]

This declaration denies the existence of a rule binding upon the United States and would permit the first use of chemicals in warfare.

This conclusion is borne out by the 1940 Army Manual, which emphasized that the United States was not a party to a treaty prohibiting or restricting the use of toxic or nontoxic gas, smoke, or incendiary materials.[162] Moreover, the express statement was made that "[t]he practice of recent years has been to regard the prohibition against the use of poison as not applicable to the use of toxic gases."[163] These Army declarations could be taken to imply that no customary or conventional rule exists to bind the United States against the use of the mentioned methods.

It may be noted that a wavering course was followed by military authorities as to biological agents. The 1914 Army Manual declared unequivocally that Article 23a of the Hague Regulations prohibiting the use of poison and poisoned weapons "extends to the use of means calculated to spread contagious diseases."[164] This was repeated as late as the 1940 Rules of Land Warfare.[165] Since Article 23a was a codification of a principle of international law, it becomes evident that a universal ban on biological weapons arose therefrom.[166] Since it was agreed that bacteriological warfare fell within the meaning of poison, a United States conviction that a legally binding rule was in being seemed to be present. Yet in the 1956 Army Manual a flip-flop was made and the restriction on biological weapons was relaxed. The new manual makes no reference to the question of whether biological warfare against human beings is against customary international law, although it does except the use of chemical or bacterial agents harmless to man used to destroy crops intended for the armed forces.[167] Moreover, it goes on to say that the United States is not bound by any treaty banning or restricting the use of gas, smoke, incendiary materials, or bacteriological warfare.[168] These statements are, at best, of a fence-straddling variety. But the change from a former flat prohibition to the present reading, plus the fact that bacterial as well as chemical agents harmless to man, if used against crops intended for consumption by armed forces, are not prohibited, would be some indication that the Army no longer believes that the use of any biological or chemical agent is subject to a customary international law rule. Various reasons, none of which appear very satisfactory,[169] were set forth for the change as to biological agents. Possibly the most important one given for the deletion of a reference to biological agents as illegal is that the United States has reserved its position because of the Senate refusal to ratify the Geneva Gas Protocol. This makes some sense until one remembers that a prohibition of bacteriological warfare was carried over in the 1940 manual, which came out some years subsequent to the 1925 Geneva Gas Protocol and the United States Senate's rejection thereof.

Some doubt as to the Army's position concerning the existence of a customary rule is felt, however, for the words that the United States is not prohibited from use by treaty do not assert expressly the absence of a customary rule restricting the employment of gas and biological methods. In the case of atomic and incendiary weapons the manual is positive, stating that their use violates no rule of international law.

The 1955 United States Law of Naval Warfare does not clarify the issue when it states that although the use of poisonous or asphyxiating gases and bacteriological methods has been frequently condemned by states, including the United States, it remains doubtful that

in the absence of a specific restriction established by a treaty, a state legally is prohibited at present from resorting to their use. However, it is clear that the use of poisonous gas or bacteriological weapons may be considered justified against an enemy who first resorts to the use of these weapons.[170]

A note to this paragraph goes on to say, "It is difficult to hold that the use of these weapons is prohibited to all states according to customary international law."[171]

It will be remembered that the General Board of the Navy at the time of the Washington Conference had condemned the use of all gases as violative of international law.[172] The Navy had retreated from this position in 1935 when the Naval War College would find only those gases which cause unnecessary suffering banned and would exclude tear gas from the prohibition.[173] Now in 1955 the Navy points out that it is difficult to hold that *poisonous* or *asphyxiating* gases or bacteriological methods are prohibited according to customary international law.

Note should also be taken of the positive assertion by the Naval Manual that poisonous gases as well as biological weapons are justified against an enemy who makes first use of them. Retaliation or reprisals with gas has generally been admitted, but retaliation or reprisals by biological means has been questioned on the ground that the use of such means would affect everybody, combatants and noncombatants, and that they were to be considered as too revolting and foul to use.[174]

In the years following World War I certain Presidents of the United States[175] and their civilian advisers evinced a determination to abolish gas as a weapon, but the impression is gained from a reading of statements and documents of the period that there was no real belief that a customary prohibition had developed. The abolition was sought by treaty, as evidenced by the antigas treaty of the 1922 Washington Conference.[176] Again at the 1925 Conference for the Supervision of the International Trade in Arms and Ammunition in Implements of War, the Department of State sought to prohibit international trade in asphyxiating gas by treaty provision. Its real desire here was to prohibit the use of gas in war.[177] This would signify no customary rule; but again there is contradiction, for the instructions of the department declared that the United States and other governments are committed to the principle that gas should not be used in war. If governments are committed to a principle that a weapon is not to be used, and if they believe that it is not to be used because legally prohibited, then an *opinio juris* necessary to support a customary rule is present. That the United States delegate was convinced of the existence of a binding customary rule barring biological warfare is manifest in his strongly censorious terminology to the effect that biological warfare was so revolting and foul as to meet with the condemnation of all civilized nations.[178]

Despite the negative attitude of the Senate in failing to ratify the Geneva Protocol resulting from this conference, the United States continued to participate in subsequent League of Nations proceedings which would ban the use of chemical and incendiary weapons in war, except as reprisals, and would prohibit wartime use of bacteriological weapons absolutely. Moreover, preparations for warfare with these agents were to be forbidden.[179] The United States delegate did at one point during these proceedings indicate disagreement with a rule barring the use of gases causing no real suffering or permanent disability.[180] Here again is a shift from the viewpoint held by the preceding naval report, by General Pershing, and by the Advisory Committee at the time of the Washington Conference. This viewpoint denounced all gases and made no attempt to select certain types which would be prohibited while others would be permitted.

President Roosevelt was most hostile to gas warfare and expressed his opposition forcefully in a statement in 1937 which, while recognizing the "defensive necessities" which demanded United States study of the use of chemicals, went on to say that "[i]t has been and is the policy of this Government to do everything in its power to outlaw the use of chemicals in warfare. Such use is inhuman and contrary to what modern civilization should stand for."[181]

When World War II commenced there was some thought that it would be advisable for the United States to declare its intention to abide by the Geneva Protocol. The secretary of war advised against it on the ground that the deterrent to enemy use of gas would be fear of United States retaliation and not declarations. No declaration was made.[182] The basic United States policy, however, was set forth later by President Roosevelt, who called poisonous or noxious gases inhumane and barbarous and made it clear that the United States was committed to making no first use of these agents. He stated:

Use of such weapons has been outlawed by the general opinion of civilized mankind. This country has not used them, and I hope that we never will be compelled to use them. I state categorically that we shall under no circumstances resort to the use of such weapons unless they are *first used* by our enemies.[183] [Italics supplied]

There was some attempt to change the policy during World War II so as to permit use of gas against the Japanese, where tactical considerations would have permitted its effective employment. In the end, however, fear of the reaction of hostile world opinion, particularly in the light of President Roosevelt's strong condemnation, prevented a change of policy,[184] and with the use of the atomic bomb against Japan and the consequent Japanese surrender the question became no longer relevant.

One can deduce from President Roosevelt's words a belief in a rule of customary international law prohibiting any use of poisonous or toxic gases except as reprisals against a previous and hence illegal use by the enemy. Words declaring that such weapons had been outlawed by the general opinion of civilized mankind would be some indication that outlawry had become a part of the law of civilized nations. Although the general opinion of civilized mankind is not to be considered a source or law-creating process of international law, still it would seem permissible to infer that a general opinion of civilized mankind would be evidence of an *opinio juris* of civilized states, inasmuch as the civilized mankind of civilized states would be influential in forming the conviction of states.

President Roosevelt's exception to the ban would be after first use by the enemy. This appears to be a recognition of the right of reprisal against an illegal use of such weapons and expresses a conviction that a first use by the United States or any other nation would be violative of a rule of law.

The communist charges of United States use of biological warfare in the Korean war brought forth statements by United States officialdom relating to biological warfare and chemical warfare as well. The United States commenced research in biological warfare in 1941. This nation was thus a Johnny-come-lately, for Germany, Russia, and Japan are reported to have started their investigations on the subject in the 1930s. Once started, however, the United States and its Allies were soon prepared for retaliation if the enemy had made use of biological agents during the war.[185] Apparently no nation resorted to such methods during World War II, but there was discussion among United States officials as to such use. Admiral Leahy mentions a conversation with President Roosevelt wherein the admiral expressed the opinion that the use of germs and poison would "violate every Christian ethic . . . and all of the known laws of war."[186]

The United States course of action with reference to the communist charges of use of biological warfare in Korea has been said to signify a United States conviction that an international customary rule did ban biological warfare. Here the United States, in answer to the Soviet charges, did not assert a legal right to use biological weapons, which it could have done if no customary rule existed, for it was not bound by treaty on the matter. On the contrary, the United States representatives, after stating the abhorrence felt by public opinion in the United States and the rest of the free world at the thought of use of these weapons, categorically denied that the United States had resorted to such weapons in conflict.[187] The failure of the United States to adhere to the Geneva Protocol was excused because the protocol was said to be a paper guarantee ineffective in its prohibition, since enforcement provisions were lacking. Greenspan, after taking note of the United States denial, concludes: "Obviously quite apart from treaty obligations, bacteriological warfare is regarded as a disgraceful and impermissible weapon, whose proven use would bring down on the user the merited obloquy of mankind."[188] And O'Brien declares that

it would have been quite easy to answer the Communist BW charges with a simple denial of their truth, and a reiteration of the position that the United States would be legally free to use BW if it wanted to do so. But such a response would have brought down a storm of adverse criticism on the United States as the Communists well knew.[189]

Neinast disagrees with any conclusion that the failure of the United States to assert a legal right to use biological warfare in Korea manifests a customary rule forbidding such use. He first points out that since the discussions were largely of a propaganda nature, it becomes difficult to attribute to them any legal significance. After examining the statements of the United States, he then reaches the opinion that the United States position was to deny and disprove false charges and to seek to advance the cause for the creation of a really effective prohibition of all weapons of mass destruction, with adequate controls and inspection. Moreover, until such effective prohibition was forthcoming the United States would not renounce the use of biological agents.[190]

It is difficult to judge the United States conviction as to customary rule in this case. But there is something to be said of the fact that the United States, being chary of the adverse reaction of world opinion, would have been hesitant to come forth and exert a right to use these weapons. It may be that a bow to public opinion was made because it was expedient to do so or because a moral obligation was felt, or it may be that the conviction had come into being that a legal obligation against use had developed.

A 1952 statement of Ambassador Benjamin V. Cohen, Deputy United States Representative, in the Disarmament Commission on the Elimination of Germ Warfare does nothing to clear up his country's way of thinking. He declared: "The United States as a member of the United Nations had committed itself, as have all other members, to refrain from not only the use of poisonous gas and the use of germ warfare but the use of force of any kind contrary to the law of the charter."[191] This statement gives us no clue as to the United States stand on the legality of chemical or biological weapons. It simply expresses that force and weapons are forbidden under the charter. One permissible use of force under the charter is in the exercise of the right of individual and collective self-defense. Query: where such force may be legitimately used, can resort be legally had to chemical and biological weapons, or are they barred by a customary international rule as forbidden weapons even when force and other types of weapons may be legitimate? To add to the confusion, one need but look at the following statement by Secretary of State Dean Acheson, also made in 1952: "We will not commit aggression with chemical weapons or biological weapons, which we have been falsely and slanderously accused of using."[192]

Since aggression itself is forbidden at international law, it would be assumed that the United States would not commit aggression with any kind of weapons—chemical, biological, or conventional. Moreover, this statement does not shed any light on whether the United States would use chemical or biological methods in cases where the United States would not be committing aggression.

Later in the 1950s, in certain military quarters at least, there began to be reports and statements intimating a belief that a change in United States policy had come about or was needed. A civilian committee on Chemical Corps Mission and Strategy came up with a recommendation for the development of chemical agents for their deterrent effect in war, and for their actual use in war as concepts and policies may change. This could be a recommendation of a shift from the no first use policy. Following this report the United States Army secretary called for its implementation.[193]

Fearing that the Department of Defense was seeking to relax or change United States policy on the use of chemical and biological agents in war, United States Representative Robert W. Kastenmeier introduced into the House of Representatives a resolution which would call for a reaffirmation of "the longstanding policy of the United States that in the event of war the United States shall under no circumstances resort to the use of poisonous or obnoxious gases unless they are first used by our enemies."[194]

In 1960 President Eisenhower was questioned as to the truth of Representative Kastenmeier's suggestion that there might be a change in the traditional policy of the United States of no first use of chemical or biological warfare, inasmuch as Army people had indicated a belief "that maybe we should change our policy and use these first, either in a large war or even in a small war." President Eisenhower responded: "I will say this: no such official suggestion has been made to me and so far as my own instinct is concerned, is to not start such a thing as that first."[195]

The House resolution failed. There was opposition including that of the Defense Department and the Department of State. The spokesman for the former said:

Similar declarations might apply with equal pertinency across the entire weapons spectrum, and no reason is perceived why biological and chemical weapons should be singled out for this special declaration. . . . Effective controls on biological and chemical weapons, as in the case of other weapons, may have to await international agreements with necessary safeguards.

It must be considered that biological and chemical weapons might be used with great effect in a future conflict. Available evidence indicates that other countries including Communist regimes, are actively pursuing programs in this field. Moreover, as research continues, there is increasing evidence that some forms of these weapons, differing from previous forms could be effectively used for defensive purposes with minimum collateral consequences.[196]

The Department of State repeated Ambassador Cohen's ideas discussed earlier and went on to say that the United States must recognize its responsibility to free world security which would "involve, among other things, the maintenance of an adequate defensive posture across the entire weapons spectrum, which would allow us to defend against acts of aggression. . . ."[197]

Despite President Eisenhower's earlier statement that there had been no change in United States policy, these statements indicate that the United States was contemplating possible use of these methods in future conflict—even first use, although albeit defensively against aggression. In any event, the words can hardly be taken to show any belief in a customary rule of international law forbidding use of these methods. Thus, the customary international legal status of chemical and biological weapons as gleaned from official civilian and military United States statements over the years from the end of World War I to 1960 is confused and contradictory. The degree of conviction or lack of conviction that a legally binding obligation exists appears to be ever changing, and the words used are seldom clear-cut or demonstrative of a firmly held position.

Official statements on chemical and biological warfare have also arisen as a result of the Vietnam conflict and the use in that conflict of certain chemical agents—herbicides and tear gas. Here again one feels a sort of Alice-in-Wonderland quality about the terminology used. It was pointed out, for example, by William C. Foster of the United States before the First Committee of the General Assembly that the Geneva Protocol was "intended to prohibit the use in war of deadly gases such as mustard gas and phosgene." And although the United States had not ratified the Geneva Protocol, still the fundamental line or policy of the United States was that the use of weapons of gas warfare would not be resorted to under any circumstances unless they were first used by the enemies of the United States.[198] A short time earlier Deputy Defense Secretary Cyrus Vance had stated in a letter that "national policy does proscribe the first use of lethal gas."[199] Mr. Foster, however, in his statement distinguished the first use of nonlethal gases like tear gas and herbicides, for he went on to say that no distinction could be made with respect to the use of tear gas by national authorities for the purpose of riot control against their own nationals which was "not contrary to accepted norms of behavior and use of the same gas in Vietnam for humanitarian purposes, *i.e.,* to save life and not destroy it." Such use did not violate any norm of international conduct and law, nor did the use of chemicals in Vietnam to clear weeds and control vegetation. He also pointed to the possession by the Viet Cong of tear gas and tear grenades and their use against forces of the United States.[200]

Secretary of State Rusk took the same view. He stated:

We are not embarking upon gas warfare in Viet-Nam. There has been no policy decision to engage in gas warfare in Viet-Nam. We are not talking about agents or weapons that are associated with gas warfare in the military arsenals of many countries. We are not talking about gas that is prohibited by the Geneva Convention of 1925 or *any other understandings about the use of gas.* [Italics supplied][201]

As in the case of the charges of United States use of biological agents in the Korean conflict, the United States again failed to assert that it had a legal right to use gas merely because it had not ratified the Geneva Protocol. On the contrary, the United States *excepted* the employment of tear gas and herbicides from any prohibitory rule or norm of international law. The fact that the United States insisted that these agents were exceptions to the rule and hence could be legitimately employed would seem to imply a conviction that a first use of lethal or severely injurious gases (which is, of course, against established United States policy) would be prohibited by a rule of international law, which would have to be a *customary* rule, since the United States is not bound by any of the prohibitory treaties.

This would seem to be borne out by the words of Secretary of State Rusk when he pointed out that he was not referring to gas prohibited by the Geneva Convention or "any other understandings about the use of gas." Again, since the United States is not a party to the Geneva Protocol he could only be talking, insofar as the United States is concerned, about a customary prohibitory rule if by "understandings" he meant legal understandings.

It would then appear permissible to assume that certain gases—lethal or severely injurious ones—are prohibited by the Geneva Convention or other understandings, i.e., customary international law. In any event, it should be stressed that the existence of a customary international rule barring the first use in war of lethal or severely injurious chemical agents has not been denied. It should be noted that Secretary Rusk would place the psychochemical gases within a military classification which he would consider forbidden. It is difficult to follow his reasoning here if these gases are incapacitants of a temporarily disabling nature only. If they are of such nature, they would appear to fall under the same category as tear or riot control gases for purposes of international law.

Some further uncertainty as to the United States position was engendered by the United States statements and actions concerning the United Nations General Assembly resolutions of December 5, 1966, which called on all nations to observe the principles and objectives of the Geneva Protocol as to the prohibition of the use in war of asphyxiating, poisonous, or other gases and of bacteriological methods in warfare. The United States supported this resolution, after the United States representative in a statement pointed out that it did not apply to tear gas and herbicides, as "it would be unreasonable to contend that any rule of international law" prohibits such use. A statement was also made that the United States had "always observed the principles and objectives which the Protocol sought to achieve," and "had repeatedly endeavored to find adequate means to attain these objectives."[202]

It would scarcely be daring to assume that support of the resolution calling for observation of the principles of the Geneva Protocol and statements that the United States had observed such principles could be considered as tantamount to a conviction that observance is believed to be necessary—legally necessary, in that a legal obligation has been created. Since the United States is not a party to the protocol, the creation would have to come about by a customary rule. At any rate, the United States must feel some compulsion to observe. If this is not a legal compulsion, the observation is occasioned by a moral compulsion or by military or diplomatic expediency. Deputy Secretary of Defense Vance spoke of "*de facto* limitations" on United States use of chemical and biological weapons. Ambassador Goldberg, however, spoke of legal limitations in commenting on the use of gases in the Yemen conflict, for he admitted that the use of poison gas was contrary to international law. It can be reasoned that he was speaking of customary international law, for he made the statement in relation to the United States position, and this would refer to a customary prohibition, since the United States is not a party to a conventional prohibition. Moreover, if Yemen is not bound by the Geneva Protocol, as is possibly the case since she has not adhered to it, then a use of gas in that conflict would perforce have to violate a customary norm to be considered illegal.[203] About all that can be said is that the United States seems to fear to deny the existence of a rule forbidding dangerous chemical or biological agents; but its practice of never having resorted to the use of biological agents and of not having resorted to lethal or severely injurious chemical agents since World War I, taken together with these recent statements (some of which are admittedly obfuscatory and contradictory), is indicative of a prohibitory customary rule against first use of biological agents and first use of anti-personnel chemical agents of a lethal or severely injurious nature.

An American position was again propounded on November 25, 1969, by President Nixon, who reaffirmed support for the principles and objectives of the Geneva Protocol and renounced the first use of lethal chemical weapons. To this degree the statement was consistent with previous United States policy; but the President went on to extend this renunciation to the first use of incapacitating chemical weapons. Excepted, however, was the use of tear gas or riot control agents and chemical defoliants. Either from the standpoint of customary law or from various interpretations of the Geneva Protocol, it is difficult to sustain legally the inclusion of incapacitants and the exclusion of tear gas and plant defoliants. As we have seen, either the Geneva Protocol condemns all chemical agents or it condemns lethal or severely injurious agents only. Moreover, if incapacitants are neither lethal nor severely injurious they would not appear to fall within the customary ban of international law or automatically within the unnecessary suffering principle, upon which the customary prohibition is often based.

As to biological weapons, the President renounced all use of these by the United States even in retaliation in kind. Previously, United States policy had apparently barred only first use of these weapons. There was an implication of an intention to use them in retaliation if necessary. President Nixon announced not only renunciation of use but an intention to dispose of existing United States stocks of biological agents. The United States, he said, would confine its research in the biological area to defensive measures to counteract possible biological attacks—measures such as immunization and other public health activities.

The President's statement does not seem to represent an *opinio juris* as to customary international law. Rather, it is a unilateral statement of present United States policy. The call for ratification by the United States of the Geneva Protocol, and for United States association with the draft convention of the United Kingdom which would prohibit use of biological methods of warfare and their acquisition once necessary safeguards are included, emphasizes the need for conventional law to assure legal control.[204]

THE UNITED KINGDOM

As early as the Crimean War the British government indicated its belief that the use of gas in war is illegal. In 1855 a British general proposed that vapors of sulphur dioxide could be wafted toward Sebastopol during the siege of that city. Its effects, he declared, would be instantaneous and highly deleterious to the Russians. After due consideration, the War Ministry rejected the proposal, declaring that "an operation of this nature would contravene the laws of civilized warfare."[205]

It might be thought that the failure of the United Kingdom to sign the Hague Gas Declaration showed a belief that no rule of international law should or did exist on the subject; but, in reality, its refusal to agree at that time was based upon the refusal of the United States to adhere to the declaration, thereby destroying the unanimity in acceptance which the British believed to be necessary. The United Kingdom did later, at the time of the 1907 Hague Conference, adhere to this declaration, thus becoming bound by it.[206]

During World War I the British position was ambivalent. British words manifested a belief that the German use of gas violated international law. Britain failed, however, to protest the first big German cloud gas attack. Technically this attack was outside the scope of the Hague Declaration, which prohibited projectiles with the sole purpose of diffusing gas. Britain did protest the later German use of shells or projectiles emitting gas. It was said that such use violated the laws of civilized warfare. Despite the failure to protest, certain British opinion was convinced that the earlier cloud gas attack also violated the laws of civilized warfare, on the ground that gas caused superfluous injury or unnecessary suffering.[207]

That the British regarded gas, whether from shells in violation of the Hague Declaration or as generated in clouds from cylinders or otherwise, as a breach of international law is evidenced also by the fact that British words expressed the thought that British retaliation in kind was a legitimate reprisal against an illegal use of gas by the enemy. British retaliation with gas, however, may have gone beyond the rules of proportionality and therefore beyond legal reprisals. About the best that can be said is that when Germany resorted to gas warfare legal restraints, if any existed with respect to such warfare, did not make themselves felt.[208] One can hardly contend that the British or the other participants in the warfare believed that gas warfare was forbidden by customary or conventional international law. Hyde states that the Allied use of gas

may have been attributable at the outset, to a design of retaliation, [b]ut the employment of gases perfected in England and America proved of so great offensive value as to convince military opinion in those countries that such instrumentalities were generally desirable for use in land warfare.[209]

Although the British representative on the subcommittee of technical experts of the Washington Conference agreed with the United States representative that gas warfare should not be forbidden, the British did later agree to the treaty which emerged from the conference and which sought to prohibit poisonous or other gases.[210] They also subsequently became a party to the Geneva Gas Protocol of 1925 which condemned the use of gases in war as well as bacteriological methods. As we have seen, this agreement has created something of a quandary as to the outlawry of chemical and biological warfare, and this quandary remains with respect to the British attitude. The treaty might be thought from its language to be a codification of an existing rule of customary international law. It speaks of the uses of gases in warfare as condemned by "the general opinion of the civilized world."[211] It does not say the same thing as to bacteriological methods, but British manuals of military law had previously provided that germ warfare was prohibited by the antipoison article 23a of the Hague Regulations,[212] which was a codification of international law. Thus, it could be contended that the British were convinced of the existence of a customary rule of international law barring both methods.

The force of such a contention is largely nullified, however, by the fact that the Geneva Protocol itself goes on to say that its purpose is to create a prohibition universally accepted. If a customary rule was thought to be in being, it would already be accepted. Further, the parties were bound as between themselves only, and Britain added a reservation confining the binding effect on the British government to states which have ratified or acceded to the protocol. Such reservation also calls for the cessation of obligation as to any state failing to respect its terms.[213] Couple this language with that of the British manual, which declares that the Geneva Protocol and certain other agreements are "strictly speaking binding only on the states which have agreed to them and have not subsequently denounced them,"[214] and one gets an impression that a customary prohibitory rule is not in existence, but that states, if bound, are bound only by the treaty law of the Geneva Protocol. This is further borne out by a 1933 British draft convention to the Conference for the Reduction and Limitation of Armaments, wherein it was stated that a provision banning the use of chemicals, incendiary, or bacterial methods in war is accepted as an established rule of international law.[215] This would appear superfluous if such a provision had already been accepted, and it seems to state that the provision would be accepted as a rule only by those ratifying the draft treaty.

That the Geneva Protocol and the British reservation to it created the only British rights and duties with respect to gas warfare can further be surmised from the Churchillian policy of what Kelly calls "disproportionate reprisal" during World War II.[216] Churchill promised to carry on gas warfare "on the largest possible scale" against Germany if Germany resorted to the use of gas.[217] A disproportionate or unlimited use would not be a valid reprisal at international law and hence would be violative of a universal customary rule of war if there were such a rule. It can be argued, however, that such use would be permitted under the British reservation to the protocol, which obligated the British only if the enemy respected the protocol's ban.

The British attitude in relation to a customary rule forbidding chemical and biological warfare remains difficult to pin down in the years following World War II. The British government has continued preparation for and study of chemical as well as biological methods of warfare. Since Britain is a party to the Geneva Protocol, it is said that such preparation is to provide defense against the use of such methods by other countries.[218] Some writers point to continued preparation for these methods of warfare as evidence of there being no customary prohibition.[219] This hardly follows, for even if there is a norm, reprisals may well be permitted and preparation so as to be capable of such retaliation would be necessary. Insofar as Britain is concerned, however, British preparedness means very little with respect to the existence or nonexistence of a customary rule, inasmuch as Britain has accepted the Geneva Protocol with a reservation which permits reprisals, and possibly even disproportionate ones. It is the treaty law which appears to be what Britain regards as controlling. This is again emphasized by the 1969 British draft treaty prohibiting use of biological methods of warfare.

Statements made by British representatives before United Nations organs are not too helpful in reaching a conclusion as to a British *opinio juris*. For example when, in 1952, the Security Council considered the "Question of an appeal to States to accede to and ratify the Geneva Protocol of 1925 for the prohibition of the use of bacterial weapons," the British representative stressed the Geneva Protocol as expressive of the prohibitory rule and spoke of "political, legal and moral obligations assumed by states under the agreement."[220] In what the British representative said there appears to be some deprecation of the protocol as a restraint on the methods of warfare prohibited by it, inasmuch as it was said to rest only upon the good faith of the governments party to it. Something more was believed needed, according to the British representative, and that was international control to assure that the protocol's terms would be carried out. Since international law, customary or treaty, is largely based on the good faith of states, the value of all international prohibitory rules in and of themselves was thus questioned.

FRANCE

The French attitude, as garnered from certain evidence, is largely that obligation to refrain from the use of chemical and biological weapons in war rests upon treaty law, not customary international law. France was a party to the 1899 Hague Gas Declaration, which forbade the use of projectiles having as sole object the diffusion of *asphyxiating* or *deleterious* gases.[221] Thus, she early became obligated to a limited degree by international convention. Despite this treaty obligation the French did, prior to World War I, develop a cartridge filled with a tear gas which was employed to quell civil disturbances at home, but which was reported to have been used in the war prior to the first German cloud gas attack.[222] The French claimed that use of this shell in war would not violate the terms of the declaration because the shell did not contain an asphyxiating or deleterious gas.[223] If the French did actually resort to this weapon, it can also be assumed that they believed no customary rule of international law barred tear gas either. When France later, along with Britain, used lethal gases, such widespread use might have been considered reprisals, if carried out on a limited and proportionate scale, a fact which certain authors have refuted. In any event, French language would denote that the only binding international rule was the treaty rule. This is borne out in a reply to a Red Cross protest[224] against the employment of asphyxiating gases by the belligerents. A French statement on behalf of the Allies declared, in speaking of the use of poisonous gases, that the Allied Powers had believed at the beginning of the war that civilized nations would not employ such cruel methods of warfare, since these nations "had through international conventions solemnly engaged not to employ such instrumentalities."[225] Stress here is placed upon international agreements as the basis of obligation.

Following World War I, France was amenable to the creation of a gas prohibition by treaty. France did fail to ratify such a treaty prepared by the 1922 Washington Conference, but not because she was not opposed to gas.[226] Her opposition was to those portions of the treaty dealing with submarine warfare.[227] Later, at the Conference for the Supervision of the International Trade in Arms and Ammunition and in Implements of War, the French representative emphasized again that duty to forbear the use of gas rested on treaty. M. Paul-Boncour declared in this connection:

The military regulations of France on the conduct of the larger units begin with these words: "Faithful to the *international undertakings which France has signed,* the French Government will, on the outbreak of war, and in agreement with the allies, endeavour to obtain from enemy Governments an undertaking that they will not employ gas as a weapon of war." [Italics supplied][228]

A French military representative repeated this idea at the conference by stating:

The Government of France had proclaimed in all its military regulations its desire to observe *international agreements* concerning recourse to chemical warfare. The French delegation accordingly felt the utmost sympathy for any proposal calculated to achieve the object on which all the delegates appeared to be agreed. [Italics supplied][229]

Here again obligation appears to come from treaty law only, for French military men are instructed to observe international treaties as to any French recourse to chemical warfare. France signed and ratified the Geneva Protocol of 1925 which resulted from the conference and which prohibited not only gas, but also bacteriological methods of warfare. The French representative expressed skepticism as to the effectiveness even of a treaty ban in the absence of effective sanctions. He was of the opinion that international morality was not sufficient in case of war to assure respect for the engagement contracted by the terms of the protocol. If he doubted the restraining influence of an express ban by international agreement, he could hardly believe that a rule of customary international law existed.[230] The French skepticism is reflected in the French ratification, which made the protocol binding upon France only as to other states parties to it; and even as to them its binding effect was to cease as to an enemy state or the allies of an enemy in case they failed to respect its obligations.[231] The emphasis is placed entirely upon the protocol as the creator of French obligations.

At the beginning of World War II, France joined with the United Kingdom in a declaration reaffirming determination to abide by the Geneva Protocol, but only if the enemy did likewise.[232] Customary international law was not mentioned.

France had opportunity to speak again on the subject during the 1952 United Nations Security Council considerations on the topic, "Question of an appeal to the States to accede to and ratify the Geneva Protocol of 1925 for the prohibition of the use of bacteriological weapons."[233]

Here the French representative, in speaking of the reservations of France to the protocol, stated:

These reservations . . . merely constitute the explicit formulation of the implicit conditions for carrying out any bilateral or multilateral engagements entered into in good faith. Such engagements can have validity only in relation to contracting parties which themselves respect them. The violation of an engagement by one of its signatories sets free the obligations which they may have contracted in relation to that signatory.[234]

This language is concerned only with treaty law, contract law. It is this type of law which is binding and which if breached will leave the other party free to act. Complete and unlimited freedom to act would not ensue from a breach of an obligation imposed by a rule of customary international law. That no such customary rule is in being is further indicated by the French representative's later words where he declared that the Protocol is binding only "on those states which have signed and ratified it."[235] Some confusion is engendered, however, by subsequent words, for he speaks of states which have abstained from becoming parties to the protocol as not having "challenged its principles or disputed its moral values." Although failure to dispute or challenge moral values does not necessarily imply a belief in a customary rule or that a customary rule has arisen, still a failure to challenge the principles of the protocol could well show a belief, an *opinio juris*, that those principles are accepted implicitly as a rule of customary law.

A final French statement was made before the General Assembly's First Committee concerning a draft resolution which would, among other things, demand compliance by *all* states with the Geneva Protocol, and would condemn any action aimed at the use of chemical and biological warfare.[236] The French representative, in speaking to the draft resolution, could not agree that the protocol could be extended to condemn chemical weapons in general, for this could not be derived from the text.[237] This attitude is somewhat reminiscent of the French viewpoint expressed at the time of World War I and prior to the coming into existence of the protocol, to the effect that the Hague Gas Declaration which forbade asphyxiating or deleterious gases did not apply to tear gas.[238] On the other hand, as noted previously, French opinion, expressed in 1931 before the League of Nations Disarmament Conference, was that the language of the Geneva Protocol covered at least all toxic gases, whether those like tear gas causing temporary irritation or those causing serious or fatal lesions.[239] There appears to be some ambivalence here. Aside from this, however, the French delegate's language is directed strictly to the protocol and its meaning, and he largely denies the existence of any French *opinio juris* of a customary rule when he queries: "How could states which had not signed or ratified a treaty be required to undertake to observe its provisions, as laid down in operative paragraph 1 of the draft resolution?"[240]

GERMANY

Manifestations of a German conviction concerning the existence of a customary rule of international law denying a right to use chemical-biological weapons in war are scarce. As a party to the Hague Gas Declaration, Germany did seek to remove her use of gas in World War I from the provisions of that instrument on the ground that she was not employing projectiles with the sole object of diffusing gas. Germany also sought to justify her action legally on the ground of reprisals and on the ground that customary international law did not propound a restraining rule.[241] There is a contradiction here, for Germany's justifying her action as reprisals indicates the existence of a rule subject to an exception, namely, the taking of reprisals. These differing and contradictory positions which were advanced thus make a conclusion as to the German position hard to reach.

As a result of World War I, Germany was specifically forbidden by treaty to use gas.[242] She also became a party to the Geneva Protocol, ratifying that instrument without reservations. A statement by the German representative at the conference where the protocol was drafted may be some slight indication that Germany believed a treaty rule to be necessary to control and regulate. He declared that Germany would adhere without reservations "to any international regulations adopted in order to bring about the disappearance of chemical warfare."[243] It can be argued that if a rule had arisen through custom, an express treaty rule would not have to be adopted to effect the disappearance.

Since Germany was bound by the protocol, her non-use of gas during World War II can, insofar as legal grounds are concerned, be attributed to the obligations imposed by the instrument. At the beginning of that war, Germany made it known that she would observe the protocol, subject to reciprocity.[244] Inasmuch as Germany did not reserve rights to reciprocity in the protocol, either she was taking advantage of the British, French, and Russian reservations with respect to it, or she believed reciprocity to be implied. In any event Germany does rely on the treaty, not customary law; and this appears to be true also as to bacteriological methods, since the West German army manual merely sets forth the prohibition against use of this method contained in the Geneva Protocol.[245]

The Allies by agreement prohibited Germany from producing certain lethal or destructive gases after World War II; and in 1948, when Germany became a party to the Western European collective defense treaty, she agreed not to manufacture chemical or biological weapons and accepted supervision to assure that she did not.[246] Therefore, it becomes obvious that since Germany is bound by international agreements against use and production of such agents, German *opinio juris* as to a customary rule does not make itself felt.

ITALY

As a party to the Hague Gas Declaration of 1899, Italy was in the same legal position concerning the use of gas as her Allies at the time of World War I; i.e., she was prohibited by treaty from employing projectiles with the sole object of diffusing asphyxiating or deleterious gases. During the war however, gas was used on the Austrian-Italian Front by both Austria and Italy, but to a much lesser extent than on the Western and Eastern Fronts.[247] Outside the treaty provisions of the Hague Declaration, there is evidence of an Italian conviction that no rule of international law customary or otherwise obligated nations to refrain from the use of gas in warfare, for as late as 1925 an Italian representative at the Conference for the Supervision of the International Trade in Arms and Ammunition and Implements of War stated unequivocally that "[u]p to the present there could be no guarantee that a country would not have recourse to chemical warfare" and that "international law contained no provision prohibiting the use by countries of gas." Therefore, he thought that "a perfectly clear undertaking by all countries to abandon chemical warfare should be obtained."[248]

Such an undertaking in the form of a treaty, the Geneva Protocol, was forthcoming from the conference and Italy became a party to it without reservation, binding herself against the use of gas as well as bacterial methods in war. As we have seen, the protocol's ban did not prevent the Italians from employing lethal gases in their war against Ethiopia. Italy acknowledged the obligation of the treaty, but sought to justify this use of gas as legitimate reprisals.[249] Thus Italy emphasizes treaty law, not customary international law, as the basis of obligation to refrain from the use of these forbidden methods. This is further borne out by the Italian War Regulations of 1938, which incorporate the prohibitions of the Geneva Protocol and make the observance of these provisions dependent upon treaties or reciprocity.[250] Later evidence from which Italian conviction can be garnered appears to be wanting.

UNION OF SOVIET SOCIALIST REPUBLICS

Imperial Russia was a strong exponent of the treaty method for the regulation of arms, and, as we have seen, sponsored at the turn of the century a series of international conferences which culminated in conventions with respect to arms regulations. Specifically as to chemical warfare, the Hague Gas Declaration of 1899, which was presented to the Hague Conference of that year by the Russian representative, was accepted by Russia;[251] and thus, at the time of World War I, Russia like most of the other belligerents was bound by this treaty rule. She therefore stood in the same position as her Allies when Germany resorted to the use of gas against her on the Eastern Front. Like her Allies, Russia made no protest against this German use; but thereafter she in turn waged gas warfare against the enemy.

Little evidence of a Soviet attitude toward chemical warfare can be found in the years following World War I and the Russian Revolution. The Soviets were not present at the 1925 Conference for the Supervision of the International Trade in Arms and Ammunition and in Implements of War; but later, in 1928, they did become a party to the Geneva Protocol which emerged from that conference. As a result the Soviet Union was bound by international convention to refrain from gas and also bacteriological warfare as proscribed by the treaty. Soviet statements at the time point to conventional law, not customary law, as the basis of obligation. This would appear to be exemplified by the Soviet Union's reservation to the protocol wherein it was stipulated that the Soviet Union was obligated only as to other states parties to the Protocol, and further that the protocol would cease to be binding upon the Soviet Union with regard to any enemy state whose armed forces or whose allies *de jure* or in fact did not respect the protocol's prohibitions.[252] If it had been believed that a customary rule did exist over and above the treaty rule, obligation would not have been regarded as existing only as to contracting states. Furthermore, if such were the case obligation would not cease as to hostile states and their allies not respecting the rule.[253]

At the League of Nations Disarmament Conference the Soviet representative on various occasions called upon governments to ratify the Geneva Protocol and spoke of proposals for prohibiting chemical warfare.[254] If chemical warfare had been thought by the Soviets to have already been prohibited by a customary rule, it is hardly likely that they would have stressed ratification and thereby acceptance of the rule by all states, and further they would hardly have called so vehemently for proposals to prohibit if customary international law already prohibited.

The Soviet attitude toward customary international law itself has ranged from lukewarm acceptance to downright hostility. It is quite clear that international treaties are regarded by Soviet authorities as the fundamental or primary source of international law. Tunkin states: "In contemporary conditions the *principal* means of creating norms of international law is a treaty. This is the point of view held by the great majority, if not by all, of the Soviet authors who have treated this subject." (Italics supplied)[255] Custom, on the other hand, has been looked upon by many Soviet jurists as an unreliable source of international law, particularly international customary law which might be rooted in pre-Soviet days or which is maintained by the non-Soviet world. Vyshinski, for example, set forth the view that the treaty was the basic and the only valid source of international law.[256] Other jurists have adopted international custom as a second source of international law, but custom is definitely regarded with suspicion and is relegated to a less important position.[257]

The Soviet Union did not employ gas in the Russo-Finnish War or in World War II. She was prepared, however, to engage in chemical and biological warfare in retaliation if the enemy had made use of these weapons. In 1938 Marshal Voroshilov said:

Ten years ago or more the Soviet Union signed a convention abolishing the use of poison gas and bacterial weapons. To that we still adhere, but if our enemies use such methods against us I tell you we are prepared and fully prepared to use them also and to use them against aggressors on their own soil.[258]

In speaking of the Geneva Protocol, to which the Soviet Union adheres, the marshal accepted that instrument as imposing a legal duty upon the Soviets. Because it convicted certain Japanese nationals for use of bacterial weapons during World War II, it might be concluded that the Soviet Union had come to accept a point of view that such methods had come to be banned by customary international law, in the face of the fact that Japan had not ratified the Geneva Protocol. The British manual notes this possibility.[259]

In 1952 the Soviet Union cast some additional doubt on the existence of a customary rule of international law, or at least of one banning the use of bacterial weapons. In discussing bacterial methods of warfare before the Security Council of the United Nations, the Soviet representative stated repeatedly that there was "some difference of opinion among statesmen and public figures in various countries concerning the admissibility of using bacterial weapons."[260] Since this difference of opinion prevailed, and because the continuing production not only of bacterial but also of chemical weapons created a threat to international peace and security, it became, in the view of the Soviet delegate, requisite "that the United Nations should adopt appropriate measures to prevent the use of such weapons."[261] The measure advanced was the adoption of the Geneva Protocol by the states not yet a party to it.[262]

To state the obvious, the Geneva Protocol can apply only to ratifiers and adherents. It does not apply to non-parties. Any disagreement among statesmen as to the use of chemical or biological methods of warfare must be with respect to use by those who are not parties to the protocol. But they could be bound by customary law, so it becomes necessary to find a customary prohibition. If disagreement prevails among statesmen concerning the admissibility of these methods, it is difficult if not impossible to advance the existence of a customary rule. It follows then that the Soviets would believe that no such rule exists, and as a result it becomes necessary for those not bound by the protocol to accede to it.

It might be noted that the Soviet Union has sought in post-World War II conferences to obtain weapons bans, inclusive of bacterial and chemical weapons, by general declaratory treaties like the Geneva Protocol which merely prohibit the use of such weapons and which do not provide methods of inspection or enforcement. Soviet representatives have stated the belief, for example, that the Geneva Protocol contributed greatly to the non-use of gas in World War II.[263] Despite this faith in prohibitory treaties, doubt as to their effectiveness as a restraining influence has been expressed by Soviet military authority. In 1956 Marshal Zhukov anticipated that a "future war, should it be unleashed, will be characterized by the massive use of air forces, various rocket weapons, and various means of destruction such as atomic, thermonuclear, chemical and bacteriological weapons."[264] Military officials have also stated that in staging a surprise attack such weapons would be of value.[265] If there is little faith in the effectivity of a treaty rule, some doubt would be turned on Russian belief in a customary rule or at least in an effective customary rule.

Ex-Premier Khrushchev, in addressing himself to the problem of chemical and biological warfare at a 1959 meeting of the Pugwash Conference, first emphasized the fact that the military use of chemical and biological agents was prohibited by international agreement—the Geneva Protocol. He did state, however, that these methods had been condemned by mankind, and he concluded with a declaration that the use of chemical and biological weapons "runs counter to humane principles, the rules of international law, and the conscience of all peoples."[266] Here one feels that something more than the Geneva Protocol is involved. The use of these weapons, it was said, runs counter to the principle of humanity. This is a fundamental precept of international law itself over and above treaty law. Rules of international law are also mentioned. Although the treaty rule is a rule of international law, it could only be violated by adherents. Nonadherents could run counter to a customary rule only if one happened to exist. Khrushchev must have been using the term "rules of international law" in a sense broader than mere treaty law. Finally, if the use of these weapons runs counter to the conscience of all peoples and is condemned by mankind then surely such conscience must have made itself felt upon the states in which all peoples dwell, so as to create a customary rule of international law. A Soviet writer, Kozhevnikov, bears this out when he speaks of the Geneva Protocol as expressive "of the legal conscience of all mankind."[267] It can then be deduced from these statements that a Russian *opinio juris* as to a customary rule is present, unless the words were uttered for propaganda effect only.

An ambiguous statement was also made before the General Assembly's First Committee by the Soviet representative in 1966, when that body was considering the Hungarian draft resolution calling upon all nations to accede to the Geneva Protocol. Here it was declared: "Decisive steps were . . . required to prohibit the use of weapons of mass destruction, such as chemical and bacteriological weapons . . ."[268] in view of the fact that the United States was using chemical weapons in Vietnam. This language could be regarded as indicative of a view that no customary rule existed and that all nations including the United States should adhere to the Geneva Protocol so that the use of these weapons would be prohibited and legally so by treaty binding upon all states, again inclusive of the United States. However, the Soviet delegate went on to say that the Hungarian draft which deplored the use of chemical and bacteriological weapons was based on generally accepted principles of international law.[269] Consequently either principles or rules of international law apart from treaty would appear to be considered as existing and as binding upon all states. A statement at a later meeting conforms to this thought: the Russian representative at that meeting set forth in a negative way his point that a customary prohibitory norm as to chemical and biological weapons had come to exist by declaring that in sponsoring amendments to the Hungarian draft certain Western Powers were "trying to deny the obvious fact that the Geneva Protocol had created a norm of international law."[270]

Although these Soviet statements tend to be equivocal, a tentative conclusion can be reached that the Soviets have in recent times come to understand that the Geneva Protocol has now become a customary rule of international law, and that it prohibits first military use of all chemical and biological agents. That they consider all such agents to be banned is deduced from the fact that the Soviets have denounced the use not just of lethal or severely injurious chemicals, but also, in relation to the Vietnam situation, of incapacitating or riot control types such as tear gas and antiplant agents such as herbicides. The Soviet Union does not appear to have made exemptions as to certain agents of a less lethal type from the meaning of the language of the Geneva Protocol. That the Russians believe the rule to extend to first use only appears to be shown by the Russian reservations to the Geneva Protocol and by Russian statements at the time of World War II which call attention to the fact that the Soviet Union would resort to such methods if the enemies of the Soviet Union did so.[271]

Some incertitude is felt in reaching this conclusion, for as Taracouzio has pointed out, custom is regarded by the Soviets as an authoritative source "whenever the interests of the Soviets call for this concession."[272]

JAPAN

The Japanese ratified the Hague Gas Declaration of 1899, and by so doing became bound to the limited extent of that treaty to refrain from gas warfare.[273] Whether this treaty inhibited Japan from the employment of gas in the Russo-Japanese War is hard to say. In any event she did not resort to gas in that war, although it has been reported that a British chemist in Japan suggested to the Japanese government that gas be used against the Russian forces.[274] During World War I Japan did not resort to the use of gas in the Pacific area. Kelly points out that the kind of war conducted in this region did not lend itself to gas warfare as did the trench warfare in Europe.[275]

Although Japan was present at the Conference for the Supervision of the International Trade in Arms and Ammunition and in Implements of War and signed the Geneva Protocol of that Conference which would prohibit the use of gases and bacteriological agents, she, like the United States, failed to ratify this convention.[276] Japan, therefore, was not bound by it at the time of her war with China or during World War II. Her fairly well substantiated use of gas in these conflicts[277] could then be considered violative of law only if one concluded that gas methods of war fall within the principles codified by the Hague Regulations prohibiting poison and unnecessary suffering, or the old Hague Gas Declaration of 1899, or a customary rule of international law specifically banning gas. Excluding the Hague Gas Declaration from consideration, the same can be said with respect to bacteriological warfare, the use of which was charged to Japan by the Soviet Union.[278] Unless Japan considered herself a lawbreaker, which is doubtful, it would be concluded that this nation regarded none of these principles or rules as applicable to forbid her use of these agents. Thus there would be indicated a Japanese belief that no customary international rule existed which would preclude her legal use of gas or biological methods.

In the years immediately following World War II, Japan as a defeated nation appeared little concerned with war and weaponry. For example, the postwar Constitution of Japan renounced war and the right of belligerency.[279]

At the time of the United Nations 1966 discussion of the Hungarian draft calling upon nations to accept the Geneva Protocol, the Japanese representative set forth the belief of the Japanese delegation "that in any circumstances of war the use of chemical and bacteriological weapons should be most strictly avoided."[280] These words echo a Japanese position taken before the Bureau of the League of Nations Disarmament Conference in 1932, when the Japanese delegate called for an absolute prohibition of chemical warfare without exception. He stated at the time that "not only defensive material and training but also recourse to the use of chemical weapons should be prohibited even by way of reprisals."[281] This statement could hardly be expressive of an *opinio juris* as to the existence of a customary rule, for Japan at this time was attempting to create a treaty rule to this effect. The 1966 statement of a belief that chemical and bacteriological agents should be avoided in all circumstances might be indicative of a Japanese belief that they should be avoided not only as a matter of policy, but legally as demanded by a customary rule which had come into being. The force of any such argument is somewhat negated inasmuch as the Japanese would not support the Hungarian drafts which indicate rather clearly the thought that the Geneva Protocol has come to be a customary norm.[282] The Japanese supported the amendments to the draft which finally prevailed in the General Assembly's resolution. The resolution straddles the fence by calling for observance "by all states of the principles and objectives of the Protocol" and "condemns all actions contrary to those objectives."[283] While it does not deny a customary rule, neither does this language necessarily express the thought that such a rule exists. The Japanese representative in the 1969 disarmament conference indicated Japan's willingness to ratify the protocol. This would appear to emphasize conventional rather than customary law.[284]

CONCLUSION

The state of customary international legal limitations on the use of chemical and biological methods in war is not easily determined from the practices of states as evidenced by the conduct and the statements of the powers which have resorted to the use of chemical agents or which would appear to be most capable of resort to the use of chemical or biological agents. From the practice of states it can be said that chemical incendiary weapons, including flamethrowers and napalm weapons, and smokes are accepted as legal today. Disagreement does prevail as to the use of other lethal or severely injurious antipersonnel chemical agents. But it would seem that the conclusion can be reached that the practice of almost complete abstention from their use in World War II and the complete abstention from the use of such agents in major conflicts which have occurred since that time, plus the evidence adduced from the recent words of statesmen and national leaders including those of the United States, the most important nation not to have ratified the Geneva Protocol, indicate a belief in the existence of a binding customary norm prohibiting at least the first use of the lethal or severely injurious types of chemical agents. How effective this rule would be in standing up to the challenge of a situation where chemical weapons, for example nerve gas, might be considered decisive is another matter.

In the case of biological agents it is more difficult to reach a conclusion as to a customary legal status from the practice of states. State conduct of abstention can be taken to mean merely abstention because of considerations of doubtful military utility of such agents rather than because of legal conviction. On the other hand, abstention from use if biological means are militarily feasible could well indicate a belief in a customary rule. Moreover, the two superpowers, the United States and the Soviet Union, indicate an *opinio juris* that biological means or at least certain of them are banned by customary international law. Support for this statement is found particularly in the attitude demonstrated by these nations' representatives in relation to the United Nations' General Assembly resolutions of 1966, which called upon all nations to observe the principle and objectives of the Geneva Protocol.

After these determinations have been made, many issues and questions still remain. What, for example, is the status of antipersonnel incapacitating or riot control chemical agents—those of a nonlethal character—which only disable temporarily, or of the antiplant and antimateriel agents? Opinions as to a customary international legal limitation on these agents differ, and the practices of states do not offer a firm basis for conclusion. The same can be said as to biological agents. Finally, the no first use rule is troublesome. Is it applicable to the use of biological agents at all? If it is applicable to both chemical and biological methods, what is its meaning? After first use of chemicals or first use of some other forbidden weapon, to what extent and by what method is retaliation permitted? These and other issues remain unclear as to applicable law from a consideration of the practices of states as bearing upon customary international law and norms emanating therefrom. It therefore becomes necessary to proceed to a consideration of another law-creating source of international law and the law of war, the principles of the law recognized by civilized nations, and to certain secondary sources of international law such as the writings and opinions of jurists, in order to pursue the possible existence of further international legal restrictions on chemical and biological warfare.

CHAPTER SEVEN

GENERAL PRINCIPLES OF LAW RECOGNIZED BY CIVILIZED NATIONS

RELATIONSHIP BETWEEN CUSTOMARY INTERNATIONAL LAW AND GENERAL PRINCIPLES OF LAW RECOGNIZED BY CIVILIZED NATIONS

EVEN THOUGH chemical and biological weapons may not be completely outlawed by treaties or rules of customary law, this does not mean that belligerents are free to utilize such weapons without restriction, for the majority of international jurists agree that there is yet a third law-creating process on the international level which is independent of, although supplementary to, custom and treaty, namely the general principles of law recognized by civilized nations.[1] It is said that these principles are a source of law independent of convention and custom because, in virtue of their rational character, they belong to a common legal fund recognized in *foro domestico* by all civilized nations.[2] Consequently, international law shares with the municipal law of independent states a substructure of basic propositions of a most generalized character, because all systems of law, being a reflection of the interests and needs in a human society, have many legal propositions and fundamental legal policies in common.[3]

Nevertheless, there is dispute whether or not such general principles are in fact law-creating. Some international publicists like Tunkin[4] of the Soviet Union maintain that general principles add nothing to what is already covered by treaties and custom, for these authorities hold that general principles of national law are part of international law *only* to the extent that they have been adopted by states in treaties or recognized in state practice. At the other end of the spectrum are jurists like Verdross[5] of Austria who say that general principles in effect incorporate "natural law" into international law and who even claim that positive rules of international law are invalid if they conflict with natural law. In between these two extremes stand the majority of jurists[6] who do not accept the view that general principles of law recognized by civilized nations incorporate "natural" law in the sense of "ideal" law in international law; nor do they at the same time consider that general principles which have already found concrete expression and recognition in national systems of law must necessarily have had prior recognition in treaties or state practice before they are available for application on an international level. They take the line that general principles recognized in national law constitute a reservoir of basic propositions of a most generalized character which may be referred to in order to complete the system of international law. Accordingly, general principles of law recognized by civilized nations are considered to be a law-creating process in their own right, separate from treaties and custom. A word of caution must be uttered that this does not signify a wholesale borrowing of domestic *rules* based on some sort of census-taking of the law in each state. The selection would be limited to generalized municipal principles applicable to international relations rather than an incorporation of specific rules of municipal law.[7] The principles indicate a legal policy to be applied by analogy to make the international legal system a more viable one. Furthermore, there is no antithesis between general principles and custom. They are concordant elements of the same system, with man as the starting point and the states as the machinery for devising and maintaining a judicial pattern which is necessary if intercourse between nation and nation is to work to man's good.[8]

Is There a Fourth Law-Creating Process in International Law?

DE MARTENS CLAUSE—ITS NATURE AND EFFECT

Although most internationalists limit the law-creating process on the international level to these three sources (treaties, custom, and general principles of law recognized by civilized nations), a few claim there is yet a fourth law-creating process, namely "the general principles of international law."[9] All internationalists recognize that there is a distinction between *general principles of law recognized by civilized nations* and *general principles of international law.*[10] The latter phrase generally denotes what are considered to be particularly important and deep-rooted principles of international law—principles which could be called the "constitutional" principles of international law, such as those surrounding the independence and equality of states or the freedom of the seas. But it is normally accepted that this constitutional type of principle does not have a legal basis different from other principles of international law. The most that the phrase "general principles of international law" implies is that certain principles are well settled and fundamental, but their formal source still comes from customary law, treaty law, or general principles of law recognized by civilized nations.[11] Their legal status is simply that of a customary rule, or a general multilateral treaty rule, or a general principle of law recognized by civilized nations.

Nevertheless, as far as international limitations on weapons of war are concerned, there are some authorities who feel that certain principles of international law are in and of themselves a law-creating process.[12] They base their reasoning on the de Martens clause which appeared in the Preamble to the IV Hague Convention of 1907 Concerning the Laws and Customs of War. This preamble stated:

According to the views of the High Contracting Parties, these provisions, the drafting of which has been inspired by the desire to diminish the evils of war, so far as military requirements permit, are intended to serve as a general rule of conduct for the belligerents, in their mutual relations and in their relations with the inhabitants.

It has not, however, been found possible, at present, to concert stipulations covering all the circumstances which arise in practice.

On the other hand, the High Contracting Parties clearly do not intend that unforeseen cases should, in default of written agreement, be left to the arbitrary opinion of military commanders.

Until a more complete code of laws of war can be drawn up, the High Contracting Parties deem it expedient to declare that, in cases not covered by the rules adopted by them, the inhabitants and the belligerents remain under the protection and governance of the *principles of the law of nations,* derived from the usages established among civilized peoples, *from the laws of humanity,* and from *the dictates of the public conscience.*[13] [Italics added]

Following this language, it is argued that in addition to treaties, custom, and general principles of law recognized by civilized nations, there are two other law-creating sources on the international level, namely (1) principles derived from the laws of humanity and (2) principles derived from the dictates of public conscience.

Those who accept this point of view are of the opinion that the essence of war is that it signifies a breakdown of all order, hence the restraints placed on the conduct of hostilities by the law of war can only have as their purpose the mitigation of human suffering. War may prove completely destructive of all political order—national and international—but the requirements of humanity are alleged to remain imperative and unyielding in a total war, in a limited war, or even in guerrilla warfare. On this basis it is reasoned with respect to the laws of war that certain nonlegal, moral-ethical ideals are converted into legal rules governing weapons and the means of conducting war. It is then deduced that certain new weapons, including chemical and biological weapons, are so inhumane and bestial that the thought of their use is morally abhorrent to all mankind, and they are therefore condemned in conscience by all people. These new weapons would then be automatically outlawed because their use would be so horrible as to constitute (1) a crime against humanity and (2) a violation of the dictates of public conscience. In other words, any resort to such weapons for any reason whatsoever would be inherently criminal as *malum in se.*[14]

If this line of reasoning is correct, then it would seem that at least the lethal and severely injurious chemical weapons, such as the nerve or choking agents as well as others, and such potential biological agents as those which cause anthrax, botulism, glanders, pneumonic plague, to name but a few (all of which are virulent and have a high mortality rate when the infecting organism enters the body via a route which differs drastically from its natural form or when the intensity of the dose concentration has increased the organism's potential capacity for injury or death), would come within the scope of a crime against humanity or would be included within the class of weapons whose use violates the dictates of public conscience and would therefore be *mala in se.*[15]

Nevertheless, most orthodox authorities would question this reasoning. First, they approach the law of war from a completely different point of view, contending that war is not or at least need not and should not be the negation of all order but rather should be acknowledged as a method —a tragic method—for effecting change within the international order. The nations participating in war must accept limitations upon their behavior, not to protect human rights or to mitigate suffering, but to insure that at least the very minimum foundations of international order will be preserved even in war. Without such minimal order, war would degenerate into complete anarchy which could lead to the ultimate destruction of all mankind. This minimal order is derived in part from the general principles of law of all civilized nations. This does not mean that those holding this view are unconcerned with or inimical to humanitarian considerations, but rather they stress that the law of war is primarily aimed at attempting to preserve at least some semblance of international order even in the grim situation of violent conflict. Consequently the distinctly humanitarian purpose of the restraint on weapons and methods is not derived from new and distinctive law-creating sources such as the "laws of humanity" and the "dictates of public conscience," but rather enters the international legal arena as one of the component elements of either customary law or general principles of law of all civilized nations.[16]

As to the "dictates of public conscience," it is argued that this factor cannot be a law-creating source in and of itself in view of the differences in the philosophical and ideological opinions adhered to by the nations of the world. Public conscience, to be a guide, must be formed on the basis of correct information, uncolored by transitory emotions; but the complexity of factors (physical, technical, military, political, legal, etc.) involved in possible resort to severely injurious or lethal chemical weapons or virulent biological weapons is such that it would be impossible to say that any worldwide consensus could be arrived at based absolutely upon correct information and without reference to transitory emotions.[17] Common public conscience today is becoming more, not less, difficult to form. Objective truth has, to some extent, become nationalized. Stone has characterized this trend as follows:

Indeed, increasingly in our century human judgment is being reduced within the insulated chambers of state societies, from the free exercise of the intellectual and moral faculties to the acceptance of the authoritatively promulgated version of the state society.[18]

It is possible for "public conscience" under modern methods of propaganda to be channeled into the changing currents of public opinion. In such a case it could not then become a logical or consistent, let alone an infallible method of establishing the legality or illegality of a certain weapon. For example, the same "public conscience" which tried to outlaw gas in the 1920s was relatively unmoved by indiscriminate submarine warfare or saturation bombing in World War II.[19]

It would be almost impossible to derive universal principles from such a nebulous concept which conceals an unchartable area of discretion, and hence gives an appearance of being too unreliable to bind states legally to a pattern of conduct for the future. For these reasons it is generally not considered to be a separate mode of creating norms of international law. Rather it has been maintained that the phrase "dictates of public conscience" is merely an awkward rephrasing of the *opinio juris* of nations; if so it enters into international law as an element of customary law but not as a component of general principles of law recognized by civilized nations.[20]

As to the principle of humanity, the traditional approach acknowledges that even though it is not a law-creating source in and of itself, it is one of the very vital constituents of the general principles of law recognized by civilized nations, and for that reason it will be discussed in conjunction with other elements included within those principles.

The orthodox position with reference to both of these elements is bolstered by referring to the background and purpose of the de Martens clause. De Martens, one of the Russian delegates at both Hague conferences, drew attention to the fact that although the Hague conventions were codifications of the customary laws of war, they were by no means a complete codification thereof. He suggested that the clause which bears his name be inserted in the preamble to the treaty, to safeguard those rules—most of them derived from customary international law or by the general principles of law recognized by civilized nations—which were not covered in the Hague deliberations. If the principles of humanity or the dictates of the public conscience had led or in the future would lead to the creation of rules of warfare in the form, for instance, of customary law or of general principles of law recognized by civilized nations, such rules were not affected by ratification of the Hague convention on land warfare. The de Martens clause, it is contended, was not meant to establish with binding force the sources of the rules of warfare. Its only purpose was to preserve intact any preexisting rules of warfare, or any later developing rules of warfare, including those relating to weapons or methods of warfare, no matter which of the three law-creating processes brought them into being.[21] Since it was not intended by the parties to the treaties or by the author of the clause to establish new sources of international law with relation to the weapons or means of warfare, it would appear to be incorrect to assert that there exists an automatic limitation, such as *malum in se*, against the possession or use of any or all chemical or biological weapons because they constitute a crime against humanity or violate the dictates of the public conscience.[22]

MAJOR PRINCIPLES OF LAW OF WAR RECOGNIZED BY CIVILIZED NATIONS GOVERNING WEAPONS AND METHODS OF WARFARE

Even among those jurists who accept the orthodox view that international law is derived only from three law-creating sources, there is still not complete unanimity on which general principles of law recognized by civilized nations have become international legal principles governing weapons and methods of warfare. Some stress one set of values protected by municipal law of all civilized nations, while others stress different sets of values. But a composite picture of all approaches would indicate that the following have evolved into major principles of the international law of war:

(1) The principle of military necessity, which can be traced to such municipal law principles as the doctrine of reasonableness or the prohibition of the abuse of rights.

The doctrine of reasonableness connotes action which the actor feels is suitable and necessary in a particular case, not necessarily what is best but rather what is fairly appropriate to the purpose, in view of all the attendant circumstances.

The prohibition of the abuse of rights is derived from a recognition that in the complexities of human society, either of individuals or nations, law cannot precisely delimit every right in advance. Thus it is stated that rights granted by law are not absolute. They must be exercised reasonably and moderately in a manner compatible with the general rules and principles of the legal order. Each case must be judged according to its particular circumstances by looking either at the intention or motive of the doer or the objective result of the act, in the light of practice and human experience. When either an unlawful intention or design can be established, or the act is clearly unreasonable, there is an abuse of right prohibited by law.[23]

(2) The principle of humanity, which can be traced to such policies as *salus populi suprema lex est* and the use of municipal police power to help certain classes of citizens.

The ancient maxim *salus populi suprema lex est* implies that the welfare of the people is the supreme law. It is interpreted to mean that there exists an implied agreement of every member of society that his own welfare shall, in case of necessity, yield to that of the community, and that his property, liberty and life shall under certain circumstances be placed in jeopardy or even sacrificed for the public good.

The police power of a state embraces its whole system of internal regulation by which a state seeks to promote order, safety, health, morals and general welfare of society. It may be used to control private property and private interests for the public welfare of certain classes of society such as women and children, laborers, indigents, etc.[24]

(3) The principle of chivalry, which, although a relic of medievalism and knighthood, introduced from the municipal law the idea of honor, fair play, and mutual respect between opposing forces.[25]

(4) The principle of reprisal, which can be traced to the criminal law of all civilized nations which recognizes the right to take coercive measures to force respect for the law;[26] and

(5) The principle of self-defense, which is derived from the municipal law principle that a private individual may protect himself against an illegitimate attack, commenced or imminently impending, when organized law-enforcement forces are unavailable or unable to halt the attack.[27]

THE PRINCIPLE OF MILITARY NECESSITY AND THE PRINCIPLE OF HUMANITY

PURSUIT OF VICTORY VERSUS DESTRUCTION AND SUFFERING

The major military objective of any nation at war is to bring about a successful conclusion of hostilities. In order to accomplish this solution, military men speak of the "requirements" or "necessities" of the situation. Some solutions may actually be necessary in that they present the sole means of attaining the end. Other solutions may only be preferable or more convenient. Some solutions may be appropriate, but there may be more desirable alternatives. But not all potential solutions are legally permissible.

The laws of war derived from principles recognized by civilized nations were founded upon the theory that the ultimate end of the war was not to do all the harm possible to an enemy with a view to wiping him off the face of the earth, but rather to defeat him, to bring him to terms, and make him accept peace. Therefore as a principle of the law of war, military necessity is distinct from uninhibited military utility. Legitimate military necessity bears a positive meaning in that presumably it is a guide to a military commander telling him how far he is permitted to go in the conduct of legally regulated warfare. Therefore the international law doctrine of military necessity authorizes such destruction and suffering and only such destruction and suffering as is necessary, relevant, and proportionate to the prompt realization of legitimate belligerent objectives. It declares, among other things, that a belligerent is justified in using any type of weapon, except those prohibited by the laws of war, which is necessary for the realization of the purpose of the war, namely the overpowering of the enemy in the shortest time with the least possible expenditure of life and money. Conversely, all kinds and degrees of violence and all resort to weapons not necessary for the overpowering of an opponent are not permitted to a belligerent; to resort thereto would be viewed as an abuse of right.[28]

The principle of humanity in war attempts to insure respect for the individual and his well-being by regulating hostilities to attenuate human hardships insofar as military necessity permits. It stresses the fact that because of humanity considerations wanton destruction and unnecessary human suffering not needed for the defeat of the enemy are prohibited. In other words, you may not cause as much destruction and suffering to your enemy as you can, but rather, you may not inflict more harm on your enemy than the object of the war demands. Although the principle of military necessity and the principle of humanity represent divergent social values, in effect they do not differ too radically. It has been succinctly stated:

The principle of necessity does not allow the employment of force unnecessary or superfluous to the purposes of war. Nor does the principle of humanity oppose human suffering or physical destruction as such. It is the unnecessary infliction of human suffering and the wanton destruction of property that is opposed both by the principle of military necessity and by the principle of humanity.[29]

With reference to chemical and biological weapons as viewed from the doctrine of military necessity and the doctrine of humanity, the pertinent questions then appear to relate to the issue of whether or not such weapons cause *wanton* destruction of property or *unnecessary* human suffering. These questions bring in their wake an evaluation of whether or not the destruction and suffering caused by such weapons serve a military purpose, whether or not the destruction and suffering even though they did produce certain military advantages could have been avoided; and finally whether or not the destruction and suffering were proportionate to the military advantages gained.

REGULATON OF CB WEAPONS USED AGAINST AN ENEMY'S RESOURCES

Chemical and biological weapons can be used against resources and human life. Among the rules distilled from the general principles of the law of war recognized by civilized nations is that which states that weapons may not be used to cause wanton destruction of property not justified by military necessity. In other words, the devastation "pure and simple" of enemy property as an end in itself, as a self-contained measure of war, is illegitimate. Destruction of property by chemical and biological weapons must be militarily relevant; it must have a reasonably close connection with the securing of a legitimate belligerent objective in order to be lawful. Devastation of property by such methods must be imperatively demanded by the necessities of war.[30]

The difficulty arises when one attempts to determine whether a particular chemical or biological agent caused devastation of property beyond military necessity. Would the spraying of herbicides to destroy the food crop of an enemy or the use of antiplant or antianimal biological agents for the same purpose fall within the ban? It has long been accepted that a besieged city might be starved into submission,[31] and in both World War I and World War II economic blockades and indiscriminate submarine warfare were used against food supplies of the enemy.[32] Furthermore, during World War II the Germans retreating from Finland, after evacuating civilians, used fire weapons in a "scorched earth" policy burning and destroying all food supplies, houses, and installations that could afford shelter and all means of transportation and communication in various towns and villages to impede the progress and lower the combat efficiency of advancing Russian troops.[33] The war crimes tribunal declared that such a general destruction of property ordered as an incident of broad military strategy did not constitute devastation beyond military necessity and was hence permissible.[34] Thus it could be argued that in ordinary military operations the use of antimateriel, or antiplant, or antianimal chemical or biological weapons does not clearly exceed the limits of military necessity and hence becomes permissible. On the other hand, Hyde has stipulated that if the devastation against property was of a nature or intensity calculated to cast "a permanent or long enduring blight" it might become impermissible.[35]

Now under certain conditions it has been claimed that herbicides used to destroy an enemy's food crop will linger in the soil for long periods, leak into streams killing fish by poisoning the microscopic fauna on which they feed, and cause other ecological imbalances in nature which will cause permanent or long-enduring damage.[36] Would such uses then be considered illegal? They might and they might not, depending on whether or not such destruction clearly exceeded the limits of military necessity. And to speak of military necessity or the lack of it is to raise the question, necessary or unnecessary to what? The use of a chemical or biological weapon in a particular combat operation can be deemed necessary or unnecessary only in relation to the attainment of a specific objective. Therefore clarification of the principle of military necessity as it relates to the use of chemical and biological weapons against the resources of an enemy must be in part contingent upon a definition of legitimate belligerent objectives.[37] However, defining legitimate military objectives is no easy task. Most internationalists speak of legitimate objectives as "securing the ends of the war." But does this relate to the ultimate object of war, i.e., the overpowering of the opponent, or does it relate to some purely military objective during the course of the war? Most authorities feel that from a standpoint of utilitarianism or hard-headed reality it cannot be limited to the latter, and yet agree that under the former it would cover every combat aim and would substantially render illusive any limitation upon military necessity. Therefore the legitimate military objectives implied in the limitation of military necessity are generally interpreted by some verbal variation of the shadowy, nebulous line of reasonableness. McDougal and Feliciano call it "a rational policy oriented toward a public order of human dignity."[38] Schwarzenberger refers to it as "the standard of civilization,"[39] while O'Brien would use the phrase "the commands of natural law."[40] But they all come down to the basic reality that in the abstract without a view of the whole context of the use it would be impossible to judge whether or not the destruction of an enemy's resources by chemical or biological agents was so unreasonable and disproportionate as to violate international law. One can conclude that where chemical or biological weapons are used merely for senseless destruction of an enemy's resources, irrelevant to the military objectives of war, their use would be illegal.[41]

CHARACTERISTICS OF CHEMICAL AND BIOLOGICAL WEAPONS AND CLASS OF INDIVIDUALS INVOLVED

In General

When chemical or biological weapons are used directly or indirectly against enemy personnel, their use is governed by those international rules which relate to the fundamental protection of human life, primary among which is the rule which prohibits resort to weapons which cause unnecessary suffering.[42]

Various answers have been given to the question of whether or not chemical and biological agents cause unnecessary suffering and hence are outlawed. About the only area of agreement is that it would be clearly illegal to use a particular chemical or biological agent solely because it causes suffering or to use one that causes more suffering than another agent equally effective from a military standpoint.[43]

There are some authorities who categorically state that all chemical and biological agents automatically violate the prohibition against weapons which cause unnecessary suffering and hence all are illegal. Under such a view the use of a temporary incapacitating agent such as tear gas is placed on the same plane as the use of a lethal agent such as nerve gas. This approach would seem inaccurate in logic as well as law, for in the process of lumping all together they seem to be ascribing to all chemical and biological weapons the suffering-causing characteristics of the most injurious or most lethal, refusing to admit that there is a broad spectrum in the suffering potentials of such weapons.[44] Other critics[45] of these weapons are more discriminating. They argue, for example, that the suffering caused by the modern lethal or severely injurious chemical agents is far more intense and acute than suffering caused by conventional weapons. As to the gases used in World War I, although statistics might seem to indicate that such gases caused fewer serious casualties and deaths and hence less suffering than conventional weapons, these statistics are said to be misleading[46] in that one of the most important military uses of gas in that war was to force enemy troops out of protective fortifications into areas of high explosive fire. The most painful of all injuries are those caused by fire weapons such as flame-throwers or napalm, and hence it is argued that they fall within the ban on unnecessary suffering. Even the nonlethal chemical agents may cause agonizing suffering in infants, elderly people, and those already afflicted with serious diseases. Although the long-range effects of psycho- and physico-incapacitants are still in doubt, if they bring on such things as permanent brain injury the suffering they cause will be unending, and would then presumably fall within the ban against unnecessary suffering. It has been contended that chemical herbicides and antiplant biological agents used against the food crop of the enemy are more apt to bring about long-term suffering, through the acute anguish of starvation, to civilian populations than to enemy military personnel.[47] As to other potential biological agents, their military usefulness lies mainly in the misery and suffering they cause, ranging from acute but short-term agony to lifelong pain and distress or prolonged, lingering death. An attack by a biological agent on a city may tie up all medical facilities and thereby bring unnecessary suffering and death to those not directly injured by the attack. Some biological agents may cause worldwide epidemics, bringing unnecessary suffering to people and nations having no relation to the conflict, and may wipe out whole civilizations.

Diametrically opposite arguments are made by certain military men and legal authorities who claim that some of the chemical and biological weapons cause less suffering than conventional weapons. For example, the internationalist Lawrence observes:

It is not easy to see how quick asphyxiation exceeds in cruelty the blowing of a human body to pieces by the bursting of a shell. Slow torture by chemical methods might well be forbidden; but immediate death after inhaling deleterious fumes is comparable to drowning which is often the fate of seamen in a naval engagement. If gas kills a combatant almost immediately, or puts him out of action, without needless pain or permanent evil results, it is not unnecessarily cruel.[48]

Furthermore, it is alleged that the lethal gases do not mutilate the body and seldom cause extreme pain.[49] There even appears to be controversy over whether quick death by napalm or flamethrowers necessarily causes more suffering than death from the crush blast effects of high explosives. Nonlethal chemical and biological agents which produce merely temporary, even though distressing, effects entailing no enduring damage to the human organism are claimed to be less likely to cause unnecessary suffering than nonlethal injuries by conventional weapons because the survivors of the latter may remain permanently crippled or maimed, as survivors of the former might not.[50]

It has also been implied that resort to chemical and biological weapons may be more humane than a prolonged conflict fought with less efficient weapons, for the use of chemical and biological weapons may shorten the war and thereby bring about a return to peace and the ending of general suffering caused by the war.[51] Military advocates attest that chemical and biological weapons produce casualties with a minimum destruction of ancillary targets such as roads, houses, hospitals, and the like. The reconstruction of a battered city, it is claimed, is thereby made easier and the suffering of the civilian population correspondingly mitigated.[52] It has even been advanced that in the future the rule against unnecessary suffering will demand that wars be fought by means of nonlethal chemical or biological agents, since such weapons would shorten fighting time and prevent the indiscriminate killing and maiming of both belligerent armies.[53]

Actually all these statements on whether or not a chemical or biological weapon causes unnecessary suffering are misleading, for without a careful comparison between all the potential effects of each chemical or biological agent and all the potential effects of conventional weapons, no accurate judgment can be reached as to whether or not chemical or biological weapons do in fact cause unnecessary suffering and hence fall under the ban established by the law of war. Such a comparison would involve diagnosing each possible degree of suffering caused by chemical or biological agents and balancing it against that inflicted by conventional weapons; analyzing the length of the period of suffering caused by biological or chemical weapons to see if their painful effects are longer or shorter than those resulting from wounds caused by conventional weapons; studying the length of incapacitation caused by chemical or biological agents and comparing it with that caused by conventional weapons; and finally reviewing the permanent effects caused by chemical or biological agents and those caused by conventional weapons.

Enemy Military Personnel

But even if such a comparison were made, one could still not definitely say that a particular chemical or biological agent would be illegal because it caused unnecessary suffering, for it must be remembered that all weapons of war are designed to incapacitate, kill, or destroy enemy military personnel. A device which does not do one or more of these has no military value.[54] Weapons remove enemy military personnel by injuring them or killing them, and there would seem to be no objective standard which could be applied to a weapon in the abstract, if the decision is to be based solely on physical results, saying this weapon causes more than an acceptable amount of suffering. Quantitative results are also important.[55] The relevant point of this approach is not that a chemical or biological agent causes more or less suffering than a conventional weapon, but rather that the legitimacy of a chemical or biological weapon must be judged in part by its quantitative results. In the words of Spaight:

> The test of lawfulness of any weapon or projectile is practically the answer one can give to the question "what is its 'bag'?"—does it disable so many of the enemy that the military end thus gained condones the suffering it causes.
>
> It is certain that the employment of a projectile capable of destroying an army at one blow would be legitimate under the actual principles of the law of war.[56]

This has meant that no militarily decisive weapon has ever been regarded as causing superfluous injury, no matter how painful the suffering resulting from its use, for the fact that it was militarily decisive would prove that the suffering was necessary.[57] As Schwarzenberger points out:

> The legality of hand grenades, flame throwers, napalm, the incendiary bombs in contemporary warfare is a vivid reminder that the suffering caused by weapons with sufficiently large destructive potentialities is not *unnecessary* in the meaning of this rule.[58]

Of course, once an enemy soldier has been placed *hors de combat*, if the chemical or biological weapon which brought about this result was used or designed in such a manner as unnecessarily to increase his suffering, i.e., "to uselessly aggravate the suffering of disabled soldiers," it would be illegal.[59]

Enemy Noncombatants in Limited Wars

Even though the unnecessary suffering doctrine as it applies to military personnel gives no clear, decisive, or instantaneous guide to the legality or illegality of resort to chemical or biological weapons, there are other approaches which may lead to an answer. It has been said, for example, that these two classes of weapons must be distinguished legally on the basis of their distinctive properties.[60] Militarily speaking, chemical agents are thought to be more predictable and apparently can be limited to legitimate targets with a minimum of spill-over effects; hence, they are deemed to be tactical armaments.[61] On the other hand, biological agents are of strategic significance because there is a time lapse between their introduction and subsequent infection and because of their unique spill-over effects.[62] When biological agents are used against enemy troops, there is said to be little possibility of controlling or limiting any ancillary destruction.[63] Hence, from the viewpoint of permissible suffering as it applies to enemy military personnel, chemical weapons can be legally justified but biological weapons cannot. This is the distinction between the use of weapons counter-force, i.e., against enemy military personnel, and the use of uncontrollable weapons which become counter-people, i.e., weapons which by their nature cause superfluous suffering to enemy civilian personnel.[64] Such a blanket condemnation is correct only if it is assumed that the armed forces of a belligerent are the sole legitimate military objectives and hence that noncombatants are inviolable and may not under any condition become the object of a military attack.

For many years the military power center of a nation was its armed forces; consequently these forces were the main military target of the enemy. Noncombatants therefore occupied a protected status under the laws of war. On the battlefield of yesteryear, the distinction between combatant and noncombatant was relatively easy to make, and persons in the latter protected category were not a legitimate object of attack, unless they happened to be within a narrowly defined military target zone and their injury was unavoidable.[65] But the modern concept of total war has enlarged the battlefield considerably, so that its limits are not nearly so clearly defined as when wars were fought with sword or musket. Even in limited war the power center has shifted from the army to industry, communications, and transportation; the outcome of the conflict is no longer decided by the victory of an army but depends in large measure on the industrial communications and transportation capacities of the belligerents.

In order to distinguish between combatants and noncombatants, it is again necessary to determine what are ultimate legitimate military objectives in modern warfare. These in turn depend upon whether a war is a limited war, a total war, or a guerrilla war. In a limited war (a war fought for limited purposes between a limited number of belligerents who mutually refrain from exercising their full capabilities for destruction),[66] persons connected with military operations or the production of war material must be expected to be treated as objects of war irrespective of whether they are members of armed forces or civilians.[67] Thus if it is permissible to use a chemical or biological weapon against enemy troops in such circumstances, it would also be permissible to use such weapons against these enemy noncombatants. Civilians present in actual or likely theaters of war or target areas, such as centers of communication, large industrial centers, or administrative establishments, even if they are persons not connected with the war effort, such as the infirm, the aged, or children, are not immune from being attacked by chemical or biological weapons if resort to such weapons is not for the *sole* purpose of attacking the civilians regardless of any connection with military objectives.[68] Thus persons not engaged in military operations or the production of war material and living in places sufficiently remote from target areas are probably the only enemy civilians considered inviolable from attack by chemical or biological weapons.[69] And in this, of course, lies the danger of resort in a limited war to chemical and biological weapons, which because of their inherent nature may by their effects cause death and suffering among the small group of enemy civilians who still remain under the protection of international law.

The issue, of course, revolves about the controllability of chemical and biological agents. The controllability of chemical agents depends upon a number of factors such as the methods of dissemination (e.g., whether they are disseminated by bursting type munitions or by spray devices), the weather (including temperature in the target area, the speed and direction of the wind, the humidity, and the amount of precipitation), the nature of the terrain (its contours, vegetation, and type and condition of soil), the persistency of the agent to be used, and the location and composition of the target.[70] Military authorities declare that commanders trained in the art of chemical weaponry are normally able to analyze all of these factors, compensate them with a certain margin of safety, and calculate with a high degree of assurance that chemical weapons will not cause needless suffering or death to those noncombatants who remain under the protection of international law.[71]

But this argument may not be applicable to potential biological agents, for it has been said that they are uncontrollable because after the first impact they are designed to lead to successive impacts such as mass epidemics.[72] Undoubtedly this is true of such potential biological agents as those causing bacillary dysentry, cholera, diphtheria, pneumonic plague, typhoid fever, paratyphoid fever, tuberculosis, influenza, smallpox, hepatitis, and the like. This being the case, it would seem that in *limited wars* no guarantee could be made that they would not attack those enemy civilians who still remain in the protected category under international law, and consequently their use would be illegal.[73]

Nevertheless there are some potential biological weapons which are noncontagious; toxins, for example, cannot be communicated from man to man. Other diseases such as undulant fever, San Joaquin fever, histoplasmosis, are also considered to be noncontagious.[74] In a limited war, if it is possible by means of a multi-factor analysis to program these noncontagious potential biological weapons for use on a specific legitimate military target without endangering that class of enemy persons to whom international law still offers shelter from the extreme violence of war, these weapons could not be outlawed under a blanket indictment of causing unnecessary suffering because of uncontrollability—though of course they might be outlawed for other reasons. For example, toxins have been said to fall under the ban against poison.[75]

Enemy Noncombatants in Total Wars

In total war situations civilians seem to be even less protected. Total war is a struggle of entire nations and groups of nations thoroughly organized against each other, a struggle as much of military prowess of armies as of supplies, working activities, raw materials, industrial capacity, food production, moral propaganda, and mental ouslaught.[76] In total war, every person is a prospective participant in the war, and hence every person becomes a prospective victim of weapons of war. Since long distance artillery, air warfare, and long range missiles have made the enemy hinterland accessible as a target area, the concept of noncombatant has undergone a remarkable process of shrinkage. Correspondingly, the notion of legitimate military target has become expanded. Under such conditions, it has been questioned whether the distinctions between combatant and civilian and between military and nonmilitary objectives remain a valid standard of reference. Von Knieriem, for example, in discussing the laws of war *re* unnecessary suffering of civilian populations in total war situations, claims that such laws belong to a past age. They are "erinnerungen an eine versunkene Welt"—reminiscences of a lost world.[78] This was even recognized in the Nuremberg trials when the tribunal stated: "Technical advancement in weapons and tactics used in the actual waging of war may have rendered obsolete or inapplicable certain rules relating to the actual conduct of hostilities and what is considered legitimate warfare."[79]

Total war has been compared to ancient cities under siege where all within the city, combatants or noncombatants, able-bodied, infirm, children, or aged, could be legitimately killed, injured, starved, or terrorized by besieging forces, until surrender. No matter how horrible the suffering, it was considered necessary suffering.[80]

Some would say that the only limitation on chemical and biological weapons in a total war situation would be a prohibition of the use of such weapons for the sole purpose of terrorization, for in such a case the civilian population becomes the direct object of attack regardless of any connection with military objective. A weapon of terrorization can be one which causes an almost incredible amount of death and destruction or one whose psychological effects are out of proportion to the purely physical results.[81] The spectrum of chemical and biological weapons would include both types. Nevertheless, World War II demonstrated that an important element in victory in total war is the breaking of the morale of an enemy's labor force by any means including terror weapons. Civilians thus became military objectives, under the theory that the use of terror weapons would in the long run cause less needless suffering than the use of conventional weapons.[82] The effect of disrupting the enemy's will to fight by terror weapons was amply demonstrated by the aftermath of dropping the atom bomb on Japan, which surrendered within a few days after the use of the bomb.[83] The terror effect, according to all accounts, was no less important than the actual devastation caused. To a lesser extent, this was true of terror bombing of civilian populations and sink-on-sight submarine warfare.

Some international lawyers maintain, and this may well be the actual case, that while the use of weapons for terrorization in World War II was violative of international law on a grand scale, such use did not impair the validity of the law of war with reference to terror weapons even in the case of analogous conduct by both belligerents.[84] For example, Lauterpacht declares that only in the prohibition against the intentional use of weapons of terror against a civilian population lies the last vestige of the claim that war can be legally regulated.[85] Without that irreducible principle of restraint, there is no limitation on the types of weapons which may be used in warfare, and hence the prohibition against weapons of terror not incidental to lawful operations must be regarded as an absolute rule of law.

In rebuttal it is stated that in an area such as this, law closely follows the practice of states, particularly in view of the fact that in World War II all of the powerful military nations were involved and all, at one time or another, resorted to the use of weapons for the purpose of terrorization.[86] It is noted, furthermore, that the fact that the postwar crimes tribunals so completely failed to raise the issue of terror weapons in and of itself is a strong indication that the practice has been ratified and absorbed into the legal modes of warfare.[87]

Under the first view, the use in total war situations of chemical and biological weapons to create stark terror and panic among the civilian populations would be illegal. Under the second, resort in total war to chemical and biological weapons, whether such weapons were of the lethal or nonlethal variety, for the purpose of terrorization to shatter the enemy's will to fight would now no longer be illegal.

There is one other view with reference to the use of weapons for the purpose of terrorization, namely, the utilitarian view which holds that utility is the underlying principle of all legal regulations applying to weapons in warfare.[88] There must be a relationship between true utility and law. This school is also divided on its opinion as to the legality of chemical and biological agents as utilitarian weapons of terror. Some hold that in total war an attack by lethal chemical or biological agents would have the same terrorization effect as the attack on Japan by atomic weapons in World War II, and hence their use must be considered legal.[89] The other view holds that you do not win wars by terrorizing people, but by destroying targets; targets are something tangible, not something in people's minds, hence pure terror weapons are nonutilitarian in total war and are illegal.[90]

There are some internationalists who maintain that even in total war the traditional legal distinction between combatant and noncombatant still survives, both as to the concept of military objective to be gained by the resort to a chemical or biological agent and as to the "incidental" injury that may be inflicted upon noncombatant populations in the course of attacking military objectives by such weapons. They point out that international law does not give an absolute protection to noncombatants, but only a relative protection determined by the concrete circumstances of the war.[91] With a sufficiently elastic definition of what constitutes a legitimate military objective, and with a sufficiently broad interpretation of what constitutes permissible "incidental" injury of the civilian population caused by resort to chemical or biological weapons, there would apparently be no need to deny the continued validity of the principle distinguishing between combatants and noncombatants.[92]

Friendly Troops and Friendly Civilians

Although the humanitarian requirements established by the prohibition against unnecessary suffering would seem to be a blanket prohibition in that human suffering is human suffering wherever it occurs, nonetheless this interpretation is not universally accepted.[93] Some human lives are considered to be more important than others. There has been a propensity among nations at war to insist that the prohibition against unnecessary or needless suffering begins at home with one's own troops, with the troops of friendly forces, or with one's own population or the population of allied nations. Under this approach the prohibition against unnecessary suffering would not be violated if chemical or biological weapons were used with the purpose of saving friendly troops or friendly civilians from death or injury, no matter what other effects such weapons might have. In other words, if resort to chemical or biological weapons would quickly end a war by disabling or killing a multitude of enemy forces or civilians, without proportionate injury or suffering among one's own forces or civilians, it would not be prohibited by the rule against unnecessary suffering.[94]

Guerrillas

The Geneva Conventions of 1949 indicated that armed bands carrying on irregular warfare should be dealt with as legitimate belligerents if they are commanded by a responsible person, wear a fixed distinctive sign, carry arms openly, and comply with the laws of war.[95] In such case, whatever international law rules relating to chemical or biological weapons applied to regular forces of the enemy would also apply to such irregular forces.[96] But only a minor portion of modern guerrilla warfare is carried on in the fashion outlined by the Geneva Conventions. The problem of how to make the laws of war apply to guerrillas carrying out secret partisan warfare has not yet been solved. When civilians become soldiers at night, committing acts of terror and destruction, the distinctions between combatants and civilians and correspondingly between military and nonmilitary objectives lose meaning and certainty. If there is no clearly distinguishable front and rear in the traditional sense, or no clearly distinguishable combatant and noncombatant, or no clearly distinguishable friend and enemy, there can be no clearly distinguishable international law rule which prohibits the use of chemical or biological weapons in guerrilla warfare. Nondisciplined bands which do not observe the laws of war themselves lose their claim to have such laws applied to them.[97]

In such situations the internal law (criminal or martial) of the nation on whose territory the guerrilla operations were taking place would apply. Under this law guerrillas fall within various classifications of criminals—murderers, saboteurs, robbers, arsonists, terrorists, etc. Few, if any nations have restrictions on internal governmental uses of chemical weapons against such criminals. Riot control weapons are standard in governmental arsenals, and where the death penalty is permitted, a number of nations use lethal gas for this purpose. This would indicate that in such nations municipal law has no aversion to the use of gas as such.[98]

Resort to certain chemical weapons is not unknown in counter-guerrilla operations. Because of the many unknown factors involved in the use of biological weapons, in situations where it is impossible to distinguish friend from foe, governments would not be inclined to use such weapons. From a practical standpoint guerrillas might effectively employ biological weapons against a legitimate government under certain conditions, but the reverse is not true. Hence there is apparently as yet no nation with internal laws which would sanction the use of biological weapons against guerrillas.

Neutrals

The law of neutrality as it developed during the eighteenth and nineteenth centuries revolved mainly about the law of neutral rights in maritime warfare and was based on the idea of nonpartisanship in wars between other nations.[99] But during World I and World War II, the fact that neutrals often were the main supply lines of the belligerents virtually wiped out the rights of neutrals on the high seas and in neutral airspace. The miniscule rights of neutral states still remaining in international law related to the inviolability of neutral territory.[100] As chemical and biological weapons are no respecters of boundaries, would their use violate the rights of states not parties to the conflict? Clearly a chemical or biological weapons attack directed at a neutral state would be illegal, because it would be an act of war. But what is one to say of death and destruction within neutral borders resulting from the use of chemical or biological weapons between belligerents originating within the belligerent jurisdiction?

In the nineteenth century the indifference of neutrals to the outcome of the war was possible because the solidarity of the international society was great enough, even in war, to make the outcome of a conflict not a matter of deep concern to the nonparticipants. But in the twentieth century the great ideological total conflicts fought for control of major parts of the earth completely destroyed the sense of international community and also the whole basis of nonpartisan disinterestedness. The laws of war are apparently impotent in such situations, and neutrality, being the other side of the coin of the law of war, must also fail. Kunz declares:

> Violations of the law of neutrality by belligerent states, retreat of neutrals by renunciation of rights, and violation of neutral duties in the form of so-called non-belligerency—a purely political, not a legal concept—have brought about a chaotic condition, have produced a constant oscillation between a pretended abolition and a strong reaffirmation of neutrality, and have rendered the law of neutrality at present one of the most uncertain parts of international law.[101]

Still, not all modern conflicts result in total war, and in limited conflicts it is generally stated that international law imposes the duty upon belligerent nations to refrain from actions which would cause injury to citizens or property on neutral territory.[102] Nonetheless some authorities argue that if chemical or biological weapons are legitimately used within the territory of a belligerent, the fact that thereafter they may affect neutrals would not make their original use illegal, for it is said that the belligerent has only the duty to pay compensation for the injury.[103] Reparation for the immediate effects of chemical or biological agents which are neither lethal nor severely injurious could probably be accurately assessed. But when a belligerent uses a lethal or severely injurious chemical or biological agent the long-range effects of which are unknown or unpredictable, the payment of reparation might then appear to be an incomplete answer to the neutral state. Certain chemical and biological weapons might affect neutral rights to such an extent that no compensation in adequate terms would ever be conceivable. It would seem that in such cases, if there were no reasonable doubt as to the fact that irreparable injury would occur to neutrals, the belligerent would be prohibited from resort to such weapons.

Some authorities[104] argue that the plea of necessity may excuse the nonobservance of neutral rights. If the excuse is valid, it excludes international responsibility. Necessity does not give any right; it only provides an excuse. It does not imply a denial of the law but is invoked to justify actions which otherwise would be outside the law.[105] The plea of necessity has been distinguished from the plea of military necessity in the following manner:

> An accused might object: "I acted in military necessity *and therefore my act was not a war crime.*" Here the doctrine of military necessity is followed, a doctrine

which purports to provide a criterion for what is allowed in war and what is not.

Distinct from this plea is the objection: "I committed a war crime, but I acted out of necessity, for my soldiers, or even my father land, were in danger; therefore I should not be punished for the crimes I committed."[106]

This latter, of course, is the German doctrine that in case of necessity, the laws of war yield to this necessity. This, of course, has been harshly condemned as illegal. But in spite of its illegality, certain writers[107] maintain that it is the only realistic view of warfare. In time of war can it ever be expected that the law of war will actually prevail over vital national or military interests?

There is one other argument relating to the legality or illegality of the use of chemical and biological weapons and the rights of neutrals, and that is that the issue would have to be based on the degree of anticipated risk to the neutral state, with the criterion of proportionality used to weigh the military advantage of a chemical or biological attack against the possible damage to the neutral state.[108]

Mankind in General

Resort to chemical and biological weapons may involve the issue of the survival of the human race, and consequently it has been argued that because of the many unknown factors involved in the residual injurious effects of such weapons, in the self-interest of all mankind they must be considered unlawful.[109] For example, it is argued that defoliation or extensive napalm attacks on tropical forested areas may produce ecological disturbances affecting the environmental niche of rodents and other wild animal reservoirs of disease and thus set off a chain reaction in plague and other epidemic diseases over a large sector of the globe. Epidemic biological agents may also spread disease to areas of the world where populations have no history of exposure to a particular agent, and this may have awesome results.

It was with this in mind that the 1956 draft rules of the International Committee of the Red Cross recommended that a specific legal prohibition should be established banning weapons whose harmful effects, resulting in particular from the dissemination of incendiary, chemical, or bacteriological agents, could spread to an unforeseen degree or escape, either in space or time, from the control of those who employ them.[110] The fact that this recommendation was made would seem to indicate that no legal ban on use of chemical or biological weapons as yet exists, for if these weapons were in fact already illegal, an express prohibition against them would be unnecessary.[111]

It has been argued that the reason the nations failed to follow the advice of the Red Cross in this instance was that the ban was far too broad to be practical.[112] Certainly nonlethal agents, and those not severely injurious, whether chemical or biological, cannot be classified as unlawful solely on the basis of their threat to mankind in general. For example, the knowledge gained from intensive and extensive use of incendiary weapons during all major wars would indicate that even though they spread havoc over a large area, they would not do so to "an unforeseen degree," and neither would they "escape in space or time."[113] Furthermore, certain military men argue that the most lethal or injurious chemical agents can be used as selectively and controllably as conventional weapons, and that even lethal biological agents can be used selectively or with reduced pathogeneity and hence would not "escape the control of those who employed them." If this be true, and it must be acknowledged that there is a great deal of dispute over the validity of such military assertions, then resort to such weapons would be considered illegal only if their employment caused suffering or death to mankind in general disproportionate to any legitimate military objective.[114]

THE DOCTRINE OF PROPORTIONALITY

A chemical or biological weapon may be "efficient" in the sense of causing indiscriminate mass destruction, but that efficiency which is relied upon as a factor in establishing the lawfulness of a weapon is military efficiency in the controlled destruction of lawful military objectives. It is therefore necessary to balance the net military advantage against the amount of devastation caused by resort to a particular weapon. Thus the *major* legal limitation on the use of any weapon in war is that of proportionality.[115] Proportionality requires a decision on whether resort to a particular weapon is proportionate to the legitimate military end sought. The lawfulness of a chemical or biological weapon cannot be judged only by the level of destruction effected; the judgment must include an evaluation of its reasonableness in the total context of a particular use, considering not only the physical characteristics of the weapons (including the extent and duration of their effects), but also the time and place of use. A chemical or biological weapon not immediately indispensable for and wantonly or grossly disproportionate to a legitimate military end is forbidden.[116] Thus it can be seen that approached in this manner it is not the particular weapon of destruction that is important but rather the amount of destruction in the light of the objectives sought to be gained. Even the use of a conventional weapon may become unlawful when its use is superfluous. Hence the rule of proportionality changes the perspective on chemical and biological weapons from the approach of whether they are legal or illegal per se, to the issue of whether their use is legal in a particular situation.[117] If there is no specific legal rule prohibiting the resort to chemical or biological weapons, the relevant question is not whether resort to such weapons is against the law, but whether their use in a particular situation is proportionate to a legitimate military end, when the possible consequences of alternative courses of action are taken into consideration.

In a hypothetical military combat situation, one might conclude that the achievement of a clearly legitimate objective would permit under a given set of conditions in a specified place at a particular moment the application of a special controllable chemical or biological weapon for a particular but no longer period of time against a particular base of enemy power. But in times of hostility such perfection is not achievable; hence the requirement of proportionality does not necessarily mean what weapon is best, but rather what is fairly appropriate or reasonable under all attendant circumstances.[118]

The principle of proportionality as it applies to chemical or biological weapons is, consequently, rather nebulous when it comes to the question of at what point the actual or expected level of destruction by a chemical or biological agent may be judged to deprive its use of further justification because such use would be disproportionate. It would seem to depend, for one thing, on the legitimate objectives which are sought to be gained.

In total war situations, unless annihilation of the enemy society itself has been accepted as a legitimate military objective,[119] there must be some minimal limitation of proportionality of weapons. This minimum, as far as chemical or biological weapons are concerned, is usually stated to be limited to weapons "which are uncontrollable in the hands of their belligerent users."[120] It is said that resort to such weapons cannot be justified as lawful even under the most expanded conception of military necessity, since they do not achieve military objectives without disproportionate ancillary injury. Although certain military men contend that chemical and biological weapons can be precisely tailored to specific military needs, still it would seem that at least certain lethal epidemic biological agents might turn out to be uncontrollable, and hence their first use would be banned even in total war.[121] Beyond that the requirement of proportionality would preclude the use of chemical and biological weapons only if they caused great suffering without a corresponding military utility.[122]

Even though an extensive amount of ancillary injury through chemical and biological weapons might be acceptable as proportionate in total war, an equivalent amount of injury by the same weapon might be unacceptable and consequently unlawful in limited war. In limited war situations the tactical controllability of chemical or biological agents must be consistent with the limited military objectives which are postulated.[123] The test of lawfulness of a particular chemical or biological weapon in limited war involves mainly a determination of the *reasonable* proportionality of the weapon and the ancillary suffering or destruction of values caused by its use. It would seem that if biological or chemical weapons are to be used lawfully in limited war they must be weapons of very limited destructive power which are employed under the most rigid technological and tactical controls. Precision delivery of tactical chemical or biological weapons which accomplish military objectives without disproportionate suffering or damage would appear to meet the accepted juridical criteria of proportionality in the lawful use of weapons.[124]

Under this approach, chemical riot control agents and smokes would generally appear to be proportionate in limited war situations. All other chemical antipersonnel weapons such as flamethrowers, incendiary bombs, napalm, or lethal gases might or might not be proportionate depending upon the amount of suffering or destruction effected and the military value of the objectives sought in the operation being appraised.[125] Disproportionate destruction is by definition unnecessary destruction and includes in its reference a whole continuum of degrees. All that can be derived from past formulations and experience is that the disproportion should be minimal and not gross and that the connection between the injury or destruction caused and the military objective postulated should be reasonably proximate and not remote.[126]

As to nonepidemic and perhaps nonlethal epidemic antipersonnel biological weapons in limited war, they might under the correct circumstances be legitimate under the rule of proportionality, provided that there was no possibility of prolongation of the diseases far beyond the period of hostilities. But lethal epidemic biological weapons would appear to be disproportionate, for resort to their use would appear to be a deliberate abandonment of an effort to apply force in a discriminating manner because these weapons are of such a nature that serious doubt exists as to whether they can be applied with discrimination.[127] Hence they would appear to be disproportionate and contrary to the principle of legitimate military necessity.

The best that can then be concluded is that there can be no blanket acceptance or condemnation of all chemical or biological weapons based on the doctrine of proportionality. Their use in a given context at a particular place and time and aimed at a particular target might well conform to the requirements of military necessity; on the other hand, there are some military situations relative to place, time, and short-range and long-range effects of specific chemical or biological weapons which make their use clearly disproportionate by any standard of reasonableness. Clearly *unlimited* lethal or severely injurious chemical warfare or lethal or severely injurious biological warfare would be inadmissible because its predictable effects would threaten the physical existence of mankind while at the same time offering no commensurate military utility.

THE USE OF CHEMICAL OR BIOLOGICAL AGENTS FOR PSYCHOLOGICAL PURPOSES

The military might of a nation consists not only of its armed forces and economic potential but also of the psychological-ideological factors comprising the collective predisposition or will to fight loosely summed up as "enemy morale."[128] Psychological intimidation of the enemy population—both civilian and military—as a means of bringing about the surrender of the enemy armies has long been an incident of warfare. Measures of psychological intimidation range from visual or verbal propaganda to the intentional violent dissemination of terror through indiscriminate methods of warfare with military weapons.[129] It has been argued that the latter is probably illegal, for to accept as lawful the deliberate violent terrorization by military instrumentalities of the enemy community comes close to legitimizing the annihilation of the enemy society itself and may also bring about a situation in which the enemy masses become entirely incapable of political behavior necessary to bring about the termination of the war.[130]

With the advent of psychochemical agents, a new weapon of psychological warfare entered the picture. Although military views on the feasibility of psychochemicals as weapons range from scorn to approbation,[131] it would seem safe to assume that there is at least a possibility that through the dispersal of psychochemicals over enemy territory, stark terror and panic might be created among the enemy population without concomitant widespread physical damage or death. This type of psychological warfare would vary from previous methods of psychological warfare in which enemy soldiers and civilians still had freedom of choice and will and could use their intelligence, courage, loyalty, or honor to defeat the psychological attack, and the enemy government could impose measures of penalty or discipline in order to prevent the complete destruction of the morale of its society.[132]

The new psychochemicals are depersonalizing agents, in that they destroy freedom of choice and will and break down enemy morale not by exhaustion through the war effort, or consent, or physical defeat, or by an act of cowardice, but rather through the means of a biochemical reaction.[133] (The same could probably be said for physicochemicals which act as a strong anesthesia or produce temporary paralysis, blindness, or deafness in their victims.) Would such psychochemicals then fall within a class of prohibited weapons outlawed either by the doctrine of military necessity or by that of humanity?

First it must be reemphasized that the novelty of a weapon cannot be equated with illegality. Furthermore, it would be difficult to contend that psychochemical weapons threaten to destroy the very foundation of civilization or would cause complete annihilation of the enemy society. With these lines of inquiry closed, other questions concerning the legality or illegality of these weapons would involve the rule that military necessity does not include any act of hostility which makes the return of peace unnecessarily difficult if not impossible. The question then to be asked is, "Do the enemy masses subjected to a psychochemical attack become entirely incapable of the political behavior necessary to bring about the termination of the war?"

Assuming that the psychochemical or physicochemical agent used had only a temporary effect, this certainly would not be true, because once the enemy territory was occupied and the effects of the agent on the populace wore off, peace could be negotiated. The use of such an agent has been compared with the ancient ruse of placing narcotics in the enemy's wine and thereafter conquering him while he was under their effects. This tactic has apparently never been considered illegal under the laws of war, either as contrary to the principle of humanity or contrary to the prohibition against poison.[134]

On the other hand, if the psychochemical agent caused a permanent altering of the minds of a majority of the population by damaging the brain or central nervous system, clearly the return to peace would be unnecessarily difficult, and, such an agent would seem to be illegal as not protected by military necessity or by humanity, for the suffering would continue long after hostilities had ended.[135]

As for the humanitarian aspects of resort to temporary disabling psychochemical agents, beyond the obvious one of minimum destruction,[136] it must be emphasized that only exceptionally are dignity, personality, honor, conscience, or voluntary will of enemy individuals protected by the rules of war, the exceptions being in occupied territory or when they are prisoners of war. Otherwise the morale or psychological state of enemy civilians or military men is said not to be a juridically protected object.[137]

Nevertheless there is apparently some question as to whether or not resort to psychochemical weapons would be legal in limited war situations. In a news conference on March 24, 1965, United States Secretary of State Dean Rusk attempted to distinguish between military gases and riot control agents by defining riot control agents as those which (1) have no lethal effects; (2) have a minimum disabling character; and (3) are normal to police forces the world over. Such agents, he implied, were not covered by any conventional, customary, or other ban relating to gas warfare, and conversely there was the implication that first use of military gas would be illegal. When questioned as to the status of psychochemical agents, he placed them in the military gas category.[138]

Although psychochemicals may have no lethal effect, and may have a minimum disabling character, they are not as yet weapons normally used by police forces. Suggestions that they should be used by them have been seriously made.[139] If the psychochemicals contemplated as potential weapons of war do not fit into the category of lethal or severely injurious gases, and if Secretary of State Rusk by his statement meant that they were illegal under the laws of war, then they would have to be considered as illegal under some other ban than that of military necessity or the principles of humanity. Of course, he might merely have been implying that from a policy as distinct from a legal point of view, he felt that psychochemicals should be placed in the war weapons category. But if his words meant that psychochemical agents were legally banned, this prohibition could only arise from some other principle of the law of war such as chivalry or poison.

THE PRINCIPLE OF CHIVALRY AND RESORT TO CHEMICAL OR BIOLOGICAL WEAPONS

IN GENERAL

The principle of chivalry as recognized by the laws of civilized nations demanded a certain amount of fairness in offense and defense and a certain mutual respect between opposing forces; it denounced and forbade resort to dishonorable means, expedients, or conduct. Chivalry represented a quality of forbearance, a holding back from the ultimate in combat.[140]

It has been asserted that potential chemical and biological weapons permit men to kill an enemy not only at ever increasing distances but also in ever increasing numbers.[141] By what appears to be a curious psychological inversion, a radical increase in the number of victims at a sufficient distance serves to destroy any feeling of chivalry in mankind. The destructive power of weapons of sufficient magnitude used at sufficient distance transforms the act of killing into an abstraction. One cannot give concrete meaning to enormous casualty figures which cannot be directly witnessed. Some have even questioned whether killing in the abstract is killing at all.[142] Under such conditions, of course, any rules which might be derived from the principle of chivalry would seem to have little application in total war situations, for the whole concept of total war is contrary to the chivalrous ideal of holding back.

The rules derived from the principles of chivalry which may still be applicable in limited war situations are the prohibitions against treacherous wounding or killing of the enemy and the prohibition against the use of weapons which aggravate the suffering of disabled men or render death inevitable.

TREACHERY

It is forbidden to resort to treachery in the waging of hostilities, but belligerents are permitted to resort to surprise ruses or deceits to gain victory.[143] Yet it has been almost impossible to establish general criteria that could be applied to all possible acts of surprise and deception in order to determine whether such acts may be regarded as permissible ruses or constitute forbidden treachery.

Tucker concludes that resort to lethal or severely injurious chemical agents which are colorless and odorless and hence give no prior warning constitutes a form of treachery and is outlawed.[144] Apparently he would exclude from this ban riot control agents and temporarily incapacitating agents such as psychochemicals and physicochemicals.

Osgood and Tucker assert that there is a marked persistence in identifying a treacherous act with a clandestine act and therefore they feel that "[t]he special category in which biological weapons for example, are placed probably is the result in part of the belief that such weapons are by their very nature clandestine and that their use therefore amounts to treachery."[145]

O'Brien would disagree with the idea that resort to such weapons constitutes a form of treachery. He points out that the mere fact that a weapon is clandestine in nature and gives no prior warning is not sufficient to constitute treachery, for snipers, land mines, booby traps, long-range artillery, and V-2 bombs (to name but a few) give no prior warning and yet are considered conventional weapons.[146] Brungs would agree with O'Brien in emphasizing the fact that the element of surprise has long been considered one of the first principles of warfare.[147]

The most accurate view would seem to be that of Meyrowitz, who contends that the prohibition against resort to treachery is not a normative principle of the law of war but rather an explicative principle which clarifies the genesis, foundation, and *ratio legis* of certain positive rules of the law of war.[148] He arrives at this conclusion by demonstrating that both in the dictionary sense and in the military sense as set forth under the established laws of war, acts of treachery consist of measures of deceit which involve a breach of faith with the enemy. Treachery comes about when there has been an implicit or explicit change in the relationship of the belligerents which has substituted for a completely injurious relationship a relationship of obligation or confidence, such as that which comes about in situations of capture, surrender, armistice negotiations, capitulations, or work under the emblem of the Red Cross. Therefore the prohibition against treachery is limited to cases of violation of the *bona fides* and is not related to stealthy or invisible or new weapons of warfare where no issue of a *bona fide* relationship exists. If resort to a chemical or biological agent complied with other legal principles such as proportionality and military necessity, even though the agents themselves are invisible and their use would probably come as a complete surprise to the enemy, their employment would not constitute treachery— rather, such employment would probably fall within a broad concept of *ruse de guerre.*[149]

Nevertheless, chemical and biological agents can be used treacherously to wound and kill when they are used to commit an act otherwise prohibited. Chemical and biological weapons are in and of themselves incapable of being treacherous per se. Whether or not any weapon is used treacherously depends upon its user. The mere fact that a weapon is capable of being used treacherously certainly does not support the proposition that its every use is necessarily treacherous. But if, for example, a belligerent has by means of a physico- or psychochemical agent temporarily paralyzed an enemy army and placed them *hors de combat* in a situation where the belligerent can take over and reduce them to prisoners of war, he is prohibited from killing or severely injuring them.[150] This, of course, assumes that the belligerent is in a position immediately to disarm the enemy and assure that his fighting days are over. If, instead, he slaughtered the helpless enemy, the violation would not consist in the employment of the psycho- or physicochemicals, but rather in the act which the employment served to prepare.[151]

AGGRAVATING THE SUFFERING OF DISABLED MEN OR RENDERING DEATH INEVITABLE

Most internationalists indicate that technological developments in the field of weaponry have drained of much of their vitality the medieval rules of chivalry against weapons which uselessly aggravate the suffering of disabled men or render their death inevitable.[152]

As to the first rule, if a chemical or biological weapon kills quickly and causes little or no suffering, it cannot be said uselessly to aggravate the suffering of disabled men. Nor would a chemical or biological weapon that causes severe suffering for a short period of time, but does not kill and leaves no aftereffects, uselessly aggravate suffering. If a chemical or biological weapon does not kill and does not produce permanent aftereffects, but does cause a great deal of suffering for a long period of time, or if it causes a great deal of suffering and permanent aftereffects, the legality of its use must still be judged from the standpoint of whether or not such aggravated suffering was useless, taking into consideration whether the suffering caused was proportional to the military objective sought to be attained.[153] If it was, it would not be banned under the uselessly aggravated suffering rule. If it was not proportional, it would be banned both by the lack of proportionality principle and the prohibition against uselessly aggravated suffering. Thus again, each use must be judged in the full light of all the circumstances which are surrounding such use.

It has been postulated that in view of the fact that for the past twenty years there has been a determined and universal effort to eradicate endemic and epidemic diseases, resort to biological agents must be condemned as useless aggravation of universal suffering because their use would be contrary to the effort to control disease, and also because their use is a threat to the origin of life.[154] Under this approach it matters not what the circumstances surrounding their use may be: they are automatically and completely prohibited. The logic of this contention is difficult to follow. Certainly all weapons are a threat to the origin of life; dead people do not procreate. Furthermore, there has long been a universal international movement seeking to eradicate the use of force, but the use of force cannot be said to cause useless aggravation of universal suffering *ipso facto* so as to be unlawful. The lawfulness or unlawfulness of force, like the lawfulness or unlawfulness of biological weapons, is not to be derived from any contention that they cause useless aggravation of universal suffering.[155]

As to the second rule against weapons which render death inevitable, it has been pointedly remarked that the efficient use of well-aimed firearms or heavy artillery will render death inevitable for exposed target troops, but no one has suggested that the laws of war require soldiers to fire only at the limbs, for example, of enemy troops.[156] The rule therefore is said not to apply to weapons "which kill or wound fatally; if it were it would be a condemnation of practically all the projectiles used in war. It is to projectiles the effect of which is to leave the individual wounded or otherwise affected with no hope of survival."[157]

Thus it might well be argued that quick-acting lethal chemical agents are not within the scope of this rule. Only those agents which bring on lingering death would be involved. Nevertheless as to those lethal chemical weapons which are classified as gases, it has been implied that they are forbidden precisely because their deadly effect, whether instantaneous or lingering, renders death inevitable.[158] But these approaches both seem to be factually inaccurate in view of the fact that the effectiveness of a lethal chemical agent depends upon a number of factors such as the method of dissemination, i.e., whether it is disseminated by bursting type munitions or by spray devices; the weather, including temperature in the target area, the speed and direction of the wind, and the humidity and amount of precipitation; the nature of the terrain, including its contours, vegetation, and type and conditions of soil.[159] Furthermore, it might be noted that protective masks and devices are available against lethal gas attacks. Consequently resort to lethal gas agents can hardly be said to render death inevitable if the factors relating to effectiveness are not favorable, or if the targets are fully masked and protectively clothed, or if there is quick and efficient medical service available for those who have been exposed to the attack. As to incendiary attacks, there too whether or not death was inevitable following their use would depend on the time, place, wind and humidity conditions, protective shelters or protective clothing, and available medical facilities.

Inasmuch as germ warfare is a potentiality rather than an actuality, the military efficiency of differing methods of biological warfare is still an unknown factor. The complete protection of the general population against an attack by biological weapons is manifestly extremely difficult. Nevertheless, any attempt to outlaw all biological agents on the basis that they make death inevitable would be factually inaccurate in view of the fact that biological agents also range from mildly incapacitating to lethal. Furthermore, even lethal agents affect different people in different ways. A pathogen which causes fatal illness in one person may only make another ill and may have no effect on a third person. The effect in each case would depend on many factors including immunity and general health of the victim, portals of entry of the pathogens, the dosage absorbed, and the availability of medical therapy. Even the highly fatal biological toxins can be effectively neutralized if they are treated in time.[160] It is difficult to see how any biological weapon could be classified as one which makes death inevitable.

POISON AND POISONED WEAPONS

The treaty rule[161] against poison and poisoned weapons was a codification not only of an ancient customary rule but also of a medieval rule of chivalry which considered resort to such weapons as unchivalrous and dishonorable conduct. The rule entered into international law primarily because medieval monarchs were often eliminated by their rivals via poison in food or drink. Poison was thus a very individualistic method of doing away with an enemy. On the field of battle poisoned weapons were hard to handle and inefficient, and because of this lack of utility agreement could be reached to outlaw such weapons.[162] In addition an opponent who was hit by a poisoned arrow or a poisoned javelin suffered not only from the weapon wound but also from the poison, and therefore the poison was thought to fall within the scope of the chivalrous prohibition against uselessly aggravating the suffering of disabled men.[163]

The ban against poison and poisoned weapons was unqualified. Undoubtedly all antipersonnel chemical weapons except incendiary weapons and smoke, and all antipersonnel biological weapons could fall within an ample definition of poison.[164] Some international authorities feel that this particular rule can, in consequence, be relied upon as establishing an unequivocal ban prohibiting resort to such weapons.[165] Nonetheless, there are others who feel that the rule has relevance only to ancient weapons and ancient manners of assassination and consequently reflects only the past, having no application to modern technological developments in weaponry.[166] It is stated that chemical and biological weapons were never considered to fall within the classification of poison or poisoned weapons, for if they had been so classified there would have been no need to draw up the 1925 Geneva Protocol attempting to ban them specifically by an international treaty. It is claimed that the preponderance of the evidence would indicate that there was no prohibition against chemical or biological weapons prior to 1925 either in customary law or under the general principles of law recognized by civilized nations.[167]

Others argue that as the historic prohibitions upon the use of poison and poisoned weapons were based in large part upon their inefficiency, an analogy to such ancient weapons does not seem particularly helpful in ascertaining the lawfulness of antipersonnel chemical or biological weapons, since such an analogy does not take into consideration the issue of the efficiency of chemical or biological weapons.[168] The fact that such weapons are in the stockpile of many of the major powers indicates a probability that they are considered to be efficient, and consequently the analogy to ancient inefficient weapons would have no contemporary relevance. In addition, the very difficulty in securing explicit agreement about the effective prohibition of such weapons must suggest at least expectations of their military effectiveness.[169]

It would seem, therefore, that it would be difficult and perhaps dangerously illusionary to conclude that the total elimination or limitation as a matter of law of the use of chemical or biological weapons can be established by way of a restatement of the chivalrous ban against poison and poisoned weapons. Such a restatement denying the legality of such weapons would, of necessity, be based on controversial deductions from supposedly fundamental principles established in conditions vastly different from those obtaining in modern scientific warfare.

REPRISALS

The principle of reprisal becomes of import to any consideration of the legality of means and methods of warfare.[170] Reprisals are possibly the most effective sanction of the international law of war and are employed to bring about compliance with it. They are defined as repressive, retaliatory measures, otherwise unlawful, taken against an illegal act of warfare committed by the enemy to force abandonment of the illegal act and to compel future compliance with the rules of warfare by the delinquent. Under the principle of reprisal, justification may be had for the use of an illegitimate weapon or act in retaliation for a previous illegitimate act of warfare by the enemy. Reprisals are not to be considered as acts of punishment, however, but as acts to force compliance with the law by deterring future illegal acts. They indicate to the law-breaking state that the illegality will not be permitted, and, further, that the one against whom the illegality has been directed will not be placed at a disadvantage in the conflict because of the violator's breach of law.

Applying the principle to chemical and biological methods of warfare, it must first be stressed that the act of reprisal must be illegal itself except as employed in retaliation against a former illegality. Thus if resort to chemical and biological weapons has not been made illegal by international law, the principle of reprisal would have no applicability to them, for their use would be a legal use over and above any legality which might be conferred upon them when resorted to in the exercise of proper reprisals. If chemical or biological means have been made illegal in whole or in part by the international law of war, use of these weapons might still be considered as legitimate as a reaction to a former violation of the law by the enemy to deter repetition of such prior unlawful act or acts.

Some jurists would, however, refuse to admit of the right of reprisal with an inhumane weapon of war, for such would be considered as *malum in se*.[172] If chemical and biological methods of war were so identified, they could never be legally justifiable even when used as reprisals against a breach of the law of war. Chemical agents and those biological agents which are toxins have been stated to be poisons, and thus banned from use by the international rule which prohibits poisons and poisoned weapons. As such they could still be employed as reprisals unless the use of poison is considered *malum in se*. This position has been taken,[173] but not widely.

Over and above the poison prohibition, an instrument might be considered completely banned because it is thought to be inhumane or cruel. The spreading of biological agents has been stated by some to be so inhumane as to be completely prohibited.[174] However, and as has been noted, there would seem to be no automatic and complete *malum in se* restriction on weapons derived from a special principle of humanity as an independent source of law, and most authority seems to recognize that there is no real limit on weapons used as reprisals.[175]

The law of war does place certain limitations upon the use of reprisals which must be observed if such reprisals are to be legitimate acts. Since they are taken to force the enemy to desist from an illegal act, it is obvious that there must be a prior illegitimate act of warfare by the enemy. After infraction of the law has been determined, the victim should use all means other than reprisal to obtain redress from the wrongdoer and cessation of his illegal act. Complaint should be filed with the enemy calling upon him to cease and to grant redress. Public warning should be given to the effect that if the illegality is not abandoned retaliation will be forthcoming.

As we have seen, the Allied Powers sought to justify their use of gas in World War I as legitimate reprisals.[176] Some issue might be taken with this point of view, for they made no complaint after the first big use of gas by the Germans at Ypres, but instead retaliated with gas at a later time. Although it may not always be necessary to resort to the alternative and preliminary procedures if great damage would ensue to the victim by delay in taking reprisals, still the Allies could hardly excuse themselves, for several months elapsed following the German attack before they themselves made use of gas warfare.[177]

If the enemy does not abandon his illegal activity and when there is no longer reasonable hope for such abandonment, the countermeasures which would otherwise be illegal may be legally taken in retaliation provided those measures are not disproportionate to the wrong done— the original illegal activity. This is widely admitted in the literature, and with respect to chemical and biological agents those jurists who would view first use of such weapons as illegal would, if they are not considered as *mala in se*, admit of the legality of their use as reprisals in kind.[178] On the other hand, the position is not so firm as to the use of chemical or biological methods to retaliate against other illegal methods or acts of warfare which do not involve first use of chemical or biological means. In the general law of reprisals the notion seems to prevail that reprisals to be legitimate need not be identical to the method first used by the enemy. Stone, for example, states in this connection "that international law permits measures to be of an entirely different kind from the original illegality."[179] Greenspan is in accord:

The form which reprisals take is a matter within the discretion of the party instituting them, and is not laid down by any rule of law. A reprisal, therefore, need not be identical with the offense which provoked it, although the two acts are generally of a similar nature in order to bring the matter forcibly to the attention of the offender.[180]

Castrén states in this connection:

A belligerent has a *wide choice* of appropriate *countermeasures* and is not forced to adopt the same methods as the enemy. If this were the case, reprisals might not be sufficiently effective, nor is it always even possible to take similar measures.[181]

It will be remembered that the Italians sought to justify their first use of gas against the Ethiopians as legitimate reprisals in retaliation for illegal barbaric methods of warfare practiced against the Italians by the Ethiopians.[182]

Speaking specifically with respect to chemical and biological weapons as reprisals and despite the general rule that identical reprisals are not required, legal retaliation with chemical and biological means other than in kind is questionable. Lauterpacht, for example, would limit reprisals with chemical agents to retaliation in kind because these weapons cause cruelty and incalculable suffering.[183] The International Law Association in 1962 concluded that to the extent that chemical and biological weapons were considered poisons they were absolutely forbidden by international law and "because of this incompatibility with the standard of civilization, reprisals involving disregard of absolute prohibitions are, at the most, lawful as a form of identical reprisals."[184] This conclusion is somewhat strange in the light of the *malum in se* idea discussed above.[185] If a weapon is absolutely prohibited and incompatible with standards of civilization, it should probably not be permitted at all even for use as reprisals in kind. The report of this association, however, determined that an enemy who resorted to first use of chemical and biological weapons would have demonstrated to all its own barbarian character. Consequently identical reprisals would be permissible against such barbarism.

United States policy as enunciated so often would proscribe a first use of lethal or severely injurious chemical or biological weapons. This policy, as we have seen, has probably crystallized into a conviction of the existence of a customary rule to this effect. If this be correct, then the rule as viewed by the United States would limit the use of reprisals with lethal or severely injurious chemical and biological agents to retaliation after their first use by the law-breaker—reprisals in kind. Nevertheless, President Nixon's 1969 statement would indicate a changed United States policy which would bar the use of biological weapons for any purpose including reprisals.[186] The Soviet Union could possibly be said to share a similar point of view as to customary law.[187]

In any event, reprisals must not be excessive; they must not be disproportionate to the original wrong committed. If proportionality is measured in relation to the original illegal act and must not exceed the degree of violation committed by the delinquent, then, if chemical and biological reprisals are not restricted to identical methods of retaliation, it would seem that at the most lethal or severely injurious chemical and biological agents could be used only against some barbaric or shocking previous illegal act, in view of the fact that these agents have been so heartily condemned in many quarters. Nevertheless, the position is usually taken that reprisals are to be regarded primarily as acts to deter future illegality, and the proportionality should be looked upon as the amount of violence requisite to prevent the continuation of the former conduct. Therefore, it would be permissible at times to retaliate with stronger measures if necessary to bring about cessation of the illegality.[188] Even here, however, the reprisals should not be "so gross as to have no reasonable relationship to the postulated deterrent effect."

Following this line of thought, and again if reprisals with chemical and biological agents are not limited to identical measures, then a broad use of chemical and biological agents would be permissible against almost any serious breach of the laws of war.

The question has been raised whether chemical and biological instruments could be employed in retaliation for a first use of nuclear weapons.[189] If use of the latter is outlawed by the laws of war and if use of chemical and biological methods as reprisals is not restricted to retaliation in kind, then their use against a use of nuclear weapons could hardly be thought to be illegal as disproportionate. But, it is exceedingly doubtful whether the international law of war proscribes the use of nuclear weapons.[190] As against a legitimate weapon of war reprisals cannot be taken; accordingly, if chemical and biological agents are illegal methods, resort could not be had to them in reprisal against a legitimate use of force with nuclear means.

Allied conduct in World War I after German use of gas has been cited as an example of a disproportionate use of gas as reprisal, for the Allies adopted an approach which pointed to an unlimited right to resort to the use of gas after the initial German use, rather than an approach in accordance with the law of reprisals which would demand appropriate limited measures designed to make the law-breaking state desist.[191] The Allies, it is said, indicated by their course of resort to unlimited gas warfare that they felt themselves free to abandon the laws of war after the first German use of gas. This has been called a contract approach to the laws of war which would find no continuing obligation after first breach. This is an incorrect view, for customary rules of law continue to be binding after breach. They are not to be likened to contract, and they continue to demand after violation of the laws of war that reprisals be proportionate and limited, not unlimited.[192] It might be argued, however, with respect to the Allied use of gas in World War I, that the so-called unlimited use of gas by the Allies would be proportionate to the German use, which appears also to be unlimited, for German use was persistent and long-continued prior to the first use by the Allies. Several German gas attacks occurred before the first use by the British, and after the first British attack German attacks were many prior to the second Allied attack.[193] It can be said that use of gas in this war by both sides was largely unlimited.

Certain persons or property may not be subjected to reprisals with chemical or biological means or with any other means. Proscriptions as to persons would include prisoners of war,[194] wounded and sick of the armed forces,[195] enemy civilians found in the territory of the state subjected to the wrong, and inhabitants of the territory of the enemy occupied by that state.[196] Property exempt from reprisals is that of enemy aliens in the victim state's territory and property under that state's belligerent occupation,[197] as well as medical buildings, ships, transports, and equipment.[198] Cultural property registered as required by international convention for the protection of such property is also free from reprisals under certain conditions.[199]

As to authorization of reprisals, the law demands that superior officers are required to command their use. The United States Army Manual requires consultation of the highest accessible military authority before reprisals are taken unless immediate action is demanded, when a subordinate officer may give the order.[200] This United States rule as to reprisals in general has apparently been changed with respect to the use of chemical and biological weapons, for it is ruled that only the President of the United States must make the decision to use these instruments of war.[201]

SELF-DEFENSE

A major principle derived from the laws of civilized nations is that of self-defense, which empowers a state to take necessary measures to protect the nation against illegal external dangers.[202] This right has never been questioned, but it has been approached from two different angles. From a circumscribed point of view, a state, like an individual, may protect itself against an illegitimate forceful attack, commenced or imminently impending.[203] From a wider point of view, a state may exercise a right of self-defense not only against an illegitimate attack but also against any serious delictual conduct (even though no armed force is employed) when there is an absence of other means of protection for the essential rights of the state subjected to the wrong.[204]

Would it be legal for a state to resort to chemical or biological weapons in exercising its right of self-defense? Since riot control agents and incendiary weapons may be considered as conventional weapons, they can probably be used wherever conventional weapons may be legally employed in the right of self-defense.[205] If the first use of lethal and severely injurious chemical and biological agents has now been banned by customary international law, these weapons would not be permissible for first use in any situation of self-defense.[206] Nonetheless, there are some jurists[207] who are of the opinion that no such customary legal ban exists; consequently consideration must be given to this problem from their point of view.

The issue of the right to employ lethal or severely injurious chemical and biological agents in exercising the right of self-defense revolves not only around the nature of the weapon used, but also around the object to be defended. There has never been complete unanimity among international jurists on what is a nation's "self" in the exercise of the right of self-defense.[208] Some limit this "self" to territory and population,[209] while others take a broader view, pointing out that even if territory and population remain, the nation itself may not survive, and consequently the collective existence known as "self" in a nation has dimensions other than mere physical attributes.[210] It is asserted under this wider view that a nation may act in self-defense to preserve certain values and to protect the political and social institutions that embody these values. Since there is this uncertainty with respect to the scope of the legally protected interests comprising the state's security and independence, an equal uncertainty also prevails with respect to the measures which may be used in the right of self-defense. For example, may a state legitimately employ chemical or biological weapons to defend the state's "self" against illegal acts which do not involve the use of force but which do seriously imperil the self? Or may a state use such weapons only against an illegitimate armed attack, commenced or imminently impending? If a state's "self" is interpreted to involve only its territory and people, then it has been contended that only armed attack would threaten its vital interests, and therefore self-defense would have to be restricted to instances where there was an illegitimate resort to force, commenced or imminently impending, against that territory or the state's population. A nonforceful illicit act would not give rise to the right of "self" defense.[211] If a state's "self" is something more, then it has been stated that the right of political independence may be deprived of any real meaning if a state is not permitted to take, if necessary, forceful measures of self-defense, possibly including resort to chemical and biological weapons, against such illicit nonforceful threats.[212]

To be lawful, the exercise of force in self-defense requires that the danger (whether that danger come from forceful or nonforceful illicit acts) be immediate and of such a nature as to leave no reasonable possibility of recourse to alternative means of protection.[213] This stipulation might well exclude any resort to biological weapons in self-defense against either forceful or nonforceful illicit acts. The fact that biological weapons are by nature delayed-action weapons would indicate that a state had a reasonable possibility of recourse to other weapons which would act with more immediacy; and furthermore, if a state resorted to delayed-action weapons such as biological agents, it would seem to indicate that the danger was not "immediate."[214]

But this argument would not be applicable to resort to most chemical weapons, for their effects are generally felt within a short time after the weapon's use. The major restriction on chemical weapons then would be that the measures taken must be in proportion to the danger and must never be excessive or go beyond what is strictly required for the protection of the state's substantive rights which are endangered.[215] Force in excess of this purpose is forbidden, since action taken in self-defense is held to be strictly preventive in character. If resort to chemical weapons fulfills the requirements of proportionality, the form the immedate danger takes—whether forceful or nonforceful—would seem to be immaterial. It is not clear, however, whether the requirement of proportionality limits the act taken in self-defense to the *repelling* of the immediate danger or permits action directed to *removing* the danger altogether. The latter interpretation is not unreasonable, given the circumstances attending the situation in international society today, yet this approach would indicate that there can be no legal restraint on measures that may be taken if they do in fact *remove* a threat to a state's independence.

A further confusion as to when and by what means the right of self-defense may be exercised today arises from Article 51 of the United Nations Charter, which states in part:

> Nothing in the present Charter shall impair the inherent right of individual or collective self-defense if an armed attack occurs against a Member of the United Nations. . . .[216]

If this means that no member of the United Nations can take action in the nature of "anticipatory" self-defense before an armed attack is actually launched, in view of the speed and destructiveness of modern weapons it might well be that a law-abiding nation could be destroyed before it could save itself. General international law permitted the exercise of the right of self-defense not only in face of actual armed attack but also against a *threatened* attack when the danger was imminent.[217] As well known an authority on the Charter as Hans Kelsen is of the view that the right of self-defense is now limited to action *after* an armed attack has occurred.[218] Thereafter he would permit any proportional forceful reaction—which presumably would include reaction by chemical weapons, if such weapons are not otherwise banned by international law.

The major objection to this restrictive view is simply that a state may be unable to protect its vital interests, above all its political independence, if self-defense is legitimate only where the measures taken to endanger such interests take the form of an armed attack. To deny states the right to respond to illicit nonforceful measures jeopardizing a state's independence by employing, if urgently necessary, forcible measures in self-defense may well be to turn the right of political independence into little more than a sham. Presumably the purpose of the Charter's article was to enable nations to protect their essential rights when gravely threatened and not to insure that their epitaph would be able to testify to their lawful behavior.[219]

Consequently, the better view would seem to be that when the Charter speaks of an *inherent* right of self-defense, it implies that the right is inalienable, incapable of being surrendered in whole or in part.[220] If it is truly inherent, the right of self-defense can then be applied wherever it was permitted under general international law, not only against an actual attack, but also against a *threatened* attack when the danger is imminent; not only against a forceful illicit act, but also against a threatened nonforceful illicit act which threatened the political independence of a nation.[221] If resort to chemical weapons is not disproportionate to the danger threatened, and if they are not banned by other stipulations in the law of war, they may be legally resorted to in self-defense, under general international law and under the Charter of the United Nations.

Lauterpacht[222] apparently would go even farther. He implies that where the threatening nation is clearly intent upon dominating the world and imperiling the ultimate values of human freedom not only in a single state but also in the international community, a threatened nation may assume the responsibility of self-defense as well as the supreme right of self-preservation for itself and for the international community even by resorting, in a disproportionate manner, to any and all weapons of mass destruction including lethal or severely injurious chemical and biological weapons (whose first use he would ordinarily assume was banned) to defeat such an enemy.

O'Brien[223] would add a slight limitation to Lauterpacht's view. He indicates that if a state and its people are threatened by a menace which intends to destroy the state and wipe out the people physically and spiritually, that state could take any measure of self-defense necessary to counter such a threat except massive reprisals with weapons which would do the same to the enemy as the enemy sought to do to the reacting state.

Schwarzenberger[224] would disagree, pointing out that each major nation feels that its political system represents the ultimate values of society, and assertion of the right of self-preservation or the right to be the self-appointed guardian of humanity for the international community would merely function in advance as a semilegal justification for indiscriminate, uncontrolled, and illegal use of any weapon against another nation.

CHAPTER EIGHT

SUBSIDIARY MEANS FOR DETERMINATION OF LEGAL LIMITATIONS ON CB WARFARE

INTRODUCTION

ARTICLE 38 of the Statute of the International Court of Justice speaks of (1) judicial decisions and (2) the teachings of the most highly qualified publicists of the various nations, as *subsidiary* means for the determination of rules of law. As law-determining agencies, juristic works and judicial decisions are not considered as *sources* of international law. They are, however, regarded as important evidences of international law.

In this connection the works of publicists are not in and of themselves authority, but they do shed light on what the rules of international law may be through their scrutiny and analysis of the usages of nations. One judge has referred to juristic works as being "resorted to by judicial tribunals . . . for trustworthy evidence of what the law really is."[1]

Judicial decisions fall into two categories—those of international tribunals and those of national tribunals. Decisions of international tribunals are not considered as judicial precedents. As a result, they are not a direct source of international law. They have been called an indirect or a subsidiary source. Previous opinions are given weight in that they are relied upon in argument and in later decisions. Thus they are influential as evidences of the correct interpretation of the law. Judicial decisions of a particular nation also have value as evidence of international law, for, although they do not bind the state in which they are rendered to a rule or rules of international law, a uniform accumulation of decisions of the courts of many states can afford evidence of customary law.[2]

Finally, although not mentioned in the Statute of the International Court of Justice as a subsidiary means for the determination of international law, still the opinions of certain influential private groups offer some evidence of what the law is and possibly what the law ought to be. In a democratic state there is no doubt but that such private groups do contribute to the formation of an *opinio juris* by the state, and thus they may have some importance in the creation of customary rules of international law.

JURISTIC WORKS

CHEMICAL AGENTS

When one considers the works of publicists as evidence of prohibition of chemical and biological methods of warfare as based on customary norm or principle, one finds something of the same cleavage and lack of agreement as is found in the opinions of statesmen. Publicists writing general texts in the field of international law tend to treat the problem in a cursory fashion, lumping chemical and biological warfare together. This is well exemplified by certain Latin American writers. Podesta Costa of Argentina simply mentions the various treaties banning the use of asphyxiating or toxic gas and bacteriological methods and lets it go at that.[3] Antokoletz, another Argentine, does the same, but apparently believes no rule of customary law or prohibitory principle exists, for he states that the prohibitions of the treaties are respected among contracting parties, but not among the noncontractors.[4] Accioly of Brazil sheds no light on any customary rule. He confines himself to an observation of the various existing prohibitory conventions.[5] Sierra, a Mexican jurist, follows suit and then declares that as a result of the treaties asphyxiating and poisonous gases were not used in World War II.[6]

Turning to writers who express more definite views, we shall first consider jurists who regard gas warfare as being today universally prohibited between and among nations by international customary norm or by international principle.

Among post–World War II American writers, Greenspan concludes that the practice of states since the end of World War I indicates that gases are now to be considered as illegal weapons. He bases his conclusion primarily on the practice of states, but reinforces it with a statement that gas warfare is also to be regarded as a violation of the prohibition of the use of poison or poisonous weapons in war.[7]

Tucker, writing the 1955 United States Naval War College study, and again in 1966[8] in revising and editing Kelsen's *Principles of International Law*,[9] advances a belief that the practices of states do forbid the use of poisonous and asphyxiating gases to all states, not just those bound by treaty. These practices of states are said to be composed of treaties and proposed drafts of treaties as well as of the peacetime and wartime pronouncements of states. This customary rule would prohibit first use only, for the legality of reprisals to enforce the gas ban is admitted. Tucker doubts the applicability of either the customary rule or the treaty rule of the Geneva Protocol to all forms of chemical warfare. He would apparently confine the inhibition to what he calls asphyxiating or poisonous gases, which would probably be considered the lethal or severely injurious types.

Also mentioned by Tucker as possible bases for the gas prohibitions are the principle against unnecessary suffering and prohibition of the use of poison, as well as the noncombatant principle. Since Tucker believes that the use of gas can be confined to combatants only, he limits his discussion to such use and goes on to say that it is doubtful whether such suffering when judged by military purposes is unnecessary and therefore inhumane. In the 1966 work it is bluntly stated that poisons or asphyxiating gases would fall under the antipoison forbiddance, but earlier, in 1955, a hedging statement is made to the effect that the rule against use of poisons in warfare is applicable to gas only by analogy and implication. In a note Tucker qualifies this statement by limiting the application of the rule to odorless and colorless gases, since their use would constitute a form of treachery.

Another publicist, O'Brien, in an extended article sets forth the opinion that the fact that chemical warfare has not been resorted to since 1925, the year of the Geneva Protocol, is evidence of a customary rule against it. He finds that international practice has, therefore, given rise to a customary rule which prohibits the first use of chemical weapons. It is not clear whether he believes that the customary rule applies to all gases, including those that only temporarily disable. But he is of the belief that *all* chemical agents *should* be prohibited. Such a complete ban is justified, in his opinion, on the escalation theory, in that the use of any such means would ultimately result in the use of all. Possibly this theory may lead O'Brien to believe that all such means *are* actually forbidden by the customary rule.[10]

Sack, in an article written in 1950, makes the broad statement that chemical warfare is illegal for all states, inasmuch as the Geneva Protocol is said to be "an unwritten rule of international law . . . formally accepted as binding by the vast majority of civilized nations."[11]

Two of the most eminent of British publicists follow this line of thought. Lauterpacht speaks in a confused fashion of the "cumulative effect of customary law" combined with the binding force of the various treaties as rendering the ban on chemical warfare legally effective upon practically all of the states. He also grounds his opinion on the inhumaneness of the chemical weapon which he describes as a cruel method with a high degree of capability to impose such great suffering upon combatants and noncombatants alike that resort to it would make reprisals criminal unless taken as retaliation in kind. No discrimination would apparently be made between the various kinds of gases. All would be considered barred, for the British view presented in the 1930s which would make no differentiation is cited in his work.[12] Schwarzenberger also believes that the restraints of the Geneva Protocol have become declaratory of customary international law obligating all states, in that poisonous gas falls within the antipoison norm. He does not make note of any distinction between gases, but would admit the right of chemical reprisal after illegal first use.[13]

Castrén, the Finnish writer on the laws of war, makes no clearcut statement as to the existence of a customary norm banning chemical agents. He does find, however, that certain poisonous gases—and he distinguishes poisonous from asphyxiating gases—fall into the poison prohibition. Basing the antipoison rule on the principle of chivalry which rules against treachery, he is of the belief that only completely odorless or invisible poisonous gases would be treacherous and thus prohibited, together with those gases against which a gas mask does not give necessary protection. He also states that the unnecessary suffering principle would prohibit gas warfare behind the fighting lines, for its use would cause disproportionately large suffering to civilians. Use against combatants would be legitimate insofar as the unnecessary suffering principle is concerned, for the military benefits to be gained would presumably be proportionate to the suffering caused.[14]

Meyrowitz, a French author, in a recent and very well-reasoned article on chemical warfare, decides that a customary rule of international law does exist prohibiting the use of chemical asphyxiating or toxic weapons. His opinion is founded primarily on the nonuse of such weapons during World War II, particularly by the United States, which did not ratify the Geneva Protocol. He sees this abstention as an important element going to the affirmation of a customary rule, inasmuch as it demonstrates respect for and consolidation of the norm. Both the customary rule and the conventional rule forbid first use only, and neither is applicable to prohibit the production or stockpiling of or preparation for chemical warfare. However, Meyrowitz believes the customary rule to be more restricted than the conventional rule of the Geneva Protocol, in that the latter through its extensive language applies to prohibit all chemical substances in the solid, liquid, or gaseous state, while the customary rule, in his opinion, applies only to those substances that are deadly or harmful to health. He states expressly that the customary rule would not forbid the use of psychochemicals. He imposes a narrower customary rule because he sees the origin of the rule as going back to the antipoison and unnecessary suffering inhibition of the Hague Regulations. Since temporarily disabling agents would not cause unnecessary suffering and since he defines poison as death-dealing or injurious to health, only lethal or severely injurious anti-personnel agents would fall within the norm. To strengthen his argument he declares the field of application of the customary norm to be analogous to the Hague Declaration of 1899, which speaks of *asphyxiating* or *deleterious* gases.[15] He then states: "Pertinent as they may be, the arguments that since 1919 have influenced the codifiers to include non-deleterious chemical substances, arise from a reasoning too subtle and too technical to be expressed in the content of the customary rule."[16]

Guggenheim, a Swiss jurist, in a brief coverage of chemical warfare, bases his prohibition largely on international convention, but he does equate it with the Hague Regulations forbidding the use of poison in war, which would of course create a prohibition over and above treaty law. In a footnote he speaks of a statement by a Swiss delegate to the effect that the Geneva Protocol had become an integral part of international law.[17]

Singh, of India, condemns gas warfare vehemently as immoral and uncivilized, and then cites with approval the views of Lauterpacht and Schwarzenberger who find, as we have noted, that the prohibition has become a customary rule of international law.[18]

Finally, Soviet writers, although stressing the Geneva Protocol as the law-creating element which interdicts chemical warfare, do go further and accept a prohibition based on other sources. For example, certain Russian publicists refer to the demands of the public conscience as set forth in the de Martens clause as playing a leading role in the formulation of the legal prohibition of chemical warfare.[19] Kozhevnikov speaks of the Geneva Protocol as expressive of the legal conscience of mankind and concludes that it is declaratory of international law.[20]

Arrayed against these jurists who find a universal obligation are other authors of note who express a contrary point of view or who doubt that all states are bound by a prohibition. Hyde[21] and Fenwick,[22] two American writers, do not indicate the existence of a customary restraint. Fenwick takes note of the Geneva Protocol and then says that it cannot be relied upon because important states have failed to ratify it. This clearly dashes any belief in a customary rule. Hyde even questions the effectiveness of any treaty prohibition and believes that fear of retaliation only will prevent future use of chemical weapons. Fuller, writing in 1966, doubts the existence of a customary rule, stating: "The legal status of chemical and biological warfare is still uncertain for efforts are still made to have it declared illegal in a treaty or resolution."[23]

Kelly, in a lengthy and thorough article, refutes the existence of any customary rule forbidding gas warfare. He believes that the noncombatant principle would prevent the use of gas directly against noncombatants and that the principle of proportionality would forbid the use of gas against a military target if the benefit to be obtained would not be proportionate to the suffering.[24] Bernstein, writing in 1942, also would find no prohibition except upon those nations which had ratified a treaty like the Geneva Protocol.[25]

The Australian publicist Julius Stone is cited as accepting the view that customary international law forbids gas warfare, but[26] upon careful reading, his position appears equivocal. He agrees that the Lauterpacht view mentioned above has much in its favor and that this is reinforced by the fact that international organizations have assumed that the "use of toxic gases . . . is condemned by international law." But he hastens to state that this is not decisive and then continues:

Whether such preparations [for gas warfare] are directed to the principle of reciprocity under the Geneva Protocol, or under the general rule of international law now said to have emerged, or to retaliatory protection against a weapon not prohibited except to certain treaty-bound states in their mutual relations, it is clear that international law does not prohibit either the *retaliatory* use of poison gas against an enemy who has used it, or preparations for such retaliation.[27]

Kunz, in 1935,[28] found no universal rule prohibiting gas. And he stands by this conclusion in 1957, stating that such a prohibition is possible only by international agreement to which militarily important states are parties.[29]

McDougal and Feliciano take note of the positions of certain writers who have assumed that the Geneva Protocol is declaratory of a customary norm, but they find such a viewpoint not easy to rationalize. Indeed, they refute unnecessary suffering as a basis of the norm and believe the language of the Protocol which permits writers to extend it to certain nonlethal chemical agents is much too broad to be practical.[30]

Rousseau of France does not speak of a customary rule, but bases interdiction upon the Geneva Protocol.[31] The same is true of certain German authorities.[32] Moritz, although admitting that the language of the Geneva Protocol would lead to a conclusion that it was declaratory of customary international law, goes on to say that official doubts as to its binding quality raise a question as to its declaratory nature and the legal status of chemical warfare at international law.[33]

This sampling of juristic works shows authority on both sides of the fence. No definite conclusion drawn from the evidence presented by the writings of publicists as to the imposition of universal obligation upon all states to refrain from the use of chemical agents in war is possible. There is a further complication in that many of the writers who take a stand for the existence of a universal obligation do so after treating the subject matter in a very perfunctory manner, with little reasoning or authority to back them up.

Taking note of certain of the authors who have given thoughtful and reasoned attention to the problem, one might hesitantly and with some trepidation reach the point of view that a customary rule binding upon all states has come into being which would serve to make the first use of lethal and severely injurious or harmful chemical antipersonnel agents illegal.

BIOLOGICAL AGENTS

The legality or illegality of biological warfare is given even more sketchy treatment than is chemical warfare by many of the publicists mentioned above. Certain of these writers, particularly authors of general international law treatises, fail to mention bacterial or biological agents as methods of war at all.[34] Others simply call attention to the Geneva Protocol, which is said to prohibit gas as well as bacterial methods.[35] This sheds no light on the existence or nonexistence of any customary rule. Other writers do make brief mention of biological warfare and venture an opinion as to legal control other than by international convention. Schwarzenberger[36] and Singh[37] agree that the Geneva Protocol of 1925 is now declaratory of international customary law and makes biological as well as gas methods illegal. They also liken biological agents to poisons. Sack would be in accord.[38] The former two writers would apparently admit the use of biological means as reprisals.[39] The latter makes no mention of this point.

Greenspan would also find biological agents barred quite apart from treaty obligation, for to him they are "disgraceful and impermissible" and violative of the general prohibition against poison.[40] Spaight, in speaking of alleged spreading of pathogenic germs during World War I, states this to be a grave offense against the laws of war and later calls bacteriological warfare contrary to the laws of humanity.[41] Lauterpacht directs his attention in the main to gas warfare, and in speaking of this method he admits that the Geneva Protocol has come to be almost universally effective. As to bacteriological warfare, he is content to rest with the observation that the Geneva Protocol includes this method also. In his words as to gas he admits that this method can be used as reprisals, but only in kind.[42] Can these words, one wonders, be extended to biological agents?

Tucker, writing in 1955, was not sure of the existence of a customary rule as to biological warfare, for he could find no practice of states extant which would compare with the impressive evidence of practice prohibitory of gas.[43] He admitted, however, a trend toward outlawry, and by 1966 he finds the crystallization of a prohibitory customary rule to be deduced from treaties, drafts of treaties, and pronouncements of states.[44] To the extent that biological agents are toxic he would believe them barred by the antipoison rule.[45] Possibly he too would admit reprisals with biological agents, although he makes no express statement on them, for he recognizes them in regard to gas.[46]

The Soviet writers mentioned above in connection with the discussion of chemical agents take the same position as to biologicals as they do as to chemicals. They believe that the Geneva Protocol is a codification of international law, and further that the de Martens clause, in banning methods of warfare violative of the public conscience, had much to do in the creation of a norm barring bacteriological and chemical methods.[47] A German author also would proscribe first use of bacteriological as well as chemical or atomic weapons, but he gives no reasons for the prohibition other than the Geneva Protocol.[48]

Three authorities agreeing that biological methods of warfare are outlawed have written on the subject somewhat more extensively, and have set forth more detailed reasons for their conclusions. Castrén, the Finnish publicist on the laws of war, sets forth a minimum standard of warfare principle which he declares proscribes brutal methods of warfare, the extent of which may be unpredictable. He uses as his example chemical and bacteriological means which are prohibited if condemned by prevailing public opinion.[49] He becomes somewhat more definite at a later point in his work when he advances the notion that biological warfare *should* be prohibited *entirely* in all theaters of war, inasmuch as noncombatants could not be afforded protection from infection. He then points out that "general opinion condemns bacteriological warfare even more severely than the use of gas" and refers to the opinions of others who regard it as a treacherous method like poison or even assassination.[50] Castrén is not really clear in setting forth his own opinion as to the existence of a forbidding principle or customary norm. Another statement does little to clarify his position in this respect, for he advances the idea maintained by the Geneva Disarmament Conference to the effect that bacteriological warfare must be absolutely prohibited even as reprisal because of the danger to humanity from the spread of dangerous biological agents.[51]

Meyrowitz, the French authority, in an article devoted to biological weapons advances the opinion that use of certain of such weapons would be contrary to the principle of the immunity of the civilian population, the antipoison norm, and the superfluous injury principle, as well as an express customary norm of international law. With regard to the first he distinguished chemical warfare, the effects of which can be confined to enemy forces, and which is therefore not outlawed under the noncombatant principle except as used directly against noncombatants. Despite the fact that he recognizes that biological agents could conceivably be limited to combatants, Meyrowitz believes the possibility of such limitation would be exceptional; therefore, since biological warfare violates or is capable of violating the noncombatant immunity because of its "contagiousness, delayed effects, insidious action, unpredictable effects and difficulty of detection and identification," it is prohibited.[52] As to the rule forbidding the use of poison or poisoned weapons in war, this author would forbid the use of those biological agents which fall under the classification of toxins, for they fit the definition of poison.[53] He would also consider the proportionality rule of the superfluous or unnecessary injury principle violated by the use of such agents, for the large and unpredictable extent of harmful effect on the civilian population would be out of reasonable proportion to the military advantage to be gained, and therefore would constitute unnecessary suffering.[54]

This writer also believes that a customary international rule has arisen through practice—that is, through abstention from use in recent years and in recent conflicts and from a conviction or *opinio juris* of nations that biological warfare is illegal. He relies heavily for this conviction on the General Assembly resolution adopted in 1966, which he believes in affirming the principle of the Protocol recognizes a universally binding prohibition of chemical and biological methods of warfare.[55]

Meyrowitz would forbid only first use of this instrument of war; reprisals against such use even with biological agents would be permitted.[56] Note should be made of an important limitation made as to both the conventional rule of the Protocol and the customary rule as to chemical and biological warfare. First use of these methods is proscribed, Meyrowitz believes, only as directly aimed *against human targets.*[57] He states in speaking of the Protocol that the language is so general as to encompass and prohibit use against all targets, persons as well as plants, animals, and materiel. Nevertheless, he concludes that this generality has been restricted in interpretation and that the proscription is to be considered applicable only to direct use against human beings. He is not completely sure of his ground, for later he speaks of an ambiguity in the Protocol and states that it is not clear whether it would also prevent use of chemical or biological agents against livestock or plant life. To support the restricted version that the Protocol only proscribes as against human beings, the author falls back on the general principles of the laws of war which do not make illegal, for example, defoliation of plant life not necessary for sustenance of people when the defoliation is not harmful to the human or animal organism. Moreover, it is said that no rule forbids destruction of foodstuffs in an area where enemy forces are fighting.[58] Again the author is somewhat uncertain of his own viewpoint, for he mentions that a *general* prohibitory interpretation of the Protocol may be the correct one and a restricted version dangerous, inasmuch as the considerations which have caused the general character to be attributed to the language with reference to chemical warfare and to biological apparently as well are "on the one hand the practical impossibility of maintaining the distinction between merely incapacitating weapons, pathogenic weapons and lethal weapons; and on the other hand the risk of escalation by the mechanism of reprisals."[59] These considerations could well be thought to offset any reasons for tolerance of a less restrictive rule mentioned above.

Finally, Meyrowitz maintains the same distinction as to biological methods that he made with respect to chemical methods, to the effect that the customary rule is narrower than the conventional rule as to the type of agent. The conventional rule would prohibit all biological methods of war used directly against human targets, while the customary rule "probably does not cover merely incapacitating agents."[60]

The American writer Brungs, in a detailed article on biological warfare, finds no international norm which forbids biological methods of war per se. He does conclude that the use of those agents classified as toxins is illegal, for they poison a victim rather than infect him with disease and thus would be considered as poison. As such, toxins would be forbidden by the universal antipoison rule. He does not state an opinion as to the validity of reprisals with biological toxins, but he does recognize reciprocity between ratifiers of the Geneva Protocol. Anticrop and antianimal agents are to him lawful, an opinion based on an analogy to blockades, scorched earth policies, and sieges, all of which also cut off supplies.[61]

On the other side of the coin, important jurists see no customary rule of international law banning biological agents in war and no other principle or rule which in and of itself condemns absolutely the use of such agents. Certain writers such as Kunz,[62] Fenwick,[63] Rousseau,[64] and Hyde[65] treat the matter summarily, basing any prohibition on the Geneva Protocol. Fuller, after extensive discussion and analysis of the policy and practices of states, believes the legal status of both chemical and biological methods to be uncertain.[66] Moritz takes a categorical position that there is no customary rule applicable to forbid the use of biological agents, since there has been no resort to such agents in war, and that, although from the wording of the Protocol it might be contended that chemical weapons were prohibited by international law prior to that instrument, still the same argument cannot be made as to biological agents, since there had been no previous treaties as to this form of warfare.[67]

O'Brien adopted the viewpoint that from the abstaining practices of states a rule has evolved inhibiting chemical warfare. He refuses to take a similar position with respect to biological warfare because there has been no widespread capability to use biological weapons, and therefore the abstention from use of these agents is based not on conviction of illegality, but on pure military considerations. He declares:

We know that some kind of capability for waging biological warfare exists today, but it has never been tried. Certainly it cannot be said that failure to use a means not adequately developed is proof of an intent to have such means prohibited. Consequently, there can be no customary rule against biological warfare based on non-use.[68]

Direct attacks on noncombatants by biological methods as well as their use to cause injury to the people of a neutral state would appear to this author to be illegal. The unnecessary suffering principle would apply, but only as it would apply to any means of warfare not specifically forbidden. The antipoison rule would not be applicable to biological instruments, for they were not a type of weapon known at the time the rule was propounded.[69]

Neinast, writing on biological warfare, concludes that there is no customary rule forbidding this type of warfare. His reasoning is founded primarily upon the fact that preparation for such warfare through stockpiling of weapons is evidence that the nations believe this method legal. Moreover, the fact that the United Nations has not been able to secure a prohibitory convention is to him additional evidence of legality. The only two principles of importance to this author, proportionality and reprisals, are considered. He would say that since the principle of proportionality applies to the use of any legal weapon, it would forbid the indiscriminate use of biological as well as other legal weapons. If biological are considered illegal, then the principle of reprisals would still permit their use against violations of the laws of war.[70]

Stone, while somewhat doubtful as to a customary antichemical warfare rule, refutes definitively any such antibiological warfare rule binding upon all states. The fact that the text of the Geneva Protocol itself extended a treaty prohibition to bacteriological warfare would to him be an admission that no limitation had come into existence in customary international law at the time of the treaty. This would be strengthened by the fact that biological weapons have been developed so recently. He goes on to state: "Nor is there as yet a sufficient line of treaty undertakings to suggest the growth of any such rule. Its scope therefore must be limited to those states who are parties to the Gas Protocol within the limits of reciprocity and the like there laid down."[71]

Recognizing the fact that biological warfare is "widely assumed to be a particularly disgraceful and odious activity," McDougal and Feliciano still doubt the development of a universally binding prohibition. They do not see the acceptance of a customary rule by states not ratifying the Protocol. To them it is difficult to base an interdiction on the antipoison rule, apparently on the ground that that rule was meant to apply to simpler weapons of a former time, like poisoned spears and javelins. They do not believe any more unnecessary suffering to be caused by the use of biological agents than by the use of bullets; and they feel that no conflict with the noncombatant principle should occur, for they state that the virulence of biological agents can be controlled and thus would not necessarily spread to noncombatants. The fact that complete protection of noncombatants is almost impossible anyway is another factor militating against referral to the noncombatant principle. Also noted by these authors is the broad and general language of the Protocol which prohibits bacteriological warfare. They then ask whether the Protocol or any customary rule would or should apply to ban all bacteriological methods— for example, those not directed against human beings, but against plants and animals. Deprivation of supplies through a food blockade has been an international practice and the use of antiplant and antianimal agents could be analogous.[72]

This lack of agreement among authors not only as to the legal status of a prohibitory norm or principle applicable to biological warfare over and above a conventional rule, but also as to the scope of the prohibition pertaining to biological warfare makes evidence formulated upon the juristic works of publicists inconclusive. When we look at the works of those writers mentioned above who have given the most profound consideration to the matter in their analyses, taking into account the fact that some find an all-inclusive prohibition, while others find none and still others something in between, it would seem that a balance can possibly be reached, and thus it might be said that evidence points to some restrictive proscriptions of the use of biological methods in war.

There seems to be some common theme running through certain of the writings to the effect that the noncombatant principle could or can be violated by biologicals if their virulent effects cannot be controlled so that noncombatant immunity could not be effectuated. Disagreement prevails, as we have seen, as to this latter point.

Several of the authors find that the biological agents which are classified as toxins are prohibited under the antipoison rule, while other biological agents would have to find forbiddance elsewhere if at all. The distinction based solely upon a technical classification of poison seems a rather foolish one. Death or injury by a toxin or by an infectious disease is still death or injury. A better argument, as we have mentioned earlier, is that the antipoison rule was not thought to encompass biological or bacteriological methods: if it was, why was it necessary to create a special conventional rule relating to these methods through the Geneva Protocol?[73]

If one can accept the fact that the abstention by states from use of biological warfare is abstention through legal conviction, not on the incomplete development of the biological method as an instrument of war, then it would be logical to agree with Meyrowitz that a customary norm prohibiting at least some aspects of biological warfare has come into being. It can then be contended that a circumscribed customary rule limited to a prohibition of antipersonnel biological agents would exist. Antiplant, antianimal, and antimateriel agents would not be banned, because other rules of international law permit destruction of supplies and food of the enemy in time of war until his territory is actually occupied. Moreover, in an analogy to the customary prohibition of chemical agents and the fact that norms of civilization have been said to forbid weapons of mass destruction, which may be interpreted to mean mass human destruction,[74] then the customary rule would cover those virulent epidemic agents which are harmful in high degree to the human organism. Temporary disabling incapacitants would be excluded from the rule.

Jurists who discuss the matter and who favor a prohibitory rule on biological methods would in general permit reprisals after first use by the other party.

INCENDIARY WEAPONS

The legality of fire weapons such as napalm, flamethrowers, and incendiary bombs has upon occasion been questioned, although there is something of a dearth of writing on the subject. Upon the employment by Germany of flamethrowers in World War I, the French government offered strong protest against the use of such a barbarous and inhumane instrument, and France and her British and American allies thereafter retaliated in kind.[75] Garner, writing immediately after the war, saw no illegality in the use of this weapon, for he did not believe that it violated any of the Hague Conventions, including the superfluous injury or unnecessary suffering principle. In relation to this latter point he had this to say:

> While the effect may be more deadly than bullets or shells, we can hardly say that it is any less permissible. Indeed, owing to its very limited radius of action and the visibility of the flame, the chances of escape are greater than where the instruments employed are projectiles or shells.[76]

On the other hand, a very few publicists have been found who would condemn fire weapons. Lauterpacht, in speaking of the German flame projectors of World War I, declared in a brief footnote that a practice of throwing burning liquid on the enemy would violate the unnecessary suffering principle.[77]

Writing more extensively on the subject of fire in war, Noel-Baker concludes that the use of fire in war was forbidden by the unnecessary suffering principle before 1914 and up to World War II. He also notes the unsuccessful effort of the Geneva Disarmament Conference of the 1930s, which sought to incorporate an express prohibition against incendiary weapons as having base on this principle. The extensive use of fire weapons—incendiary bombs and flamethrowers—in World War II and Korea force this author to a conclusion that the old laws of war abolishing such means had been "completely demolished." Consequently, in the absence of an existing prohibition he calls for abolition of fire weapons by international agreement.[78]

Greenspan believes that the use of fire in war to kill or disable human beings is still violative of international law.[79] Use of fire weapons to destroy military objectives other than human beings, such as fortifications, buildings, and equipment, would be permitted. Antipersonnel weapons, however, are considered as impliedly forbidden by the Declaration of St. Petersburg of 1868[80] which barred the use of small projectiles charged with fulminating or inflammable substances. The broader principles of this declaration, such as the use of weapons which uselessly aggravate the sufferings of disabled men and which render death inevitable, would also forbid. To Greenspan, fire weapons do both. Fire can also be considered analogous to the prohibitions of the Geneva Protocol (gases and analogous liquids and materials) in that fire can cause damage to skin and tissue such as gas can cause, and can also asphyxiate.

Singh, like Noel-Baker, has stated that flamethrowers were considered illegal before World War II as impinging on the unnecessary suffering rule, but their extensive use in that war and in Korea demonstrates that the use of incendiary agents is not now thought to be violative of international law.[81] Schwarzenberger is cited to the effect that these and other weapons with large destructive possibilities would not automatically be illegal under the unnecessary suffering rule.[82]

Spaight[83] and Tucker[84] also are of the opinion that particularly since World War II fire weapons are to be regarded as legitimate weapons of war. Stone would find no prohibitions against them which can be derived from the practice of the twentieth century. He states that their use has not been "seriously questioned."[85] Castrén would agree, stating that the use of these instruments should be confined to the fighting area, but behind the lines they should be used only against military objectives that could not be destroyed by other means. He admits, however, that the use of fire weapons was indiscriminate in World War II.[86]

McDougal and Feliciano, in commenting upon flamethrowers and napalm bombs, would seem to adopt the United States Army Manual position to the effect that their use against military targets does not violate international law, but that they should not be used so as to cause unnecessary suffering to individuals. These writers can find no more unnecessary suffering from a use of these weapons for a reduction of bunkers, for attacking tanks, or for removing the enemy from certain places of an inaccessible nature than from the use of regular artillery shells. To them "the nature and situation of the target would seem the factors of decisive significance."[87]

From this review of the attitude of publicists, the conclusion can be reached that no matter what might have been the thought prior to World War II, the use of incendiary weapons is now considered legitimate subject only to whatever effect the restraints of proportionality in the unnecessary suffering principle as well as the noncombatant and other principles might have.

JUDICIAL DECISIONS

Judicial decisions are not helpful in arriving at a conclusion as to a prohibition of chemical or biological warfare apart from treaty law. The only reference which an international tribunal has made concerning these methods of warfare is one made by way of dicta in 1930 by the German-Greek Mixed Arbitral Tribunal in *Kiriadolou* v. *Germany*. This case involved the death of a Greek from a conventional air bombing of Bucharest by the Germans in 1916. In speaking to Article 26 of the Hague Regulations, which required warning before commencement of bombardment, the tribunal stated:

The dispensation from preliminary notification would enable aeroplanes and dirigibles to poison the non-combatant population of an enemy town by permitting them to drop, by night and without warning, bombs filled with asphyxiating gas, spreading death or causing incurable diseases.[88]

As Neinast points out, the meaning of this statement is not clear.[89] It is directed to a use of gas against noncombatants only. Unanswered is the question of whether gas can be used against enemy personnel. Even as to noncombatants the question may be posed as to whether it would be permissible to use the weapon through air bombing if a previous warning was given. What is meant by the use of the words "incurable diseases"? Do they relate back and condemn the spreading of incurable diseases by bombs filled with asphyxiating gas, or is this a condemnation of gas as well as biological methods of war? Moreover, all the states involved—Greece, Rumania, and Germany—were parties to the Geneva Protocol, so that the court might have been influenced by a treaty prohibition. These words uttered by way of dicta can hardly be pointed to in reaching a conclusion as to the existence of a prohibitory rule.

None of the international tribunals created to deal with the war crimes of World War II concerned themselves with gas or biological warfare. A count of the indictment brought before the Tokyo War Crimes Tribunal accused Japanese commanders of using poison gas against China contrary to the Hague antigas declaration of 1899 and the antipoison provision of the Hague Regulations as well as the Treaty of Versailles.[90] As we have seen, reliance on these treaty rules is rather questionable as against Japan, but in any event such reliance shows little belief in the existing of a binding inhibition over and above treaty law.[91] The final judgment did not concern itself with this charge.[92]

One judicial decision is extant concerning biological warfare—that of a Soviet Military Tribunal in Khabarovsk which convicted and sentenced certain Japanese army officers for using bacteriological agents (typhoid, paratyphoid, cholera, anthrax, and plague) against the Mongolian Peoples Republic in 1939 and against China during the period between 1940 and 1942.[93] O'Brien refers to a comment from the British Manual to the effect that this charge and decision against Japanese nationals would be evidence of a conviction on the part of the court of a customary prohibition on bacteriological methods of warfare, because Japan was not a party to the Geneva Protocol.[94] This could point to a Soviet *opinio juris*, for the decision was that of a national rather than an international court.[95] It would not, however, be so valuable as evidence of a universal *opinio juris*. The Soviets did attempt in 1950 to obtain the creation of a special international tribunal to try the Japanese emperor and certain Japanese generals on these and similar charges, but nothing ever came of this Soviet effort.[96]

PRIVATE GROUPS

THE INTERNATIONAL LAW ASSOCIATION

The International Law Association has considered the problem of the legal prohibition of chemical and biological methods of warfare on various occasions. As early as 1921 a Chemical Warfare Committee was created by the association "to consider how an international agreement not to use poison gas in war, nor to manufacture it at any time for use in war, nor to engage in experiments or research work with the object of producing such gas in war, could be enforced."[97]

At the Thirty-First Conference of the association in 1923, the committee, in its report and in certain draft articles, stated that the production, manufacture, or preparation of poisonous or asphyxiating gases for use or intended for use in war is declared unlawful and prohibited. States violating this prohibition as well as the prohibition of subsidizing production, manufacture, or preparation of poison war gas would be deemed to have breached international law and to have incurred the penalties set forth in Article 16 of the Covenant of the League of Nations. Any individual who, even under superior orders, violated such provisions was to be considered guilty of a war crime and upon conviction by an International Criminal Court would be punished as a war criminal. Further forbidden was the manufacture or attempted manufacture of any projectile or vessel to distribute poison gas, the erection of any plant or machinery for the purposes of poison gas, or the erection of or use of any station to make tests for the use of poison gas. The last article of the draft provided that its provisions were to be a part of municipal law, and a national of a state charged with a war crime in violating the provisions would be liable to arrest in any of the contracting states and could be sent to trial before an international Criminal Court.[98]

It is evident from this report and draft that the members of the committee were attempting to create new law by international agreement. Thus the action does not indicate the existence of a customary rule or prohibitory principle.

This organization considered the problem of chemical and biological warfare again in 1938 at its Fortieth Conference in connection with a Draft Convention for the Protection of Civilian Populations Against New Engines of War.[99] Although the draft was concerned with the protection of noncombatants, it sought to forbid by a blanket proscription chemical, incendiary, or bacterial weapons. Chemical weapons prohibited were those of any natural or synthetic substance (solid, liquid, or gaseous) harmful to the human or animal organism by reason of its being toxic, asphyxiating, irritant, or vesicant. Explosives, smoke, or fog not likely to produce harmful effects were excepted, as was tear gas. Incendiary weapons forbidden were those specifically intended to cause fire, except those used in defense against aircraft. Certain other exceptions were set forth, such as flamethrowers employed to attack individual combatants. Bacterial weapons interdicted were methods for disseminating pathogenic microbes or filter-passing substances in order to bring them into contact with humans, animals, or plants in any manner, by polluting either the atmosphere, water, foodstuffs, or any other objects of human use. Like the previous consideration by the association, this was an attempt to create law by treaty, and as such it does not demonstrate the existence of a rule.

The most recent deliberations in this field by the International Law Association are those of the Fiftieth Conference held in 1962.[100] Here a report concluded that legal limitations on chemical-biological methods of warfare apart from treaty limitations were imposed by the antipoison rule, which was said to have come into being as a customary rule of international law. If a particular chemical or biological weapon could be classified as poison, then it would be prohibited. It would appear that almost any chemical or biological agent would be included within the poison classification, for poison was defined broadly and nontechnically as that which "destroys life or injures health by the introduction of substances . . . into, or their absorption by a living organism."[101] The prohibition was based upon the poison rule rather than upon the character of the weapon as one of mass destruction, for no real prohibition by principle or customary rule could be found against weapons of mass destruction as such. Their use would apparently be permitted if military necessity were served. Moreover, arguments based on the illegality of chemical and biological weapons because of the indiscriminate effects upon combatants and noncombatants alike were no longer thought decisive because of the indiscriminate character of modern air warfare as practiced by states.

Even though chemical and biological weapons were barred by the antipoison rule, the report would permit their use by way of reprisals. At one point it was argued that because these weapons might be considered incompatible with standards of civilization, reprisals should be lawful only as identical reprisals or reprisals in kind.

This report, then, would find chemical and biological weapons banned by the customary antipoison rule except as to reprisals. It must be pointed out that any evidentiary value of this finding is curtailed by the sharp disagreement with this viewpoint which we have discussed previously.

THE PUGWASH CONFERENCES AND OTHER SCIENTIFIC GROUPS

The Conference on Science and World Affairs, commonly called the Pugwash Conference, composed of scientists from different parts of the world, has also considered the problem of chemical and biological weapons.[102] A meeting of 1959[103] was devoted to an assessment of chemical and biological warfare and its threat to humans, animals, and plants.

Attention was also given to the ways and means to prevent the production and use of chemical and biological instruments in war. The scientists agreed that the only way to alleviate world apprehension concerning these weapons was to assure that they will not be produced and that if produced they will not be used. At the same time the difficulty of international control through a system of inspection and verification was recognized. Nevertheless it was believed that some progress could be made in averting the danger of chemical and biological warfare and alleviating world fears by "(a) a general agreement to prohibit the use of such weapons, and (b) the renunciation of official secrecy and security controls over microbiological, toxicological, pharmaceutical, and chemical-biological research."[104]

Biological and chemical agents in war were subjected to further discussion in 1965,[105] and here a total ban on such weapons under strict international verification was said to be required. It was noted that no distinction could be made between lethal agents and those which were merely incapacitating. Finally all states were called upon to adhere to the Geneva Protocol, but it was pointed out that additional arrangements were needed to avoid development and production of these agents.

Another group speaking with reference to the use of gas in Vietnam condemned the employment of this instrumentality in war in any part of the world. Even the temporary incapacitating gases were condemned, for it was believed that once any gas is used there is danger of escalation to the use of all gases. Moreover, it was stated that temporarily incapacitating gases would probably be directed toward the civilian populations in cases where more destructive gases would not be used.[106]

In 1967 the Pugwash groups concerned themselves primarily with the study of the technical problem of fast detection of microbiological agents which would include viruses and toxins and which might be employed in biological warfare.[107] Also of concern were the control of such weapons by voluntary inspection and conditions for a ban on the testing of these weapons. At the conference of September, 1967,[108] the nations not parties to the Geneva Protocol were once again called upon to adhere to this instrument, and a treaty was urged which would forbid both the use of chemical and biological weapons and their transfer to other nations.

In analyzing these deliberations of the Pugwash Conference one finds that the group has stressed the fact that chemical and biological agents *should* be banned for use in war by international law. It would be doubtful that they are already considered banned to all nations, for all are urged to adhere to the Geneva Protocol. Finally, this group feels the need of something more than a ban on use. They want also the prohibition of preparation, production, and transfer of these weapons. A system of control and verification is thought to be needed. Such a complete regime is not now law; it is yet to be established.

The Federation of American Scientists has also spoken on the use of chemical and biological weapons in war. It has called for a no first use policy, an abandonment of mass production of biological weapons, and a cessation of the development of new biological and chemical weapons. Moreover, this organization has urged an international agreement to prohibit the use of these instruments of war and to renounce their development.[109]

Other scientists have expressed concern over the use of chemicals in the Vietnam War, and have called for a no first use policy and stressed the need for ratification of the Geneva Protocol.[110] The opposition of these persons to chemical and biological weapons is marked, but since they emphasize the urgent need for United States ratification of the Protocol or of prohibitory international agreement, they seem to doubt the existence of any other legally binding obligation.

CHAPTER NINE

CONCLUSION

TO RECAPITULATE briefly, a large number of the states of the world are parties to the Geneva Protocol of 1925 which prohibits the use in war of asphyxiating, poisonous, or other gases and of analogous liquids, materials, or devices as well as bacteriological methods of warfare. Other prohibitory treaties as to chemical and biological weapons do exist binding various members of the international society which have ratified them, but the Geneva Protocol is the most widespread in its effect in that the greatest number of states may be counted among its adherents.

Apart from treaty law, one can arrive at the conclusion that a more restricted rule of customary international law has come into being which has universal obligation and which would forbid the first use of antipersonnel lethal or severely injurious chemical and biological agents. As a result, it can be concluded that all nations are legally bound by either treaty or custom to refrain from resort to chemical and biological agents, or some of them, in war.

To make this statement is not in reality to say very much, for a good lawyer before an unbiased international tribunal acting on behalf of a defendant client who *had* or a plaintiff who *had not* resorted to the use of chemical or biological weapons could win or lose his case with equal ease.

First, although evidence can be marshaled as to the existence of a customary rule from the practice of abstention from resort to such weapons or from the statements of policy-makers banning certain chemical and biological agents, still the evidence is far from overwhelming, and it is quite possible to reach, with complete intellectual honesty, a differing determination. The split of authority among reputable international jurists makes evidence of the existence of a customary rule doubtful, and, if it is in existence, evidence of its extent equivocal.

If states in a case involving the use of chemical and biological weapons were all parties to the Geneva Protocol, obstacles would still exist to attempt to pin guilt upon a party alleged to have breached the treaty. It is true that a prohibition exists, as to use, but there is disagreement as to the use of what and against whom. Some aver that the broad and general language of the Protocol denies the use of *all* chemical agents in the form of gas and all biological agents. Others would limit the meaning to lethal or severely injurious agents. Some maintain the use of these agents

246

is prohibited against persons, animals, plants, and materiel; others assert that the restriction of use applies only against human beings.

Even if agreement could be found on a common meaning of the language of the Protocol itself, the reservations to it have created such a confused status of legal relationship between and among ratifiers and adherents, that extreme problems of interpretations are unavoidable.

Whatever treaty limitations on chemical or biological weapons could be derived from the St. Petersburg Declaration and the Hague Conventions may have been outmoded on the basis of *rebus sic stantibus,* i.e., the doctrine that a treaty is intended by the parties to be binding only as long as there is no vital change in the circumstances assumed by all the parties at the time of the conclusion of the treaty. It has been alleged[1] that these treaties were based on theories that war would be fought in two dimensions: land and sea. The development of new military techniques and new weapons changed the character of warfare, which is now fought in three (air) and possible four (space) dimensions. Therefore those treaty prohibitions which could be derived by analogy from these instruments are no longer valid, for those prohibitions were created with respect to very different weapons in a very different world.

An additional stumbling block in ascertaining the legality or illegality of resort to chemical or biological weapons is met in the basic question of the current status of the international law of war. Although the law of war stipulates that the right of belligerents to adopt means of injuring the enemy is not unlimited, this circumscription as it relates to new weapons has been interpreted in an exceedingly broad manner during the two world wars of this century—so broad, in fact, that some have contended that the whole law of war is now obsolete.[2] The opinion has even been expressed that since war, in the legal sense, has been abolished by such treaties as the League of Nations Covenant, the United Nations Charter, and numerous antiwar conventions adhered to by a large number of states, there is no longer scope for the laws of war.[3]

Those who still uphold the existence of the international law of war have been unable to agree on the existence or extent of limitations on chemical and biological weapons derived from customary law or from the general principles of law derived from the practices of civilized nations. There are proponents of the view that the use of such weapons is prohibited because their massive destructive power makes impossible the maintenance of any humanitarian rules such as those relating to the distinction between combatant and noncombatant or to neutrals, or the unnecessary suffering prohibition, or the rule against the useless aggravation of the suffering of disabled men. Some believe and others deny that these instruments of war fall within the definition of poison or are forbidden because their use is treacherous.

There are advocates of the view that the legality of resort to chemical or biological weapons can only be judged on the basis of a minimum destruction of values—that is balancing the military necessity for the obtaining of legitimate objectives against humanitarianism to discover whether the destruction of values is disproportionate or irrelevant. Objection to this has been voiced on the ground that decision-makers have never been able to mark out with precision the legitimate objectives of violence in relation to the degree of destruction permissible under military necessity, or even the exact scope and extent of "military necessity."

Some say that the legal issue involved in resort to chemical and biological weapons does not and cannot differ in substance from the legal justification of conventional forms of violence, that normative standards applied to judge the one class must be applicable to judge the other, since chemical and biological weapons simply add a new quantitative measure of destruction in war. The legality of the use of such weapons, therefore, must be resolved by the reasonableness of the action in the total context of the particular use. In rebuttal it is stated that if each particular use of a chemical or biological weapon rests on its own merits, the policy-makers of a state or the commanders in the field are free to make their own subjective determinations whether to engage in chemical or biological warfare and to what extent. An irresponsible government or an irresponsible commander could precipitate all-out chemical or biological warfare.

It has been asserted and disputed that such weapons may be used only against an enemy who has seriously violated the rules of war; or only in a case where the ultimate values of humanity are imperiled by an aggressor intent upon dominating the world and the nations threatened consider themselves bound to assume the responsibility of exercising the supreme right of self-preservation; or only in a final situation where the choice is to surrender to an aggressor or to employ chemical or biological weapons.

While some authorities are of the opinion that there is an absolute ban prohibiting any resort to chemical or biological agents no matter what the military situation is, others declare that such a broad prohibition applies only to biological weapons. There are jurists who say that the principles of the laws of civilized nations do nothing in reality to prohibit the use of these weapons, but on the contrary, simply condition their use. Thus the principle of reprisal permits the use of chemical and biological weapons as a retaliation in kind against a previous use, and possibly also retaliation in a proportionate manner against any previous breach of the laws of war whether or not use of chemical or biological agents was involved. Others would say that reprisals by chemical or biological weapons are permissible only if such weapons are capable of being directed with precision against armed forces or military objectives. Although reprisals are really the only effective sanction of the law of war, they are of limited value, for they generally lead to counter-reprisals, the end result of which may be, as Lauterpacht has pointed out, in effect a new law-creating source:

In the First and Second World Wars reprisals have been the legal cloak for the departure, some of which was unavoidable, from many of the accepted rules of warfare . . . In a sense, reprisals have often fulfilled the function which would normally have been left to an agreement between states namely that of adaption of the law to changed conditions of modern warfare. For this reason, it is not always profitable to enquire whose original legality opened wide the flood gates of retaliation.[4]

Under such a view, if lethal or severely injurious chemical and biological agents were employed in reprisal and counter-reprisal situations they might establish a new unquestionable rule that they were legal.

A pragmatist would determine the utility of chemical or biological weapons, and if such weapons were found to be nonutilitarian would claim the laws of war require the use of other weapons which did have utility. Or he might well claim that resort to lethal or severely injurious chemical or biological weapons which were limitless in time and space would be irrational, in that resort to such weapons may destroy the very end for which war is waged: the preservation of freedom bought at the destruction of a large portion of humanity.

That the present state of international law is inadequate to govern the use of chemical or biological weapons in a limited or total war is easily discernible from the foregoing. And there is absolutely no rule of international law which prohibits the possession or manufacture of such weapons. It would thus appear that the total elimination, or limitation as a matter of law, of the possession, manufacture, and use of chemical and biological weapons cannot be accomplished by way of a restatement of existing rules of law based on controversial deductions.

The chaotic state of the international law governing limitations on chemical and biological weapons is hardly of its own making. On a global scale the shortcomings and peculiarities of international law reflect the extreme societal character of international relations, the power hierarchies and the divisions of a split world. In a world distracted and disunited beyond human experience, science has placed in the hands of governments chemical and biological weapons systems far beyond the imagination of the founders of international law. But there has been no concomitant development of the legal process which should control and direct those in positions of supreme authority with reference to such weapons. That we strive for a sophisticated system of international controls on chemical and biological weapons and for a prohibition or a limitation on their use is demanded by humanitarian and moral considerations of the most compelling character. Any effort in that direction is not likely to be greatly aided by controversial assertions as to the present illegality of the use of chemical or biological weapons in general or because of some specific treaty or law of war.

Admittedly any international and universal arms control negotiations on chemical and biological weapons should be cautiously approached and any resulting agreement closely scrutinized and viewed with a certain amount of skepticism. Such an agreement will not usher in peace, for peace is a legal postulate, the principle of the unity of the international legal system. So long as international wars are legal or tolerated; so long as there is little homogeneity of states, little kinship of ideas; so long as states suspect each other of the worst intentions and are willing to resort to force to impose their will upon all others, peace will be an illusion. But an agreement to prohibit the possession, manufacture, and use of lethal or severely injurious chemical and biological weapons may at least prevent the human race from destroying itself so that some future generation may remain to bring about that unity which is peace.

NOTES

CHAPTER ONE

1. For list of major chemical agents and their characteristics used in World War I, or stockpiled in World War II, or presumably available in the arsenals of various nations today, see Departments of the Army and the Air Force, Technical Manual, Military Chemistry and Chemical Agents (TM 3-215, AFM 355-7, December, 1963, hereinafter referred to as TM 3-215).

2. Robinson, "Chemical Warfare," 3 Science Journal No. 4 p. 33, at 34 (April, 1967).

3. *Ibid.*

4. Summerson, "The Chemical Warfare Threat," in Nonmilitary Defense Chemical and Biological Defenses in Perspective (Advances in Chemistry Series No. 26) p. 15, at 18 (1960).

5. In the United States chemical warfare has been officially defined in various ways:

a. The tactics and techniques of conducting warfare by use of toxic chemical agents (Department of the Army, Dictionary of United States Army Terms [AR 1958]).

b. Employment of chemical agents by weapon systems to produce casualties or damage (TM 3-215, *op. cit. supra* note 1, at p. 2).

c. Employment of chemical agents (excluding riot control agents) to: (1) kill or incapacitate, for a significant period of time, man or animals; (2) deny or hinder the use of space, facilities, or material (U.S. Army CBR Weapons Orientation Course, Glossary of Terms 2 [Dugway Proving Ground, Dugway, Utah, August, 1966]).

d. Employment of chemical agents to influence combat operations by producing casualties (death or incapacitation) or threat of casualties among enemy troops (Departments of the Army, the Navy, and the Air Force, Employment of Chemical and Biological Agents 3 [FM3-10, NWIP 35-2, AFM 335-4, FMFM 11-3, March, 1966]).

e. Employment of chemical agents to influence combat operations by producing death, incapacitation, confusion, or threat thereof among enemy troops. (Subcommittees on Disarmament of the Committee on Foreign Relations of the United States Senate, Chemical-Biological-Radiological-CBR Warfare and Its Disarmament Aspects, 86th Cong. 2d sess. [1960]).

f. The intentional employment of toxic gases, liquids, or solids to produce casualties, and the use of screening smoke or incendiaries. (Committee on Science and Astronautics, U.S. House of Representatives, 86th Cong. 1st sess., Research in CBR 5 [House Report 815, August 10, 1959]).

g. Employment of chemical agents to produce casualties in man or animal, damage to plants or materiel, to make hazardous the occupation of certain areas, or to produce a screening or signalling smoke. (U.S. Army Chemical School, Fort McClellan, Alabama, The Story of Chemical and Biological Agents and Weapons 17 [June, 1964]).

From this can be seen that there is a variation in official definitions of chemical warfare. The first covers only toxic chemical agents, apparently omitting incendiaries and smoke. The second is much more inclusive, in that it includes all chemical agents. The third attempts to exclude riot control agents. The fourth and fifth make no mention of damage to materials, and thus might be thought of as excluding antimateriel chemical agents. The sixth, again, is more comprehensive, while the seventh is probably the most comprehensive. Therefore, for the purpose of this study, the definition used will attempt to include all of the major ideas set forth in the above definitions. See also Brophy, Miles and Cochrane, The Chemical Warfare Service: From Laboratory to Field 49-74 (1959).

6. TM 3-215, *op. cit supra* note 1.

7. For a table setting forth U.S. chemical munitions and their weapons delivery systems see Departments of the Army, Navy, Air Force Field Manual, Employment of Chemical and Biological Agents (FM 3-10, NWIP 36-2, AFM 355-4, FMFM 11-3, March, 1966, hereinafter referred to as FM 3-10).

8. Departments of the Army and the Air Force, Military Chemistry and Chemical Agents, Change No. 1 p. 2 (TM 3-215, AFM 355-7A, C1, March 16, 1965, hereinafter referred to as TM 3-215, C1). The military viewpoint that toxins should be retained in the field as chemical agents was reaffirmed in December, 1969, by U.S. Secretary of Defense Melvin R. Laird with reference to President Nixon's decision in November, 1969, to stop military production of biological agents. New York Times, Dec. 17, 1969. Nevertheless, after two months of discussion, President Nixon, on Feb. 14, 1970, also banned military production and use of toxins, thereby overruling the military viewpoint. N.Y. Times, Feb. 15, 1970.

The manuals of the United States armed forces also use the phrase "toxic chemical agents" when they refer to those agents which cause death or serious injury. As even riot control or incapacitating agents have toxic qualities, this terminology seems to be confusing. Hence for the purpose of this study the phrase "lethal or severely injurious chemical agents" will be used.

9. Stedman's Medical Dictionary, Unabridged Lawyers' Edition, "Toxins" p. 1660 (21st ed. 1966).

10. The Department of the Army Field Manual, Soldier's Handbook for Chemical and Biological Operations and Nuclear Warfare p. 83 (FM 21-41, April, 1963), lists the following lethal or severely injurious chemical agents which it feels a soldier should protect himself against:

Nerve Agents: G-Agents and V-Agents
Blood Agents: AC (Hydrogen Cyanide) and CK (Cyanogen Chloride)
Choking Agent: CG (Phosgene)
Blister Agents: HD (Mustard), HN (Nitrogen Mustard), L (Lewisite), and
    CX (Phosgene oxime).

The discussion in this study is therefore limited to these agents. Some would contend that only the nerve agents, mustard, the incapacitating agent BX, and perhaps phosgene (on the basis of its low cost and ready availability from industry) are of military significance because Field Manual FM3-10, *op. cit. supra* note 7, on page 5 lists only these as the chemical agents which can be employed in chemical operations.

11. Chemical-Biological-Radiological (CBR) Warfare and Its Disarmament Aspects: A Study Prepared by the Subcommittee on Disarmament of the Committee on Foreign Relations, United States Senate, p. 11, 86th Cong. 2d sess. (1960).

12. TM 3-215, *op. cit. supra* note 1, at 14-18.

13. *Ibid.*

14. Robinson, *supra* note 2, at 36.

15. TM 3-215, *op. cit. supra* note 1, at 14-18.

16. U.S. Army Chemical School, Fort McClellan, Alabama, The Story of Chemical and Biological Agents and Weapons 49 (1964).

17. TM 3-215, *op. cit. supra* note 1, at 18.

18. *Id.* at 19-20.

19. *Id.* at 14.
20. *Id.* at 12.
21. *Id.* at 13.
22. *Id.* at 21.
23. *Ibid.*
24. *Id.* at 21-22, 26.
25. *Id.* at 26.
26. *Ibid.*
27. *Id.* at 23-29.
28. *Ibid.*
29. *Id.* at 26.
30. CBR Warfare, *op. cit. supra* note 11, at 12. See also Mitru, Comparative Study of Neuroparalytic and Neuropsychic (psychochemicals) Chemical Warfare Agents (1967).
31. Casualty rates from chemical agents depend upon the dosages received. The dosage received depends upon the concentration of the agent (C) and length of exposure (t) and usually is expressed as milligram minutes per cubic meter. The median lethal dosage (LCt50) is the dosage of an agent that will kill 50% of an exposed group of unprotected personnel. The median incapacitating dosage (ICt50) is the dosage of an agent that will incapacitate 50% of an exposed group of unprotected personnel.

MEDIAN LETHAL AND INCAPACITATING DOSAGES FOR
SELECTED CHEMICAL AGENTS

Agent	Median Lethal Dosages (mg-min per m³)	Median Incapacitating Dosages (mg-min per m³)	Rate of Action
Tabun	40 for resting men	30 for resting men	very rapid
Sarin	100 for resting men	75 for resting men	very rapid
Soman	Sarin-tabun range	Sarin-tabun range	very rapid
Distilled mustard	600 to 1,000 by inhalation; 10,000 by skin exposure	200 by eye effect; 2,500 by skin effect (estimated)	delayed, hrs. to days
Lewisite	1,200 to 1,500 by inhalation; 100,000 by skin exposure	300 by eye effect; 1,500 by skin effect	immediate irritation; delayed blistering
Phosgene	3,200	1,600	immediate to 3 hours
Cyanogen chloride	11,000	7,000	rapid
DM	15,000	22 for one minute of exposure; 8 for six minutes of exposure	very rapid
CS	25,000 for resting men	10 to 20	instantaneous
CN	11,000 (estimated)	80	almost instantaneous
BZ	classified	probably lower than 100	rapid

32. Robinson, *supra* note 2, at 36.

33. FM 3-10, *op. cit. supra* note 7, at 6.

34. Schwab, "Chemicals for a Non-Shooting War," 30 The Laboratory 1 (1962).

35. Hollyhock, "Weapons against the Mind," 7 Survival 166, at 168 (July, 1965).

36. Davidson, "The Hidden Evils of LSD," Sat. Eve. Post, Aug. 12, 1967, p. 21.

37. Chemical, Biological and Radiological Warfare Agents, Hearings before the Committee on Science and Astronautics, U.S. House of Representatives p. 3, 86th Cong. 1st sess. (1960).

38. Flores-Trivino, A New Concept of Chemical Warfare (Psychochemical Warfare) 11 (Joint Publications Research Service No. 25,001, June 9, 1964); see also, Rinkel, "Psilocybine, A New Psychotogenic Drug," 262 New Eng. J. Med. 295 (Feb. 11, 1960).

39. Davidson, *supra* note 36, at 20.

40. Summerson, "More on Chemical Warfare," 16 Bull. Atomic Sci. 252 (1960).

41. Davidson, *supra* note 36, at 21.

42. *Ibid.*

43. Rinkel, *supra* note 38, at 298.

44. Hollyhock, *supra* note 35, at 168.

45. Robinson, *supra* note 2, at 36.

46. Dallas Times Herald, Sept. 10, 1967.

47. Robinson, *supra* note 2, at 36.

48. *Ibid.* See also Mitru, *op. cit. supra* note 30, at 10.

49. Trainor, "DOD Weighs New War Concept," 15 Missiles and Rockets 14 (Oct. 5, 1964).

50. Lieberman, "Psychochemicals as Weapons," 18 Bull. Atom. Sci. 11 (Jan., 1962). Fisher contends that this is wrong:

> Lieberman mentions that the water supply of an area could serve as a vehicle for the administration of imperceptible amounts of psychochemicals and goes on to say that chlorination does not alter the potency of LSD. This is not the case. LSD is very susceptible to destruction by chlorination as attested by Drs. A. Hoffman and A. Brack, the discoverers of LSD and psilocybin.

Lieberman replied:

> My source for the statement that ordinary chlorination does not affect the potency of LSD is General William Creasy's testimony at the congressional hearings of June 16, 1959. . . . Fischer is undoubtedly right; Creasy could be right too, *if* he was referring to variants of LSD (not so well known) which are chlorine resistant.

18 Bull. Atom. Sci. 36 (Feb., 1962). See also Chemical, Biological and Radiological Warfare Agents, *op. cit. supra* note 37, at 4.

51. FM 3-10, *op. cit. supra* note 7, at 25.

52. TM 3-215, *op. cit. supra* note 1, at 34.

53. N.Y. Times Mag., Sept. 17, 1967, p. 6.

54. TM 3-215, *op. cit. supra* note 1, at 33-38.

55. *Id.* at 31-33.

56. Fischer, Incendiary Warfare 29-37 (1946).

57. *Id.* at 34.

58. TM 3-215, *op. cit. supra* note 1, at 41; Hollingsworth, "The Use of Thickened Gasoline in Warfare," 4 Armed Forces Chemical J. 26 (Jan., 1951).

59. Kleber and Birdsell, The Chemical Warfare Service: Chemicals in Combat 213, 568-72 (1966). Baxter, Scientists Against Time 94-97 (1946).

60. Fischer points out that thermite is seldom used as a primary incendiary because its high combustion rate can only be maintained for seconds. Fischer, *op. cit. supra* note 56, at 39.

61. Brophy, Miles and Cochrane, The Chemical Warfare Service: From Laboratory to Field, 197-224 (1959). See Chemical-Biological-Radiological (CBR) Warfare, *op. cit supra* note 11, at 1, where it is stated: "Chemical warfare, in practice covers not only the use of toxic chemicals (often called gas warfare) but also smokes, flame and incendiaries in warfare. The military use of the last three agents is, in effect, a form of conventional warfare."

62. U.S. Army Chemical School, *op. cit. supra* note 5, at 18-29.

63. TM 3-215, *op. cit. supra* note 1, at 48.

64. *Id.* at 46.

65. *Id.* at 44-45.

66. *Id.* at 49.

67. *Id.* at 50.

68. TM 3-215, C 1, *op. cit. supra* note 8, at 3-6; "Soil Sterilization," 12 McGraw-Hill Encyclopedia of Science and Technology 464 (1966).

69. TM 3-215, C 1, *op. cit. supra* note 8, at 3. In spite of military contentions that herbicides and defoliants do not injure either man or animals, biologists and biochemists have continually challenged these statements. Added fuel was given to their views by a statement issued on October 29, 1969, by Dr. Lee Du Bridge, President Nixon's science advisor, relating to the chemical compound 2,4,5-T. He declared that as a precautionary measure the government was taking a series of coordinated actions to restrict the use of 2,4,5-T in both domestic civilian and military herbicidal operations.

The actions to control the use of the chemical were taken as a result of findings from a laboratory study conducted by Bionetics Research Laboratories which indicated that offspring of mice and rats given relatively large oral doses of the herbicide during early stages of pregnancy show a higher than expected number of deformities.

Although it seems improbable that any person could receive harmful amounts of this chemical from any of the existing uses of 2,4,5-T, and while the relationships of these effects in laboratory animals to effects in man are not entirely clear at this time, the actions taken will assure safety of the public while further evidence is being sought.

New York Times, October 30, 1969.

70. *Id.* at 4.

71. *Id.* at 5.

72. *Ibid.* For a strong rebuttal of the military usefulness of these chemicals see Whiteside, "Defoliation," The New Yorker, Feb. 7, 1970, pp. 34 ff.

73. *Id.* at 5-6.

74. "Soil Sterilization," *supra* note 68, at 464.

75. TM 3-215, C 1, *op. cit. supra* note 8, at 2.

76. "Biological Warfare," 3 Encyclopaedia Britannica 641 (1966 ed.).

77. Neinast, "United States Use of Biological Warfare," 24 Military L. Rev. 1 (1964).

78. "Pathogens," 9 McGraw-Hill Encyclopedia of Science and Technology 593 (1966).

79. "Virulence," 14 McGraw-Hill Encyclopedia of Science and Technology 328c (1966).

80. See Clarke, The Silent Weapons: The Realities of Chemical and Biological

Warfare app. 2 (1968) for a quick reference chart of some diseases of possible biological warfare interest.

81. "Biological Warfare," 3 Encyclopaedia Britannica 641 (1966 ed.).

82. Headquarters, Department of the Army, Fact Sheet on the Use of Chemical, Biological and Radiological Weapons in Warfare 3 (January 3, 1962).

83. "Fungi," 5 McGraw-Hill Encyclopedia of Science and Technology 561 (1966).

84. "Fungus Infections," 9 Encyclopaedia Britannica 1020 (1966 ed.); Department of the Army and the Air Force, Military Biology and Biological Agents 53-55 (TM 3-216, ARM 355-6, March, 1964, hereafter referred to as TM 3-216).

85. TM 3-216, *id.* at 53.

86. "Bacterial and Infectious Diseases," 2 Encyclopaedia Britannica 1003 (1966). "Bacteria," 2 McGraw-Hill Encyclopedia of Science and Technology 5 (1966).

87. TM 3-216, *op. cit. supra* note 84, at 36-45.

88. "Rickettsia," 19 Encyclopaedia Britannica 318 (1966 ed.); "Rickettsiae," 11 McGraw-Hill Encyclopedia of Science and Technology 567 (1966); "Rickettsioses," *id.* at 568; "Viruses and Rickettsiae as BW Agents," 16 Bull. Atom. Sci. 246 (June, 1960).

89. TM 3-216, *op. cit. supra* note 84, at 48.

90. "Viruses," 23 Encyclopaedia Britannica 189 (1966 ed.); "Virus," 14 McGraw-Hill Encyclopedia of Science and Technology 329 (1966); see also "Viruses and Rickettsiae," *supra* note 88.

91. TM 3-216, *op. cit supra* note 84, at 49-53.

92. "Toxology and Toxins," 26 Encyclopedia Americana 729 (1962).

93. "Toxicology," 14 McGraw-Hill Encyclopedia of Science and Technology 5 (1966).

94. TM 3-216, *op. cit. supra* note 84, at 14-15.

95. "Toxin, Bacterial," 14 McGraw-Hill Encyclopedia of Science and Technology 7 (1966).

96. TM 3-216, *op. cit. supra* note 84, at 56-61.

97. "Toxology and Toxins," *supra* note 92, at 729.

98. See Rothschild, Tomorrow's Weapons app. E pp. 206-50 (1964) for variables in diseases which may be of possible biological warfare interest.

99. TM 3-216, *op. cit. supra* note 84, at 37-57.

100. *Ibid.*

101. *Ibid.*

102. Sidel and Goldwyn, "Chemical and Biological Weapons—A Primer," 274 New England Journal Med. 21-27 (Jan. 6, 1966).

103. Leitenberg, "Biological Weapons," 9 Scientist and Citizen 153, at 158 (Aug.-Sept., 1967).

104. Langer, "Chemical and Biological Weapons II—The Weapons and the Policies," 155 Science 299 (1967).

105. Finland, "Emergence of Anti-biotic-Resistant Bacteria," 253 New England Journal of Medicine 745 (1955).

106. Miller and Bohnhoff, "The Development of Bacterial Resistance to Chemotherapeutic Agents," 4 Annual Review Microbiology 251 (1950).

107. Baron, "Transfer of Episomes between Bacterial Genera," 27 Transactions New York Academy Sciences 231 (June, 1965).

108. Clarke, "Biological Warfare," 2 Science Journal No. 11 p. 71 (Nov., 1966).

109. *Id.* at 72.

110. Pollock, "Drug Resistance and Mechanisms for Its Development," 16 British Medical Bulletin 1 (1960).

111. Clarke, *supra* note 108, at 72.

112. Leitenberg, *supra* note 103, at 164.

113. Tigertt and Benenson, "Studies on Q Fever in Man," 69 Trans. Assoc. Am. Physicians 98 (1956); Feiner, "If Biological Warfare Comes," 196 Harper's Magazine 1176 (May, 1948).

114. Leitenberg, *supra* note 103, at 157.

115. Granzeier, "Toxic Weapons," 7 Industrial Research 420 (1965).

116. Young and Zelle, "Respiratory Pathogenicity of *Bacillus Anthracis* Spores," 79 J. Infectious Diseases 266 (1946).

117. Wedum, "Defensive Aspects of Biological Warfare," 162 J. Am. Medical Assoc. 276 (1956).

118. Nopar, "Plagues on Our Children," 6 Clinical Pediatrics 72 (1967).

119. Mayer, "Epidemics and Bacteriological Warfare," 67 Scientific Monthly 220 (1948).

120. TM 3-216, *op. cit. supra* note 84, at 58.

121. *Id.* at 61-67.

122. *Id.* at 58-61.

123. "Fungus Infections," *supra* note 84, at 1020.

124. "Biological Warfare," *supra* note 81, at 642.

125. TM 3-216, *op. cit. supra* note 84, at 68-69.

126. *Id.* at 59.

127. *Id.* at 73.

128. "Plant Diseases," 17 Encyclopaedia Britannica 1181 (1966 ed.).

129. *Id.* at 1190.

130. Bawden, "Plant Diseases," 16 Bull. Atom. Sci. 247 (June, 1960).

131. 6 Oxford English Dictionary 434 (1933).

132. Hollyhock, *supra* note 35, at 166.

133. Rothschild, "Propaganda and Toxic War," 50 Ordnance 617, at 619 (May-June, 1966).

134. Trainor, "DOD Weighs New War Concept," 15 Missiles and Rockets 14 (Oct. 4, 1964).

135. Chemical, Biological and Radiological Warfare Agents, *op. cit. supra* note 37, at 30.

136. *Ibid.*

137. FM 3-10, *op. cit. supra* note 7, at 5.

138. *Ibid.*

139. *Id.* at 5-6.

140. "Research in CBR (Chemical, Biological, and Radiological Warfare)," Report of the Committee on Science and Astronautics, U.S. House of Representatives, 86th Cong. 1st sess., August 10, 1959 p. 11.

141. Department of the Army, Use of Agent CS in Training and Riot Control 3 (TC 3-9, May, 1960).

142. Brophy, Miles and Cochrane, *op. cit. supra* note 61, at 162.

143. Fischer, Incendiary Warfare 5-6, 52 (1946).

144. Fries and West, Chemical Warfare 347-52 (1921); Baxter, Scientists Against Time 294-97 (1946); Brophy, Miles and Cochrane, *op. cit. supra* note 61, at 139-65; see also, Miller, "Smoke 'Em Out," 48 Ordnance 61 (Nov.-Dec., 1964).

145. TM 3-216, *op. cit. supra* note 84, at 68; but see, "One Man's Meat," 151 New Republic 30 (March 23, 1963).

146. Crozier, "Survival in Germ Warfare," 49 Ordnance 530 (1965).

147. Rothschild, Tomorrow's Weapons 21-23 (1964).

148. See "Pugwash International Conference of Scientists—Statement on Biological and Chemical Warfare," 184 Nature 1018 (1959).

149. Fothergill, "The BW Threat," 16 Bull. Atom. Sci. 244 (1960).

150. Schyler, "Biological Warfare—The Final Weapon," 78 America 569 (1948).

151. MacArthur, "Biological Warfare—The Hidden Threat," 50 Ordnance 133 (Sept.-Oct., 1965).

152. Crozier, *supra* note 146, at 530.

153. *Ibid.* MacArthur, *supra* note 151, at 136.

154. Saunders, "The Biological Chemical Warfare Challenge," 91 Proc. U.S. Naval Institute 44 (1965).

155. Nunn, "The Arming of an International Police," 2 J. of Peace Research 187 (1965).

156. Miller, "The Use of Chemicals in Stability Operations," 46 Mil. Rev. 43 (Dec., 1966).

157. Departments of the Army and the Air Force, Field Behavior of Chemical, Biological and Radiological Agents 2 (TM 3-240, AFM 105-7, May, 1963, hereafter referred to as TM 3-240).

158. *Id.* at 15.

159. *Id.* at 33.

160. *Ibid.*

161. FM 3-10, *op. cit. supra* note 7, at 11.

162. TM 3-240, *op. cit. supra* note 157, at 35.

163. TM 3-10, *op. cit. supra* note 7, at 11.

164. TM 3-240, *op. cit. supra* note 157, at 37.

165. *Id.* at 38.

166. *Id.* at 39.

167. *Ibid.*

168. *Ibid.*

169. *Id.* at 43.

170. *Id.* at 44.

171. *Id.* at 45.

172. *Id.* at 45-46.

173. Chemical-Biological-Radiological (CBR) Warfare, *op. cit. supra* note 11, at 28. "Gas, Germs, May Decide Result of Nuclear War," 80 Science News Letter 224 (Sept. 30, 1961).

174. Lieberman, "The Ethical Neutrality of LSD," 18 Bull. Atom. Sci. 41 (1962).

175. Lieberman, "Psychochemicals as Weapons," 18 Bull. Atom. Sci. 11 (1962).

176. Balestieri, "The Problem of Tolerance to Hallucinogen Drugs," Scientific Abstracts 40 (1960). See also section on "Effects of Chemical Warfare Agents," Emergency Manual Guide, U.S. Department of Health, Education and Welfare, July 31, 1959.

177. "The Germs of Porton Down," 204 The Economist 127 (July 14, 1962).

178. Saunders, *supra* note 154, declares:

One cannot help being impressed by the economic aspects of biological and chemical weapons. In terms of over-all national effort required to develop and produce a specific warfare capability, the ratio of BW/CW weapon requirements to nuclear weapon requirements is overwhelmingly in favor of the former. The production of nuclear material by the United States required the establishment of an entirely new industry and absorbed a large percentage of the national productive effort. Costs related to production of nuclear materials and related hardware are still very high. On the other, the production of biological and chemical agents involves only a fraction of these costs and is directly associated with large industries already in existence. Associated research is often the by-product of efforts originally directed elsewhere.

179. "Army Permits Peek at Nerve Gas Facilities," 65 Chemical Engineering 74 (Sept. 22, 1958).
180. Langer, "CBW: Weapons and Policies," 9 Survival 163 (May, 1967).
181. FM 3-10, *op. cit. supra* note 7, at 15.
182. *Id.* at 18.
183. Brophy, Miles and Cochrane, *op. cit. supra* note 61, at 396.
184. Kleber and Birdsell, The Chemical Warfare Service: Chemicals in Combat 293 (1966).
185. "Army Permits Peek at Nerve Gas Facilities," *supra* note 179, at 74.
186. Kleber and Birdsell, *op. cit. supra* note 59, at 631.
187. "Elements of Aerial Warfare: Weapons," 3 Air Science 38 (1953).
188. "The Germs of Porton Down," *supra* note 177, at 127.
189. Smith, "The Microbiological Research Establishment, Porton," Chemistry and Industry 338, at 341 (March 4, 1967).
190. Orphan, "The Three Deadly Faces of Modern Warfare," 39 Today's Health 21 (March, 1961).
191. Clarke, *supra* note 108, at 73.
192. *Ibid.*
193. As stated by Kaplan, "Communicable Diseases and Epidemics," 16 Bull. Atom. Sci. 237 (1960):

While epidemiologists can formulate as generalities the set of circumstances which determine epidemics, the great number of biological variables involved in the host-parasite-environment complex frustrates attempts at quantitative or qualitative prediction of individual epidemics.

194. Calder, "Ambivalent Pests," 64 New Statesman 163 (August 10, 1962). It is stated in "A Weapon for UNO," 190 The Economist 699 (Feb. 21, 1959): "It may be true that 8-1/2 lb. of botulinus could wipe out humanity if it queued up for injections. But the practical difficulties of delivering and disseminating these agents of genocide remain as intractable as ever."
195. "The Germs of Porton Down," *supra* note 177, at 127. See also the statement of the Federation of American Scientists on Biological and Chemical Warfare, set forth in 20 Bull. Atom. Sci. 46 (Oct., 1964):

Biological weapons are potentially very cheap and their dissemination, particularly among the nonnuclear nations, would have the effect of providing these nations for the first time with a striking power comparable to that afforded by nuclear weapons. Research, development, and preparation of such weapons can be accomplished in ordinary microbial and chemical laboratories. Thus, most nations, small and large, could easily and secretly acquire a significant biological and chemical capability, which, furthermore, would be much less susceptible to inspection and control than are nuclear weapons.

The following chart was prepared by the American Chemical Society's Committee on Civil Defense and appeared in 38 Chemical and Engineering News 39 (April 18, 1960):

RELATIVE EFFECTS OF CBR WEAPONS

	Nuclear Agents	Chemical Agents	Biol. Agents
Immediate effective area	75-100 sq. miles	100 sq. miles	34,000 sq. miles at the very least and with only 450 lb. of agent

	Nuclear Agents	Chemical Agents	Biol. Agents
Human lethality (or morbidity) in immediate area (unprotected)	98% lethality	30% (not necessarily lethal)	25%-75% (morbidity, not necessarily lethal)
Residual effect	Six months fallout with an additional 1000 sq. miles of area	3-36 hours (nearly same area)	Possible epidemic or epizootic spread to other areas
Time for immediate effect	Seconds	7½ seconds to 30 min.	A few days to 14 days
Real property damage, immediate area	Destroyed (nearly 36 sq. miles)	Undamaged	Undamaged
Variation in effect	Little	Wide—need not kill, only incapacitate	Wide—need not kill, only incapacitate
Time an aggressor is able to invade area after attack	3-6 months	Immediate	Immediately after incubation period
Human protection that could be available	Evacuation (?) Shelters; civilian masks (fallout)	Civilian mask, CD-V-805 Shelters with filters	Civilian mask, CD-V-805; immunization Shelters with filters
Current defense for U.S. population (physical devices)	Some, but can be greatly improved	Nearly non-existent	Nearly non-existent
Cost of protection	Shelters ($150-$800/person)	Mask—$2.50-$8 Filters in shelters ($15-$20/person)	Mask—$2.50-$8 Filters in shelters ($15-$20/person) Immunization(?)
Covert application	Little	Some	Great
Detection and identification	Simple	Complex but fairly effective and rapid	Difficult, complex, slow
Medical countermeasures	Little	Good if immediate	Some, much more needed. High health and sanitation standards help
Would attack trigger retaliation?	Yes	Yes	Doubtful if covert, slow at best
Capital equipment costs to produce agents	Very expensive	Somewhat expensive	Relatively inexpensive
How does agent attack target?	Direct impact, then some "seeking" with fallout	"Seeks" out	"Seeks" out target

196. Langer, "Chemical and Biological Warfare: American Research," 9 Survival 128, at 130 (April, 1967) points out: "Aerobiology is of particular relevance to biological warfare, however, because the idea of disseminating infectious agents by aerosols—suspensions of small particles in the air—seems to be displacing earlier no-

tions." And Goggins declares in "Is Russia Outstripping Us in Weapons of Mass Destruction?" 26 Vital Speeches of the Day 263 (Feb. 15, 1967):

> One of the most effective methods of biological attack is by means of an aerosol. Today aerosols can be delivered by any point on the earth's surface by generators incorporated into aerial bombs, airplane spray tanks, submarine mines, and guided missiles. These generators are containers of highly concentrated cultures of bacteria, viruses or toxins, which are fitted with fog nozzles from which the contents are sprayed into the air under pressure to form a fine mist. Spreading rapidly downwind, the mist quickly becomes invisible. Under neutral or inversion conditions, 50 gallons of slurry is capable of blanketing 60 or more square miles with a high concentration of infectious particulates.

197. Smith, *supra* note 189, at 341.

198. FM 3-10, *op. cit. supra* note 7, at 44.

199. "The Ultimate Weapon?" Newsweek, March 4, 1963, p. 56:

> The second school of thought at Fort Detrick is bent on improving nature, by juggling with the genetic material. This involves trying to blend the worse attributes of different bacteria—ideally for instance, the virulence of the plague with the resistance to anti-biotics of *Staphylococcus aureus*. The results of such research are known informally as "Frankenstein monsters." Altering a species is a difficult process. Genetic material can be passed from one strain to a closely related one, but so far not from a markedly different organism. "You can't cross a mouse with an elephant," one Detrick scientist said last week. "But we have not yet exhausted the possibilities."

200. TM 3-216, *op. cit. supra* note 84, at 7.

201. TM 3-240, *op. cit. supra* note 157, at 47.

202. FM 3-10, *op. cit. supra* note 7, at 44.

203. Rothschild, Tomorrow's Weapons 46 (1964).

204. TM 3-216, *op. cit. supra* note 84, at 21.

205. "The Germs of Porton Down," *supra* note 177, at 128.

206. Smith, *supra* note 189, at 340.

207. Hersh, "Just a Drop Can Kill: Secret Work on Gas and Germ Warfare," New Republic, May 6, 1967, p. 12. But see Imshenetsky, "Modern Microbiology and the Biology Warfare Menace," 16 Bull. Atom. Sci. 241, at 242 (1960) where it is stated:

> The functional peculiarities of a microbial cell are not always stable under storage conditions. Theoretical research in this field has shown that when any one method of conservation is used, some of the microbes preserve their virulence and others lose it. However, by combining various methods of conservation (lyophilization, low temperatures, etc.), it is possible to preserve the material for long periods of time without inactivation.

208. *Ibid.*

209. Kaplan, *supra* note 193, declares at 238:

> . . . it may be concluded that for human beings there is insufficient knowledge for any quantitative accurate predictions of events resulting from BW attack, except perhaps for a limited area where very large amounts of disease agents would have to be delivered to insure an "adequate" dose for each individual. Any national power using BW agents would therefore act with great imprecision.

210. Langmuir, "The Potentialities of Biological Warfare Against Man: An Epidemiological Appraisal," 66 Public Health Reports 13 (1951).

211. Kaplan, *supra* note 193, at 239:

. . . other possible consequences, perhaps more far-reaching in the long run, should not be overlooked. These pertain to disturbance of the fine ecological balances achieved as a result of evolution over eons of time between human, animal, and plant life, and between such life and their microorganisms. Sudden disbalances in numbers, or the insertion of new infective elements into evolutionally unprepared animal and plant life could, if done to a sufficient degree, produce an indefinite period of an unrecognizable and perhaps unmanageable world from the standpoint of communicable diseases.

212. ". . . dissemination by spreading virus-carrying insects . . . is rather inefficient." "Viruses and Rickettsia as BW Agents," 16 Bull. Atom. Sci. 246, at 247 (1960).

213. Or as Nunn, *supra* note 155, at 190 pointedly queries: "Another important series of questions is that connected with the treatment of prisoners. . . . In plain language, what do you do with the troops when they wake up?"

214. Lieberman, *supra* note 175, at 13; Hollyhock, *supra* note 35, at 167.

215. Trainor, *supra* note 49, at 14 declares: "Political acceptance of this type of warfare must be established"; and General Rothschild, in "Propaganda and Toxic War," 50 Ordnance 617 (May/June, 1966) declares:

> When the Germans launched the first large-scale gas attack in World War I . . . the Allies had nothing with which to combat this new weapon. . . . After the success of the attack, they then resorted to the historic method used against innovations in war—they declared the weapon inhumane and barbarous . . . and the propaganda campaign was successful. . . . The statistics on casualties during World War I do not support the description of "inhumane" as applied to gas when compared with other weapons of war.

216. Beecher, "Chemicals vs. the Viet Cong—'Right' or 'Wrong'?" The National Guardsman 1 (1966), points out:

> VC propagandists insist that the defoliants, commonly sprayed from helicopters or light aircraft, are highly poisonous. Frequently their troops refuse to go into an area that has been sprayed. And they tend to attribute any sudden illnesses to exposure to the "toxic" chemicals . . . this has led one chemical warrior to suggest, only half kiddingly, that we ought to spray harmless, foulsmelling water all over the jungle of Viet Nam and "leak" word to the Viet Cong that it's a new secret weapon. Their propaganda machine would do the rest.

217. See for example discussion on use of gas in Yemen *infra* pp. 151-53.

218. Miller, "The Use of Chemicals in Stability Operations," 46 Military Review 43, at 45 (1966) declares: ". . . the mere threat of the use of chemical agents has a demoralizing effect on the enemy. Man fears most what he cannot see. Soldiers would no longer feel the relative security of bunkers, caves or pillboxes if the real threat of a chemical attack existed." See also New York Times, Aug. 9, 1959: "House Committee Views CB Warfare," which states, "Leading military officials are trying to overcome public horror of chemical, biological and radiological warfare." See also Schneir, "The Campaign to Make Chemical Warfare Respectable," 24 The Reporter 1 (October 1, 1959).

219. Oldendorf, "On the Acceptability of a Device as a Weapon," 18 Bull. Atom. Sci. 35, at 36 (1962).

220. *Ibid.*

221. "Gas and Germ Warfare: Balance of Terror," 192 The Economist 516, at 517 (Aug. 22, 1959).

222. Savitz, "Gas and Guerrillas—A Word of Caution," New Republic, March 19, 1966, p. 13.

223. Rosebury, "Biological and Chemical Warfare: Some Historical Considerations," 16 Bull. Atom. Sci. 235 (1960).

224. In determining the legality or illegality of any weapon, two things must always be kept in mind, first, the laws of war are not precise, and second, that in the words of Dr. Schwarzenberger, The Legality of Nuclear Weapons 58 (1958),

> if it should ever come to an all-out contest by force between the super-Powers of our age, it would be sheer day-dreaming to expect that in their fight for survival, and so necessarily world hegemony, they would refrain from the use of any weapon in their arsenal . . . the first, and most self-denying, duty of the international lawyer is to warn against the dangerous illusion that his findings on the legality or illegality of . . . weapons are likely to influence one way or the other the decision on the use of these devices. . . .

225. McDougal and Feliciano, "International Coercion and World Public Order: The General Principles of the Law of War," 67 Yale L.J. 771 (1958).

226. Neinast, "United States Use of Biological Warfare," 24 Military Rev. 1, at 3 (1964).

CHAPTER TWO

1. For a description of the categories which comprise the substantive or normative body of law see Pound, "Hierarchy of Sources and Forms in Different Systems of Law," 7 Tulane L. Rev. 475 (1933).

2. On the development and nature of the law of war see Greenspan, The Modern Law of Land Warfare pt. I (1959); Castrén, The Present Law of War and Neutrality ch. I (1954); 1 Wright, A Study of War 1952-65 (1942); Bordwell, Law of War (1908); Marin, "The Evolution and Present Status of the Laws of War," 92 Recueil des Cours 633 (1957); Edmunds, "The Laws of War: Their Rise in the Nineteenth Century and Their Collapse in the Twentieth," 15 Va. L. Rev. 321 (1929).

3. See Marin, *id.* at 651, 657.

4. On the laws of war at this time see Keen, The Laws of War in the Late Middle Ages (1965).

5. Edmunds declares that it is "absurd to speak of the Laws of War" at this time. Edmunds, *supra* note 2, at 324.

6. Stone, Legal Control of International Conflict 337 (2d imp. rev. 1959); Schwarzenberger, "The Standard of Civilization in International Law," 8 Current Legal Problems 212, at 219-20 (1955).

7. Schwarzenberger, *id.* at 222; 2 Oppenheim, International Law sec. 67 (7th ed. Lauterpacht 1952).

8. McDougal and Feliciano, Law and Minimum World Public Order 522 (1961).

9. Mérignhac, "Les Téories du Grand État-Major Allemand Sur Les 'Lois de la Guerre Continentale'," 14 Revue Générale de Droit International Public 197, at 203 (1907). See also Bordwell, The Law of War 114 (1908) wherein he sets forth the following as the first official expression of the German doctrine:

> Perpetual peace is a dream, and not even a good dream. War is an element of the world's order established by God. . . . Without War the world would stagnate and lose itself in materialism. . . . The greatest benefit in war is that it can be terminated promptly. It ought to be permitted in view of this end, to use all means save those which are positively condemnable. I by no means agree . . . that the enfeebling of the military forces of the enemy constitutes the only legitimate mode of proceeding in war. No, it is necessary to attack all the resources of the enemy's government, his finances, his railroads, his provisions, his prestige. . . .

10. The German authorities on this subject are listed and discussed in 2 Garner, International Law and the World War 195 *et seq.* (1920) and in O'Brien, "The Meaning of 'Military Necessity' in International Law," 1 World Polity 109, at 119 *et seq.* (1957).

11. See for example O'Brien, *id.* at 127 *et seq.*; Rodick, The Doctrine of Necessity in International Law 59-60 (1928); Greenspan, *op. cit. supra* note 2, at 313; Castrén, *op. cit. supra* note 2, at 66; Dunbar, "Military Necessity in War Crimes Trials," 29 Brit. Yb. Int'l L. 442 (1953).

12. Dept. of the Army Field Manual, "The Law of Land Warfare" 4 (FM 27-10 1956).

13. 2 Scott, The Hague Peace Conferences of 1899 and 1907 p. 389 (1909).

14. See authorities cited note 11, *supra.*

15. Tucker, "The Law of War and Neutrality at Sea," U.S. Naval War College International Law Studies 1955 p. 33 n. 21; p. 45 (1957).

16. For discussion of this concept and law see Taylor, The Masks of Society 256 *et seq.* (1966).

17. *Ibid.* See also Kelsen, Principles of International Law 291-92 (2d ed. Tucker 1966).

18. Tucker, *supra* note 15, at 45 *et seq.*; Kelsen, *id.* at 112 *et seq.*; Castrén, *op. cit. supra* note 2, at 187; O'Brien, *supra* note 10, at 152 speaks of limitation according to the laws of war and *natural law.*

19. Kelsen, *id.* at 113.

20. These law-creating processes are subsidiary means and are those to which the International Court of Justice must refer. Art. 38 (1), Statute of the International Court of Justice.

21. Davis, "Dr. Francis Lieber's Instructions for the Government of Armies in the Field," 1 Am. J. Int'l L. 13 (1907).

22. Lieber's code is set forth in 2 Lorimer, The Institutes of the Law of Nations 303-36 (1884).

23. See *infra* pp. 49-57 on the nature of poison.

24. Holland, Studies in International Law 85-90 (1898).

25. Bordwell, The Law of War 113-14 (1908).

26. The various changes in U.S. manuals relating to the employment of weapons will be discussed *infra* pp. 155 *et seq.*

CHAPTER THREE

1. Art. 38 (1) of the Statute of the International Court of Justice lists treaties as one of the principal law-creating processes to which the International Court of Justice must refer.

2. On the lawmaking treaties see 1 Oppenheim, International Law 27-29, 878-80 (8th ed. Lauterpacht 1963); Brierly, The Law of Nations 57-59 (6th ed. 1936); Thomas and Thomas, International Treaties 24-28 (monograph 1950); Starke, "Treaties as Sources of International Law," 23 Brit. Yb. Int'l L. 342 (1946); Levi, "Law-Making Treaties," 26 Minn. L. Rev. 252 (1944); McNair, "The Functions and Differing Legal Character of Treaties," 11 Brit. Yb. Int'l L. 112 (1930).

3. See Kelsen, Principles of International Law 97 (2d rev. ed. Tucker 1966); Stone, Legal Controls of International Conflicts 335 *et seq.* (2d imp. rev. 1959).

4. The Declaration of St. Petersburg of 1868 is contained in Scott, Documents Relating to the Program of the First Hague Peace Conferences 30 (1921). For general discussion of the Conference and Declaration see Bordwell, Law of War 87-88 (1908); 1 Garner, International Law and the World War 14-15 (1924); Taylor, International Public Law 46-47 (1901).

5. Scott, *id.* at 30.

6. *Id.* at 31.

7. *Ibid.*

8. See 2 Oppenheim, International Law 344 (7th ed. Lauterpacht 1952); U.S. Naval War College, International Law Situations 102, 106 (1935). For discussion see O'Brien, "Biological/Chemical Warfare and the International Law of War," 51 Geo. L. J., at 18-20 (1962); Neinast, "United States Use of Biological Warfare," 24 Military L. Rev. 1, at 22-25 (1964); Brungs, "The Status of Biological Warfare in International Law," 24 Military L. Rev. 37, at 57-58 (1964).

9. See *supra* pp. 40-42; and *infra* ch. VII.

10. See 2 Westlake, International Law 84 (1907); Stone, *op. cit. supra* note 3, at 551 n. 27.

11. Greenspan makes such a statement in his treatise, "The Modern Law of Land Warfare" (1959) at 360. Castrén would disagree. See Castrén, The Present Law of War and Neutrality 190 (1954).

12. O'Brien points out that present-day states still adherents are Belgium, Denmark, France, Germany, Great Britain, Greece, Italy, The Netherlands, Norway, Austria, Persia, Portugal, Sweden, Switzerland, Turkey, and Brazil. Hungary's position is anomalous depending upon whether she admits to succession of Austria-Hungary's obligation. Russia no longer admits succession to treaties signed by the Czar. O'Brien, *supra* note 8, at 18.

13. See *infra* ch. VII.

14. The Project is set forth in Scott, *op. cit. supra* note 4, at 32. See also Actes de la Conférence de Bruxelles 297 (1874). A summary of the Conference may be found in 2 Lorimer, The Institutes of the Law of Nations 337 *et seq.* (1884).

15. Art. 13(a) of the Project, *id.* at 34.

16. For discussion of the various proposals on this matter at the conference see Brungs, *supra* note 8, at 47-48.

17. The Final Protocol of the Conference at Brussels was signed by Russia, Germany, Austria-Hungary, Belgium, Denmark, Spain, France, Great Britain, Greece, Italy, The Netherlands, Portugal, Sweden and Norway, Switzerland, and Turkey.

18. On the two Hague Peace Conferences see 1, 2 Scott, The Hague Peace Conferences of 1899 and 1907; Scott, The Hague Conventions and Declarations (1915); Scott, The Hague Peace Conferences, American Institutions and Reports (1916); White, The First Hague Conference (1905); Choate, The Two Hague Conferences (1913); Hull, The Two Hague Conferences (1908); Davis, The United States and the First Hague Peace Conference (1962).

19. Declaration (IV 2) Concerning Asphyxiating Gases is contained in Scott, The Hague Conventions and Declarations of 1899 and 1907 pp. 225-26 (1915). On poison and poisoned weapons see *infra* pp. 49-57 and as a general principle in ch. VII.

20. *Ibid.*

21. Prentiss, Chemicals in War 686 (1937). For discussion on the work of this subcommittee apropos the Gas Declaration see Davis, *op. cit. supra* note 18, at 117-21; Hull, *op. cit. supra* note 18, at 87-90; Bernstein, "The Law of Chemical Warfare," 10 Geo. Wash. L. Rev. 889 (1942); Kelly, "Gas Warfare in International Law," Military Law Rev., July 1, 1960 (Da Pam. 27-100-9, July 1, 1960) p. 1, at 21-23.

22. Scott, *op. cit. supra* note 19, at 226 lists those adhering: Austria-Hungary, Belgium, China, Denmark, France, Germany, Greece, Italy, Japan, Luxembourg, Mexico, Montenegro, Netherlands, Norway, Persia, Portugal, Roumania, Russia, Serbia, Siam, Spain, Sweden, Switzerland, Turkey, Great Britain, and Nicaragua.

23. See Hull, *op. cit. supra* note 18, at 87-88.

24. These instructions are set forth in Scott, The Hague Peace Conferences, American Institutions and Reports 6-9 (1916). Those pertaining to weapons and applicable here are as follows:

> The second, third, and fourth articles, [of the Russian topics for discussion] relating to the non-employment of firearms, explosives, and other destructive agents, the restricted use of existing instruments of destruction, and the prohibition of certain contrivances employed in naval warfare, seem lacking in practicality, and the discussion of these propositions would probably prove provocative of divergence rather than unanimity of view. It is doubtful if wars are to be diminished by rendering them less destructive, for it is the plain lesson of history that the periods of peace have been longer protracted as the cost and destructiveness of war have increased. The expedience of restraining the inventive genius of our people in the direction of devising new means of defense is by no means clear, and considering the temptations to which men and nations may be exposed in a time of conflict, it is doubtful if an international agreement to this end would prove effective. The dissent of a single powerful nation might render it altogether nugatory. The delegates are, therefore, enjoined not to give the weight of their influence to the promotion of projects the realization of which is so uncertain.

25. As contained in 2 Scott, The Hague Peace Conferences of 1899 and 1907 p. 37 (1909).

26. Hull, *op. cit. supra* note 18 discusses this position at 90.

27. For discussion of these deficiencies of the Declaration see Castrén, *op. cit. supra* note 11, at 193; 1 Garner, *op. cit. supra* note 4, at 273-78; Greenspan, *op. cit. supra* note 11, at 355; Spaight, Air Power and War Rights 189 (3rd ed. 1947).

28. Kunz, Gaskrieg und Volkerrecht 26 (1927).

29. See Meyrowitz, "Les Armes Psychochimiques et le Droit International," 10 Annuaire Français de Droit International 81, at 92 n. 31 (1964).

30. Gas Declaration, Scott, *op. cit. supra* note 19, at 225.

31. Fenwick has stated that it has limited validity because of the insufficient number of states agreeing thereto. Fenwick, International Law 557 (3rd ed. 1948).

32. E.g., Oppenheim, *op. cit. supra* note 8, at 342; Singh, Nuclear Weapons and International Law 154-55 (1959).

33. See O'Brien, *op. cit. supra* note 8, at 20-21; Spaight, *op. cit. supra* note 27, at 189.

34. These conventions are set forth in Scott, *op. cit. supra* note 19, at 100 *et seq.*

35. *Id.* at 116.

36. *Ibid.*

37. See *infra* ch. VII.

38. Lawrence, The Principles of International Law 438 (3rd ed. rev. 1909); Schwarzenberger, The Legality of Nuclear Warfare 35 (1958).

39. See Scott, *op. cit. supra* note 19, at 129-31. It should be pointed out that Articles 1 and 2 of the Hague Convention IV of 1907, to which the Hague Regulations are annexed, read as follows:

Article 1

The Contracting Powers shall issue instructions to their armed land forces which shall be in conformity with the Regulations respecting the laws and Customs of War on Land, annexed to the present Convention.

Article 2

The provisions contained in the Regulations referred to in Article 1, as well as in the present Convention, do not apply except between Contracting Powers, and then only if the belligerents are parties to the Convention.

If the customary law rule absolutely forbids poison, then this would seem to be an attempt to change the customary law rule, something which can only be done by parties as among themselves but not as to third states. See discussion on this point *infra* pp. 78-79.

40. Schwarzenberger, *op. cit. supra* note 38, at 27-36.

41. See e.g., Schwarzenberger's critical statement: "Consultation of standard textbooks and military manuals on the meaning of poison and poisoned weapons further confirms how little explored this field is. Definitions excel by their absence." *Id.* at 27. See also "Poisons," Scientific American, Nov., 1959, p. 76.

42. The Oxford English Dictionary vol. 7 (1933) defines poison as "any substance which when introduced or absorbed by a living organism, destroys life or injures health, irrespective of mechanical means or direct thermal changes."

Webster's Third International Dictionary (1961) defined poison in the following way: "A substance (as a drug) that in suitable quantities has properties harmful or fatal to an organism when it is brought into contact with or absorbed by the organism: a substance that through its chemical action kills, injures, or impairs an organism."

10 McGraw-Hill Encyclopedia of Science and Technology (1966) defines poison at 434 as follows: "A substance which by chemical action and at low dosage can kill or injure living organisms. Broadly defined, poisons include chemicals toxic for any living form: microbes, plants or animals."

43. See Schwarzenberger, *op. cit supra* note 38, at 27.

44. "Toxicology," 14 McGraw-Hill Encyclopedia of Science and Technology 5 (1966).

45. *Ibid.*

46. See Departments of the Army and the Air Force, Military Chemistry and Chemical Agents (TM 3-215, AFM 355-7) pp. 12-30 (December, 1963).

47. Mimeographed Glossary of Terms, U.S. Army CBR Weapons Orientation Course Dugway Proving Ground, Dugway, Utah, August, 1966. Chemical operations are described as the "employment of chemical agents (excluding riot control agents) to (1) kill, or incapacitate for a significant period of time man or animals; (2) delay or hinder the use of space, facilities or material."

48. Rothschild, Tomorrow's Weapons 39 (1964).

49. See, e.g., an article signed by Leary, Litwin, Hollingshead, Weil, and Alpert entitled "The Politics of the Nervous System," 18 Bull. of the Atomic Scientists 26 (May, 1962). This article would seem to say that an enemy would do us a favor by introducing such "conscious-expanding drugs" among our leaders. An article in The Economist (Nov. 28, 1959) concerning psychochemicals calls them "Humane and not Killers," at p. 869.

50. See Meyrowitz, *supra* note 29, at 88 *et seq.* (1964).

51. See Hollyhock, "Weapons Against the Mind," New Scientist (April 22, 1965) p. 166, at 168.

52. See Lieberman, "Psychochemicals as Weapons," 18 Bull. of the Atomic Scientists 11 (Jan., 1962); see also Lieberman, "The Ethical Neutrality of LSD," 18 Bull. of the Atomic Scientists 41 (1962), where he states that such drugs are "toxic and intoxicating."

53. "Poison," 10 McGraw-Hill Encyclopedia of Science and Technology, *supra* note 42, at 434. Lysergic acid is also classified as an alkaloid. *Ibid.* On bufotenine see Webster's Third New International Dictionary 291 (1961).

54. "Mushroom," 8 McGraw-Hill Encyclopedia of Science and Technology 661 (1960). Psilocybine is called a toxin, 6 Chambers Encyclopaedia 112 (1966).

55. TM 3-215, *op. cit. supra* note 46, at 31; Rothschild, "Chemical Warfare" Ordnance (Sept.-Oct., 1966) p. 168 speaks of the effects at pp. 169-70; for effects of tear gas and an example resulting in death from overexposure see Gonzalez, Vance, Halpern, and Umberger, Legal Medicine, Pathology and Toxicology 690 (2d ed. 1954); and see *supra* p. 11 for discussion of these agents.

56. See *supra* pp. 45-46 for discussion of the Brussels Conference.

57. Dept. of the Army, Military Biology and Biological Warfare Agents 2 (TM 3-216, 1956). The new manual of 1964 would narrow biological operations to the employment of biological agents "to produce casualties or damage." Biological agents are specified as living microorganisms unless otherwise specified. And see *supra* pp. 18-19 *re* toxins.

58. For description of antimateriel agents see *supra* p. 16.

59. Military Biology and Biological Agents 14 (TM 3-216, AFM 355-6) (1964) hereinafter referred to as TM 3-216.

60. Brungs, *supra* note 8, at 58-59 n. 49.

61. *Ibid.* On these two types of toxins see TM 3-216, *supra* note 59, at 56-57. An American case has spoken of a technical distinction between infection and poison, stating that "illness produced by bacteria themselves is referred to as infection, while that occasioned by the poisoning produced by such bacteria is referred to as poisoning." The court, however, in deciding the case was not impressed with the distinction. N.Y. Life Ins. Co. v. Mariano, 102 Colo. 18, 76 P.2d 417, 418 (1938).

62. The Columbia Encyclopaedia 575 (3rd ed. 1963).

63. Webster's New International Dictionary 735 (2d ed. 1940).

64. Neinast, *supra* note 8, reaches this conclusion at 27. Disease is said to presuppose "a shifting of the normal balance [of substances making up the chemical composition of the body] and usually a decrease or an increase in their quantity." "Disease," 4 McGraw-Hill Encyclopedia of Science and Technology 236 (1960).

65. See 9 Encyclopedia Americana 161 (1963).

66. See *supra* p. 50 for definition of poisons.

67. Fenwick, International Law 667 (4th ed. 1965). Greenspan, *op. cit. supra* note 11, at 317.

68. Such agents are described in TM 3-216, *op. cit. supra* note 59, at 58, 68.

69. Holland, Lectures on International Law 316 (1933).

70. U.S. Dept. of the Army Field Manual, 27-10, The Law of Land Warfare 18 (1956).

71. Garner would take this position. See 1 Garner, *op. cit. supra* note 4, at 289. He discusses there the South African charges of the poisoning of wells by the Germans in World War I. Greenspan, *op. cit. supra* note 11, agrees with Garner at p. 317.

72. Castrén, *op. cit. supra* note 11, at 192. The British Manual would accept this view. British Manual of Military Law pt. III para. 112 (1958).

73. Garner, *op. cit. supra* note 4, at 291; Holland, *op. cit. supra* note 69, at 316.

74. Garner, *ibid.*

75. Art. 23, Geneva Convention Relative to the Protection of Civilian Persons in Time of War of Aug. 12, 1949, 1 Final Record of the Diplomatic Conference of Geneva of 1949.

76. On general devastation and requisition see Greenspan, *op. cit. supra* note 11, at 285, 300.

77. 2 Oppenheim, *op. cit. supra* note 8, at 419.

78. Fenwick so states, *op. cit. supra* note 67, at 667.

79. Schwarzenberger, *op. cit. supra* note 38, at 38; Greenspan, *op. cit. supra* note 11, at 359.

80. Kelsen, *op. cit. supra* note 3, at 117.

81. Stone, *op. cit. supra* note 3, at 553-54 and 557; McDougal and Feliciano, Law and Minimum World Order 634-36, 637-38 (1961).

82. McDougal and Feliciano, *id.* at 665.

83. *Id.* at 663.

84. O'Brien, *supra* note 8, at 21-23.

85. *Id.* at 22.

86. *Ibid.*

87. *Ibid.*

88. Neinast, *supra* note 8, at 27-28.

89. Kunz states categorically: "The Hague Conventions could, of course, not regulate methods of warfare unknown at the time." Kunz, "The Chaotic Status of the Laws of War and the Urgent Necessity for Their Reviison," 45 Am. J. Int'l L. 37, at 38 (1951). Stone softens this and thinks it depends on whether a rule "*may* have been framed wisely enough to catch a new weapon." (Italics supplied) Stone, *op. cit. supra* note 3, at 550 n.

90. See *supra* pp. 45-46.

91. Prentiss, *op. cit. supra* note 21, at 686.

92. It has been said that it was not so intended at the time of the Hague Conventions to include poison gas within the meaning of the poison proviso of Art. 23(a) and that practice has borne this out. Kelly, "Gas Warfare in International Law," *supra* note 21, at 44.

93. O'Brien, *supra* note 8, at 22.

94. See *supra* p. 45.

95. See Brungs, *supra* note 8, at 40. He discusses the attitude of the delegates on this matter. One was of the opinion that the issue of the spread of contagious diseases should be the subject of a sanitary convention. Another mentioned that it was up to occupying armies and their commanders to observe sanitary regulations.

96. U.S. Department of the Army Field Manual, *op. cit. supra* note 70, para. 38. Various explanations have been given for the change in the U.S. position. The army's statement was a confusing one, but seemed to rest primarily on the fact that the United States had reversed its position on biological warfare by failing to adopt the Geneva Protocol of 1925. See Neinast, *supra* note 8, who at 19-21 discusses the Army's attitude and the inconsistencies in its reasoning. He himself states at 21 that the Army's previous stand condemning biological warfare (the spread of contagious disease) was wrong, and the Army persisted in error until the change was made, and realized in Neinast's words that "biological warfare is not illegal." Brungs in discussing the new United States position that no treaty to which the United States is adherent restricts uses in war of bacteriological warfare reasons that this language would apply "only to treaties specifically prohibiting bacteriological warfare by name and only to disease-producing bacteria." Since the United States is a ratifier of the Hague Convention of 1907, its present statement and stand would not refer to biological toxins (poisons) which would be prohibited by Art. 23(a) of the Hague regulations. This carries out his distinction between microorganisms which produce toxins and those which produce disease by direct contact with the victim. See Brungs, *supra* note 8, at 90-91, 58-59.

97. U.S. Dept. of the Army Field Manual, Rules of Land Warfare para. 177 (1914 as corrected 1917); U.S. Dept. of the Army Field Manual 27-10, Rules of Land Warfare para. 28 (1940). However, decision as to whether CB weapons are to be employed is the sole prerogative of the President. Armed Forces Doctrine for Chemical

and Biological Weapons Employment and Defense (FM 101-40, NPW 36 C, AFM 355-2, LFM 03) p. 3 (April, 1964).

98. On the Geneva Gas Protocol, see *infra* pp. 71-85. Stone, *supra* note 3, at 557 in discussing bacteriological warfare and the later Geneva Protocol declares: "The very text of this Protocol purporting as it does to 'extend' the gas warfare prohibition to bacteriological warfare, seems to admit that no such restriction was to be found in customary international law." See also Neinast, *supra* note 8, at 28, 29.

CHAPTER FOUR

1. For a complete history of the peace conference see the six-volume set, A History of the Peace Conference of Paris, edited by Temperly (1920-1924). See also the four volumes of Foreign Relations of the United States, The Paris Peace Conference 1919 (1943). See also, Von Muralt, From Versailles to Potsdam 9-32 (1948).

2. The Treaty of Versailles is set out in 3 Temperly, *id.* at 100-336.

3. The Treaty of Saint-Germain-en-Laye is set out in 5 Temperly, *id.* at 173-302.

4. The Treaty of the Trianon is set out in 5 Temperly, *id.* at 173-304. See also, Bethlem, The Treaty of the Trianon and European Peace (1933).

5. See Treaty of Neuilly-sur-Seine as set out in 5 Temperly, *id.* at 305-58.

6. 3 Foreign Relations, *op. cit. supra* note 1, at 469.

7. 1 Temperly, *op. cit. supra* note 1, at 253.

8. *Id.* at 255.

9. Statement following concluding Article 381 of Treaty of Saint-Germain-en-Laye; and following concluding Article 364 of the Treaty of the Trianon, and protocol following concluding Article 296 of the Treaty of Neuilly-sur-Seine.

10. 1 Temperly, *op. cit. supra* note 1, at 266.

11. *Ibid.*

12. 6 Temperly, *op. cit. supra* note 1, at 553.

13. 4 Foreign Relations, *op. cit. supra* note 1, at 232. See also, Kessler, Germany and Europe 58-75 (1923).

14. *Id.* at 363.

15. *Ibid.*

16. *Id.* at 388.

17. Naval War College, International Law Situations 1935, at 102 (1936). And see *infra* pp. 73-78 for further discussion of opposing contentions.

18. O'Brien apparently adopts this view. "Biological/Chemical Warfare and the International Law of War," 51 Georgetown Law Journal 1, at 24 (1962).

19. Van Eysinga, "La Guerre Chimique et le Mouvement pour sa Répression," 16 Recueil des Cours 329, at 349 (1927). But see Ewing, "The Legality of Chemical Warfare," 61 American Law Review 58, at 68, who flatly states: "This treaty did not purport to be a pronouncement of international law; it was merely a penalty directed against Germany alone."

20. 5 Temperly, *op. cit. supra* note 1, at 5.

21. 4 Foreign Relations, *op. cit. supra* note 1, at 102; 2 Temperly, *op. cit. supra* note 1, at 136, 4 Temperly, *id.* at 143.

22. 5 Temperly, *id.* at 209.

23. Almond and Lutz, The Treaty of St. Germain 2-8 (1935).

24. 4 Temperly, *op. cit. supra* note 1, at 150.

25. Weller, Weapons and Tactics: Hastings to Berlin 91 (1966).

26. See *infra* ch. VII.

27. Holt, Treaties Defeated by the Senate 249-307 (1964).

28. The Treaty of Peace between the United States and Germany is set forth in

170 International Conciliation 3 (Jan., 1922). The Treaty of Peace with Austria is set forth in the same publication at 8, and with Hungary at page 13.

29. ". . . 'the use in war of asphyxiating, poisonous, or other gases, and of all analogous liquids, materials or devices' . . . should have been sufficient to cover bacteriological warfare." League of Nations Document A.13.1925.ix. Proceedings of the Conference for the Supervision of the International Trade in Arms and Ammunition and in Implements of War (Geneva, May 4 to June 17, 1925) at 341. See also Greenspan, The Modern Law of Land Warfare at 358-59 (1959); Singh, Nuclear Weapons and International Law 165 (1959).

30. ". . . biological warfare has unique characteristics which distinguish it from chemical warfare and other related systems; therefore, biological warfare is not subject to the same legal considerations as chemical warfare." Neinast, "United States Use of Biological Warfare," 24 Military Law Review 1, at 43 (1964).

31. See *supra* pp. 28-36.

32. "Mr. Lansing said that the difficulty had arisen with regard to exacting from the Germans the disclosure of their secret processes for the manufacture of ingredients for the inhuman conduct of war . . . Baron Sonnino pointed out that the British proposal demanded the surrender of all chemical processes out of which gases had been or could be made, and for the production of all substances from which gases or other destructive agencies could be produced." 4 Foreign Relations, *op. cit. supra* note 1, at 479.

33. *Id.* at 480. "Baron Sonnino agreed that the Germans might reveal their second best secrets, but would probably succeed in keeping their best ones. President Wilson said that they would certainly not reveal their new ones. . . ." *Ibid.* The Council of Ten requested their military advisers to state the military advantages of exacting from the Germans the revelation of their secret processes for the manufacture of lethal gases, pointing out, "It is to be observed:—That no means of supervision exist capable of guaranteeing the veracity of the statements the Germans might make on this subject." *Id.* at 481. Temperly points out in volume 2, *op. cit. supra* note 1, at 135, "Articles 171 and 172 are also most important, but their strict execution will be more difficult to check and enforce, especially as regards the manufacture of gases or similar materials."

34. The United States, Great Britain, France, Italy, Japan, Belgium, Bolivia, Brazil, Cuba, Ecuador, Greece, Guatemala, Haiti, The Jedjaz, Honduras, Liberia, Nicaragua, Panama, Peru, Portugal, Roumania, The Serb-Croat-Slovene State, Siam, Czechoslovakia, and Uruguay, 3 Temperly, *id.* at 100.

35. "The Treaty thus drawn up was signed by all the Powers, Great and Small, with the single exception of the Chinese, whose empty places were a protest against the Shantung settlement." 1 Temperly, *id.* at 271.

36. Holt, *op. cit. supra* note 27, at 334.

37. McNair, The Law of Treaties 518 (1961).

38. Tillman, Anglo-American Relations at the Paris Peace Conference of 1919, at 161 (1961).

39. Buell, The Washington Conference ch. II (1922).

40. Hosono, International Disarmament 210 (1926). See also 4 Naval War College, International Law Documents 1921, "Conference on the Limitation of Armaments" 24 (1923).

41. Hosono, *id.* at 176.

42. The text of the invitation is set out in Senate Doc. No. 126, 67th Cong. 2d sess., 1921-1922, Conference on the Limitation of Armament pp. 17-18 (1922).

43. Hosono, *op. cit. supra* note 40, at 177.

44. *Id.* at 212.

45. See Report of the Sub-Committee on Poisonous Gases, Senate Doc. No. 126, *op. cit. supra* note 42, at 384-88.

46. *Ibid.*

47. Hosono, *op. cit. supra* note 40, at 215.

48. *Ibid.*

49. Senate Document No. 126, *op. cit. supra* note 42, at 386.

50. The French version of the resolution again varied from the English: it uses the phraseology "gaz asphyxiants, toxiques ou similaires"—for discussion of this point see *supra* p. 59 and *infra* pp. 73-78.

51. Senate Doc. No. 126, *op. cit. supra* note 42, at 165.

52. See Note, "The Binding Force of League Resolutions," 16 Brit. Yb. Int'l L. 157 (1935); 1 Podesta Costa, Derecho Internacional Publico 367 (3rd ed. 1955).

53. Fenwick, International Law 205 (3rd ed. 1948).

54. Customs Regime between Germany and Austria (Protocol of March 19, 1931), P.C.I.J. Series A./B.—No. 41 (September 5, 1931).

55. For an excellent discussion on the potentialities of instruments signed at international conferences see Johnson, "The Conclusions of International Conferences," 35 Brit. Yb. Int'l L. 1 (1959).

56. 5 Hackworth, A Digest of International Law 33 (1927).

57. The English and French versions of the treaty are set forth in Naval War College Documents, *supra* note 40, at 352.

58. See *supra* pp. 44-45.

59. See *supra* pp. 45-49.

60. See *supra* p. 60.

61. This conclusion is supported by Rodgers, "The Laws of War Concerning Aviation and Radio," 17 Am. J. Int'l L. 629 (1923) when he states:

> . . . it was apparently the intention of those who were chiefly responsible for the resolution and the terms of the treaty to have these matters definitely put into the international law accepted by the world. Or at least, by getting the treaty and resolution accepted by five great armed Powers, they felt they were making a long step in that direction.

62. Naval War College Documents, *op. cit. supra* note 40, at 251.

63. "The Washington Treaty seems to overstate the case about previous condemnations of gas warfare. Such overstatement is common on this subject." Fuller, "The Application of International Law to Chemical and Biological Warfare," 10 Orbis 247, at 252 (1966).

64. "The Washington Treaty is also interesting because it is the only treaty containing limitations on chemical warfare ever ratified by the United States Senate." *Ibid.*

65. Rodgers, *supra* note 61, at 629; Naval War College Documents, *op. cit. supra* note 40, at 283.

66. Moore, International Law and Some Current Illusions and Other Essays p. 182 (1924).

67. Senate Doc. 126, *op. cit. supra* note 42, at 423.

68. *Id.* at 421-22.

69. Moore, *op. cit. supra* note 66, at 238.

70. Garner, Proposed Rules for the Regulation of Aerial Warfare, 18 Am. J. Int'l L. 56 (1924).

71. Spaight, Air Power and War Rights 197 ff. (3rd ed. 1947).

72. Moore, *op. cit. supra* note 66, at 238.

73. 9 Bemis, The American Secretaries of State and Their Diplomacy 266 (1958).

74. Cox, Nicaragua and the United States 769 (1927).

75. The complete treaty is set out in 189 International Conciliation 96 (August, 1923).

76. 2 Hudson, International Legislation 1922-1924 p. 942 (1931).

77. Article 18 of the Covenant of the League of Nations. This Covenant can be found in Part I of the Treaty of Peace signed at Versailles June 28, 1919, and of the other peace treaties signed in 1919 and 1920. It is also set forth in Sohn, Basic Documents of the United Nations 277 (1956).

78. According to McNair, The Law of Treaties 183 (1961):

> The duty to register undertaken by the parties in Article 18 was not merely a duty to one another—if that were all it could validly be waived—but a duty toward all the other members of the League, and they had a direct interest in its fulfillment. In view of the language of Article 18 it is difficult to escape the view that non-registration was a fatal defect and affected the essential validity of the treaty.

79. Lockley, "Diplomatic Futility," 10 Hispanic American Historical Review 265 (1930).

80. Thomas and Thomas, The Organization of American States 3-18 (1963).

81. Wilgus, "James G. Blaine and the Pan American Movement," 5 Hispanic Historical Rev. 662 (1922).

82. Thomas and Thomas, *op. cit. supra* note 80, at 19.

83. Scott, "The Fifth International Conference of American States," 17 Am. J. Int'l L. 518 (1923).

84. Scott, The International Conferences of American States 1889-1928 p. 291 (1931).

85. Thomas and Thomas, Non-Intervention: The Law and Its Import in the Americas 109-10, 117-18 (1956); Fenwick, "The Inter-American Regional System," 39 Am. Pol. Sci. Rev. 496 (1945).

86. Woolsey, "The Leticia Dispute between Colombia and Peru," 27 Am. J. Int'l L. 317 (1933). PAU, Actas y Antecedentes de la Quinta Conferencia Internacional Americana 89 (1923).

87. League of Nations Document, Report of the Secretary General to the First Assembly of the League on the Work of the Council 20/48/37 (1920).

88. *Ibid.*

89. *Id.* at 11-12.

90. This was an idea ascribed to Lord Cecil; see De Madariaga, Disarmament 187-88 (1929); Committee on Intellectual Co-operation p. 109 (1922). See also 2 League of Nations Record of the 3rd Assembly, Plenary Meetings (1922).

91. On the Temporary Mixed Commission and its establishment see League of Nations, Annex 164, Resolutions of the Assembly with Regard to Armaments 21/41/22 pp. 104 *et seq.* (1921).

92. 2 League of Nations, Records of the 3rd Assembly Plenary Meetings, Annex 24, Reduction of Armaments p. 160, at 164 (1922).

93. League of Nations, Records of the 5th Assembly, Minutes of the Third Committee, Spec. Supp. No. 26 pp. 120-26 (1924).

94. *Id.* at 121.

95. *Id.* at 122.

96. *Id.* at 126.

97. *Id.* at 125.

98. *Id.* at 126.

99. 1 League of Nations Records of the 3rd Assembly Plenary Meetings 238

(1922). Discussion of these early League efforts in the field of CB warfare are contained in League of Nations Secretariat, Ten Years of World Cooperation 118 (1930); Fradkin, "Chemical Warfare—Its Possibilities and Probabilities," Int. Concil. No. 248 pp. 162 *et seq.* (March, 1929).

100. The Conference and Proceedings are set forth in League of Nations Proceedings of the Conference for the Supervision of the International Trade in Arms and Ammunition and in Implements of War, A 13.1925.IX (1925).

101. Text of the Draft Convention, *id.* at 17-26.

102. The Department of State declared:

> The Department would desire to see an article inserted absolutely prohibiting international trade in asphyxiating, poisonous or other gases for use in war . . . as this Government and various other governments are clearly committed to the principle that poisonous gases should not be used in warfare, there is every reason for you to press for the inclusion of an article prohibiting the shipment of such gases in foreign trade for possible use in time of war.

1 Foreign Relations of the U.S., 1925 pp. 35-36 (1940).

103. Proceedings of the Conference, *op. cit. supra* note 100, at 739.

104. *Ibid.*

105. *Ibid.*

106. *Id.* at 779.

107. De Madariaga, *op. cit. supra* note 90, at 188-89.

108. Proceedings of the Conference, *op. cit. supra* note 100, at 313.

109. See on this point remarks of certain of the delegates, *id.* at 162, 306, 529, 530, 533, and the proposal of the drafting committee, *id.* at 307.

110. *Id.* at 339.

111. *Id.* at 340-41.

112. *Id.* at 341.

113. *Ibid.*

114. *Id.* at 77, 365.

115. The Congressional debates will be found in 68 Cong. Rec. 141-54, 226-29, 363-68, 1969, 2090 (1926). For discussion see Kelly, "Gas Warfare in International Law," Mil. L. Rev., July, 1960 (DA Pam 27-100-9, 1 July 60) p. 1, at 34; Fradkin, *supra* note 99, at 176. See also Senate Subcommittee on Disarmament, 84th Cong. 2d sess., Disarmament and Security: A Collection of Documents 1919-1955 pp. 700-704 (1956).

116. 68 Cong. Rec. 142 (1926).

117. The following countries have ratified or acceded to the Geneva Protocol. Those marked with an asterisk ratified or acceded with reservations:

°Australia	January 22, 1930
Austria (ratified)	May 9, 1928
°Belgium (ratified)	December 4, 1928
°Bulgaria (ratified)	March 7, 1934
°Canada (ratified)	May 6, 1930
Ceylon	December 18, 1953
°Chile (ratified)	July 2, 1935
China	August 7, 1929
Cuba	June 24, 1966
Cyprus	December 12, 1966
°Czechoslovakia (ratified)	August 16, 1938
Denmark (ratified)	May 5, 1930
°Estonia (ratified)	August 28, 1931

Ethiopia	September 18, 1935
Finland (ratified)	June 26, 1929
*France (ratified)	May 9, 1926
Gambia	November 16, 1966
Germany (ratified)	April 25, 1929
Ghana	May 3, 1967
Greece (ratified)	May 30, 1931
Holy See (Vatican)	October 18, 1966
Hungary	November 11, 1952
Iceland	November 2, 1967
*India (ratified)	April 9, 1930
*Indonesia	October 31, 1930
Iran	July 4, 1929
*Iraq	April 7, 1931
*Ireland	August 18, 1930
Italy (ratified)	April 3, 1928
Latvia (ratified)	June 3, 1931
Liberia	April 2, 1927
Lithuania (ratified)	June 15, 1933
Luxembourg (ratified)	September 1, 1936
Madagascar	August 12, 1967
Maldive Islands	January 6, 1967
Mexico	March 15, 1932
Monaco	January 6, 1967
*Netherlands (ratified)	October 31, 1930
*New Zealand	January 22, 1930
Niger	April 19, 1967
Norway (ratified)	July 27, 1932
Pakistan	1947
Paraguay	1933
Poland (ratified)	February 4, 1929
*Portugal (ratified)	July 1, 1930
*Romania (ratified)	August 23, 1929
Rwanda	June 25, 1964
Sierre Leone	March 20, 1967
*Spain (ratified)	August 22, 1929
Sweden (ratified)	April 25, 1930
Switzerland (ratified)	July 12, 1932
Tanzania	April 22, 1963
Thailand (ratified)	June 6, 1931
Tunisia	July 12, 1967
Turkey (ratified)	October 5, 1929
Uganda	May 24, 1965
*Union of South Africa	January 22, 1930
*United Kingdom (ratified)	April 9, 1930
*USSR	April 5, 1928
UAR	December 6, 1928
Venezuela (ratified)	February 8, 1928
Yugoslavia (ratified)	April 12, 1929

The ratification of the Protocol by the Netherlands on October 31, 1930, included Surinam, the Netherlands Antilles, and the Netherlands Indies (Indonesia). On December 27, 1949, sovereignty over Indonesia was transferred from the Netherlands to the Republic of Indonesia. The Agreement on Transitional Measures adopted by the Round Table Conference at The Hague on November 2, 1949, provides that treaties and other international agreements concluded by the Netherlands are in force for the Republic of Indonesia.

In 1933 Paraguay sent to France a note of accession to the Protocol, but there is no record that France notified the other signatories of the accession.

Yugoslavia is a party by virtue of the ratification in the name of the Kingdom of Serbs, Croats and Slovenes on April 12, 1929. The Kingdom changed its official title to "Kingdom of Yugoslavia" in 1928 and in 1954 to the "Federal People's Republic of Yugoslavia."

On July 13, 1952, the People's Republic of China issued a statement recognizing as binding upon it the accession to the Protocol "in the Name of China" on August 17, 1929.

In 1959 Czechoslovakia transmitted to France, the depositary government, an instrument of adherence from the German Democratic Republic.

Tanganyika acceded to the Protocol on April 22, 1963. In a note dated May 6, 1954, the United Republic of Tanganyika and Zanzibar informed the U.N. secretary-general that all international agreements formerly in force between either country and other states would continue in force for the United Republic.

The following countries have signed the Protocol but have not ratified it to date:

> United States
> Brazil
> El Salvador
> Japan
> Nicaragua
> Uruguay

118. It is stated in 2 Oppenheim, International Law (7th ed. Lauterpacht 1952) at p. 344 in speaking of the Geneva Protocol and other instruments that "[t]hese drafts and pronouncements, which have not so far, all acquired the force of law, bear witness to the tendency to universality in the prohibition of chemical warfare."

119. Meyrowitz, "Les Armes Psychochimiques et le Droit International," 10 Annuaire Français de Droit International 81, at 93 (1964).

120. *Ibid.*

121. Spaight, Air Power and War Rights 19 (3rd ed. 1947).

122. For exposition of these reasons see Meyrowitz, *supra* note 119, at 94-95.

123. U.K. Memorandum on Chemical Warfare to the Preparatory Commission for the Disarmament Conference, Part. Pap. Misc. No. 17 (1930) Cmd. 3747.

124. Tucker mentions these agents in U.S. Naval War College International Law Studies 1955 p. 53 n. 16 (1957).

125. See Greenspan, The Modern Law of Land Warfare 361 (1959).

126. For discussion see McDougal and Feliciano, Law and Minimum World Order 634-37 (1961).

127. McDougal and Feliciano doubt the application, or at least the present-day application, of the Protocol, to such nonlethal agents. *Ibid.* And Kunz points out that the Geneva Convention lifted both the English and French versions on the use of gas verbatim from the Treaty of Versailles. Consequently, he contends that one must refer back to the circumstances surrounding that treaty to see what was the intention of the parties in order to interpret the phrase. The drafters of the Versailles Treaty were concerned only with the choking, blood, and blister agents used in World War I. It was these that they wished to prohibit Germany from importing, manufacturing, exporting, or employing. Consequently the ban applied only to lethal and severely injurious gases and not to incapacitating or riot control agents. If the participants in the Geneva Protocol had truly desired a more extensive ban on the use of gas in war, they could easily have constructed a new formula; failure to do so, in spite of what the delegates said throughout the proceedings, means that the majority realized their

governments would not go beyond the Versailles formula, and hence the Geneva Protocol must apply only to lethal or severely injurious gas agents. Kunz, Gaskrieg und Volkerrecht 36-49 (1927).

128. Stone points out that the British position (to the effect that innocuous gases should be prohibited, for if they were not states could arm themselves with equipment which could easily be used for poisonous gases) "has been overcome by the facts for [s]tates continue so to arm themselves even under a prohibition ranging over all gas warfare." Stone, Legal Control of International Conflict 556-57 (2d imp. rev. 1959).

129. Proceedings of the Conference, *op. cit. supra* note 100, at 76.

130. See, e.g., Naval War College International Law Situations 1935, pp. 101-2 (1936).

131. See *supra* pp. 51-52.

132. Meyrowitz, *supra* note 119, at 94.

133. See *infra* p. 89.

134. See *supra* p. 16.

135. See *supra* pp. 17-19.

136. Proceedings of the Conference, *op. cit. supra* note 100, at 340.

137. See *supra* p. 70.

138. McDougal and Feliciano, *op. cit. supra* note 126, at 638.

139. Proceedings of the Conference, *op. cit. supra* note 100, at 779.

140. *Id.* at 340.

141. See *supra* pp. 46-49.

142. See *supra* p. 60.

143. See *supra* pp. 68-69.

144. See *supra* p. 67.

145. For the early reservations see 94 League of Nations Treaty Series 67 *et seq.* (1929).

146. For discussion along these lines see Meyrowitz, "Les Armes Psychochimiques et le Droit International," 10 Annuaire Français de Droit International 81, at 97-100 (1964).

147. International law rests upon the common consent, express or tacit, of the members of the family of nations, and from this principle of common consent it is deduced that states are equal. See Thomas and Thomas, "Equality of States in International Law—Fact or Fiction?" 37 Va. L. Rev. 791, at 806-7 (1951).

148. 2 Oppenheim, International Law—Disputes, War and Neutrality 561 (7th ed. Lauterpacht 1952). Meyrowitz, *supra* note 146, at 100 n. 51, poses an additional question: Suppose in the course of the last war, Japan, a nonsignatory of the Protocol, employed chemical weapons against the United States, also a nonsignatory. In view of the wording of their reservations, could Russia and Great Britain, Russia not even being at war with Japan, have resorted legally to the same weapons against the forces of Germany, an ally of Japan?

It might be contended that there is little significance in the second paragraph of the French reservation, because it appears to be a restatement of the commonly accepted rule of treaty law which permits an aggrieved party to suspend performance of a treaty's obligations or even terminate the agreement toward another party who materially breaches the treaty. But the terms of the reservation are much broader than this customary rule of international law. The reservation is not limited to material breach but covers *any* breach, material or nonmaterial. Would not any use of gas or bacteriological methods of warfare constitute a material breach?

If, as many authorities contend, the Geneva Protocol prohibits not only those agents classified as toxic, lethal, or severely injurious, but also nonlethal agents such as riot-control and incapacitating agents, then the use of even a small quantity of tear gas in a war by a contracting party would be a breach of the treaty. Under treaty law, without the reservation, the use of a nonlethal, not severely injurious agent such as tear gas would not be accepted as such a *material* breach of the treaty to permit complete abrogation or suspension of its terms. But the reservation would definitely change this. It would relieve from obligation in the case of such a nonmaterial breach as well as in the case of a material breach.

A further possible significance of reservations such as that of the second paragraph of the French reservation which makes obligation cease upon a failure of a contracting party to respect the prohibition is that such reservations apparently do away with the law of reprisal. The reservation stresses the contractual nature of the protocol and sanctions in advance *any* use, not just a *proportional* use as required by the law of reprisal.

Normally the laws of war that have become effective between parties to a treaty do remain subject to the right of reprisal to enforce the terms of the treaty, for treaties forbidding resort to certain weapons in war are not looked upon as being purely contractual as regards the right of reprisal. In other words, if a contracting party breaches the treaty, normally another contracting party may equally resort in a proportionate manner to a forbidden weapon as an enforcement measure to stop the breach of the treaty. But the reservation can be interpreted to permit *unlimited* use of forbidden weapons subject to no necessity first to take actions in the nature of reprisals only, for once a breach occurs the other party is free from all obligation. So the reservations can establish a completely different rule from that normally occurring under the international law of warfare. As Oppenheim, *supra* p. 235, points out:

> The effect [of this type of reservation] might be that in a war in which a considerable number of belligerents are involved, the action of one state, however small in a distant region of war, might become the starting point for a general abandonment of the restraints of the Convention.

149. League of Nations, *op. cit. supra* note 145, at 71. Attention should be called to the fact that Triska and Slusser in their work, The Theory, Law, and Policy of Soviet Treaties p. 82 (1962) translate, apparently from the Russian version, the phrase "whose Allies *de jure* or in fact do not respect the restrictions" as *"the formal or factual allies* of which would ignore the prohibition." (Italics added) This translation is a transposition of the English version which is one of the two authentic languages (French being the other) established in the treaty itself. Grammatically speaking, as far as the English version is concerned, from their location in the text the words *"de jure* or in fact" would normally modify the phrase "respect the restrictions." If these words were clearly designed to modify "allies" they should have been placed before rather than following the word "allies," as Triska and Slusser's wording indicates. Therefore here is another potential ambiguity which might arise in interpreting the Geneva Protocol.

150. 5 Hackworth, Digest of International Law sec. 482 (1943). See also McNair, The Law of Treaties 159 (1961); 1 Oppenheim, International Law 517 (6th ed. Lauterpacht 1944); 1 Fauchille, Droit International Public, pt. 3 para. 823 pp. 312-13 (1921); Spiropoulos, Traité de Droit International Public 45 (1933); Saba, "Certains Aspects de l'Evolution de la Technique des Traités et Conventions Internationales," 54 Revue Générale de Droit International Public 417 (1950); 2 Hyde, International Law 442 (1957); Fourteen Diamond Rings v. U.S., 183 U.S. 176 (1901); Statement by Sir Hartley Shawcross, I.C.J. Pleadings, Oral Arguments, Documents: Reservations to the Convention on the Prevention and

Punishment of the Crime of Genocide, Advisory Opinion of May 28, 1951, pp. 358-401.

It might be possible to argue that failure of any party to the Geneva Protocol to object to any reservation for a period that now exceeds thirty-five years must be construed as tacit consent among all the parties, particularly in view of the fact that the International Law Commission of the United Nations in its final version of the Law of Treaties, Article 19, section 5 (2 Yearbook of the International Law Commission 1966, Doc. A/CN.4/L. 117 and Add. 1 p. 116) declares that

> a reservation is considered to have been accepted by a State if it shall have raised no objection to the reservation by the end of a period of twelve months after it was notified of the reservation or by the date on which it expressed its consent to be bound by the treaty, whichever is later.

Additional weight is given to this proposition by the Advisory Opinion of May 28, 1951, of the International Court of Justice on Reservations to the Convention on Genocide, p. 10:

> Extensive participation . . . has already given rise to greater flexibility in international practice concerning multilateral conventions. More general resort to reservations, very great allowance made for tacit assent to reservations, the existence of practices which go so far as to admit that the author of reservations which have been rejected by certain contracting parties is nevertheless to be regarded as a party to the convention in relation to those contracting parties that have accepted the reservations – all these factors are manifestations of a new need for flexibility in the operation of multilateral conventions.

This point of view was supported by the United States before the International Court in this case, although Sir Hartley Shawcross in his oral argument before the Court pointed out that "the view which is now apparently contended for on behalf of the State Department is wholly opposed to what has hitherto been the clear trend of American authority on this matter." (Shawcross, *supra* 358)

In this connection it might be well to bear in mind McNair's warning that "the diversity of views now held upon . . . the practice of making reservations, and the best method of controlling it within reasonable limits render it unusually necessary to be sure whether a particular pronouncement on the subject is made *de lege lata* or *de lege ferenda*." (McNair, The Law of Treaties 159-60 [1961]). And Dr. Schwarzenberger has again reemphasized in his most recent Manual of International Law (5th ed. 1967) p. 171, with reference to acquiescence to reservations to multilateral treaties:

> *Acquiescence.* Tacit consent cannot be presumed. Thus acquiescence may be inferred only if, in good faith, any other interpretation of silence is impossible.

As Hackworth's approach is accepted by McNair as *lege lata*, then silence on reservations would have other interpretations than acquiescence. In the opinion of Covey T. Oliver, all of the proposals of the International Law Commission with reference to the problem of reservations are *de lege ferenda*, going outside any known precedents or practice . . . " (Oliver, "Contemporary Problems of Treaty Law," 88 Recueil des Cours 477-78 [1958]). Thus it would seem that Hackworth's statement was probably *lege lata* at the time of the making of the Geneva Protocol, at the time the reservations were deposited, and will probably remain the correct rule of international law until formal adoption by all of the nations of the world of the UN Convention of the Law of Treaties. Vienna Convention on the Law of Treaties, UN Doc. A/Conf.39/27, May 23, 1969.

151. League of Nations, *op. cit. supra* note 37, 67 *et seq.*

152. See McNair, *op. cit. supra* note 144, at 650.

153. See O'Connell, "The British Commonwealth and State Succession After the Second World War," 26 Brit. Yb. Int'l L. 454-63 (1949) and Schermers, "The Suitability of Reservations to Multilateral Treaties," 6 Nederlands Tydschrift voor Recht 350 (1959).

154. Cotran, "Some Legal Aspects of the Formation of the United Arab Republic and the United Arab States," 8 Int'l & Comp. L. Q. 346, at 350 (1959) would call this not a succession but an amalgamation, implying that this was a new phenomenon in international life.

155. See the following authorities: Fiore, International Law Codified and Its Legal Sanction 133 (trans. Borchard 1918); O'Connell, The Law of State Succession 26 (1956); Hershey, "The Succession of States," 5 Am. J. Int'l L. 287 (1911); Cavaglieri, "Règles Générales du Droit de la Paix," 26 Recueil des Cours 374 (1929); Lauterpacht, "State Succession and Agreements for the Inheritance of Treaties," 7 Int'l & Comp. L. Q. 524 (1958).

156. Jones, "State Succession in the Matter of Treaties," 24 Brit. Yb. Int'l L. 366 (1947); Jenks, "State Succession in Respect of Law-Making Treaties," 29 Brit. Yb. Int'l L. 105 (1952).

157. Full text of the note is set out in Cotran, *supra* note 154, at 358.

158. Arab Information Center, Basic Documents of the Arab Unifications pp. 10-20 (1958).

159. Although Schwarzenberger, A Manual of International Law 88 (5th ed. 1967) contends that "it is presumed that it is the intention of parties to treaties to adjust automatically the territorial scope of their treaties to such territorial changes as may subsequently occur." O'Connell, "State Succession and the Effect Upon Treaties of Entry into a Composite Relationship," 39 Brit. Yb. Int'l L. 54, at 131 (1963) feels that this is not necessarily true. According to him, if a region remains administratively identifiable so that the area of treaty continuity can be ascertained, inconsistent territorial applications of treaties in the region would be immaterial. Nevertheless, he would probably admit that if such regional treaties affected areas of power of the central government, and hence were not susceptible of performance in a regional context, they either would be inherited by the total new entity or would lapse. With respect to limiting territorial application of multilateral treaties, the Secretariat of the United Nations has stated:

> The United Arab Republic declared in 1958 that the treaties of Egypt and Syria remained "valid within the regional limit prescribed on their conclusion and in accordance with the principles of international law." . . . Some difficulties may be anticipated from this kind of limited succession, for example, in respect of treaties which are applicable abroad or on the high seas, or which are otherwise impossible to apply on a purely regional basis; the question may also arise whether a State which recognizes itself bound by a treaty in respect of only part of its territory is able to exercise the full rights of a party in taking actions provided for in the treaty or otherwise open only to parties.

Memorandum: Succession of States in Relation to General Multilateral Treaties of Which the Secretary-General Is the Depositary. Document A/CN.4/150, 2

Yearbook of the International Law Commission 106, at 123 (1962) A/CN.4/Ser.A/ 1962.

160. See for example U.N. Doc. ST/LEG/7 p. 62; U.N. Doc. ST/LEG/ 8/3976, Annex B.

161. International Labor Conference, Provisional Record, No. 25, 42nd sess. p. x (June, 1958).

162. 1 Oppenheim, *op. cit. supra* note 2, at 524.

163. 38 Dept. State Bull. 418 (March 17, 1958).

164. Set forth *supra* note 159.

165. Anabtawi, Arab Unity in Terms of Law 173-89 (1963), Young, "The State of Syria: Old or New?" 56 Am. J. Int'l L. 482, at 486 (1962).

166. Meyrowitz, *op. cit. supra* note 146, at 100, states it thus:

Les réserves ont pour conséquence d'introduire dans l'application du protocole une complexité de régimes juridiques incompatible avec la clarté, la simplicité et la généralité de règlementation qu'exige le droit de la guerre, et en premier lieu le droit gouvernant les moyens de nuire à l'ennemi. Etant donné le nombre et l'importance des Etats qui ont formulé des réserves, il n'est pas exagéré de dire que le régime normal du protocole constitue l'exception. Dans une guerre à laquelle participeraient plusieurs puissances, les unes non parties, les autres parties au protocole, soit avec, soit sans réserves, le premier emploi d'une arme chimique ou biologique, par l'un quelconque des belligérants, risquerait d'entraîner l'écroulement de l'édifice conventionnel.

167. The Preparatory Commission consisted of representatives of certain other League members, which by reason of their geographic situation occupied a special position with respect to the problem of disarmament. Three countries not belonging to the League, the United States, Union of Soviet Socialist Republics, and Turkey, were represented. The latter two did become members. Before Germany was a member of the League she was invited to take part, and she cooperated in the Commission's work from the beginning. On the resolutions calling for a Conference on the Reduction and Limitation of Armaments and on the creation of the Preparatory Commission see League of Nations, Documents of the Preparatory Commission for the Disarmament Conference, Series I, C. 9 M. 5. 1926. IX (1925). See also on the background of the Conference and Commission League of Nations, Ten Years of World Cooperation 79 *et seq.* (1930).

168. League of Nations Official Journal, 7th year, No. 7, Annex 890 a, C. 301, 1926 IX [C.P.D. 29] 897, at 999 (July, 1926).

169. League of Nations Preparatory Commission for the Disarmament Conference, Report of Sub-Commission A, C 739. M. 278. 1926 IX C.P.P. 28 165 (1926); League of Nations Preparatory Commission for the Disarmament Conference, Sub-Commission B, Report No. 1, C.P.D. 29. 1926 IX 15 (C.P.D./ C. "B"/12.), 10 *et seq.*

170. Report of Sub-Commission A, *id.* at 175.

171. *Ibid.*

172. League of Nations Commission for the Disarmament Conference Draft Convention C. 687. M. 288. 1930. IX [C.P.D. 292 (2)] (1930).

173. *Id.* at 26.

174. A summarized report as to this provision is contained in 1 League of Nations, Conference for the Reduction of Armaments, Conference Documents pp. 52-53 (1932).

175. *Id.* at 52.

176. Remarks of the representative of the Kingdom of the Serbs, Croats and Slovenes, League of Nations, Documents of the Preparatory Commission for the Disarmament Conference, ser. VIII, Minutes of the Sixth Session (First Part) of the Preparatory Commission C. 195. M. 74. 129. IX [C.P.D. 1(g).] 49 (1929).

177. *Id.* at 51.

178. The views of the Soviet delegate, *id.* at 55.

179. Remarks of the Czechoslovak delegate, *ibid.*, and see *id.* at 82-83.

180. See, e.g., the statement of the Spanish delegate, *id.* at 50.

181. Statement of the Belgian delegate, *id.* at 51.

182. *Id.* at 211.

183. *Id.* at 72.

184. Memorandum of the British Delegation, League of Nations, Documents of the Preparatory Commission for the Disarmament Conference, ser. X, Minutes of the Sixth Session (Second Part), of the Preparatory Commission, C. 4. M. 1931 IX [C.P.D.I. (i).] 311.

185. On these views of the French and other delegates see *id.* at 311-13.

186. Proposal by the U.S. delegation, *id.* at 312.

187. See Documents, ser. VIII, Sixth Session (First Part) of the Preparatory Commission, *op. cit. supra* note 176, at 52, 53, 66-69.

188. *Id.* at 66

189. *Id.* at 68.

190. Remarks of Belgian delegate, *id.* at 68.

191. *Id.* at 64.

192. *Id.* at 63-64.

193. An excellent report on the summary of the work of the conference, including its endeavors as to chemical, bacterial, and incendiary warfare, may be found in League of Nations, Conference for the Reduction and Limitation of Armaments, Preliminary Report on the Work of the Conference, Conf. D. 171 (I), 1936 IX. 3 (1936). That relating to chemical, bacterial, and incendiary warfare is set forth on pp. 103 *et seq.*

194. League of Nations, Conference for the Reduction and Limitation of Armaments, Conference Documents vol. 1, 1932. IX. 63 pp. 210-11 (1932).

195. For discussion of the report *re* chemical weapons and methods, see *id.* 211-13.

196. *Id.* at 214.

197. *Ibid.*

198. *Id.* at 211-12.

199. For discussion of bacteriological weapons and methods, see *id.* at 213.

200. *Ibid.*

201. *Id.* at 215.

202. *Ibid.*

203. *Id.* at 213.

204. For discussion of these fire weapons, see *id.* at 213-14.

205. The draft resolution is contained in League of Nations, Records of the Conference for the Reduction and Limitation of Armaments, ser. B, Minutes of the General Commission vol. 1, IX, 1932, 64. pp. 153 *et seq.* (1932).

At 154 it was stated: "Chemical, bacteriological and incendiary warfare shall be prohibited under the conditions unanimously recommended by the Special Committee." Further, at 155 it was stated:

Rules of international law shall be formulated in connection with the provisions relating to the prohibition of the use of chemical, bacteriological and incendiary weapons, and bombing from the air, and shall be supplemented by special measures dealing with infringement of these provisions.

206. This report is contained in League of Nations, Conference for the Reduction and Limitation of Armaments, Conference Documents vol. 2, 1935, IX. 4. pp. 370 *et seq.* (1935).

207. *Id.* at 378.

208. *Ibid.* and see *supra* pp. 90-92.

209. See *supra* pp. 78-85.

210. See *supra* pp. 88-90.

211. For discussion of the merits of an absolute or relative ban see Conference Documents vol. 2, *op. cit. supra* note 206, at 372-73.

212. *Id.* at 379.

213. *Id.* at 373.

214. *Id.* at 379.

215. *Id.* at 373.

216. Conference Documents vol. 2, *op. cit. supra* note 205, at 379.

217. For discussion of the problems involved in supervision see *id.* at 374.

218. *Id.* at 376.

219. *Id.* at 379.

220. *Id.* at 376-77.

221. *Id.* at 377 .

222. *Id.* at 379.

223. *Ibid.*

224. *Id.* at 377.

225. *Ibid.*

226. Preliminary Report, *op. cit. supra* note 193, at 106.

227. League of Nations, Records of the Conference for the Reduction and Limitation of Armaments, ser. V, Minutes of the Bureau vol. 1, 1935. IX. 2 pp. 75 *et seq.* (1935).

228. The answers and discussion are contained in Conference Documents, vol. 2, *op. cit. supra* note 206, at 448 *et seq.*

229. *Id.* at 461.

230. These attitudes are set forth in the Preliminary Report, *op. cit. supra* note 193, at 109.

231. *Ibid.* See also Minutes of the Bureau, *op. cit. supra* note 227, at 136.

232. This Draft Convention is contained in Conference Documents vol. 2, *op. cit. supra* note 206, at 476 *et seq.* That pertaining to chemical, bacterial, or incendiary warfare is found at 488 *et seq.*

233. *Id.* at 488.

234. Preliminary Report, *op. cit. supra* note 193, at 109-10 sets forth these observations.

235. *Supra* pp. 90-92

236. See remarks of U.S. delegate, League of Nations, Conference for the Reduction and Limitation of Armaments, ser. B, Minutes of the General Commission vol. 1, 1932. IX. 64. p. 569.

237. *Ibid.*

238. Conference Documents vol. 2, *op. cit. supra* note 206, at 645.

239. On this sad ending, see 2 Walters, A History of the League of Nations 541-55 (1952).

CHAPTER FIVE

1. McNeill, America, Britain and Russia: Their Cooperation and Conflict 1941-1946 (Survey of International Affairs 1939-1946) pp. 606-29 (1953).

2. *Id.* at 591-605

3. Dept. State, The International Control of Atomic Energy; Growth of a Policy 22-24 (Publication 2702, 1946).

4. U.S. Senate, Subcommittee on Disarmament, Disarmament and Security: A Collection of Documents 1919-1955 p. 80 (84th Cong. 2d sess. 1956).

5. Dept. State, *op. cit. supra* note 3, at 29.

6. Bechhoefer, Postwar Negotiations for Arms Control 54-77 (1961).

7. 1 U.N. GAOR pt. 2, 847 (1946).

8. 1 U.N. GAOR pt. 2, 894 (1946).

9. 2 U.N. SCOR, 105th Meeting, No. 13 (1947).

10. U.S. Dept. State, The International Control of Atomic Energy: Policy at the Crossroads 69 (Publication 3161, 1948).

11. 3 U.N. SCOR, No. 3, at 32, Rev. 1 and 3 U.N. SCOR, No. 3, at 32, Rev. 1, Corr. 1 (Aug. 12, 1948). See also Yearbook of the United Nations 1947-48 pp. 476-80 (1949.)

12. Yearbook of the United Nations 1948-49 pp. 370-71 (1950).

13. 4 U.N. SCOR, 450th Meeting, No. 46, at 14 (1949).

14. *Id.*, 452nd Meeting, No. 48, at 25. But some authors insist that the Security Council adopted the definition. See, for example, Noel-Baker, The Arms Race 315 (1958): "This definition was endorsed by the Security Council in August 1948." Kelly, "Gas Warfare in International Law," 9 Military L. Rev. 1, at 30 (1960), states: "In August 1948 the Security Council of the United Nations endorsed the . . . definition submitted by the UN Commission on Conventional Armaments . . ." and Fuller, "The Application of International Law to Chemical and Biological Warfare," 10 Orbis 247, at 258 (1966) says: "In 1948, the UN Security Council resolved that 'weapons of mass destruction' should be defined to include atomic explosive weapons, radioactive material weapons, and lethal chemical and biological weapons . . . "

15. Tammes, "Interaction of the Sources of International Law," 10 Nederlands Tydschrift voor International Recht 225, at 233 (1963).

16. 1 U.N. GAOR pt. 2, First Comm. Doc. No. A/C. 1/101; Official Records of the First Session of the General Assembly: First Committee: Political Security Questions including Regulation of Armaments: Summary Record of Meetings: 2 November - 13 December 1946: Thirty-fourth Meeting, 222, U.N. Doc. A/C. 1/101 (1946).

17. N.Y. Times, Dec. 3, 1946.

18. Annual Report of the Secretary-General on the Work of the Organization 1 July, 1947 - 30 June, 1948. 3 U.N. GAOR Supp. 1 at xiii, UN Doc. A/565 (1948).

19. Trygvie Lie, "UN v. Mass Destruction," Scientific American 11-13 (Jan., 1950).

20. 6 U.N. GAOR 295 (1951).

21. 6 U.N. SCOR, 577th Meeting 15 (1952). See also Yearbook of the United Nations 1952 pp. 323-27 (1953).

22. Yearbook, *id.* 323.

23. *Id.* at 325.

24. 6 U.N. SCOR, 581st Meeting 18 (1952).

25. *Id.*, 578th Meeting 9 (1952).

26. *Id.* at 6.

27. *Id.*, 583rd Meeting 2, 6 (1952).

28. D.C. Official Records, 8th Meeting 17 (1952).

29. *Id.*, 1st Meeting 5 (1952).

30. 6 U.N. SCOR, 577th to 583rd Meeting (1952). See also statement by Hon. C. W. Mayo, Alternate U.S. Delegate to the General Assembly, to the Political Committee of the General Assembly; U.S. Mission to the United Nations, Press Release 1786, Oct. 26, 1953. D.C. Official Records, Special Supplement No. 1 p. 15 (1952).

31. 6 U.N. SCOR, 583rd Meeting (1952).

32. D.C. Official Records, 24th Meeting 14 (1952).

33. G.A. Res. 704 (VII), 7 U.N. GAOR (1953).

34. G.A. Res. 715 (VIII), 8 U.N. GAOR (1953).

35. G.A. Res. 808 (IX), 9 U.N. GAOR (1954).

36. 14 U.N. GAOR, 799th Meeting (1959).

37. This Committee consisted of the following states: U.S.S.R., U.S., U.K., France, Canada, Italy, Poland, Czechoslovakia, Bulgaria, and Rumania. It had no organic connection with the United Nations. It did, however, proceed with UN blessing and made use of UN services and facilities.

38. Ten Power Disarmament Committee, Verbatim Records, First Meeting (March 15, 1960); N.Y. Times (March 16, 1960).

39. "Letter dated 2 June 1960 from the Permanent Representative of the Union of Soviet Socialist Republics to the United Nations addressed to the Secretary General," G.A. Doc. A/4374 (June 2, 1960).

40. Ten Power Disarmament Committee Verbatim Records. Thirty-seventh Meeting pp. 689 ff. (June 13, 1960); N.Y. Times, June 14, 1960.

41. Yearbook of the United Nations 1960 pp. 7-15 (1961). See N.Y. Times, June 29, 1960.

42. 16 U.N. GAOR, Annexes, Agenda Item No. 19. 19 U.N. Doc. No. A/4879 (1961).

43. Yearbook of the United Nations 1961 p. 16 (1962). Yearbook of the United Nations 1962 pp. 5-14 (1963).

44. 21 U.N. GAOR, First Committee, Agenda Item No. 27, U.N. Doc. A/C. 1/L. 374 (1966).

45. *Id.* at 151.

46. See debates during meetings 1451-62 of 21 U.N. GAOR First Committee of General Assembly (1966).

47. *Id.* at 158.

48. *Ibid.*

49. UN Monthly Chronicle, Dec., 1966, p. 31.

50. 21 International Organization 345 (Spring, 1967).

51. 21 U.N. GAOR, First Comm., 1461 Meeting (1966).

52. *Ibid.*

53. *Ibid.*

54. 21 International Organization 347 (Spring, 1967).

55. *Ibid.*

56. 21 U.N. GAOR, First Comm., 1461 Meeting (1966).

57. *Id.*, 1457 Meeting.

58. 21 U.N. GAOR, First Comm., Agenda Item No. 27, doc. A/C. 1/L. 381 (1966).

59. UN Monthly Chronicle, Dec., 1966, p. 32.

60. 21 International Organization 346 (Spring, 1967).

61. *Ibid.*

62. 21 U.N. GAOR, First Comm., doc. A/C. 1/L. 382/Rev. 2.

63. 21 U.N. GAOR, First Comm., 1462nd Meeting (1966).

64. 21 U.N. GAOR 17 (1966).

65. *Id.* at 26.

66. *Id.* at 21.

67. 21 U.N. GAOR, G.A. Res. 2162, pt. B p. 5 (1969).

68. See *supra* pp. 64-65.

69. For summary of these activities see *Report of the Secretary-General on Chemical and Bacteriological (Biological) Weapons and the Effects of Their Possible Use,* 24 U.N. GAOR, Doc. A/7575 (1969) [hereinafter cited as *Report*]; 23 International Organization 386-88 (Spring, 1969).

70. *Report, id.* at x.

71. *Id.* at xii.

72. Conference of the Eighteen Nation Disarmament Committee, ENDC/255 (July 10, 1969).

73. The explanatory remarks of the U.K. representative are set forth in ENDC/PV. 418 (July 10, 1969).

74. *Id.* para. 19.

75. *Id.* para. 20.

76. *Id.* para. 21.

77. *Id.* para. 23.

78. For summation of the various views see 23 International Organization 386-88.

79. See, e.g., the words of the Swedish delegate before the Conference of the Eighteen Nation Disarmament Committee, ENDC/PV. 425 pp. 7-8 (Aug. 5, 1969).

80. *Report,* pp. 7-10.

81. Remarks of the U.K. representative, CCD/PV. 431 para. 40 (Aug. 26, 1969).

82. Remarks of the U.K. representative, ENDC/PV. 418 para. 15 (July 10, 1969).

83. Remarks of the Nigerian representative, ENDC/PV. 430 para. 53 (Aug. 21, 1969).

84. Remarks of the Bulgarian representative, ENDC/PV. 422 para. 19 (July 24, 1969). But see remarks of the Swedish and U.K. representatives, ENDC/PV. 425 para. 16 (Aug. 5, 1969) and CCD/PV. 431 para. 41 (Aug. 26, 1969) respectively where the use of the term "biochemical" is attacked with reference to chemical and biological warfare as misleading for biochemistry has another meaning, a scientific discipline on the borderline of chemistry and biology.

85. Meyrowitz, Les Armes biologiques et le droit international; droit de la guerre et désarmement 34 (1968) as quoted by the Bulgarian representative ENDC/PV. 422 para. 17 (July 24, 1969).

86. Remarks of the Bulgarian representative, *id.* para. 26.

87. ENDC/PV. 422 para. 40 (Aug. 5, 1969).

88. Revised draft convention for the Prohibition of Biological Methods of Warfare and accompanying draft Security Council Resolution, ENDC/255/Rev. 1 (Aug. 26, 1969). For the remarks of the U.K. representative on the amendment see CCD/PV. 431 paras. 38-53 (Aug. 26, 1969).

89. For example that of Canada, ENDC/266 (Aug. 26, 1969).

90. *Working Paper on a Proposed Declaration by the United Nations General Assembly Regarding Prohibition of the Use of Chemical and Biological Methods of Warfare,* ENDC/265 (Aug. 26, 1969).

91. Such a proposal was later adopted by the General Assembly. G.A. Res. 2603 A, 24 U.N. GAOR (1970). The vote was 80 to 3 with 36 abstentions. The United States cast a negative vote. See 52 Dept. State Bull. 97 n. 7 (1970). The United States objected because the resolution attempted to interpret international law as set

forth in the Geneva Protocol, such interpretation by the General Assembly being considered as inappropriate. The United States also objected in the attempt by the General Assembly to embody the prohibition of the Geneva Protocol into international law by including in the prohibition a ban of all chemical and biological agents. Such a ban was thought to be too comprehensive in view of continuing arguments as to whether international law did or did not prohibit riot control agents and chemical herbicides. See statement by Ambassador James F. Leonard, United States representative to the Conference of the Committee on Disarmament as contained in 52 Dept. State Bull. 95-97 (1970). Another resolution was also adopted by the General Assembly on the same date which would call for strict observance of the Geneva Protocol and invite all nonparties to that agreement to ratify it. Further, the Conference of the Committee on Disarmament was requested to give urgent consideration to reaching agreement on the prohibition of the development, production and stockpiling of such weapons. This resolution was adopted unanimously. G.A. Res. 2603 B, 24 U.N. GAOR (1970). See also 52 Dept. State Bull. 96 n. 4 (1970).

92. "UN Calls on States to Refrain from Orbiting Weapons," 49 Dept. State Bull. 753 (1963).

93. 55 Dept. State Bull. 952 (1966).

94. 56 Dept. State Bull. 577 (1967); N.Y. Times, Oct. 11, 1967.

95. This principle was best stated by Judge M. Max Huber in 1924 in the case of the *Spanish Zone of Morocco Claims (Reclamations britanniques dans la Zone espagnole du Maroc,* 2 R.I.A.A. 626):

Dans ces circonstances, le Rapporteur a résolu d'attendre avant de donner ses décisions sur l'arbitralité de chacune de ces affairs, la production par les Représentants des Gouvernements intéressés de tous renseignements sur la genèse et sur signification de la clause ci-dessus rappelée. Ces renseignements devraient en premier lieu comprendre tout information, notamment documentaire, sur les négociations ayant abouti à l'insertion de ladite clause, ainsi que les thèses juridiques soutenues par les deux Gouvernements, à la lumière de cette information au sujet de l'interprètation de la clause.

Of course, if the text is clear, there is no need to consult preparatory work. This was emphasized by the International Court in the *Lotus Case,* P.C.I.J., ser. A., No. 10 p. 16 (1927): "The Court must recall in this connection what it has said in some of its preceding judgments and opinions, namely that there is no occasion to have regard to preparatory work if the text of a convention is sufficiently clear in itself."

96. See *supra* p. 103.

97. Webster's International Dictionary (2d ed. 1934) defines mass, when used as a noun, as a large body of persons and when used as an adjective as being characteristic of or involving a mass or the masses; it defines destruction as slaying. The Oxford English Dictionary (1933) defines mass as a large number of human beings, the generality of mankind, or a formation of troops in which battalions, etc., are arranged behind one another as opposed to line; and destruction as the action of putting to death multitudes of men.

98. Jarvis argues that CB weapons are "weapons of minimum destruction," for weapons inflicting maximum destruction affect not only living things but material objects as well. Jarvis, "Take the Mystery Out of CBR," Army, Oct. 1957, p. 44, at 46.

99. N.Y. Times, Nov. 4, 5, 1967.

100. "Fobbing Off FOBS," 225 The Economist No. 1481 p. 622 (Nov. 11, 1967).

101. Fitzmaurice, "The Law and Procedure of the International Court of Justice:

Treaty Interpretation and Certain Other Treaty Points," 282 Brit. Yb. Int'l L. 1 (1951).

102. Fitzmaurice, "The Law and Procedure of the International Court of Justice, 1951-4: Treaty Interpretation and Certain Other Treaty Points," 33 Brit. Yb. Int'l L. 203 (1957).

103. "A Treaty is to be interpreted in the light of the general purpose which it is intended to serve," Art. 19(a), Harvard Research in International Law on Treaties, 29 Am. J. Int'l L. Supp. 948-53 (1935).

104. McNair, Law of Treaties 399 (1961).

105. "The Treaty is based upon the resolution of the Congress of the United States, accepted and adopted by Germany. The language, being that of the United States, and framed for its benefit, will be strictly construed against it." Lusitania Claim, U.S.-Germany Mixed Claims Commission, A.D. 1923-4, No. 198 (1923).

106. Royal Institute of International Affairs, Documents on Germany under Occupation 1945-1954 p. 25 (1955).

107. *Id.* at 381.

108. 20 Dept. State Bull. 530 (1949), and Schedule B, Control Council Law No. 43, Dec. 20, 1946, Official Gazette, Control Council for Germany 234, at 239 (1946).

109. *Ibid.*

110. Subcommittee on Disarmament, U.S. Senate Committee on Foreign Relations, Disarmament and Security: A Collection of Documents 1919-1955, Treaty of Peace with Italy p. 459; Treaty of Peace with Bulgaria p. 462; Treaty of Peace with Hungary p. 470; Treaty of Peace with Rumania p. 474; Treaty of Peace with Finland p. 476, 84th Cong. 2d sess. 1956.

111. *Ibid.*

112. "A material breach of a bilateral treaty by one of the parties entitles the other to invoke the breach as a ground for terminating the treaty or suspending its operation in whole or in part." 1 Y.B. Int'l L. Comm'n 127 (Law of Treaties — Article 42, Termination or Suspension of the Operation of a Treaty as a Consequence of its Breach), A/Cn. a/Ser. A/1966.

113. State Treaty for the Re-Establishment of an Independent and Democratic Austria, May 15, 1955, 32 Dept. State Bull. 916 (1955).

114. Robertson, "The Creation of Western European Union," 2 European Yearbook 125 (1956); Dept. State, In Quest of Peace and Security (Pub. No. 4245, Oct., 1951).

115. Marchal, "The Consultative Assembly of the Council of Europe and the Political Problem of European Defense," 2 European Yearbook 100 (1956); 1 Basic Documents, American Foreign Policy, 1950-1955 pp. 1139 *et seq.* (Dept. State Pub. 6446, 1957).

116. Subcommittee on Disarmament, *op. cit. supra* note 110, at 504, 509.

117. *Id.* at 509-10.

118. *Id.* at 513.

119. Article 7 of the Protocol No. IV on the Agency of Western European Union for the Control of Armaments, *id.* at 514-15.

If all the measures for control had ever been implemented and thereafter the Agency found that stocks did exceed the agreed levels, or that Germany was in fact manufacturing prohibited weapons, it was to report this to the Council of Western European Union, which could then take the matter up to the member concerned or, acting by simple majority, take such other action as it deemed necessary.

120. Article 11, *ibid.*

121. Protocol No. III on the Control of Armaments, Article 1, *id.* at 509.

122. Annex II to Protocol No. III, *id.* at 511.

123. *Ibid.*

124. The Assembly of Western European Union, Proceedings, First Session, Second Part, October, 1955 p. 197.

125. Assembly of Western European Union, Proceedings, Fifth Ordinary Session, First Part, June 1959, I — Assembly Documents pp. 35-38; 127-29. *Id.*, Sixth Ordinary Session, First Part, June 1960, I — Assembly Documents pp. 19-25.

126. Assembly of Western European Union, Proceedings, Sixth Ordinary Session, First Part, June 1960, I — Assembly Documents pp. 19-25.

127. *Id.* at 23.

128. Assembly of Western European Union, Proceedings, Twelfth Ordinary Session, First Part, June 1966, I — Assembly Documents p. 25.

129. Assembly of Western European Union, Proceedings, Sixth Ordinary Session, First Part, June 1960, I — Assembly Documents p. 23.

130. *Id.* at 24.

131. *Ibid.*

132. *Ibid.* para. (a).

133. *Ibid.* n. 1.

134. See for example, the warning of the Assembly's Committee on Defence Questions and Armaments, in Assembly of Western European Union, Proceedings, Fifth Ordinary Session, First Part, June 1959, I — Assembly Documents p. 129:

> . . . The Committee is left with the impression that . . . the control of armaments, as provided for in the treaty . . . [is not] being pursued with vigour. The Committee views this with some concern because there is always danger that if one part of an international Treaty is allowed to fall into abeyance, sooner or later the other parts will follow.

135. London Times, Dec. 18, 1959.

136. Debate in House of Commons, Dec. 17, 1959, Statement by Mr. William Marbey (Ashfield), London Times, Dec. 18, 1959.

137. Ferreri, "L'Agence de L'U.E.O. Pour le Contrôle des Armements," 5 European Yearbook 30 (1959); see also Assembly of Western European Union, Proceedings, Eleventh Ordinary Session, First Part, June 1965, I — Assembly Documents p. 84 n. 3: "See *e.g.*, Speech by Mr. Gaston Palewski, Minister of State for Scientific Research and Atomic and Space Questions, on 29th May 1962: 'As you know, France is the fourth atomic power . . . we have gone beyond the research stage and are now in the full industrial era.'"

138. Fletcher, "Existing Arrangements for International Control of Warlike Material in Western European Union," Disarmament and Arms Control 151-52 (Autumn, 1963).

139. The worldwide International Red Cross consists of the International Committee of the Red Cross (the founding body and intermediary in time of war) and the League of Red Cross Societies (the federation of the national Red Cross societies). The highest deliberative authority of the International Red Cross is the International Red Cross Conference which meets every four to eight years, to which all governments send representatives and in which each government is given one vote. Guggenheim and Verdross contend that the Red Cross is a particular subject of international law. 1 Guggenheim, Traité de Droit International Public 288-89 (1953); Verdross, Volkerrecht 110-11 (3rd ed. 1955).

140. Werner, La Croix Rouge et les Conventions de Genève (1949); Kunz, "The Geneva Conventions of August 12, 1949," in Lipsky (ed.), Law and Politics in the

World Community 279 (1953); Gutteridge, "The Geneva Conventions of 1949," 25 Brit. Yb. Int'l L. 294 (1949); Pictet, "La Croix Rouge et Les Conventions de Genève," 76 Recueil des Cours 5, at 36 (1950).

141. Kunz, "The Laws of War," 50 Am. J. Int'l L. 313, at 332 (1945).

142. "The Geneva Diplomatic Conference of 1949 continuously emphasized its lack of competence within the realm of the 'Hague' laws of war; yet it is clear that such rules as the prohibition of reprisals, prohibition of taking hostages, prisoner-of-war status, under certain conditions, of members of resistance movements, even in occupied territories, profoundly influence the rules concerning the actual conduct of warfare." Kunz, "The 1956 Draft Rules of the International Committee of the Red Cross at the New Delhi Conference," 53 Am. J. Int'l L. 133, at 134 n. 10 (1959).

143. *Id.* at 134.

144. International Committee of the Red Cross, Draft Rules for the Protection of the Civilian Population from the Dangers of Indiscriminate Warfare with Commentary p. 5 (June, 1955).

145. *Id.* at 30.

146. *Ibid.* See also, Castrén, "La Protection Juridique de la Population Civile dans la Guerre Moderne," 50 Revue Générale de Droit International Public 121 (1959).

147. Kunz, *supra* note 142, at 134.

148. International Committee of the Red Cross, The Draft Rules, 1956, for the Limitation of the Dangers Incurred by the Civilian Population in Time of War with Commentary (1956).

149. 19th International Conference of the Red Cross, New Delhi, October-November 1957, Final Record Concerning the Draft Rules for the Limitation of Dangers Incurred by the Civilian Population in Time of War p. 21 (1958).

150. *Id.* p. 36.

151. Pictet, "The XXth International Conference of the Red Cross: Results in the Legal Field," 7 Journal of the International Commission of Jurists 3, at 12 (Summer, 1966).

152. *Id.* at 13.

153. *Id.* at 14.

CHAPTER SIX

1. Art. 38, Statute International Court of Justice. See 1 Whiteman, Digest of International Law 75 *et seq.* (1963) for discussion. See also 1 Oppenheim, International Law secs. 16, 17 (8th ed. Lauterpacht 1955); Starke, An Introduction to International Law 33 *et seq.* (5th ed. 1963); 1 O'Connell, International Law 15 *et seq.* (1965).

2. See Friedmann, The Changing Structure of International Law 121 (1964).

3. See O'Connell, *op. cit. supra* note 1, at 1-6; Starke, *op. cit. supra* note 1, at 24-29.

4. See 1 Schwarzenberger, International Law as Applied by International Courts and Tribunals 39 *et seq.* (3rd ed. 1957); Kelsen, Principles of International Law 440 (2d ed. Tucker 1966). In the Colombian-Peruvian Asylum case the International Court of Justice set forth the two elements. See I.C.J. Reports 1950 p. 276.

5. I.C.J. Reports, *ibid.*

6. For discussion see Kunz, "The Nature of Customary International Law" 47, Am. J. Int'l L. 662, at 666 (1953).

7. Wright, "Custom as a Basis for International Law in the Post-War World,"

7 Indian J. Int. L. 1, at 5 (1967). Authors take issue with this positivist viewpoint. See, e.g., Starke, *op. cit. supra* note 1, at 25-29; Brierly, The Law of Nations 49-56 (6th ed. 1963); Kelsen, *op. cit. supra* note 4, at 442 *et seq.*

8. Brierly, *id.* at 61.

9. Kunz, *supra* note 6, at 666. And see Kelsen, *op. cit. supra* note 4, at 444-45.

10. Brierly, *op. cit. supra* note 7, at 59.

11. P.C.I.J., ser. A No. 10 p. 28 (1927).

12. See Kunz, *supra* note 6, at 668.

13. For discussion of the history of chemical warfare prior to World War I see Fradkin, "Chemical Warfare — Its Possibilities and Probabilities," No. 248 Int. Conc. 113, at 116-18 (Mar., 1929); Wachtel, Chemical Warfare 20-24 (1941). Prentiss in his work Chemicals in War (1937) states at p. xvi that Greek fire was the only early use of chemicals which produced important results. On Greek fire see 10 Encyclopaedia Britannica 82 (1951 ed.); Partington, A History of Greek Fire and Gunpowder (1960).

14. Discussions of the employment of gas in World War I are contained in Prentiss, *id.* at 51-54, 80-82, 688-89; Fradkin, *id.* at 128-52; Garner, International Law and the World War 271-87 (1920); Kelly, "Gas Warfare in International Law," Military L. Rev. 5-12 (July, 1960). An excellent summation is made by the latter article on the types of gases used and developed. See also Bernstein, "The Law of Chemical Warfare," 10 Geo. Wash. L. Rev. 889, at 905-8 (1942).

15. Prentiss, *id.* at 688-89.

16. Graphic descriptions of this first attack are set forth by Fradkin, *supra* note 13, at 125-26; Garner, *op. cit. supra* note 14, at 271-72.

17. The principal gas attacks, the method of dispersal, the amount and kind of gas used, and the number of casualties are set forth in a chart by Prentiss, *op. cit. supra* note 13, at 663-66. See also casualty chart, *id.* at 653.

18. For discussion of the Hague Gas Declaration see *supra* pp. 46-49.

19. Prentiss, *op. cit. supra* note 13, at 689.

20. Bernstein, *supra* note 14, at 905.

21. See *supra* p. 89.

22. See *infra* p. 177.

23. Prentiss, *op. cit. supra* note 13, at 689.

24. See Kelly, *supra* note 14, at 37 n. 171. The Red Cross in 1918 did protest the use of gas by both sides. This protest is contained in 1918 U.S. For. Rel. Supp. 2, at 779-81 (1933).

25. The British Foreign Office made this charge on April 21, 1915. As noted by Garner, *op. cit. supra* note 14, at 284-85.

26. *Id.* at 285.

27. See, e.g., Holland, Lectures on International Law 323 (1933); and Singh, Nuclear Weapons and International Law 154-55 (1959); 2 Oppenheim, International Law 342 (7th ed. Lauterpacht 1952).

28. See Garner, *op. cit. supra* note 14, at 277, 285; Castrén, The Present Law of War and Neutrality 195 (1954).

29. See *supra* pp. 40-41 for commentary on "Kriegsraison."

30. Garner, *id.* at 280-82; Kelly, *supra* note 14, at 40.

31. For example, the German war office spoke of previous use of gas by the Allies. See Garner, *op. cit. supra* note 14, at 173 n. 2, 285 n. 2; and Kelly, *supra* note 14, at 8 n. 28, 39-40. On reprisals, see Greenspan, The Modern Law of Land Warfare 407 *et seq.* (1959); Tucker, The Law of War and Neutrality at Sea, U.S. Naval War College International Law Studies 1955 pp. 150 *et seq.* (1957).

32. See Garner, *op. cit. supra* note 14, at 273 n. 2, 286; Stone, Legal Controls

of International Conflict 564 (2d imp. rev. 1956); Prentiss, *op. cit. supra* note 13, at 688; 2 Buchan, A History of the Great War 46 (1922).

33. A German author stated the view that inasmuch as the Allies did not protest the German use of gas they were "agreed it would be better to spread the adoption of the new chemical warfare and hit back with it, rather than inveigh against its use." Leipmann, Poison in the Air 65 (1937) as quoted by Kelly, *supra* note 14, n. 171.

34. Bernstein, *supra* note 14, at 906.

35. Prentiss, *op. cit. supra* note 13, at 688.

36. Garner, *op. cit. supra* note 14, at 284.

37. *Id.* at 273, 287.

38. Greenspan, *op. cit. supra* note 31, at 411; O'Brien, "Biological/Chemical Warfare and the International Law of War," 51 Geo. L.J. 1, at 24 (1962).

39. O'Brien, *id.* at 24, 47-48. Fuller, "The Application of International Law to Chemical and Biological Warfare," 10 Orbis 247, at 251, 269 (Spring, 1966).

40. 3 Hyde, International Law Chiefly as Interpreted and Applied by the United States, states at 1819 n. 4 (2d rev. ed. 1957):

> While this procedure on the part of the enemies of Germany *may* have been attributable, at the outset, to a design of retaliation, the employment of gases perfected in England and America proved of so great offensive value as to convince military opinion in those countries that such instrumentalities were generally desirable for use in land warfare.

And see O'Brien, *supra* note 38, at 29 where he stated that no customary rule survived World War I for "[a]t the first opportunity, without even an obeisance to the right of reprisals the participants in World War I engaged in what amounted to unlimited warfare."

41. League of Nations, Official Journal, 17th yr., No. 4 (pt. II), 91st Extraordinary Session of the Council, April, 1936 pp. 370-72. For various Ethiopian telegrams and memorandums on such use see *id.* at 241-42, 465, 474, 476, 479.

42. *Id.* at 479.

43. League of Nations, Official Journal, Spec. Supp. No. 151, Records 16th Session of the Assembly, Plenary Meeting (pt. III), June 30-July 4, 1936 p. 22, at 23.

44. League of Nations, Official Journal, 17th yr., No. 6 (pt. I), 92nd Session of the Council, June, 1936 p. 653, at 654.

45. *Id.* at 580.

46. League of Nations, Official Journal, *op. cit. supra* note 41, at 241, 242.

47. *Id.* at 378.

48. *Id.* at 382.

49. *Id.* at 393.

50. O'Brien, *supra* note 38, at 33-34. For other discussions of the Italian use of gas see Kelly, *supra* note 14, at 13, 41; Spaight, Air Power and War Rights 192-93 (3rd ed. 1947).

51. It has, for example, been stated that Chinese charges concerning the Japanese use of gas were never definitely established. Brophy and Fisher, The Chemical Warfare Service: Organizing for War 63 n. 3 (1959).

52. Research in CBR, Report of the Committee on Science and Astronautics, U.S. House of Representatives, 86th Cong. 1st sess., H.R. No. 815 p. 4 (1959).

53. Kelly, *supra* note 14, at 13.

54. See Report, Use of Gas in World War II, Historical Office, Edgewood Arsenal, Edgewood, Maryland.

55. League of Nations, Official Journal, Minutes of the 101st Session of the Council, 19th yr. No. 5-6 p. 307 (May-June, 1938).

56. *Id.* at 378.

57. Remarks of the delegates are set forth *id.* at 378-79.

58. Appeal by the Chinese Government of May 9, 1938, Annexes, *id.* at 381.

59. League of Nations, Official Journal, Records of the 19th Ordinary Session of the Assembly, Minutes of the 3rd Committee, Special supp. No. 186 pp. 11 *et seq.* p. 21 (1938).

60. League of Nations, Official Journal, Records of the 19th Ordinary Session of the Assembly, Plenary Meetings, Special Supp. No. 183 p. 136 (1938).

61. 7 Judgment of the International Tribunal 117, Annexes (1948) (mimeographed materials) as set forth in O'Brien, *supra* note 38, at 34 n. 90. As this author points out, *ibid.*, the judgment does not concern itself with this charge of poison gas use.

62. See *supra* pp. 46-49.

63. See *supra* pp. 49-57.

64. See *supra* pp. 58-62.

65. See Chemical-Biological (CBR) Warfare and Its Disarmament Aspects, a study prepared by the Subcommittee on Disarmament of the Committee on Foreign Relations, United States Senate, 86th Cong. 2nd sess. 22 (1960); Research in CBR, Report of the Committee on Science and Astronautics, *op. cit. supra* note 52, at 4; Spaight, *op. cit. supra* note 50, at 193.

66. London Times, Sept. 4, 1939.

67. London Times, Sept. 14, 1939.

68. Brophy and Fisher, *op. cit. supra* note 51, at 48 n. 1.

69. Resolution, "Humanization of War," First Meeting of Ministers of Foreign Affairs of the American Republics, 1939, The International Conferences of American States, First Supp. 1933-1940 p. 329, at 330 (1940). This attempt to limit the use of gas and biological methods of war is in harmony with previous actions of the Inter-American System such as the resolution of the Fifth International Conference of American States, discussed *supra* p. 69; and the resolution of the 1936 Inter-American Conference for the Maintenance of Peace on the "Humanization of War," which resolved to proscribe chemical elements in war and recommended pacts regulating the use of pathogenic bacteria and poisonous gas among other things. The International Conferences of American States, First Supp. 1933-1940 p. 164, at 165 (1940).

70. See Spaight, *op. cit. supra* note 50, at 193-95 for discussion of reports and rumors of the use of gas warfare. A German military official states unequivocally that the Poles used mustard gas in the early days of the Polish campaign, but states that such use was not ordered by the Polish government. Ochsner, History of German Chemical Warfare in World War II pt. I (The Military Aspect), Historical Office of the Chief of the Chemical Corps (1949).

71. Chemical, Biological, and Radiological Warfare Agents, Hearings before the Committee on Science and Astronautics, U.S. House of Representatives, 86th Cong. 1st sess. 12 (1959). General Creasy points out that the German fears of overwhelming retaliation were groundless. The Allies would have retaliated, but only with mustard gas, which would have required huge amounts to do the same job as the nerve gas. He states that if the Germans had used the nerve gas, the Allies would not have gotten ashore, since they were not prepared for this new gas. *Ibid.* Ochsner, *op. cit. supra* note 70, points out at 22-23 the great military advantages that would have accrued to the Germans at the time of the Normandy invasion, but fears of air gas retaliation against all Germany prevented the use.

72. N.Y. Times, May 11, 1943.

73. See Spaight, *op. cit. supra* note 50, at 195.

74. On reason given see Saunders, "The Biological/Chemical Warfare Challenge," 91 Proceedings U.S. Naval Institute 44, at 46 (1965); Kelly, *supra* note 14, at 13-14.

75. Ochsner, *op. cit. supra* note 70, at 13.

76. *Id.* at 17.

77. *Id.* at 21-22.

78. *Id.* at 20-21, 23.

79. *Id.* at 24.

80. *Ibid.*

81. Kelly, *supra* note 14, at 14.

82. Stone, Legal Controls of International Conflict 558 (2d imp. rev. 1959).

83. O'Brien, *supra* note 38, at 36.

84. Kelly, *supra* note 14, at 14.

85. Rothschild, Tomorrow's Weapons 5 (1964).

86. *Ibid*; Kelly, *supra* note 14.

87. Rothschild, *id.* at 62, 63.

88. N.Y. Times, Nov. 11, 1966.

89. On riot control agents see *supra* pp. 11-12.

90. Beecher, in an article entitled "Chemicals vs. the Viet Cong — 'Right' or 'Wrong'?" National Guardsman (1966) attributes this to the Secretary of Defense at p. 1. Blumenthal, "U.S. Now Uses Tear Gas as Routine War Weapon," N.Y. Times, Dec. 6, 1969, also states that both CS and CN have been used. But see letter dated April 15, 1969, from the Director of Defense Research and Engineering to Representative Richard D. McCarthy wherein it is stated that only CS has been used although CN has been authorized. McCarthy, The Ultimate Folly 153, at 158 (1969).

91. See Getlein, "Gas and Guerrillas — A Word of Caution," New Republic, Mar. 19, 1966, p. 13; U.S. News and World Report, Jan. 31, 1966, p. 8.

92. *Ibid*; Beecher, *supra* note 90; Margolis, "Notes on Gas and Disarmament," 21 Bull. of the Atomic Scientists 30 (Nov., 1965). The latter author states that tear gas is authorized, but not vomiting agents.

93. See Getlein, *supra* note 91; U.S. News and World Report, Jan. 31, 1966, p. 8.

94. See U.S. News and World Report, *ibid*. "CB Warfare: The Terrors of the New Weaponry," Harvard Alumni Bulletin, Mar. 11, 1967, 16, at 17.

95. "CB Warfare: The Terrors of the New Weaponry," *ibid*.

96. For discussion see Greenspan, *op. cit. supra* note 31, at 332 *et seq.*

97. Art. 23(c), Regulations Concerning the Laws and Customs of Warfare, 2 Am. J. Int'l L. Supp. 97, at 106 (1908).

98. Common Art. 3(1) of all the Conventions. 1 Final Record of the Diplomatic Conference of Geneva of 1949 pp. 205, 225, 243, 297.

99. On the principle of proportionality see *infra* ch. VII.

100. On the ruses of war see Greenspan, *op. cit. supra* note 31, at 318 *et seq.*

101. On the doctrine of proximate cause in the law of torts see Prosser, Law of Torts ch. 9 (3rd ed. 1964). See specifically pp. 282-83, 309 et seq.

102. N.Y. Times, Oct. 18, 1967, Sept. 10, 1967; U.S. News and World Report, Oct. 3, 1966, p. 40. Langer, "CBW: Weapons and Policies," Science, Jan. 20, 1967, p. 163, at 167; Mayer, "Starvation as a Weapon: Herbicides in Vietnam, I," Scientist and Citizen, Aug.-Sept., 1967, p. 115; Galston, "Changing the Environment: Herbicides in Vietnam II," *id.* at 123.

103. See Statement by the Democratic Republic of Vietnam State Committee of Science and Technology on the Use of Toxic Chemicals and Poison Gas by the

Aggressive U.S. Imperialists in South Vietnam, Hanoi, Oct. 20, 1965; and see statement of the Hungarian representative before the First Committee of the General Assembly, U.N. General Assembly, Off. Rec. 21st sess., 1st Committee, 1451st Meeting, Nov. 11, 1966 pp. 150-51. For statement expressing the concern of certain scientists at such use of chemical and biological warfare, see Langer, "Chemical and Biological Warfare (II); The Weapons and the Policies," Science, Jan. 20. 1967, p. 200, at 202. For a view of a British writer see Burlop, "U.S. Chemical Warfare," Labour Monthly, Feb., 1967, p. 176. See also 1969 Letter of Protest to UN from Cambodia on U.S. Defoliation as quoted in McCarthy, *op. cit. supra* note 90, at 93-94.

104. See statement of U.S. Representative Byrnes, U.N. General Assembly, Off. Rec. 21st Sess., 1st Committee, 1452nd meeting, Nov. 14, 1966 p. 158. For discussion of the U.S. position see "Chemical and Biological Weapons: Once Over Lightly on Capitol Hill," Science, May 26, 1967, p. 1073; Jack, "The United Nations and Chemical Warfare," Christian Century, Jan. 11, 1967, p. 60. And see statement of Secretary of State Rusk, 60 Am. J. Int'l L. 102-3 (1966).

105. See *supra* pp. 75-76 for discussion.

106. See *supra* p. 89 for discussion.

107. N.Y. Times, July 9, 10, 11, 16, 1963.

108. N.Y. Times, Jan. 24, 29, Feb. 18, 1967; "Gasmasks for the Yemen," The Economist, Feb. 4, 1967, p. 133; "The Kitof Survivors," Statist, Feb. 3, 1967, p. 135.

109. N.Y. Times, June 3, 5, 6, 1967. The text of the Red Cross Report on Yemen is found in N.Y. Times, July 28, 1967. A complete report on the use of gas is compiled by Salvia, "Gas in Yemen," Scientist and Citizen, Aug.-Sept., 1967, p. 113.

110. Sulzberger, "Where the War Goes On," International Herald Tribune (Paris ed.), June 26, 1967; Rowan, "Egyptian Use of Poisonous Gas," Dallas Morning News, July 2, 1967; Alsop, "Matter of Fact," Washington Post, June 14, 1967; Alsop, "Desperate Nasser Using Gas in Yemen," St. Louis Post-Dispatch, June 18, 1967. Childs, "Egypt Stored Nerve Gas Before War," St. Louis Post-Dispatch, June 18, 1967; Childs, "Gas Bombing in Yemen Termed a Step Toward World Disaster," St. Louis Post-Dispatch, June 20, 1967. Childs, "Chemical Warfare and a Death Wish," Washington Post, June 21, 1967. Salvia, *ibid.*, questions whether it has been so clearly established that nerve gas was used. He states that mustard or a similar lethal gas was used, but that the use of nerve gas remains unresolved. *Id.* at 151.

111. N.Y. Times, July 27, 1967.

112. N.Y. Times, July 28, 1967.

113. *Ibid.*

114. Letter dated July 24, 1967, from Arthur J. Goldberg to the Honorable Lester L. Wolff, House of Representatives.

115. N.Y. Times, July 28, 1967.

116. N.Y. Times, July 30, 1967.

117. See *supra* pp. 84-85.

118. Statement by State Dept. spokesman, Robert J. McCloskey, N.Y. Times, July 28, 1967.

119. For summary of ancient use of fire and smoke in warfare see Prentiss, Chemicals in War 220-21, 249-50 (1937).

120. On the use of these weapons during World War I see Prentiss, *id.* at 221-24, 250-51; Wachtel, Chemical Warfare 262-73 (1941); Spaight, Air Power and War Rights 196 (3rd ed. 1947).

121. *Supra* pp. 92 *et seq.*

122. For smoke operations in World War II see Kleber and Birdsell, The Chemical Warfare Service: Chemicals in Combat chs. VIII, IX, X (1965); see also on smokes, 23 Colliers Encyclopedia 266 (1967 ed.).

123. Spaight, *op. cit supra* note 120, at 219.

124. On the use of incendiaries and fire bombs during World War II see Kleber and Birdsell, *op. cit. supra* note 122, at ch. XVII; Noel-Baker, The Arms Race 337-41 (1958).

125. Kleber and Birdsell, *id.* at chs. XIV, XV, XVI. See also 23 Colliers Encyclopedia 265 (1967 ed.).

126. 23 Colliers Encyclopedia 265 (1927 ed.); Noel-Baker, *op. cit. supra* note 124, at 341-42.

127. On the use of napalm in Vietnam see N.Y. Times, March 12, 1967, Dec. 17, 1967, Dec. 27, 1967.

128. See Wachtel, Chemical Warfare 15-17 (1941) for examples.

129. But see Knollenberg, "General Amherst and Germ Warfare," 41 Miss. Valley Historical Rev. 489 (1954), contending the evidence does not support the charge.

130. A. Gaffarel, Bonaparte et les Republiques Italiennes, 1796-1797 p. 80 (1895).

131. 1 W. T. Sherman, Memoirs 331 (1875).

132. Spaight, Air Power and War Rights 191-92 (3rd ed. 1947).

133. Parnell, "The Capabilities of Chemical, Biological and Radiological Warfare," Food Technology, Jan., 1962, p. 15. Research in CBR, Report of the Committee on Science and Astronautics, H.R. No. 815, 86th Cong. 1st sess. 5 (1959).

134. Research in CBR, *ibid.* Brophy, Miles and Cochran, The Chemical Warfare Service: From Laboratory to Field 101 *et seq.* (1959); Brophy and Fisher, The Chemical Warfare Service: Organizing for War 46-48 (1959).

135. 2 Oppenheim, International Law 343 n. 2 (7th ed. Lauterpacht 1952).

136. Report of the Joint Interrogation Group of Korean and Chinese Specialists and Newspaper Correspondents on the Interrogation of War Prisoners Enoch and Quinn with Supplementary Opinion, The Chinese People's Committee for World Peace, Peking 1952; Statements by Two American Air Force Officers Keith Lloyd Enoch and John Quinn Admitting Their Participation in Germ Warfare in Korea and Other Documents, Supplement to People's Chinese, May 16, 1952. For brief description of this communist allegation and for action in the United Nations, see Fuller, "The Application of International Law to Chemical and Biological Warfare," 10 Orbis 247, at 260, *et seq.* (1966); and see Chemical-Biological (CBR) Warfare and Its Disarmament Aspects, a study prepared by the Subcommittee on Disarmament of the Committee on Foreign Relations, U.S. Senate, 86th Cong. 2nd sess., Aug. 29, 1960. See also *infra* pp. 162-63.

137. Neinast, "United States Use of Biological Warfare," 24 Military L. Rev. 1, at 6 (1964).

138. See, e.g., O'Brien, "Biological/Chemical Warfare and the International Law of War," 51 Geo. L.J. 1, at 36 (1962); Brungs, "The Status of Biological Warfare in International Law," 24 Military L. Rev. 47, at 75 (1964).

139. See Rothschild, Tomorrow's Weapons ch. 5 (1964); also *supra* pp. 154-55.

140. See *supra* pp. 132-34.

141. On the two constitutive elements of custom as law see *ibid.*

142. Cheng, "United Nations Resolutions on Outer Space," 5 Indian J. Int. L. 23, at 36 (1965). But other jurists contend to the contrary and conclude that the psychological element, *opinio juris*, is unimportant and that which is important is the practice of states. See, e.g., Fischer Williams, Some Aspects of International Law 44 (1939).

143. Cheng points out that in any event it can be considered an unwritten rule of international law. *Ibid.*

144. On the various elements considered as evidence see Brownlie, Principles of Public International Law 4 (1966); Brierly, *op. cit. supra* note 7, at 61; Kunz, *supra* note 6, at 667.

145. For discussion see *supra* pp. 46-49.

146. U.S. Dept. of Army Rules of Land Warfare, 1914 para. 175 nn. 177, 185. Hosono, International Disarmament 215 (1926).

147. For. Rel. of the U.S. 1918 Supp. 2 pp. 782-83 (1933).

148. See *infra* p. 175. Prentiss, Chemicals in War (1937) shows in a chart at p. 665 German first use against the Americans.

149. Kelly, "Gas Warfare in International Law," Military L. Rev. 1, at 32 (July, 1960).

150. See Prentiss, Chemicals in War ch. XXIV, "The Effectiveness of Chemical Warfare" 647 *et seq.* (1937).

151. Brophy and Fisher, The Chemical Warfare Service: Organizing for War 18 (1959).

152. *Id.* at 16, 22-24.

153. See *supra* pp. 63-64.

154. As quoted in Brophy and Fisher, *op. cit. supra* note 151, at 20.

155. This report is contained in Naval War College, International Law Situations 1935 pp. 99-100 (1936).

156. See *supra* pp. 63-64.

157. See *supra* pp. 65-67.

158. See *supra* pp. 73-74.

159. See Fuller, "The Application of International Law to Chemical and Biological Warfare," 10 Orbis 247, at 264 (1966).

160. As quoted in Brophy and Fisher, *op. cit. supra* note 151, at 21.

161. As quoted in Brophy and Fisher, *ibid.*

162. U.S. Dept. of Army Field Manual 27-10, Rules of Land Warfare para. 29 (1940). This is repeated in the present U.S. Dept. of Army Field Manual 27-10, "The Law of Land Warfare" para. 38 (1956).

163. U.S. Dept. of Army Field Manual (1940), *id.* at p. 7.

164. U.S. Dept. of Army Manual, Rules of Land Warfare para. 177 (1914).

165. *Id.* 27-10 para. 38.

166. See *supra* pp. 49-50.

167. U.S. Dept. of Army Field Manual 27-10 para. 37 (1956).

168. *Id.* para. 38.

169. Neinast, examining the historical record of the new Manual, sets forth the reasons and then criticizes them in some detail. Neinast, "United States Use of Biological Warfare," *supra* note 137, at 18-21.

170. The 1955 U.S. Navy Manual, "Law of Naval Warfare," is set forth in the Appendix of Tucker, The Law of War and Neutrality at Sea, U.S. Naval War College International Law Studies 1955 pp. 359 *et seq.* This quotation is found at p. 612.

171. *Id.* at 415 n. 7.

172. *Supra* p. 157.

173. International Law Situations, *op. cit. supra* note 155, at 101.

174. See *supra* pp. 72, 88.

175. See Brophy and Fisher, *op. cit. supra* note 151, at 21.

176. For discussion of the Washington Conference see *supra* pp. 62-67.

177. For discussion see *supra* pp. 71-72.

178. *Supra* p. 72.

179. For discussion see *supra* pp. 86 *et seq.*

180. See *supra* p. 89.

181. As quoted in Brophy and Fisher, *op. cit. supra* note 151, at 22.

182. *Id.* at 49-50.

183. As set forth in Tucker, The Law of War and Neutrality at Sea, U.S. Naval War College International Law Studies 1955 p. 415 (1957).

184. Brophy and Fisher, *op. cit. supra* note 151, at 87-88.

185. See Neinast, *supra* note 137, at 4-5. See also Brungs, *supra* note 138, at 68 for discussion of U.S. preparation for germ warfare.

186. Leahy, I Was There 439-40 (1950).

187. See *supra* pp. 152-53.

188. Greenspan, The Modern Law of Land Warfare 358 (1959).

189. O'Brien, *supra* note 138, at 56-57.

190. See Neinast, *supra* note 137, at 33-35.

191. U.S. Mission to the U.N., Press Release 1527, Aug. 12, 1952, Statement by Ambassador Benjamin V. Cohen, Deputy U.S. Representative in the Disarmament Commission, on the Elimination of Germ Warfare pp. 4-5.

192. 27 Dept. State Bull. 641 (1952).

193. N.Y. Times, Nov. 7, 1955.

194. As contained in a study entitled Chemical, Biological, Radiological (CBR) Warfare and Its Disarmament Aspects, Subcommittee on Disarmament of the Committee on Foreign Relations, U.S. Senate, 86th Cong. 2d sess., Aug. 29, 1960 p. 20.

195. Public Papers of the Presidents, Dwight D. Eisenhower 1960-1961 p. 29.

196. Chemical, Biological, Radiological (CBR) Warfare, *supra* note 194, at 21-22.

197. *Id.* at 22.

198. U.N. General Assembly, Off. Rec. 21st sess. 1st Committee, 1452nd meeting, Nov. 14, 1966 p. 158. For discussion of the U.S. position see "Chemical and Biological Weapons: Once Over Lightly on Capitol Hill," Science, May 26, 1967, p. 1078; Jack, "The United Nations and Chemical Warfare," Christian Century, Jan. 11, 1967, p. 60.

199. Langer, "CBW: Weapons and Policies," Science, Jan. 20, 1967, p. 167.

200. Note 192, *supra*.

201. 6 Am. J. Int'l L. 102-3 (1966); see also Secretary Rusk's News Conference of Mar. 24, 1965, Dept. State Press Release No. 59.

202. 56 Dept. State Bull. 577 (1967).

203. The statement of Mr. Vance is contained in United States Armament and Disarmament Problems, Hearings before the Subcommittee on Disarmament of the Committee on Foreign Relations, 90th Cong. 1st sess., Feb. 3, 6, 7, 28 and March 1, 2, 3, 1967. For Ambassador Goldberg's statement see *supra* note 114.

204. For President Nixon's statement and discussion thereof, see N.Y. Times, Nov. 26, 1969.

205. Fradkin, The Air Menace and the Answer 9 (1934).

206. See *supra* pp. 46-49; and see Prentiss, Chemicals in War 686 (1937).

207. See *supra* pp. 136, 137-38. Holland, Lectures on International Law 323 (1933).

208. See *supra* pp. 136-38.

209. 3 Hyde, International Law Chiefly as Interpreted and Applied by the United States 1819 n. 4 (2d rev. ed. 1947).

210. See *supra* pp. 64-67 for discussion.

211. See *supra* pp. 37-38 for discussion.

212. As discussed and set forth in Neinast, *supra* note 137, at 19-20.

213. See *supra* ch. IV note 145.

214. The War Office, The Law of War on Land, Being Part III of the Manual of Military Law 4 (1958). See also Brungs, *supra* note 138, at 74-75.

215. See *supra* p. 99.

216. Kelly, *supra* note 14, at 38.

217. *Supra* pp. 142-43.

218. See comments entitled "Nothing Offensive," The Economist, May 30, 1964, p. 953; and "The Germs of Porton Downs," The Economist, July 14, 1962, p. 127.

219. See, e.g., Neinast, *supra* note 137, at 31.

220. SCOR, 7th year, 578th meeting, June 20, 1952 p. 13.

221. See *supra* pp. 46-49.

222. Prentiss, Chemicals in War 68-69 (1937); Bernstein, "The Law of Chemical Warfare," 10 Geo. Wash. L. Rev. 889, at 905-6 (1942).

223. Bernstein, *id.* at 905.

224. The text of the Red Cross protest is contained in For. Rel. of the U.S. 1918 Supp. 2 pp. 779-81 (1933).

225. As quoted in 1 Garner, International Law and the First World War 276 (1920). See also For. Rel. of the U.S., *id.* at 782.

226. See *supra* p. 67.

227. See Prentiss, *op. cit. supra* note 222, at 691.

228. League of Nations, Proceedings of the Conference for the Supervision of the International Trade in Arms and Ammunition and in Implements of War, Held at Geneva, May 4th to June 17, 1925. A. B. 1925. IX at p. 314.

229. *Id.* at 533.

230. *Id.* at 314-15.

231. See *supra* pp. 78-79.

232. See *supra* pp. 142-43.

233. SCOR, 7th year, 578th meeting, June 20, 1952 pp. 15 *et seq.*

234. *Id.* 581st meeting, June 25, 1952 p. 14.

235. *Id.* at 15.

236. See *supra* pp. 108-12.

237. GAOR, 1st Committee, 1461st meeting, Nov. 23, 1966, at 204-5.

238. See *supra* p. 135.

239. See *supra* p. 89.

240. GAOR, *supra* note 237, at 225.

241. See *supra* pp. 136-37.

242. See *supra* pp. 58-60.

243. See Proceedings of the Conference for the Supervision of the International Trade in Arms and Ammunition and in Implements of War, *op. cit. supra* note 228, at 534.

244. 2 Oppenheim, International Law 343 n. 3 (7th ed. Lauterpacht 1952).

245. 3 Handbuch des Wehrrechts para. 1519 (ed. Braunsteller 1961) as contained in Brungs, *supra* note 138, at 75.

246. See *supra* pp. 120-22.

247. See Prentiss, *op. cit. supra* note 222, at ch. XXIV.

248. Proceedings of the Conference, *op. cit. supra* note 228, at 531.

249. See *supra* pp. 138-40.

250. 2 Oppenheim, *op. cit. supra* note 244, at 343 n. 3.

251. See *supra* pp. 46-49.

252. See *supra* pp. 79-80.

253. For statement on the Soviet reservations, see Triska and Slusser, The Theory, Law, and Policy of Soviet Treaties 83 (1962).

254. See *supra* pp. 46-49.

255. Tunkin, "Co-existence and International Law," 95 Recueil des Cours 5, at 23 (1958).

256. As set forth in Triska and Slusser, *op. cit. supra* note 253, at 21.

257. On the subject of the Soviet attitude toward customary international law in general see *id*. ch. I; Taracouzio, The Soviet Union and International Law 12-14 (1935).

258. SCOR, 7th year, 577th meeting, June 18, 1952, p. 23.

259. See *supra* p. 153 and O'Brien, "Biological/Chemical Warfare and the International Law of War," 51 Geo. L. J. 1, at 34 n. 7 (1962).

260. SCOR, 7th year, 577th meeting, June 18, 1952, pp. 17, 18.

261. *Id*. at 18.

262. *Id*. at 19.

263. See, e.g., statement by Koshevnikov, a Soviet internationalist, in his book Laws and Customs of War as set forth in O'Brien, *supra* note 259, at 54. See also statement by Soviet representative, Tsarapkin, before the General Assembly's First Committee in 1961 as contained in U.S. Arms Control and Disarmament Agency, Documents on Disarmament, 1961 pp. 577-78 (1962).

264. In a 1965 address to the Party Congress as cited in Rothschild, Tomorrow's Weapons 111 (1964).

265. As quoted in Brungs, *supra* note 138, at 74; and Kelly, *supra* note 14, at 38-39.

266. The Pugwash Conference, Meeting at Pugwash, Nova Scotia, Aug. 24-29, 1959, as quoted by Fuller, "The Application of International Law to Chemical and Biological Warfare," 10 Orbis 247, at 267 (1966).

267. As quoted in Triska and Slusser, *op. cit. supra* note 253, at 431 n. 90.

268. GAOR, 21st Sess., 1st Committee, 1452nd Meeting, Nov. 14, 1966 p. 156.

269. *Id*. at 157.

270. GAOR, 21st Sess., 1st Committee, 1461st Meeting, Nov. 23, 1966 p. 207.

271. See *infra* p. 231.

272. Taracouzio, The Soviet Union and International Law 13 (1935).

273. See *supra* p. 46.

274. Kelly, *supra* note 14, at 41-42.

275. *Id*. at 42.

276. See *supra* p. 73.

277. See *supra* pp. 140-42.

278. See *supra* p. 153.

279. See chapter entitled "The New Constitution of Japan," Report of a Study Group set up by the Japanese Association of International Law 12 *et seq.* (1958).

280. GAOR, 21st Sess., 1st Committee, 1461st meeting, Nov. 23, 1966 p. 201.

281. League of Nations, Records of the Conference for the Reduction and Limitation of Armaments, ser. C, Minutes of the Bureau, vol. 1, Sept. 21, 1932-June 27, 1933 p. 59 (1935).

282. GAOR, 21st Sess., 1st Committee, 1461st meeting, Nov. 23, 1966 p. 201. The Hungarian drafts are contained in U.S. Arms Control and Disarmament Agency, Documents on Disarmament 1966 pp. 694-95, 758-59.

283. Disarmament Agency Documents on Disarmament, *id*. at 798-99.

284. ENDC/PV. 428, Aug. 14, 1969 pp. 19-20.

CHAPTER SEVEN

1. Schwarzenberger, A Manual of International Law 29 (4th ed. 1960).

2. Waldock, "General Course on Public International Law," 106 Recueil des Cours 5, at 65 (1962) states:

The phrase "civilized nations" now has an antiquated look. The intention in using it, clearly, was to leave out of account undeveloped legal systems so that a general principle present in the principal legal systems of the world would not be disqualified from application in international law merely by reason of its absence from, for example, the tribal law of a backward people. . . . Accordingly, we are quite safe in construing "the general principles of law recognized by civilized nations" as meaning today simply the general principles recognized in the legal systems of independent states.

3. Cheng, "General Principles of Law as Subject for International Codification," 4 Current Legal Problems 35, at 38 (1951).

4. Tunkin, "Co-Existence and International Law," 95 Recueil des Cours 6, at 25 (1958):

> The fallacy of the doctrine indicated becomes especially striking in the light of the co-existence of States belonging to two diametrically different economic systems. General principles of law which may be found in the legal systems of States belonging to those two systems, though sometimes containing technically similar rules, are of different juridical and class nature, *i.e.* are different as legal norms. There are therefore no general principles "common to all States." There may be common legal notions reflecting general features of legal phenomena, but not common legal norms.

5. Verdross, Die Verfassung der Volkerrechtsgemeinschaft 59 (1926). Verdross, "Les Principes Généraux dans la Jurisprudence Internationale," 52 Recueil des Cours 191 (1935).

6. Sorensen, Les Sources du Droit International ch. VI (1961); Sorensen, "Principes de Droit International Public," 101 Recueil des Cours 5, at 30 (1960).

7. "Principles are to be distinguished from rules. A rule is essentially practical and moreover, binding; . . . while a principle expresses a general truth which guides our action, serves as a theoretical basis for the various acts of our life, and the application of which to reality produces a given consequence." Cheng, General Principles of Law as Applied by International Courts and Tribunals 24 (1953).

8. Macmillian, "Scots Law as a Subject of Comparative Study," in Law and Other Things p. 114 (1938) puts it thus:

> No one can address himself to the study of comparative law without being struck by the essential similarity of the problems of human relationship all the world over, and despite the diversity in form of the solutions which each national system of law has devised, with the general resemblance in outline of their solutions.

9. Schwarzenberger, The Legality of Nuclear Weapons 9 (1958).

10. Waldock, *supra* note 2, at 68.

11. Schwarzenberger, The Frontiers of International Law 269 (1962).

12. Singh, Nuclear Weapons and International Law 60 (1959).

13. Scott, Reports on the Hague Conferences of 1899 and 1907 pp. 140-41 (1917).

14. Greenspan, The Modern Law of Land Warfare 438 (1959); Dunbar, "The Significance of Military Necessity in the Law of War," 67 Jurid. Rev. 201 (1955).

15. 2 Oppenheim's International Law 350 (7th ed. Lauterpacht 1952).

16. Schwarzenberger, "Functions and Foundations of the Laws of War," 44 Archiv fur Rechts—und Sozial Philosophie 351 (1958).

17. The French refer to "dictates of public conscience" as "Les regles telles que reconnaît la conscience juridique." In English conscience has acquired a primarily

moral and introspective connotation, while the French *conscience juridique* implies a sense of what is juridically right or wrong, distinct from any sense of morality. Thus there is even disagreement on the exact meaning of the phrase itself. Cheng, *op. cit. supra* note 7, at 8.

18. Stone, Legal Controls of International Conflict 328 (1954).

19. Lauterpacht, "The Problem of the Revision of The Law of War," 29 Brit. Yb. Int'l L. 373 (1952).

20. Schwarzenberger, *op. cit. supra* note 9, at 10.

21. 1 Rousseau, Principes Généraux du Droit International Public 889 *et seq.* (1944).

22. Schwarzenberger, *op. cit. supra* note 9, at 11. In opposition to this view see Roling, "The Law of War and the National Jurisdiction since 1945," 100 Recueil des Cours 329, at 350 (1960).

23. O'Brien, "The Meaning of 'Military Necessity' in International Law," 1 World Polity 109 (1957).

24. Vallindas, "General Principles of Law and the Hierarchy of the Sources of International Law," in Grundprobleme des Internationalen Rechts: Festschrift fur Jean Spiropoulous 425 (1957); Lauterpacht, The Function of Law in the International Community 115 (1955).

25. Verdross, "Les Principes Généraux du Droit dans La Jurisprudence Internationale," 52 Recueil des Cours 191 (1935).

26. Stowell, "Military Reprisals and the Sanctions of the Law of War," 36 Am. J. Int'l L. 643 (1942); on the history of reprisals from its private exercise in the thirteenth century to the consolidation of the modern state see Colbert, Retaliation in International Law (1948).

27. Cheng, *op. cit supra* note 7, at 77 ff.

28. O'Brien, "The Meaning of 'Military Necessity' in International Law," 1 World Polity 109 (1957).

29. Tucker, The Law of War and Neutrality at Sea, U.S. Naval War College International Law Studies 1955 p. 48 n. 8 (1957).

30. "The destruction of property to be lawful must be imperatively demanded by the necessities of war. Destruction as an end in itself is a violation of international law. There must be some reasonable connection between the destruction of property and the overcoming of the enemy forces." United States v. List, 11 Trials of War Criminals before the Nuremberg Military Tribunals Under Control Law No. 10, at 757, 1253-54 (1947). See also Greenspan, *op. cit. supra* note 14, at 278-86; and see Hall, A Treatise on International Law sec. 186 (8th ed. Higgins 1924).

31. 2 Oppenheim, *op. cit. supra* note 15, at 419.

32. Barnes, "Submarine Warfare and International Law," 2 World Polity 121, at 173-87.

33. The High Command and Hostage cases, 11 Trials of War Criminals before Nuremberg Military Tribunals Under Control Law No. 10, at 770 (1947).

34. *Id.* at 1296.

35. 12 War Crimes Trial Report 93 (1949); see also 3 Hyde, International Law 1808 (2d rev. ed. 1945).

36. See *infra* pp. 207-8.

37. Downey, "The Law of War and Military Necessity," 47 Am. J. Int'l L. 251 (1953).

38. McDougal and Feliciano, Law and Minimum World Order 528 (1961).

39. Schwarzenberger, A Manual of International Law 197, 199-200, 201, 209 (5th ed. 1967).

40. O'Brien, *supra* note 23, at 152.

41. Spaight, War Rights on Land 112 (1911).

42. Baxter, "The Role of Law in Modern War," 47 Proc. Am. Soc. Int. L. 90, at 91 (1953) states:

> Because the law of war begins to have application when armed conflict breaks out, it must work out an unhappy compromise with the use of force, and it does so by making a distinction for legal purposes between "unnecessary" and "necessary" suffering. This line is not a fixed one, and I think we must recognize that it can and does shift from time to time.

43. Brungs, "The Status of Biological Warfare in International Law," 24 Mil. L. Rev. 37, at 60, (1964); Gilchrist, A Comparative Study of World War Casualties from Gas and Other Weapons (1938).

44. See *supra* pp. 193-94.

45. Hersh, Chemical and Biological Warfare: America's Hidden Arsenal 42 ff. (1968); Clarke, The Silent Weapons: The Realities of Chemical and Biological Warfare 158 ff. (1968).

46. Romero and Leitenberg, "Chemical and Biological Warfare: History of International Control and U.S. Policy," 9 Scientist and Citizen 131, at 132 (1967).

47. Hersh, *op. cit. supra* note 45, at 153.

48. Lawrence, Principles of International Law 528 (7th ed. Winfield 1928).

49. Rothschild, Tomorrow's Weapons: Chemical and Biological 3 (1964) states: "Though a person under the effects of the nerve gases looks as though he is suffering greatly, men who have been accidentally exposed to them, and have recovered, say that they do not remember suffering at all."

50. Raymond, "Gas as Weapons: Pro and Con," N.Y. Times, March 28, 1965.

51. Krickus, "On the Morality of Chemical/Biological War," 9 J. Conflict Resolution 200 (1965).

52. Singh, "The Laws of Land Warfare and Prohibited Weapons and Practices," 7 Indian Yearbook Int'l Affairs 3, at 18 (1958); Greenspan, The Modern Law of Land Warfare 359 (1959).

53. Creasy, "War Without Death," This Week Sunday Supplement, May 17, 1959, p. 5.

54. Edson, "Weapons Systems in Relation to Foreign Policy," in National Security in the Nuclear Age 6 (1958) sets forth the "functional parameters of a weapons system," i.e., the components that are taken into consideration in appraising the military effectiveness of a weapon.

55. Royce, Aerial Bombardment and the International Regulation of Warfare 141 (1928).

56. Spaight, War Rights on Land 76 (1911).

57. Mallison, "The Laws of War and the Juridical Control of Weapons of Mass Destruction in General and Limited Wars," 36 Geo. Wash. L. Rev. 308, at 321 (1967); see also, Mallison, Studies in the Law of Naval Warfare: Submarines in General and Limited Wars ch. 4 (1968).

58. Schwarzenberger, The Legality of Nuclear Weapons 44 (1958). See *supra* pp. 151-52 for view napalm is legal.

59. See *supra* p. 152; Greenspan, The Modern Law of Land Warfare 315 (1959).

60. Matilda Gomez, "Orientaciones Modernas en la Guerra Biologica," 4 La Guerra Moderna 227, 247 (1957).

61. But see The International Law Association, Report of the Fiftieth Conference, Brussels, 1962 p. 189:

> Some . . . have expressed their faith in the distinction between tactical and

strategic . . . weapons . . . This distinction is about as useful as that of military objective. It is so vague and relative, and so capable of being indefinitely expanded, that it can hardly exercise any restraining influence on the indiscriminate use of weapons of mass destruction.

62. See *supra* pp. 32-36.

63. Cagle, "A Philosophy for Naval Atomic Warfare," 83 Naval Inst. Pro. 249, at 252 (1957).

64. Sloutzki, "La Population Civile devant la Menace de Destruction Massive" 25 (3rd ser.) Revue Générale de Droit International Public 218 (1955).

65. Nurick, "The Distinction between Combatants and Noncombatants in the Law of War," 39 Am. J. Int'l L. 680 (1945).

66. Osgood, Limited War: The Challenge to American Strategy 142 (1957). But see Kelly, "A Legal Analysis of the Changes in War," Military L. Rev., July, 1961, p. 89, at 117 who states, "There is no uniformly accepted definition of limited war at the present time."

67. Osgood and Tucker, Force, Order and Justice 307 (1967) point out:

In the practice of states the principle distinguishing between combatants and noncombatants has never been interpreted as giving the latter complete protection from the hazards of war. It has always been accepted that if war is to prove at all possible the immunity of noncombatants must be qualified and substantially so. Thus the investment, bombardment, siege and assault of fortified places, including towns and cities, have always been recognized as legitimate measures of warfare, even though such places may contain large numbers of peaceful inhabitants. More generally, belligerents have never been required to cease military operations because of the presence of noncombatants within the immediate area of these operations or to refrain from attacking military objectives simply because of the proximity of military objectives to the noncombatant population.

68. Lauterpacht, "The Problem of the Revision of the Law of War," 29 Brit. Yb. Int'l L. 360, 374 (1952).

69. The International Law Association, Report of the Fiftieth Conference, Brussels, 1962, Committee on the Charter of the United Nations, "Report on Self-Defence Under the Charter of the United Nations and the Use of Prohibited Weapons," establishes the following threefold distinction between combatants and noncombatants (p. 217):

(1) Persons connected with military operations or the production of war materiel. While engaged in these activities, they must expect to be treated as objects of warfare irrespective of whether they are members of armed forces or civilians.

(2) The same applies to persons present in actual or likely theaters of war or target areas of the types illustrated in the Geneva Conventions of 1949 and the Hague Convention of 1954 irrespective of their military or civilian status or occupation.

(3) Persons not engaged in activities mentioned in Category (1) and sufficiently remote from areas on Category (2) are the only persons who can still expect not to become objects of intentional attack by the enemy.

70. See *supra* pp. 32-36.

71. Rothschild, Tomorrow's Weapons 77 (1964).

72. See *supra* pp. 32-36.

73. See *supra* p. 199.

74. See Rothschild, Tomorrow's Weapons 211-15 (1964).

75. See Langmuir, "The Potentialities of Biological Warfare Against Man—An Epidemiological Appraisal," 66 Public Health Reports 387 (1951); Merck, Fred, Baldwin and Sarles, Implications of Biological Warfare, U.S. Dept. State Pub. No. 2661 vol. 1 pt. Y p. 65 *et seq.* (1946).

76. O'Brien, "Nuclear Warfare and the Law of Nations" in Morality and Modern Warfare 138 (Nagle ed. 1960).

77. De Visscher, Theory and Reality in Public International Law 290 (1957) states it thus:

> The two world wars . . . threw light upon the character of total war and the changes that it works in the relations between politics and recourse to war. The unlimited forces that it looses means that total war has taken on the absolute form of which its nineteenth-century theorists, especially von Clausewitz, had foreseen the possibility. Made possible by the mastery of power over the moral and material resources of the nation, prepared for in peace by extending State controls to everything needed for the conduct of hostilities, characterized by a technique of mass destruction that excludes any distinction between combatant and noncombatants, three-dimensional war knows neither localization to a combat zone nor restriction on means of destruction.

78. Von Knieriem, Nurnberg: Rechtliche und Menschliche Probleme 320 (1950).

79. I.G. Farben Trial, 10 Law Reports of Trials of War Criminals 49 (1947).

80. This has been somewhat changed by Article 17 Geneva Convention IV, 1949, which stipulates:

> The Parties to the conflict shall endeavor to conclude local agreements for the removal from besieged or encircled areas, of wounded, sick, infirm and aged persons, children and maternity cases, and for the passage of ministers of all religions, medical personnel and medical equipment on their way to such areas.

From the phraseology it can be seen that the conclusion of such agrements is entirely optional, and if any parties to the convention were to conclude such agreements, it is unlikely that these would be phrased in such a way as to interfere with the conduct of war. This may be the reason that the 1958 British Manual of Military Law pt. III para. 292, makes no mention of Article 17, Geneva Convention IV, 1949.

81. Lauterpacht, "The Problem of the Revision of the Law of War," 29 Brit. Yb. Int'l L. 378 (1952); Smith, The Crisis in the Law of Nations 76 (1947).

82. Spaight, Air Power and War Rights 34 (3rd ed. 1947); Castrén, The Present Law of War and Neutrality 404 (1953).

83. Brodie, Strategy in the Missile Age 139-42 (1959); Kecskemeti, Strategic Surrender: The Politics of Victory and Defeat ci (1958); Stowell, "The Laws of War and the Atomic Bomb," 39 Am. J. Int'l L. 786 (1945).

84. Blackett, Fear, War and the Bomb 22 (1948). Verdross, Volkerrecht 397 (3rd ed. 1955).

85. Lauterpacht, *supra* note 81, at 369.

86. Lauterpacht, "The Law of Nations and the Punishment of War Crimes," 21 Brit. Yb. Int'l L. 58, at 76 (1944).

87. Roling, "The Law of War and the National Jurisdiction Since 1945," 100 Recueil des Cours 329, at 398 (1960) states:

> The novel terror weapons (V 1 and V 2) were not made the subject of war law violation charges. It is said of the Nuremberg judgment, that it amounted to a ratification of all but the most aberrational practices of the belligerents in the

field of air warfare. Without doubt, the Allied terror-bombing, culminating in the use of the atomic bombs, contributed to that alleged ratification.

88. O'Brien, "Legitimate Military Necessity in Nuclear War," 2 World Polity 35, at 57 (1960).

89. See Ikle, The Social Impact of Bomb Destruction 198 (1958); de no Louis, "La Discriminación entre Combatientes y Población Civil en la Guerra Moderna," 3 La Guerra Moderna 237 (1956).

90. O'Brien, *supra* note 88, at 58 n. 52.

91. Smith, The Crisis in the Law of Nations 77 (1947).

92. Tucker, The Just War 92 (1960); Osgood and Tucker, Force, Order and Justice 247 (1967).

93. Thus, for example, in speaking of the right of communist nations to engage in subversion and indirect aggression against noncommunist nations, thereby bringing destruction and suffering to noncommunist people. Chinese Communist Defense Minister Marshal Lin Piao declared: "The sacrifice of a small number of people in revolutionary wars is repaid by security for whole nations, whole countries and even the whole of mankind; temporary suffering is repaid by lasting or even perpetual peace and happiness." (N.Y. Times, Sept. 4, 1965).

94. Osgood and Tucker, in Force, Order and Justice 241 (1967) state:

> What shocks the moralist . . . is the evident acknowledgement of the principle that the happiness and well-being of some justify the suffering of others. That principle, he will insist, necessarily implies the rejection of the principle that each individual must be considered a moral finality in himself, never to be used as a means for the purposes of others, however numerous. . . . War is only the most flagrant affirmation of the contrary principle, though the latter is indeed inherent in all political action . . . moral distinctions cannot literally rest on the impossible demand that the happiness and well-being of some may never be secured by the imposition of suffering on others.

95. Kunz, "The Geneva Conventions of August 12, 1949," in Law and Politics in the World Community 279 (Lipsky ed. 1953); Yingling and Ginnane, "The Geneva Conventions of 1949," 46 Am. J. Int'l L. 393 (1952).

96. Baxter, "So-Called 'Unprivileged Belligerency': Spies, Guerillas and Saboteurs," 28 Brit. Yb. Int'l L. 323 (1951).

97. The Soviet Union views the 1949 Geneva Conventions as recognizing "national-liberation wars" (their term for subversive warfare) as now having international legal character and hence raised to the full status of international wars. Ginsburgs, "'Wars of Liberation' and the Modern Law of Nations—The Soviet Thesis," in The Soviet Impact on International Law 66, at 71 (Baade ed. 1965). For description of guerrilla techniques and tactics see Levy, Guerrilla Warfare (1942); Miksche, Secret Forces: The Technique of Underground Movements (1950); Donovan, "Secret Movements, Espionage and Treachery," in Modern World Politics 308 (Kalijarvi ed. 1953); Papagpa, "Guerrilla Warfare," 30 Foreign Affairs 215 (1952).

98. Cowles, "Universality of Jurisdiction Over War Crimes," 33 Calif. L. Rev. 181 (1945) goes so far as to assimilate guerrillas to bandits and pirates. See also Wyckoff, "War By Subversion," 59 S. Atlantic Q. 35 (1960).

99. Kaplan and Katzenbach, "Resort to Force: War and Neutrality," in 2 The Strategy of World Order: International Law (Falk, Mendlovitz eds. 1966) 276, at 301 point out:

> The rules of neutrality of the "balance of power" period rested upon the premise that the neutral states had no real stake in the outcome; that is they rested upon

the assumptions that the war would not produce a predominant coalition and that fixed alignments would not persist as conditions changed. These assumptions ceased to hold shortly after the Franco-Prussian War. But it took some time for national practice to catch up with changed conditions . . . But the rule of neutrality can hardly persist in the absence of the interests that produced and supported that rule.

100. Tucker, The Law of War and Neutrality at Sea, U.S. Naval War College International Law Studies 1955 p. 198 (1957). In World War II, the territory of neutrals was also violated by belligerents. See Survey of International Affairs 1939-1946, The War and the Neutrals pp. 183-89 on German transit traffic in Sweden; pp. 336-40 on Allied occupation of the Azores (Toynbee ed. 1956).

101. Kunz, The Changing Law of Nations 890 (1968); see also Smith, The Crisis in the Law of Nations 57 (1947); Orvik, The Decline of Neutrality, 1914-1941 p. 13 (1953); Tucker, The Just War 84 n. (1960).

102. Komarnicki, "The Place of Neutrality in the Modern System of International Law," 80 Recueil des Cours 399 (1952).

103. McDougal and Feliciano, *op. cit. supra* note 38, point out that if a neutral is injured by such acts, it may engage in lawful reprisals (p. 405) or seek compensation for the damages (474), using the following test:

Potentially relevant factors may include, for example, the degree of necessity under which the user found itself in the particular use involved; the relation of the user's political objectives to the public order of the organized world community; the extent to which the neutral claimant was authorized to remain neutral; the type of damage complained of; the incidence of the ascertainable damage, that is whether the damage was limited to the neutral or shared by the user and the rest of the world and so forth.

O'Brien apparently feels that the law of neutrality is completely dead. His article, "Legitimate Military Necessity in Nuclear War," 2 World Polity 35, at 96-98 (1960), declares that the law of neutrality will not succeed in imposing legal limitations on weapons of mass destruction because in the past quarter of a century the airspace of neutral nations has been "successfully drenched with fall-out and repeatedly traversed by space flights and satellites, in such manner as to leave the revered doctrine of sovereignty *ad coelum*, in tatters, in peace as in war." From this it might be reasoned that he would make no distinction between total war or limited war, injury to neutrals from airborne chemical or biological agents. As a matter of fact he goes on to add: "It is difficult to avoid application of the working principle that new facts which challenge the very basis of an old legal order require a fairly unequivocal response, failing which it is fair to assume that the old law is extinct."

104. Laun, Haager Landkriegsordnung 37, 46 (1948); Kunz, Kriegsrecht und Neutralitatsrecht 22 (1935).

105. Rodick, The Doctrine of Necessity in International Law 1 (1928).

106. Roling, *supra* note 87, at 382.

107. Laun, *op. cit. supra* note 104, at 25-28. See also Verdross, who states that the legal position seems inconvertible and absolute, but nevertheless if one gives it a great deal of thought, some doubts as to its reality must arise. Verdross, Die Volkerrechtswidrige Kriegshandlung und der Strafanspruch der Staaten 74 (1920).

108. O'Brien, *supra* note 103, at 99: "This is not to say that general principles and older rules of the law of war are without any relevance or value . . . As we have indicated, they are invaluable guides to the assessment of reasonable proportionality. . . ." See also Brungs, "The Status of Biological Warfare in International Law," 24 Military L. Rev. 47, at 78 (1964).

109. Von der Heydte, "Atomare Kriegfuhrung und Volkerrecht," 9 Archiv des Volkerrecht 162 (1961); Singh, Nuclear Weapons and International Law 154 (1959).

110. See *supra* pp. 128-29.

111. See *supra* pp. 129-30.

112. Mallison, "The Laws of War and the Juridical Control of Weapons of Mass Destruction in General and Limited Wars," 36 Geo. Wash. L. Rev. 308 (1967).

113. Smith, "Modern Weapons and Modern War," 9 Yearbook World Affairs 222, at 238 (1955).

114. O'Brien, *supra* note 103, at 87.

115. Stone, *op. cit. supra* note 18, at 344-48.

116. Mallison, *supra* note 112, at 342.

117. O'Brien, *supra* note 103, at 76.

118. McDougal and Feliciano, *op. cit. supra* note 38, at 615.

119. Mallison, *supra* note 112, at 324.

120. Spaight, *op. cit supra* note 82, at 273-77.

121. Mallison, *supra* note 112, at 342.

122. See *supra* pp. 193-94.

123. Lasswell, "The Political Science of Science: An Inquiry into the Possible Reconciliation of Mastery and Freedom," 50 Am. Pol. Sci. Rev. 961 (1956).

124. Kaplan, "The Calculus of Nuclear Deterrence," 1 World Politics 20 (1958); McDougal and Feliciano, *op. cit. supra* note 38, at 242.

125. Kaysen, "Military Importance of the Atomic Bomb," 5 Bull. Atomic Scientists 340 (1949).

126. See *supra* pp. 193-94.

127. See *supra* pp. 196, 201.

128. Possony, Strategic Air Power: The Pattern of Dynamic Security 161 (1949).

129. "Social and Psychological Factors Affecting Morale," in Propaganda in War and Crisis 355 *et seq.* (Lerner ed. 1951).

130. Possony, *op. cit. supra* note 128, at 162.

131. Rothschild, Tomorrow's Weapons 43 (1964).

132. Lerner, Sykewar: Psychological Warfare Against Germany, D-Day to VE-Day 45 (1949); see also Holt and van de Velde, Strategic Psychological Operations and American Foreign Policy 15 (1960).

133. Research in CBR, A Report of the Committee on Science and Astronautics, U.S. House of Representatives, 86th Cong. 1st sess., Aug. 10, 1959 p. 10 (1959).

134. Meyrowitz, "Les Armes Psychochimiques et le Droit International," 10 Annuaire Français de Droit International 81, at 119 (1964).

135. McDougal and Feliciano, Law and Minimum World Public Order 637 (1961).

136. *Ibid.*

137. Spaight, Air Power and War Rights 108-9 (3rd ed. 1947).

138. Dept. of State, Press Release No. 59, March 24, 1965 p. 11.

139. Nunn, "The Arming of An International Police," 2 Journal of Peace Research 187 (1965).

140. For an account of the place of chivalry in the law of war see British Manual of Military Law 7-9 (7th ed. 1929).

141. Zuckerman, "Judgment and Control in Modern Warfare," 40 Foreign Affairs 196 *et seq.* (1962).

142. Speier, Social Order and the Risks of War 271 (1952); Osgood and Tucker, Force, Order and Justice 207 (1967).

143. Tucker, The Law of War and Neutrality at Sea, U.S. Naval War College International Law Studies 1955 p. 138 (1957).

144. *Id.* p. 52 n. 15.

145. Osgood and Tucker, *op. cit. supra* note 142, at 218.

146. Kelly, "Gas Warfare in International Law," 9 Military L. Rev. 1, at 48 (1960).

147. Brungs, *supra* note 108, at 59.

148. Meyrowitz, "Les Armes Psychochimiques et le Droit International," 10 Annuaire Français de Droit International 81, at 121 (1964).

149. Brungs, *supra* note 108, at 59.

150. Glod and Smith, "Interrogation under 1949 Prisoners of War Convention," 23 Military L. Rev. 145, at 154 (July, 1963); Verplaetse, "The Jus in Bello and Military Operations in Korea 1950-1953," 23 Zeitschrift für Ausländisches Offentliches Recht und Völkerrecht 679, at 728 (1963).

151. See *supra* pp. 193-94.

152. Stone, Legal Controls of International Conflict 615 (rev. ed. 1959) declares:

> This tolerance for air warfare of otherwise forbidden means, despite their specially cruel and mortal effects in the air, manifest the subjugation of humanity and chivalry to these very efficacies of technology . . . The tolerance is a far cry from that . . . denunciation of weapons which 'render' the death of the victim 'inevitable.'

153. See *infra* pp. 208-11.

154. Osgood and Tucker, *op. cit. supra* note 142, at 217.

155. Brierly, "The Prohibition of War by International Law," 2 Agenda 289 (1943).

156. McDougal and Feliciano, *op. cit. supra* note 135, at 636.

157. Spaight, Air Power and War Rights 275 n. 5 (3rd ed. 1947).

158. *Id.* at 275-76.

159. See *supra* pp. 32-36.

160. Rosebury, Peace or Pestilence: Biological Warfare and How To Avoid It 58 (1949); see also, Crozier, Tigertt and Cooch, "The Physicians' Role in the Defense Against Biological Weapons," 175 J. Am. Medical Assoc. 4, 8 (1961).

161. See *supra* pp. 49-57.

162. Mallison, "The Laws of War and the Juridical Control of Weapons of Mass Destruction in General and Limited War," 36 Geo. Wash. L. Rev. 308, at 318 (1967) states:

> The principal limitation upon weapons stated by Hugo Grotius in his classic study of *De Jure Belli ac Pacis* was the prohibition of the use of poison which, he stated, existed "from old times." It probably reflected the inefficiency of poison as a weapon. The Grotian interdiction was broadly formulated and included poisoning food and water as well as using weapons the points of which were tipped with poison.

163. See *infra* pp. 213-14.

164. See *supra* pp. 50-51.

165. Singh, Nuclear Weapons and International Law 154 (1959) declares that "anything" which is poisonous falls within the ban against poison and poison weapons.

166. Neinast, "United States Use of Biological Warfare," 24 Military L. Rev. 6, at 28 (1964).

167. See *supra* ch. VI.

168. Mallison, *supra* note 162, at 332.

169. O'Brien, "Biological/Chemical Warfare and the International Law of War," 51 Geo. L. J. 32-36 (1962).

170. See *supra* pp. 137-38.

171. On reprisals in general see Castrén, The Present Law of War and Neutrality 69-72 (1954); Greenspan, The Modern Law of Land Warfare 407 (1959); McDougal and Feliciano, Law and Minimum World Public Order 679-90 (1961); Tucker, The Law of War and Neutrality at Sea, U.S. Naval War College International Law Studies 1955 pp. 151-53 (1957); Albrecht, "War Reprisals in the War Crimes Trials and the Geneva Conventions of 1949," 47 Am. J. Int'l L. 590 (1953); O'Brien, "Biological/Chemical Warfare and the International Law of War," 51 Geo. L. J. 1., at 43-49, 58-59 (1962).

172. On *malum in se* see *supra* pp. 189-90 and see O'Brien, *id.* at 47 and 57.

173. Pillet in Le Droit de la Guerre—Conférences faites aux officiers de la garnison de Grenoble pendant l'année 1891-1892 as at p. 287, set forth in O'Brien, *id.* at 47 n. 134 states that poison and cruel means may not be used even in retaliation.

174. See Castrén, *op. cit. supra* note 171, at 71. This seemed to be the view of the Geneva Disarmament Conference, which sought to ban biological warfare completely and absolutely even as reprisals.

175. The writers mentioned above in note 171 see no limit on weapons used as reprisals because some might be considered inhumane or *mala in se.*

176. See *supra* pp. 137-38.

177. The first German attack was on April 22, 1915. The first British attack at Loos came on Sept. 25, 1915. See chart "Principal Gas Attacks in World War," as contained in Prentiss, Chemicals in War 663 (1937).

178. See discussion of jurists' works *infra* ch. VIII.

179. Stone, Legal Control of International Conflict 354-55 (2d imp. rev. 1959).

180. Greenspan, *op. cit. supra* note 171, at 412.

181. Castrén, *op. cit. supra* note 171, at 70. The U.S. Law of Land Warfare, Dept. of Army Field Manual 27-10 (1956) states at 177: "The acts resorted to by way of reprisal need not conform to those complained of by the injured party, but should not be excessive or exceed the degree of violence committed by the enemy.

182. See *supra* pp. 138-40.

183. 2 Oppenheim, International Law 344 (7th ed. Lauterpacht 1952).

184. International Law Association, Report of the Fiftieth Conference 1962 p. 221.

185. See *supra* pp. 189-91.

186. See *supra* pp. 160-99.

187. See *supra* pp. 182-83.

188. See McDougal and Feliciano, *op. cit. supra* note 171, at 682; Castrén, *op. cit. supra* note 171, at 70.

189. O'Brien, *op. cit. supra* note 171, at 58.

190. See, e.g., 2 Oppenheim, *op. cit. supra* note 183, at 347-49; Tucker, *op. cit. supra* note 171, at 54-55; McDougal and Feliciano, *op. cit. supra* note 171, at 659 *et seq.* But see Schwarzenberger, The Legality of Nuclear Weapons (1958).

191. See *supra* pp. 137-38.

192. See for discussion O'Brien, *op. cit. supra* note 171, at 47-48, 58; Fuller, "The Application of International Law to Chemical and Biological Warfare," 10 Orbis 247, at 251, 267-70 (1966).

193. See chart, "Principal Gas Attacks in World War," as set forth in Prentiss, *op. cit. supra* note 177, at 663.

194. Art. 13, Geneva Convention Relative to the Treatment of Prisoners of War of August 12, 1949, 1 Final Record of the Diplomatic Conference of Geneva 1949 p. 243.

195. Art. 46, Geneva Convention for the Amelioration of the Condition of the Wounded and Sick in Armed Forces in the Field of August 12, 1949, *id.* at 205; Art.

47 of Geneva Convention for the Amelioration of the Condition of the Wounded and Sick and Shipwrecked Members of the Armed Forces at Sea of August 12, 1949, *id.* at 225.

196. Art. 33, Geneva Convention Relative to the Treatment of Civilian Persons in Time of War of August 12, 1949, *id.* at 297.

197. Art. 33, *ibid.*

198. See Wounded and Sick Conventions, *supra* note 195.

199. Art. 4(4) Hague Convention for the Protection of Cultural Property in the Event of Armed Conflict of 1954.

200. Law of Land Warfare, *op. cit. supra* note 182, at 177.

201. Armed Forces Doctrine for Chemical and Biological Weapons Employment and Defense, FM 101-40, NPW 36(C), AFM 355-2, LFM 03 p. 3 (1964).

202. For a complete discussion of all the aspects of self-defense see Bowett, Self-Defence in International Law (1958).

203. Thomas and Thomas, The Organization of American States 162 (1963); Ross, A Textbook of International Law 244 (1947); Brierly, The Law of Nations 253 (2d ed. 1938).

204. Lawrence, Principles of International Law 117-18, 121-22 (5th ed. 1913).

205. See *supra* pp. 12-13.

206. See *supra* p. 185.

207. See *infra* ch. viii.

208. Osgood and Tucker, Force, Order and Justice 271 (1967).

209. Dickinson, "The Analogy between Neutral Persons and International Persons in the Law of Nations," 26 Yale L. J. 565 (1918); Baty, Canons of International Law 88 (1930).

210. Bowett, *op. cit. supra* note 202, ch. III.

211. For a discussion of the pros and cons of this view see Giraud, "La Théorie de la Légitime Défense," 49 Recueil des Cours 691 (1934).

212. Osgood and Tucker, *op. cit. supra* note 208, at 274 n. 40. Tucker, The Just War 127 (1960) states:

> Given the circumstances that normally mark the exercise of self-defense among nations, or rather the claims to the exercise of self-defense, each requirement must raise questions necessarily dependent upon complex political and military considerations. The immediacy of the danger to the security of a state need not, and indeed cannot be gauged simply in terms of overt action of an injurious nature; it is precisely the purpose of self-defense to prevent, if possible, the commission of such injurious action. Inevitably, the danger held to justify the taking of preventive measures in self-defense will depend upon an interpretation of the significance of behaviour that falls short of being overt and consequently unambiguous. Even more, if the uncertainty to be tolerated before resort to preventive measures of force must be related to the nature of the danger posed, the nature of the danger will depend not only upon the *animus* thus far manifested by the other party, but also upon the means of injury the other party has at its disposal. Hence, the nature and immediacy of the danger that may serve to justify preventive war as a measure of legitimate self-defense cannot reasonably be divorced from the technology of war. Changes in the latter cannot but affect the manner in which the requirements of self-defense are applied.

213. Thomas and Thomas, *op. cit. supra* note 203, at 244.

214. Cheng, General Principles of Law as Applied by International Courts and Tribunals 94 (1953) declares: "The existence of an 'instant and overwhelming' danger to the safety of the State or the lives or property of its nationals is the condition *sine qua non* of legitimate defense."

215. Osgood and Tucker, *op. cit. supra* note 208, at 301 point out that the principle of proportionality "is implicit in almost every conceivable justification of force. Not only does it express what may be termed the 'logic of justification,' it is compatible with almost every justification—or condemnation—of force that men have ever given."

216. Thomas and Thomas, Non-Intervention: The Law and Its Import in the Americas 123 (1956).

217. Bowett, *op. cit. supra* note 202, ch. I.

218. Kelsen, The Law of the United Nations 791 (1950); Beckett would agree; Beckett, The North Atlantic Treaty 13 (1950).

219. This is supported by the French version of the texts of the Charter which reads in part, "dans un cas où un Membre des Nations Unies est l'objet d'une agression armée," which seems to imply that there was no intention to cut down the general international law right of self-defense against an imminent threat, for aggression is a wider term than attack.

220. Thomas and Thomas, *op. cit. supra* note 216, at 213-14.

221. Bowett, *op. cit. supra* note 202, ch. III.

222. 1 Oppenheim, International Law 351 n. 2 (7th ed. Lauterpacht 1952). This, of course, is a modern version of the ancient asserted right of self-preservation of a state. The question has never really been resolved legally, although practically speaking most military men would claim that it is a duty of a nation to preserve itself at whatever cost.

223. O'Brien, "The Meaning of 'Military Necessity' in International Law," 1 World Polity 109, at 171 (1957).

224. Schwarzenberger, The Legality of Nuclear Weapons 42 (1958); Schwarzenberger, "The Fundamental Principles of International Law," 87 Recueil des Cours 195, at 343 (1955).

CHAPTER EIGHT

1. Paquete Habana, 175 U.S. 677, at 700 (1900). On the writings of publicists as evidence of the rules of international law see Fenwick, International Law 90-91 (4th ed. 1965); Brierly, The Law of Nations 65-66 (6th ed. 1963); 1 Oppenheim, International Law 33 (8th ed. Lauterpacht 1955).

2. On judicial decision as evidence of international law see Fenwick, *id.* at 91-92; Brierly, *id.* at 63-64; 1 Oppenheim, *id.* at 31-32.

3. Podesta Costa, Manual de Derecho Internacional Publico 375 (2d ed. 1947).

4. 3 Antokoletz, Derecho Internacional Publico Paz y Guerra 437 (1944).

5. 3 Accioly, Tratado de Derecho Internacional Publico 152-53 (1946).

6. Sierra, Derecho Internacional Publico 488 (3rd ed. 1959).

7. Greenspan, The Modern Law of Land Warfare 357 (1959).

8. Tucker, The Law of War and Neutrality at Sea, U.S. Naval War College International Law Studies 1955 pp. 51-53 (1957).

9. Kelsen, Principles of International Law 117 (2d ed., Tucker 1966).

10. O'Brien, "Biological Chemical Warfare and the International Law of War," 51 Geo. L. J. 1, at 36, 57, 59-60 (1962).

11. Sack, "ABC, Biological, Chemical Warfare in International Law," 10 Lawyers Guild Rev. 161, at 166-67 (1950).

12. 2 Oppenheim, International Law 342-44 (7th ed. Lauterpacht 1952).

13. Schwarzenberger, The Legality of Nuclear Weapons 37-38, 40-41 (1958).

14. Castrén, The Present Law of War and Neutrality 193-97 (1954).

15. Meyrowitz, "Les Armes Psychochimiques et le Droit International," 10 Annuaire Français de Droit International 81, at 101-15 (1964).

16. *Id.* at 111.

17. 2 Guggenheim, Traité de Droit International Public 390 (1954).

18. Singh, Nuclear Weapons and International Law 163-64 (1959).

19. Durdenevskii and Shevchenko "The Incompatibility of the Use of Atomic Weapons with the Norms of International Law," 5 Soviet State and Law 41 (1955) as translated and quoted in Brungs, "The Status of Biological Warfare in International Law," 24 Military L. Rev. 37, at 86 (1964).

20. Kozhevnikov, International Law 412 (1957) as quoted and cited in Brungs, *ibid.*, and see quote in Triska and Slussler, The Theory, Law and Policy of Soviet Treaties 431 n. 90 (1962).

21. 3 Hyde, International Law Chiefly as Interpreted and Applied by the United States 1818-1822 (2nd rev. ed. 1947).

22. Fenwick, *op. cit. supra* note 1, at 670.

23. Fuller, "The Application of International Law to Chemical and Biological Warfare," 18 Orbis 247, at 270 (1966).

24. Kelly, "Gas Warfare in International Law," Military L. Rev., July, 1960, p. 1, at 64.

25. Bernstein, "The Law of Chemical Warfare," 10 Geo. Wash. L. Rev. 889, at 914 (1942).

26. See Kelly, *op. cit. supra* note 24 at 54.

27. Stone, Legal Control of International Conflict 556 (2d imp. rev. 1959).

28. Kunz, Kriegsrecht and Neutralitatsrecht 86-88 (1935).

29. Kunz, "The New U.S. Army Field Manual on the Law of Land Warfare," 51 Am. J. Int'l L. 388, at 396 (1957).

30. McDougal and Feliciano, Law and Minimum World Public Order 632-37 (1961).

31. Rousseau, Droit International Public 559-60 (1953).

32. For a discussion of German authorities see O'Brien, *supra* note 10, at 52-53.

33. Moritz, "The Common Application of the Laws of War within the NATO Forces," Military L. Rev., July, 1961, p. 1, at 21.

34. For example Sierra, *op. cit. supra* note 6, at 488, 3 Ruiz Moreno, Derecho Internacional Publico sec. 306(b) (1941).

35. Podesta Costa, *op. cit. supra* note 3, at 374-75; Von Liszt, Derecho Internacional Publico 426 n. (1929); 2 Guggenheim, *op. cit. supra* note 17, at 390; 3 Accioly, *op. cit. supra* note 5, at 153; 3 Antokoletz, *op. cit. supra* note 4, at 437.

36. Schwarzenberger, *op. cit. supra* note 13, at 37-38.

37. Singh, *op. cit. supra* note 18, at 163-64.

38. Sack, *supra* note 11, at 166-67.

39. Schwarzenberger, *op. cit. supra* note 13, at 40-41; Singh, *op. cit. supra* note 18, at 218 *et seq.*

40. Greenspan, *op. cit. supra* note 7, at 358-59.

41. Spaight, Air Power and War Rights 191-92 (3rd ed. 1947).

42. 2 Oppenheim, *op. cit. supra* note 12 sec. 113.

43. Tucker, *op. cit. supra* note 8, at 52-53 n. 16.

44. Kelsen, *op. cit. supra* note 9, at 117.

45. *Ibid.*

46. Tucker, *op. cit. supra* note 8, at 53.

47. See notes 19 and 20 *supra*.

48. Sauer, Grundlehre des Volkerrechts 257 (1955) as quoted in Brungs, "The Status of Biological Warfare in International Law," 24 Military L. Rev. 47, at 85-87 (1964).

49. Castrén, *op. cit. supra* note 14, at 60.

50. *Id.* at 195.

51. *Id.* at 71.

52. Meyrowitz, Biological Weapons and International Law, Prohibition of the Use of Biological Weapons and Proposals for Banning the Production of Such Weapons 7-8, 9 (mimeographed article, translated from the French, April, 1967).

53. *Id.* at 8-9.

54. *Ibid.*

55. *Id.* at 9-11.

56. *Id.* at 12.

57. *Id.* at 3-4.

58. *Id.* at 6-7.

59. *Id.* at 7.

60. *Id.* at 21.

61. Brungs, *op. cit. supra* note 48, at 58-59, 90-91, 92.

62. Kunz, *supra* note 29, at 396.

63. Fenwick, *op. cit. supra* note 1, at 670.

64. Rousseau, *op. cit. supra* note 31, at 559-60.

65. 3 Hyde, *op. cit. supra* note 21, at 1818-22.

66. Fuller, *supra* note 23, at 270.

67. Moritz, *supra* note 33, at 21-22.

68. Kelly, *supra* note 24, at 55-56.

69. *Id.* at 42-43.

70. Neinast, "United States Use of Biological Warfare," 24 Military L. Rev. 1, at 31-35, 36 (1964).

71. Stone, *op. cit. supra* note 27, at 557.

72. McDougal and Feliciano, *op. cit. supra* note 30, at 637-40.

73. See *supra* p. 57.

74. See *supra* pp. 118-19, and *infra.* p. 243.

75. See 1 Garner, International Law and the World War 287-88 (1920).

76. *Id.* at 288.

77. 2 Oppenheim, *op. cit. supra* note 12, at 340 n. 3.

78. Noel-Baker, The Arms Race 335-43 (1958).

79. Greenspan, *op. cit. supra* note 7, at 360-61.

80. On this declaration see *supra* pp. 44-45.

81. Singh, *op. cit. supra* note 18, at 150-51.

82. Schwarzenberger, *op. cit. supra* note 13, at 44.

83. Spaight, Air Power and War Rights 197 (1947).

84. Tucker, *op. cit. supra* note 8, at 51, 52-53 n. 16; Kelsen, *op. cit. supra* note 9, at 116.

85. Stone, *op. cit. supra* note 27, at 550.

86. Castrén, *op. cit. supra* note 14, at 190.

87. McDougal and Feliciano, *op. cit. supra* note 30, at 620-22.

88. 10 Mixed Arbitral Tribunal 100 (1931). See also Singh, *op. cit. supra* note 18, at 186; Neinast, *supra* note 70, at 37.

89. Neinast, *ibid.*

90. 7 Judgment of the International Tribunal 117, Annexes (1948). (Mimeographed material. As set forth in O'Brien, *supra* note 10, at 34 n. 90.

91. See *supra* pp. 141-42.

92. O'Brien, *supra* note 10, at 34 n. 90.

93. 2 Oppenheim, *op. cit. supra* note 12, at 343 n. 2.

94. O'Brien, *supra* note 10, at 34 n. 90.

95. See *supra* pp. 154-55 for discussion of *opinio juris.*

96. 2 Oppenheim, *op. cit. supra* note 12, at 343 n. 2.

97. Report of the Thirty-First Conference of the International Law Association vol. 1 p. 200 (1923).

98. For report and draft see *id.* 201-9.

99. The Draft Convention is found in International Law Association, Report of the Fortieth Conference 41 (1938). The association also discussed the problem of the protection of civil populations from the spread of poison gas by aircraft in 1936. See the International Law Association, Report of the Thirty-ninth Conference 254, 264 *et seq.* (1936).

100. The International Law Association, Report of the Fiftieth Conference 218-34 (1926).

101. *Id.* at 219.

102. On the Pugwash Conferences in general see Rabinowitch, "About Pugwash," Bull. Atomic Scientists, April, 1965, p. 9.

103. For discussion of this conference see Bull. Atomic Scientists, Oct., 1959, pp. 337-39.

104. *Id.* at 339.

105. See Pugwash XIV, Bull. Atomic Scientists, Sept., 1965, pp. 41-45. As to chemical/biological discussion, see pp. 44-45.

106. *Id.* at 45.

107. Pugwash XVI, Bull. Atomic Scientists, Jan., 1967, p. 44, at 46; see also Proceedings of the Sixtieth Pugwash Conference on Science and World Affairs, "Disarmament and World Security Especially in Europe" p. 18 *et seq.* (1966).

108. Pugwash XVII, *id.* Nov., 1967, 46, at 47; see also Pugwash Newsletter, July, 1967, pp. 2-5.

109. See Bull. Atomic Scientist, Oct., 1964, p. 46.

110. See Science News, Feb. 25, 1967, p. 18; Scientific American, Nov. 19, 1966, p. 64; Science, Jan. 20, 1967, p. 302.

CHAPTER NINE

1. Kunz, "The Chaotic Status of the Laws of War and the Urgent Necessity for their Revision," 45 Am. J. Int'l L. 37 (1951); Kelly, "A Legal Analysis of Changes in War," Military L. Rev. (DA Pam. 27-100-13) p. 89 (July, 1961); Lauterpacht, "The Problem of the Revision of the Law of War," 29 Brit. Yb. Int'l L. 360 (1952).

2. Fenwick, International Law 659 (4th ed. 1965).

3. Professor Scelle has expressed the view that as the Charter of the United Nations has outlawed war there could no longer be any question of a law of war, although in his opinion there was room for regulation of hostilities waged by an international police force. Doc. A/CN. 4/SR. 6 p. 12 (1949).

4. Lauterpacht, "The Law of Nations and the Punishment of War Crimes," 21 Brit. Yb. Int'l L. 58, at 76 (1944).

INDEX

Accioly, 228, 312, 313
Acheson, 167
Adamsite. *See* Chemical agents
Advisory Opinion of Permanent Court of
International Justice, 65, 279
Africa, 146, 147
African swine fever. *See* Biological agents
Agency for the Control of Armaments,
123, 124-25, 127
Aggravation of suffering of disabled men,
45, 215-17, 239, 247
Air Warfare: 1923 Hague Rules of, 67-68
Albrecht, 310
Alexander II, Czar of Russia, 44
Almond, 270
Alpert, 267
Alsop, 295
American Civil War, 2, 155
American states, 69, 145
Anabtawi, 281
Anthrax. *See* Biological agents
Antianimal agents, 23-24, 53-55, 77, 185,
194, 195, 235, 236, 237, 238, 279. *See
also* Biological agents; Chemical agents
Antimateriel agents, 4, 16, 25, 77, 185,
194, 195, 238. *See also* Biological
agents; Chemical agents
Antipersonnel agents, 16-24, 53-55, 185,
232, 235, 238, 247. *See also* Biological
agents; Chemical agents
Antiplant agents, 4, 14-16, 27, 53-55, 75,
76, 77, 194, 195, 197, 235, 236, 237,
238. *See also* Biological agents; Chemi-
cal agents.
Antokoletz, 228, 312, 313
Argentina, 228
Army, U.S., 41-42; policy of as to CB
warfare, 161-62
Arsine. *See* Chemical agents
Asphyxiating gases. *See* Chemical wea-
pons; Gas
Atlee, 103, 118
Atomic Energy Commission, 103, 104
Australia, 82, 148, 231, 274
Austria, 58, 60, 66, 81, 122, 178, 187,
265, 271, 272, 274

Azores, 307

Baade, 306
Babesiosis. *See* Biological agents
Bacteria, 16, 17, 18, 23, 24, 77. *See also*
Biological agents
Balestieri, 258
Barnes, 302
Baron, 256
Bawden, 257
Baxter, 255, 303, 306
Bechhoefer, 284
Beecher, 262, 294
Belgium, 63, 84, 122, 265, 271, 274, 282
Bemis, 372
Bernstein, 231, 265, 291, 292, 299, 313
Biological agents: African swine fever,
23; and Agency for Control of Armaments, 125-26; analysis of Geneva Protocol with reference thereto, 76-77;
anthrax, 3, 189, 241; antianimal, 23-24,
53-55, 76-77, 185, 194, 195, 235, 236,
237, 238; antimateriel, 23, 52, 76-77,
185, 195, 238; antipersonnel, 16-23,
55-57, 185, 235, 246; antiplant, 24-25,
53-55, 76-77, 185, 194, 195, 197; babesiosis, 24; bacteria, 16, 17, 18, 22,
23, 76; botulism, 20, 24, 189; brucellosis, 18, 22, 23; cholera, 19, 23, 201,
241; classification of, 16; coccidioidomycosis, 18; dengue fever, 18; diphtheria, 18, 201; dysentery, 201; effects
of, 70; encephalitis, 18; encephalomyelitis, 23; exanthema, 23; and first
use of, 171, 183, 185-86; fungi, 16, 17-
18, 22, 23, 77; glanders, 23, 189;
hepatitis, 18, 201; histoplasmosis, 18,
201; hoof and mouth disease, 23; influenza, 18, 201; and juristic works,
232-38; lethal or severely injurious,
185, 206, 208, 210, 223-26, 235, 246,
249, 250; manufacture of, 126; microorganisms, 61-62, 77, 269; nature of,
16-25; Newcastle disease, 23; nocardiosis, 18; paratyphoid fever, 201,
283; plague, 18, 201, 241; as poisons,

317

Friedmann, 290
Fries, 257
Fuller, 231, 236, 272, 284, 296, 297, 310, 313, 314

G-agents. *See* Chemical agents: nerve
Gabon, 110
Gaffarel, 296
Galston, 294
Gambia, 275
Garner, 54, 239, 264, 265, 266, 268, 272, 291, 299, 314
Gas: and American states, 68-69; and British Draft Convention on, 99-101; Central American treaty on, 68; and Conference on Limitation of Armaments, 62-67; and Conference for the Supervision of the International Trade in Arms and Ammunition and in Implements of War, 71-74; and draft disarmament convention, 87-90; early League of Nations considerations as to prohibition of use of, 69-71; efforts of United Nations to limit use of, 103-17; and Geneva Protocol of 1925, 71-85; and Hague Gas Declaration, 46-49, 56-57; League of Nations Special Committee of Experts, 70; and Permanent Advisory Commission for Military, Naval and Air Questions of League of Nations, 69; as poison, 49-57; prohibition of use of by Washington Conference, 62-67; report of Subcommission of Preparatory Commission for Disarmament Conference, 86-90; and Treaty of Versailles, 59-62; and Treaty of Washington, 65-67; types of, prohibited, 61, 66, 73-76, 89-90, 91; use of in Italian-Ethiopian War, 141-43; use of in Sino-Japanese War, 143-45; use of in Vietnam, 148-50; use of in World War I, 137-41, 172, 175, 177, 178, 179, 183, 219, 222; use of in Yemen, 151-53. *See also* Chemical agents; Chemical warfare; Chemical weapons
General Assembly, 103, 104, 107, 109, 110, 111, 112, 117, 118
General Principles of Law Recognized by Civilized Nations, 38, 41, 187-226
Geneva Conventions of 1949, 54, 127, 149, 204, 268, 305, 311

Geneva Diplomatic Conference of 1949, 127
Geneva Protocol of 1925, 57, 71-85; as binding on states, 78-85; and biological weapons, 76-77, 232, 233, 236; and chemical weapons, 228, 229, 230, 231, 232; as codification of international law, 77-78, 173; and Conference for Supervision of the International Trade in Arms and Ammunition and in Implements of War, 71-73; defects of, 73-85, 105-6; English language version of analyzed, 74-75; failure of Japan to ratify, 73, 183; failure of U.S. to ratify, 73, 163; French language version of analyzed, 75-76; French ratification of and reservations thereto, 78-79, 176, 247, 278; and incendiaries, 239; international status of, 80-85; and Italian-Ethiopian War, 141-43; Italian ratification of, 179; Kunz on, 276-77; meaning of, 174-78, 246-47; Pugwash conferences and, 244; and question of an appeal to states to accede to and ratify, 110-12, 174, 176; reservations to, 78-85, 247, 277-80; resolution of First Committee of 1966 on, 108-12; resolution of General Assembly of 1966 on, 111-12; resolution of International Red Cross on, 129; Stone on, 332; text of, 73; U.S.S.R. ratification of and reservation thereto, 79-80, 179-80, 247-80; U.S. attitude with respect to, 161, 164, 166, 169, 170
Genocide Convention: I.C.J. advisory opinion on, 279
German-Greek Mixed Arbitral Tribunal, 240
Germany, 3, 40, 58, 59, 60-62, 66, 67, 81, 87, 99, 101, 103, 121, 122, 126, 130, 137, 138, 139, 140, 141, 145, 146, 153, 154, 155, 159, 165, 172, 175, 177-78, 179, 195, 207, 219, 220, 222, 232, 233, 239, 240, 262, 263, 264, 265, 270, 271, 275, 276, 277, 288, 291, 292, 293, 297, 307, 310
Getlein, 294
Ghana, 275
Gilchrist, 303
Ginnane, 306
Ginsburgs, 306

DATE DUE

NOV 22 1993	
FEB 22 1995	
DEC 04 1997	
DEC 14 2001	